American Indian Lives

Daniel F. Littlefield, Jr.

Alex Posey

Creek Poet,
Journalist, and
Humorist

University
of Nebraska
Press
Lincoln and
London

The paper in this book meets the minimum requirements
of American National Standard for Information Sciences
—Permanence of Paper for Printed Library Materials,
ANSI z39.48–1984.

Library of Congress Cataloging-in-Publication Data
Littlefield, Daniel F.
Alex Posey–Creek poet, journalist, and humorist /
Daniel F. Littlefield, Jr.
p.cm. – (American Indian lives)
Includes bibliographical references and index.
ISBN 0-8032-2899-6 (cl)
1. Posey, Alexander Lawrence, 1873–1908—
Biography.   2. Poets, American—20th century—
Biography.   3. Journalists—United States—Biography.
4. Creek Indians—Biography   I. Title.   II. Series.
PS2649.P55Z76   1992
811'.4–dc20   91-14538
                                                        CIP

FRONTISPIECE: *Alex Posey, about 1898, when he became
Superintendent of Public Instruction.*

Contents

List of Illustrations, vii

. . . .

Acknowledgments, ix

. . . .

Introduction, 1

. . . .

One: Tuskegee, 11

. . . .

Two: "The Winds of Boyhood," 22

. . . .

Three: Discovery of a Literary Voice, 40

. . . .

Four: Politics and Poetry, 70

. . . .

Five: Return to Possum Flat, 98

. . . .

Six: Journalism and Progress, 136

. . . .

Seven: Fus Fixico and Literary Acclaim, 160

. . . .

Eight: In Search of the Lost Creeks, 187

. . . .

Nine: Death of the Creek Nation, 209

. . . .

Ten: Land and Progress, 226

. . . .

Eleven: "Gone Over to See," 247

. . . .

Postscript, 262

. . . .

Notes, 273

. . . .

Bibliography, 309

. . . .

Index, 319

. . . .

Illustrations

Alex Posey, about 1898	frontispiece
Alex Posey, 1900	7
Map: The Creek Nation	10
Nancy Posey, 1928	60
Tuskegee Indian Baptist Church	61
Lewis Henderson (Hence) Posey	62
Alex Posey as a small child	63
The Posey ranch	64
Lydia Tiger and Lewis Phillips	65
Betsy Riley Phillips	66
Alex Posey, age twelve	67
Bacone students and teachers	68
Alex Posey	69
Creek Orphan Asylum faculty in 1896	124
The Posey home at Bald Hill	125
Bill Posey	126
Frank Posey	127
Horace Posey	128
Mendum Posey	129
Mattie Posey Howe	130
Posey family scene	131
Alex and Yohola Posey	132
James Blaine Posey	133
Pachina, Lowena, and Yohola Posey	134
George Riley Hall	135
The Posey home, 1905	207
Alex Posey, 1905	208
Alex Posey, 1908	249
Minnie and Wynema Posey, 1910	250

Acknowledgments

. . . .

For their help in the evolution of this book, I thank the archivists and librarians at the Thomas Gilcrease Institute of American History and Art in Tulsa, Oklahoma, especially Sarah Erwin, who so readily made available to me the Posey Collection, which formed the heart of this work. Special thanks also go to archivists and librarians at the Oklahoma Historical Society, particularly William G. Welge, head of the Archives and Manuscripts Division, whose knowledge of the archival holdings was indispensable to my research; the Western History Collections at the University of Oklahoma; Bacone College Library; and the Muskogee Public Library.

I also thank Ginger Blaine Moore, daughter of Wynema Posey Blaine, who gave me access to documents that she possesses concerning her grandfather; Elliott Howe, son of Mattie Posey Howe, who shared with me his knowledge of the Posey family and made available an important Posey manuscript; Hugh C. Hall, son of George Riley Hall, who so generously shared his father's memoirs; Leona

Colbert, secretary of the Tuskegee Indian Baptist Church, who assisted me with linguistic matters and church history; George Bunny, of Oklahoma City, who translated for me; Joe Johnson, mayor of Eufaula, Oklahoma, whose admiration for his granduncle's life and work encouraged me in my task; and J. O. Adams, owner of the Bald Mountain Ranch, who so kindly allowed me to climb over his fences and visit the Posey family ranch site and cemetery. Finally, I thank James W. Parins, a colleague at the University of Arkansas at Little Rock, whose collaboration a decade ago on a bibliography of American Indian and Alaska Native writers helped to establish the bibliographic base for this book.

Research for this work was funded in part by a Travel to Collections grant from the National Endowment for the Humanities.

Introduction

. . . .

It was raining, as it had been doing off and on for several weeks, when Alex Posey boarded the MK&T passenger train at Muskogee, Oklahoma, in the early morning of May 27, 1908. His destination was Eufaula, the county seat of McIntosh County, thirty-five miles to the south. In high spirits and eager to reach Eufaula, Posey hoped to complete some business that day with his traveling companion, Robert D. Howe, an agent of the Galbreath Oil Company.[1]

When the train reached the little village of Cathay, only a few miles north of Eufaula, it stopped because of reports that flood-waters were over the tracks. When Alex and Howe inquired, they found the engineer was afraid the roadbed was too weak to support the train. Although the water had undercut the rails and washed the bed from beneath five or six ties, railroad officials who had inspected the scene believed those with nerve might walk across the washout. From Cathay the tracks ran some three miles due south and across the North Canadian River to Eufaula. One could walk along the tracks and cross the railroad bridge—at least that was the theory. Alex persuaded Howe to try, and they and some others went to inspect the crossing. About half a mile south of Cathay they came to the place where the water was running over the tracks. Some of the men attempted to wade across but could not manage it.[2]

The washout was worse than expected—ten to fifteen feet wide. The North Canadian flows generally from west to east, and heavy rains to the west had swollen it to its highest point in decades. Because the raised roadbed impeded its flow, the floodwater was higher on the west side. When the water finally broke over a low place, it quickly ate away the bed so that the gap grew rapidly and the water rushed through at high speed.[3]

Alex and Howe decided to hire a boat from a local resident and row around the washout. While they waited for the boat, Alex went to a nearby farmhouse for breakfast. He was so eager to get Eufaula that he sent Howe to watch for the boat so the other men would not hire it away from them. After some three hours, Joel Scott and Tom Brannon, two black men who lived nearby, arrived with a boat they had borrowed. They planned to row southwest and make a wide arc around the break in the railroad. The current, now very swift as it rushed toward the break, was dangerous, and Howe tried to persuade Alex to let two men who were good swimmers try the crossing first. Alex refused, insisting it was safe. He had no fear of the river; he loved it, calling it Oktahutche, "sand creek," in his native Creek language. He had grown up near the river, swum in it, fished in it, written about it, and taken float trips to observe the plants and animals along its banks. In fact he and a friend, with whom he had rowed down the river many times, had plans to go up the river the next day, put in a boat, and float down to Eufaula. If he and Howe let the other men go ahead of them at the crossing, he argued, he would get to Eufaula too late to take care of his business that day. Having made that argument, Alex got into the boat, walked to the front and sat down. Howe gave in and followed.[4]

As they made their way through the swift current, disaster struck. First the boatman in the stern lost his paddle. As the current caught the boat, the other boatman panicked and lost his. The current turned the boat and propelled it sideways toward the washout. The only hope of not being carried through was to grab the railway right- 3

of-way fence, which ran parallel to the tracks. Everyone, including

of-way fence, which ran parallel to the tracks. Everyone, including Alex, grabbed for the fence, but they hit it with such force that the boat's side caved in. As the boat sank, they jumped over the fence to keep from becoming tangled in it.[5]

Once in the water, each man was on his own. Though the water was only up to their armpits, the current was so swift that the only way to keep from being swept under was to bob up and down and go with the water, which was carrying them steadily toward the break in the road. It was now flowing about a foot over the drooping tracks and several feet under them. Their only hope was to try to go over the rails; because of the rails, ties, and debris, to go under would be certain death. As they bobbed along, Alex came near Howe and grabbed his hand. Howe said they must not hold onto one another but must get on top of the water and swim over the rails in the center of the current. The first to go through the gap was Joel Scott, who went under the rails and was killed. Then Howe went over, followed by Brannon, and both swam out on the Eufaula side of the break. As he waded out of the river, Howe thought he could see Alex sitting on the railroad track on the Cathay side. But when he walked back to the break, he realized that Alex was standing in the current, holding on to what Howe described as "a little sprout not larger than the handle of an umbrella, with three small prongs on it."[6]

Howe was desperate to help his friend. He tried to persuade several spectators who had gathered on the south side of the break to run to Eufaula to bring help and some rope. No one would go. Brannon's father refused to leave his son. Another person had a sore foot and still another, rheumatism. A fourth was afraid to cross the river bridge. Howe returned to the break and asked Alex if he could hang on while he went to Eufaula himself. Alex smiled and waved Howe on with one hand. Despite a severe injury to his leg, the exhausted Howe made it to town as quickly as he could. When word spread that Alex Posey was caught in the flood, several men rushed to the scene with a boat. But they had brought no rope for mooring the boat, and while some encouraged Alex to hold on, others ran back to Eufaula. After about thirty minutes, a train backed up to the break from Eufuala with a train crew and about forty workers to see what could be done about repairing the roadbed. When he saw Alex's predicament, the engineer uncoupled the engine and raced back to Eufaula, returning in about twenty minutes with a rope. By then the crowd had grown to over a hundred.[7]

The plan was to rescue Alex with the boat, mooring it to the right-of-way fence. But the current was so strong that the rescuers could get the boat only within a few feet of him. Alex finally asked W. C. Coppick, a longtime acquaintance who had come out in the boat, to throw him one end of the rope and then pull him in. Coppick asked if Alex was scared or excited, fearing he might panic, but Alex assured him he was not. Alex took the rope in one hand and held the sapling with the other as rescuers pleaded with him not to let go of the tree unless he was certain he could hold the rope. He grabbed the rope with his other hand, but the current swept him off his feet and left him dragging about four feet behind the boat. Exhausted from his ordeal, he was unable to pull himself in, and when Coppick tried to help Alex's grip on the rope began to slip. Turning his head toward the place where Howe and the others stood helplessly watching on the bank, then toward the current rushing through the hole in the roadbed, he opened his hands and the current swept him under the railroad. His body emerged briefly near the right-of-way fence on the other side, his neck apparently broken, then disappeared as over a hundred horrified people looked on.[8]

The news of Alex Posey's death stunned the citizens of eastern Oklahoma. Though not quite thirty-five years old, he was the best-known Creek Indian in Oklahoma. Outside the state, he was better known than any except Chitto Harjo, leader of the Snake faction of Creeks, and Pleasant Porter, the late principal chief of the Creek Nation. As a poet, journalist, and political humorist, for more than a decade he had elevated, enlightened, and amused readers not only in his native Creek Nation but in the Indian Territory at large, Oklahoma Territory, the surrounding states, and other parts of America. He had been a constant player in the social and political drama that was performed in the Indian Territory during the preceding decade as the Indian national governments were dissolved and Oklahoma's statehood was established.

When a man of Alex Posey's stature dies so suddenly, he leaves a void that is sometimes filled with fictions. Over time, the sapling he had clung to in the flood was transformed in the popular mind to overhanging branches. It was mistakenly claimed that he had a fear of water and that his poem "Fancy," wrongly alleged to have been

written shortly before his death, expressed a premonition of death
by drowning:

> Why do trees along the river
>   Lean so far out o'er the tide?
> Cold reason tells me why but
>   I am never satisfied.
>
> And so I keep my fancy still
>   That trees lean out to save
> The drowning from the clutches of
>   The cold, remorseless wave.[9]

A pool of water under the river bridge near the place where he
drowned became known as the "Posey Pool" or "Posey Hole" and
was said to be haunted by the poet's ghost. Strange, inexplicable
sounds came from it in the dead of night. Awful associations were
made with the site, for during the twenty-five years after his death,
it was the scene of ten deaths by drowning or other accidents.[10] Such
stories testify to the vivid imaginations of feature writers without
access to facts.

When Alex Posey died in such dramatic fashion, his friends and
followers eulogized him so that he became fixed in Indian history as
a folk hero, romanticized as a literary artist snatched from life before he had achieved the greatness he was destined for. As a result of
such accounts, the popular concept does not always match the man.

Alex Posey's career had indeed been remarkable. Although he
claimed he did not speak English until age fourteen, he had received
sufficient American-style education at the Creek national boarding school at Eufaula to enter Bacone Indian University at sixteen.
There he acquired his literary tastes and began to write, publishing
enough works to establish a local literary reputation by the time he
left the university in 1894. The next year, at age twenty-two, he was
elected to the House of Warriors, the lower chamber of the Creek
National Council, as representative from Tuskegee, his tribal town,
and was also appointed superintendent of the Creek Orphan Asylum
at Okmulgee. At age twenty-four he had become superintendent of
public instruction for the Creek Nation; at twenty-six, superintendent of the Eufaula boarding school; and at twenty-seven, superin-

tendent of the national boarding school at Wetumka. In 1901 he left Creek national service for good.

At that time Alex Posey's career took a significant turn: he entered politics, not as an office seeker but as a journalist and political commentator. In 1902 he bought the *Indian Journal*, a weekly newspaper at Eufaula, which he edited for more than a year and a half. Then, after a brief venture in the newspaper business at Muskogee, he left journalism in 1904. Meanwhile he had distinguished himself not only for his journalistic style but as the first American Indian in the twentieth century to own and edit a daily newspaper for a sustained time. But his crowning achievement was creating the persona of "Fus Fixico," whose letters to the editor, written in the English dialect of the Creek full-blood, made incisive, humorous comment on politics, bureaucrats, and social and economic conditions in the Indian Territory. He produced seventy-two Fus Fixico letters between 1902 and his death. They were immediately popular in the Indian Territory and shortly thereafter received considerable notice in the United States press. Today they represent his most outstanding literary achievement.

In 1904 he entered another area of political activity. He became a fieldworker for the Dawes Commission, which was in the process of allotting land in severalty to members of the Creek Nation and the rest of the Five Civilized Tribes in preparation for the closing out of tribal affairs and the advent of statehood. Alex Posey had long believed that, given the historical circumstances, allotment of land and United States citizenship were necessary for the Creeks. He embraced the idea of "progress," to which private ownership of land was the key. One major item of unfinished business for the Creeks was the large number of tribesmen who could not or would not enroll for their allotments. One of his tasks, which he worked at until 1907, was to find and enroll them, and this tedious work placed him in close touch with the most conservative of his fellow Creeks. Though he arrived at a new understanding of their needs and desires, he emerged from federal service convinced that they were relics of a bygone civilization who would be unable to participate in the political and economic progress of the twentieth century. After leaving the Dawes Commission, he entered the real estate business and had just resumed editing the *Indian Journal* when he died. His remark-

Alex Posey, 1900. From the author's collection.

able career ended something over two months before his thirty-fifth birthday.

Filled with outstanding achievements though his career was, it was also marked by false starts and unfulfilled potential. His eulogists believed it was simply that his time was cut short. In reality, however, he wrote little serious poetry after 1901, when he was twenty-eight, and exerted little literary effort during the last four years of his life. Also, there were moments, had he seized them, when his literary career could have advanced. Throughout his years in Creek national service he had read voraciously and written extensively, and he produced a body of poetry unsurpassed in size by any Indian before his time and by few since. In 1900 his poetry received some national notice and was sought after by the eastern press. But by then his poetic output had slowed and, self-conscious about his work, he refused to expand his audience, stating publicly that Indians had difficulty expressing themselves poetically in English and that eastern readers would not appreciate his work as did the westerners for whom he claimed to write. There may have been other reasons for his self-consciousness about his poetry, however, reasons related to his own developing taste in literature. In like manner, when the Fus Fixico letters were picked up by the United States press in 1903, he was asked to write on national issues. He again refused, claiming an eastern audience would not appreciate his humor. Without doubt, seeking a broader audience would have pushed his literary career to a new level.

His reluctance stemmed in part from an acute sense of who and where he was. His eulogists explained it simplistically as the "natural" reticence of the Indian. In reality it was a product of the small world in which Alex Posey moved. Few days of his life were spent beyond a fifty-mile radius from his birthplace. Fewer were spent outside the Creek Nation, and fewer still outside Indian Territory. His best literary efforts were those in which he was true to the subjects he knew best—the people and landscapes of the Creek Nation.

Had Alex Posey been only a reticent idealist, dedicated to his art and loved by all who knew him, his character would have been simple—not the complex amalgam it was made by his human frailties. His materialistic side allowed him to espouse progress based on Western technology and to engage in something as mundane as the real estate business. He launched vicious verbal attacks on those he

disliked, and in his writing he expressed a virulent racism aimed at
people of African descent. He willfully participated in Creek political patronage, and though he enjoyed a rapport with Creeks in various classes of society, some of his fellow Creeks believed he had
betrayed them through his work for the Dawes Commission and his
dealings in Indian land. Despite his rapport with the conservative
Creeks, he saw them as impediments to progress or unfortunate by-
products of a changing social order. And shortly before his death,
he made distinctions between "real" Indians and those like himself
who had effectively joined the "white race." However, to say that he
suffered an identity crisis—which contemporary scholars find useful
to discover in assimilated Indians—would be inaccurate. Alex Posey
knew exactly who he was. He reached adulthood at a time when the
social and political order was changing rapidly and the landscape
of the Creek Nation was being transformed by shifting settlement
patterns. He was intensely aware of standing at perhaps the greatest
turning point in Creek history.

As one deeply involved in the changes occurring in the Creek
Nation, Alex Posey counted himself among those who understood
the old order and anticipated what the new order held in store. By
virtue of his childhood during what he called the "palmy" days of
Creek society, he believed he had had a glimpse of the old order,
and he added to his knowledge by associating with older Creeks,
among them historians, linguists, and storytellers, and by his extensive contact with culturally conservative Creeks. He understood
well why they insisted on perpetuating the old rituals, practicing
the old medicine, maintaining the common land title, and restor-
ing the Creek national government. Yet he recognized the futility of
their persistence. Like them, he weighed what life had taught him,
but he arrived at a different conclusion: that material and economic
progress, allotment of land in severalty, and United States citizenship were the only means, under the circumstances, of ensuring
Creek survival in the twentieth century.

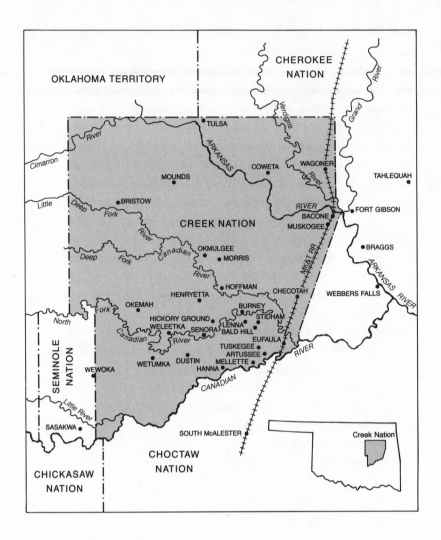

The Creek Nation.

Chapter **1** Tuskegee

· ·

Alexander Lawrence Posey—or Alex, as he preferred to be called—was born in the Creek Nation on August 3, 1873, about fifteen miles northwest of present-day Eufaula, Oklahoma, the first child of Nancy and Lewis Henderson Posey. His mother was a member of Tuskegee Canadian tribal town and his father, of Broken Arrow. Historical odds were against the idea that a child born at that time in such a remote section of the Creek Nation would become the first American Indian to receive significant notice in the United States as a lyric poet and political humorist. Yet circumstances were right for the young Posey. As was common among the Creeks, his mother's family and town would have the greater influence on him, though not because of clan law and practices, which, though greatly diminished from former times, were still viable among the Creeks during his formative years. Instead, in their religious and political activities, the Tuskegees would provide the child with models of "progressive" social change that would be bolstered by his father's political and economic ambitions.

Tuskegee, the Upper Creek town to which Nancy Posey belonged, was a white, or peace, town in the old Creek social and political tradition. After their removal from Alabama, the Tuskegees' town fire was rekindled in two places. One fire in the northern part of the nation near the Lower Creeks was called Red Water or Arkansas Tuskegee, and the other, about four miles north of Tuckabatchee on the Canadian River, was called Tuskegee Canadian. It was into Tuskegee Canadian that Nancy was born in 1848, about one mile north of the Tuskegee fire, the second child of Thlee-sa-ho-he, or Eliza, and Pahosa Harjo. Town membership was determined matrilineally.[1] Nancy was Tuskegee because Thlee-sa-ho-he was; her children would be Tuskegee because she was.

Strangely, Thlee-sa-ho-he was Chickasaw,[2] and so must have been her mother, Nancy, after whom Thlee-sa-ho-he named her first daughter. According to Thlee-sa-ho-he's sister Lydia, later known as Lydia Pah-se or Lydia Tiger, their mother was a member of Wewoka town.[3] If she was the first of her Chickasaw line to marry a Creek, it might be presumed that she belonged to the town of her husband, Otawa Harjo, who bore a distinctively descriptive Creek name. It is uncertain, however, that Otawa Harjo belonged to Wewoka town. Lydia's father was Te-wah-tah-li-che, a Tuskegee. Whether he and Otawa Harjo were the same person is not known. If so, that would explain the affiliation with Tuskegee, because women who went to live in their husbands' towns belonged to those towns. The social and culture mixture displayed by Thlee-sa-ho-he's family typified the Creeks in the early nineteenth century. Instead of being of a unified nation, as Europeans and Americans regarded them, they were an aggregate of peoples with diverse cultures and languages, sharing the same geographic region. One feature that had marked their history since contact with the whites was the absorption of one people by another.[4] However town identity came to Thlee-sa-ho-he, it was established by the time her daughter Nancy was born.

Nancy's kinship was established by her clan, the Wind, and she was related to its members, whether in Tuskegee or in other tribal towns. Like Nancy, her children and those of her sister, Winey, would be Tuskegees of the Wind clan, while the children of her brothers—Tecumseh, Benjamin, Johnson, and Lewis—would belong to the towns and clans of their mothers. Nancy and her clan kin were "People of the White," as were members of the Skunk, Beaver, Bear, Wolf, and Bird clans.[5] In those twilight years of traditional Tuskegee society into which Nancy was born, it was clan kin that determined one's identity in Tuskegee, not family lines as the Europeans understood them.

Somewhat more is known of Nancy's father. Pahosa Harjo was born about 1820 at Tallasee town in the Creek Nation in Alabama. His mother was Eu-pock-lotte-kae, a Tallasee born about 1784, and his father was Tustenuggee Chupco, born about 1778. What town Tustenuggee Chupco belonged to is uncertain, but by 1832 he was recognized as one of the "principal chiefs" of Tallasee. Pahosa Harjo had eleven brothers and one sister, Tina, born about 1812. Besides Pahosa Harjo, the sons included Narkomey, born about 1808; Takosar Harjo, born about 1810; Cheparney, born about 1822; and Tossinnichee, born about 1824. The remaining six sons included Tussekiah Hutke, Takosar, Pahose Micco, and Billy Harjo Phillips; the names of the other two are not known. As an old woman, Nancy would remember the names of only three of her father's siblings, perhaps because of failed memory, but probably in part because Thlee-sa-ho-he's family was more important in her upbringing according to clan practices.[6]

When the main body of Upper Creeks removed in 1836, Eu-pock-lotte-kae and Tustenuggee Chupco and several of their children remained in Alabama. According to Pahosa Harjo, they remained because of ill health, but there may have been additional reasons. Under the Treaty of 1832, the Creeks had given up title to all their lands in Alabama, but individuals could select lands and would receive patents after five years' residence. Under this treaty provision, over two million acres were allotted. As the head man of Tallasee town, Tustenuggee Chupco received a full section of land, 640 acres, and his sons Tussekiah Hutke and Narkomey each got a half-section. Other family members may have received allotments as well. In the wake of allotment there followed an orgy of fraud, harassment, and violence in which many Indians were dispossessed of their land. The family of Eu-pock-lotte-kae and Tustenuggee Chupco managed to retain theirs for the designated five years and, after making arrangements to sell it, removed to the West at their own expense in 1838.[7]

Like the Tuskegees, the Tallasees formed two main settlements in the West—Tulsa Canadian, not far from Tuskegee Canadian, and Little River Tulsa, farther up the Canadian. Pahosa Harjo, who by the time of removal had added "Phillips" to his name, and his brothers Takosar Harjo and Tussekiah Hutke belonged to Tulsa Canadian and ultimately settled at Tuskegee, all having married women from that town.

By the time Nancy was born in 1848, the rich ceremonial life the Upper Creeks had enjoyed before removal had been as nearly replicated in the West as it ever would be. The undisputed center of this ceremonial life was Tuckabatchee, a short distance from the Canadian River. Within a radius of five miles to the west, north, and east of Tuckabatchee town square were the square grounds of a large number of towns, among them Artussee, Tulmachussee, Tulsa Canadian, and Tuskegee.[8] The most significant ceremonial was *posketv*, literally "to fast," known commonly as the green corn ceremony or the busk. Usually held in July or August, its purpose was not only to celebrate the harvest of corn, the staple of Creek diet, but also to ensure the physical and spiritual well-being of the town through dance, song, and rehearsal of the traditional history, as well as the fast, medicine ritual, and ball game.[9]

Bolstered by their rich ceremonial life, the Creeks along the Canadian had prospered once they overcame the physical hardships of removal. Their communal farms provided for the common welfare. The Creeks had also developed vast herds of horses, cattle, and hogs. Herding, one of the many practices adopted from the Europeans, was basic to Creek economy as early as the eighteenth century. They had been good herdsmen before removal, and though the herds multiplied slowly at first in the West, by the time Nancy was born they were well established once more and growing rapidly. Creek women had rights to their own property, which at their deaths went to their children or nearest blood relatives, not to their husbands. By the time Nancy was in her teens, the women of her family owned substantial herds. In summer 1861, Thlee-sa-ho-he had 15 horses, 100 cattle, and 150 hogs, and her sister Lydia had 25 horses, 30 cattle, and 40 hogs. The livestock ran loose, and crops were protected by rail fences, diligently maintained by the town or the individual owners.[10] Nancy's childhood was not only a prosperous time for the Tuskegees but one marked by a stable domestic life, resulting in part from the cohesion of the town as a religious and political unit and from the strength of clan law and practice, though both were no doubt weaker than in former times.

The prosperity ended when the Creeks were drawn into the con-

flict that became known as the American Civil War. The split in
loyalties that characterized the Creeks as a whole also affected
the Tuskegees. Nancy's family likewise was divided, her immediate
family supporting a continued relationship with the United States,
while some of her father's brothers chose to support the Confederate
cause. She and her immediate family became refugees.

In later years Nancy told her descendants that her family was
part of Opothleyohola's famous retreat to Kansas in late 1861. A
slaveholder himself, Opothleyohola was certainly not motivated by
antislavery sentiments. Neither was he particularly pro-Union. He
and other Creek leaders had settled on the Canadian to escape
domination by the McIntosh faction, who had arrived in the West
several years before them. Old animosities that had existed before
removal were transferred to the West. It has been argued that as
the traditional red/white town division declined, it was replaced by
one based on ethnic distinctions, though at times indistinctly defined. On the one hand were the "true" Muskogees and those they
had absorbed, of whom the McIntosh Creeks were a part, and on
the other hand were non-Muskogee groups, including the Tucka-
batchees and Tuskegees, who had not been absorbed. Perhaps this
division, though unrecognized, was manifesting itself once more.
Whatever the cause, as relations between the pro-Union and pro-
Confederate Creeks deteriorated in fall 1861, the former loaded
their movables in wagons, abandoned their homes, rounded up a
few of their cattle, and gathered for mutual protection at a great
camp near the place where the Deep Fork entered the North Fork
of the Canadian. In early November, when attack by the Confeder-
ates seemed imminent, Opothleyohola led his followers—number-
ing several thousand and including a number of Seminoles, some
slaves and free blacks, and a few members of the tribes to the west—
toward Kansas. The story of these people's retreat to Kansas is a
sad one. Opothleyohola was no doubt a brilliant leader and a good
military strategist, but he was hampered by the herds and the wagons loaded with personal goods that his followers brought along.
On November 19, December 9, and December 26 the Confeder-
ates, both whites and Indians, caught up and attacked them. The
last battle, in the northwestern part of the Cherokee Nation, ended
in a rout of the Loyal Creeks. As they fled toward the Kansas border,
the people left everything they had brought. A bitter winter had set

in, with extreme cold and snow. Throughout the night and the next day they made their way to Kansas, most on foot. Many fell by the wayside and froze.[11]

During the next two and a half years subsistence was extremely difficult for the Loyal Creek survivors in refugee camps at LeRoy and other points in Kansas. Divested of their herds of hogs and cattle and of their personal property, they were dependent on Kansas officials, who were ill prepared to care for thousands of Indian refugees, or on the federal government, which was slow to respond to their needs. Thlee-sa-ho-he and her sister Lydia, young Nancy, her brothers Tecumseh and Ben, and other family members, including Tussekiah Hutke and his family, presumably suffered like the other refugees from lack of adequate food, clothing, shelter, and medical attention.[12] Somewhere in exile in 1862, Nancy's only sister, Winey, was born.

After the war, the Creeks were economically devastated and politically divided. The Loyal Creeks who had sought refuge in Kansas had followed the Union army back into Indian Territory, while the southern faction who had retreated to the Red River country during the war remained there until the war's end. Most of the Creeks did not get home until 1865, and many returned in 1866. Although the Confederate Creeks seem to have fared better in their refugee camps than the Loyal Creeks did, on their return home all found a general desolation in the land—their houses burned or fallen in, their fields overgrown, their fences down, their livestock gone, and their personal property missing or ruined. A general poverty prevailed, and the people were reduced to a subsistence economy.[13] The prosperity of the years before the war was just a memory.

Tuskegee Canadian was a microcosm of the Creek Nation. The divisive loyalties that had split the Nation had also split the community. As they struggled to survive by farming their small plots and by hunting and gathering on the public domain, the Tuskegees attempted to reestablish their town. But the town square had gone unattended for several years, the busk had not been held, and the town fire had been extinguished. The old ceremonial life was in sharp decline, and many of the Tuskegees would replace it with a new religious force—Christianity.

Despite prewar missionary efforts, the Tuskegees, like most of the Creeks on the Canadian, had remained basically non-Christian until native missionaries came to them after the war. As time approached for the green corn ceremony in 1866, a native missionary disuaded the town *micco* or headman from assembling the people for the ceremonials. Instead, they began to assemble in small groups for Christian meetings. About August of that year, Pahosa Harjo Phillips and his brothers Billy Harjo Phillips, Tussekiah Hutke, and Pahose Micco became Christians and held services in their homes. Since European contact, Creek history had been marked by cultural change; thus this change is not surprising. Why the people of Tuskegee were now susceptible to the Christian message after having so faithfully resisted is uncertain, but it no doubt had to do with the way their town had been broken up and they had been left destitute and demoralized by the war. The Confederate Creeks, who became strong leaders in the Baptist movement at Tuskegee, had been ministered to by Baptist missionaries in their refugee camps in the Red River country. Also, Pahosa Harjo and his brothers may have been more deeply touched by Anglo-American influence than is known. Some of them had, after all, remained among the whites in Alabama for two years after the main body of the tribe had gone west. That Tussekiah Hutke was a trained blacksmith perhaps reflects the extent of that influence. Under the leadership of these men, Tuskegee took a new direction in 1866, and the busk was not held there again. But the transition from traditional religious practices was not altogether smooth. The fifth brother, Takosar Harjo, vehemently opposed Christianity, believing, as his son-in-law William McCombs later said, in "Indian medicine and the old Indian tradition of the 'Green Corn Festival.'" It was said that his "medicine" was so strong he could make fire come out of his mouth. Whenever Christians met to hold services, Takosar Harjo attempted to break them up.[14]

But at last he too was converted. He fell ill, and his brothers and other Christians, including the Reverend John Smith, a Creek preacher, held services at his house. He was converted after hearing the first song in the Creek hymnal, "God Our Creator and Preserver." He was especially affected by the last verse:

> Vn nettv vhoske 'munken,
> Cesvs vm ehake 'munken,

Elkv vm oreko 'munken,
Mekusapv hakiyate.[15]

(While my day is still left,
While Jesus still waits for me,
Before my time of death comes still,
I want to become a Christian.)

The conversion of Takosar Harjo was considered by some a minor miracle.[16]

Until a church was established, services were held in homes in the Tuskegee community. One was that of Takosar Harjo, who lived near the cemetery west of the present church. Meetings were also held at the home of Thomas McWilliams near present-day Vivian. As interest grew, the people wanted a church and selected a site just east of Takosar Harjo's home. A log building with log furniture was erected and was dedicated on March 23, 1867, the Reverend Chilly McIntosh preaching the dedicatory sermon. The first pastor was Pahosa Harjo Phillips. Takosar Harjo was one of its first two deacons, and Tussekiah Hutke was one of its first exhorters.[17]

In time, mainly through the influence of Nancy Posey's father, paternal uncles, and other relatives, the Tuskegee Indian Baptist Church became the social and religious hub of the Tuskegee community. Her father served as pastor from the time the church was founded until his death nearly thirty years later. Takosar Harjo and his son-in-law William McCombs later selected a final site for the church near the old town square, and a new building was erected there in 1878. McCombs, who had been converted at a Christmas camp meeting at Tuskegee in 1866, was one of the first ministers ordained in the Tuskegee church. In time this extended family's influence was felt elsewhere in the Creek Nation: Cedar River Church at Coweta was founded by Narkomey, and Artussee Indian Church began as a splinter church from Tuskegee with Johnson Phillips, Nancy's younger brother, as pastor.[18]

Apparently from the advent of Christianity at Tuskegee, members of this family, Nancy included, worshiped their newfound God with a fervor equal to, or greater than, that they had bestowed on their traditional ceremonials before the war. According to her grandson, Nancy was once asked how she could believe in the heaven described in the white people's Bible. She replied through her interpreter that gates of pearl and streets of gold were necessary to make heaven attractive enough that the whites would want to go there. The Indians, she said, knew that heaven would have green valleys, high mountains, forests filled with game, and streams with fish. Based on her religious devotion in later years, Nancy's attachment to the church at Tuskegee must have been strong in those early years of her Christian faith. The church, along with her family, became a central focus of her life. Her family's leadership spilled over from the church into other aspects of community life, and in time those town members allied with the Phillips and McCombs families became recognized as town leaders, more intelligent than their fellow citizens.[19] The new order was firmly established in Tuskegee when Alex Posey was born into the community. It was Christian, "progressive" Tuskegee that in large measure shaped his early opinions of what the Creeks were and would become.

Equally important in shaping Alex's ideas of "progress" was his father, Lewis Henderson (Hence) Posey. The facts concerning Hence Posey's childhood and youth lie hidden in the obscure early history of the vast interior of the Indian Territory. Though in later years he would claim one-sixteenth quantum of Creek blood, those Creeks who knew him doubted the claim.[20] Was he born in Alabama as his children later claimed or in the Indian Territory as his obituary said? Had his parents drifted into the Indian Territory from Texas, and was he born in the Creek Nation? Was he, as one family legend said, stolen by the Comanches from a wagon train bound for California and sold to the Creeks? Or was he born in Missouri as he himself apparently claimed in 1860? Was he, as he may have told folklorist William O. Tuggle in 1879, the son of a Presbyterian minister?[21]

Whatever the facts of his predominantly Scotch-Irish heritage and wherever his place of birth, he was born about April 1841, the son of William and Harriett Posey, and was orphaned at an early age. He was reared near Fort Gibson in the Creek Nation by a woman variously said to be a Creek or his father's sister. Years after his death, a friend who knew him well said that Hence was "a white child found to be a waif around Fort Gibson some 20 years before the war" and was taken in and reared by a wealthy Indian family.[22]

Vague though his beginnings were, some facts have been established. That he could speak a dialect of the Creek language fluently—without a white accent, some said—was conceded by most who knew him,[23] which seems to attest either to exceptional linguistic skill or to his living among the Creeks from an early age. He was a member, probably by adoption, of Broken Arrow town, and he received a rudimentary education at one of the mission schools in the Creek Nation, becoming basically literate in English and acquiring some arithmetic skills. By age twelve he was a jockey for a racehorse owner near Fort Gibson[24] and had developed a love of horse racing that was a lifelong passion.

On the verge of the American Civil War, Hence was a laborer at the Creek Agency, west of Fort Gibson. There, at the seat of organizing efforts by Confederate agents, he enlisted in 1861, first as a private in the company headed by Captain F. B. Severs and then as a corporal in Captain William R. McIntosh's Company G of the First Regiment of Creek Volunteers. Ironically, the First Creek Regiment was among the units that fought Opothleyohola and his followers, who included members of his future wife's family. Whether Hence's company participated is unknown. Hence survived the war with only the loss of a finger.[25]

Near the beginning of the war or shortly thereafter, Hence had married into a prominent Creek family named Yargee. His wife was Polly, the daughter of Nancy of Hickory Ground town and Captain Yargee, a Tuckabatchee. The young couple lived at Tuckabatchee and had two children, who died shortly after the end of the Civil War. Polly died in March 1872, and that fall Hence married Nancy.[26]

Hence Posey, like most Creeks, was a farmer and herder. When he and Nancy married, they established their homestead on Limbo Creek in the eastern part of the Tulledega Hills about ten miles northwest of Tuskegee and not far from the North Canadian. There Hence farmed his row crops and began to develop his herd, and Nancy tended the vegetable garden and did the household chores.

This was a bountiful, wild land where they settled. The foothills on the eastern slope of the hills along Limbo Creek were a good hunting area. Along the edge of the prairies there were prairie chickens, and in the hills lived deer, turkeys, mountain lions, and huge gray timber wolves that preyed on the Creek farmers' pigs and calves. Herds of wild horses roamed the region, usually secluding themselves in the hills and canyons but sometimes ranging out onto the prairie to graze. Here, in this section of the Creek Nation, Nancy and Hence began their family. On August 3, 1873, Nancy bore their first child, and Hence named him Alexander Lawrence Posey after the world conqueror Alexander the Great.[27] On that day they could not have imagined what vast changes lay in store for the Creek Nation of the child's youth and early manhood or what public acclaim would be given their son.

Chapter 2 "The Winds of Boyhood"

· ·

By the time Alex was in his late teens, he was
acutely aware of the certainty that the national governments of the
Five Civilized Tribes would cease, that the Indian Territory would
be admitted to the Union as a state, and that a radical change in
land tenure among the Indians would result. By his mid-twenties
the Creek Nation was experiencing rapid economic growth accompanied by an influx of hordes of non-Indians from the states. Such
changes caused Alex to think of his childhood days as representative
of the "old times," what he referred to as the "palmy" days of Creek
society. By then he had already written a good deal, published a
number of works, and had enough literary ambition to consider himself a writer. He was also an inveterate romantic, and as he began to
consider the path that had led to his present success and to record his
memories of earlier times, his impressions were certainly idealized,
if not exaggerated. In later years he believed that growing up when
he did qualified him to address the changes occurring in Creek society and to relate to the Creeks who changed with the times as well
as those who were incapable of doing so.

The world of Alex Posey's childhood was that wedge of land between the north and main branches of the Canadian River west of
Eufaula, near which the rivers met. The Tuskegee hills, where many
of Nancy's relatives lived, formed the divide between the rivers. To
the south the land broke rapidly to the main branch of the Canadian,
and to the north it dropped off to broad, expansive prairies before
falling sharply to the North Canadian, or Oktahutche. The northwestern boundary of these prairies was formed by the Tulledega
Hills that run roughly north and south and span the river, Tulledega
Mountain rising above the others on the river's north side. To the
south, Limbo Creek winds its way northward through the southern
range of these hills. It was on this creek, near present-day Lenna,
that Alex was born in the summer of 1873.[1]

During his early childhood, Alex's world was that sequestered region he called Tulledega, which even in adulthood remained to him
a symbol of remoteness and natural beauty, a place

> Hedged in, shut up by walls of purple hills,
> That swell clear cut against our sunset sky.
> Hedged in, shut up and hidden from the world,
> As though it said, "I have no words for you;
> I'm not a part of you; your ways aren't mine."[2]

Alex believed it was here, in this isolated region, that he had acquired much of the character and many of the ideas that served
him well in his adult years. From Nancy and Hence he learned the
Creek language and some knowledge of Creek history and culture
and, through these, access to conservative Creek society. To Nancy
he attributed his deep love of nature and his ability to observe it
closely and intensely. From Hence he acquired his desire for formal
education, as well as his habits of dress, political views, and economic values. Here, despite the isolated setting, was the intersection
of two different, and in many ways conflicting, life-styles, two world-
views, whose boundaries Alex crossed easily as an adult. In time he
would extoll the virtues of one world and lament its passing while
enthusiastically embracing the other.

During his mid-twenties, Alex wrote a series of stories about his
childhood experiences. Under the titles "Jes 'Bout a Mid'lin', Sah"
and "Two Famous Prophets," two were published a few years later,
as were statements to the press concerning his earlier years. These

statements aimed at establishing an early date for the awakening of his poetic sensibility. At the time he recorded his memories, his romantic idealism was at its peak, and his recollections were filtered through that screen.

In memory, he passed his early childhood in a tranquil, fun-filled realm dominated by his mother. Nancy's was basically a Creek world, but one deeply touched by Anglo influence; she was a devout Christian, a charter member of the Baptist Church at Tuskegee. Though uneducated, she was an intelligent, sensitive woman to whom fell the responsibility of caring for the garden and managing the household. She kept the house neat and gave her devoted attention to the children she bore Hence—twelve in all.[3] But it was Alex, her firstborn, whom she seemed to favor, and for his first twelve years, as he looked back, she was his more influential parent.

Perhaps she was aware of a special sensitivity to life around him that set him apart from the others. Alex believed, or at least wished to project the image, that the influences that made him a poet began early. It was a family story, which he retold fondly for the press, that his love of the beautiful dated back to age two: "I slipped through the backyard fence one snowy day and ran away from home, followed by my pet dog, Shep. During my ramble I found a pretty flower under a sheltering bank and plucked it. When my mother tracked me up through the snow it so touched her heart to have me offer her a gift so sweet and welcome in so bleak a season that she dropped her switch and kissed me for my truancy."[4] In later years Nancy watched this sensitivity develop under her guidance into a quick and keen power of observation and a love for the Tulledega Hills, the rolling prairies to the southeast, Limbo Creek and the Oktahutche, and for the plants and animals of their secluded home.[5]

Nancy also instilled in her children a basic knowledge of the old times, the Tuskegee world before the whites came. According to her children she was a gifted storyteller who occupied their time during winter nights with tales of their people's creation, migration, and history and of the legendary personages and animals that peopled that mystery world of long ago.[6] Though Christian, she apparently found nothing contradictory in her newfound beliefs and the folklore of her people that she had learned as a child, perhaps from the elder man of her clan. As she passed on the stories in the language in which they had come to her, she found that Alex listened more attentively than the rest.[7]

We do not know what stories she told. Perhaps she told of that time when there was only water, before there were earth and land animals; how Crawfish dived down and was gone four days but finally returned bringing mud in his claws; and how Eagle, the chief, took the mud and made an island for the creatures to live on until the waters receded. Perhaps she told how in that old time the Controller of Breath created the clans and how her children came to be members of the powerful Wind clan, a kinship that would prove useful to Alex in later life. Perhaps she told them how the trickster Chuffee, or Rabbit, played a trick on Tie Snake, the strongest of the legendary beasts; how Rabbit played so many tricks that the other animals fashioned a tarbaby and caught him; but how he tricked Wolf into helping him escape. Or perhaps she told how Rabbit had the tables turned on him: how Turtle outwitted him and won their race, and how Opossum tricked him into butting his head against a persimmon tree and knocking himself out.[8] Alex's writing reflects familiarity with many of these traditions, though it is uncertain at what age he acquired it. Whether they were these tales or others, the stories Nancy told gave Alex a glimpse into the farthest recesses of the ancient Creek world, and as early as his teenage years he began to put this lore to literary use.

Like the Catskills of Washington Irving's stories, the Tulledegas were the dwelling place of creatures and beings of legendary proportions. They were the home of Tie Snake and the Lost Man of mythic fame and of Este Chupco, the wood spirit. There roamed *yahv*, the wolf, much feared by the Creeks. Harming him brought retribution, and children were warned not to say bad things about him. They called him *este puca rakko*, great grandfather, and *nere fulle*, night wanderer, for even to speak his name was dangerous.[9]

The Tulledegas were also the dwelling place of "medicine men" of wide fame, about whom Alex reminisced. Well learned in tribal rituals and songs, with alleged power to foretell events and to weaken enemies and strike opposing warriors blind, in former times they had been what the whites called prophets.[10] Now, in that transition period of Creek history during Alex's childhood, though still revered and held in awe by some, they were dismissed by many unbelievers as quacks, charlatans, or foolish old men. One was Chalogee, whose log cabin was on a tributary of Limbo Creek not far from the Posey farm. As Alex remembered him, Chalogee was dark, tall, thin, and somewhat stooped and dressed characteristically in a red shirt and red shawl turban. "I remember him well," Alex wrote years later, "for he passed our place almost daily on his way to the next settlement to blow medicine for the sick or locate by divers strange signs and mutterings a lost hog or cow or horse." An "unbeliever" himself, Alex attributed these men's success to keen observation. According to him, Chalogee "was a close student of nature and in all his life lived alone, mingling very little with other men except in a professional way. The full-bloods, among whom he was most popular, mistook his intimate acquaintance with natural facts and laws for divine knowledge, and he, like other prophets, was shrewd enough not to let them know any better."[11] Chalogee's greatest power lay in rainmaking, and during Alex's childhood it was common knowledge that there was a deep pool in the creek near his cabin where he kept his medicine stone and the thunderbolts he had captured and used to make it rain.[12]

Of wider fame than Chalogee was the Alabama Prophet, who lived in seclusion in the western fastness of Tulledega. He was said to have pulled the horns from the dreaded Tie Snake, and his power was undisputed. Possessing great medicine, he could cure disease by blowing in water through a hollow cane or by administering herbs. His medicine bag, according to Alex, was said to contain, "in profound secrecy, the dust of ages, the tooth and hoof of things without name or record." And like Chalogee, he had thunderbolts at his command to make rain.[13] That men like the Alabama Prophet and Chalogee peopled the Tulledega of Alex's childhood is a certainty, though as he recalled them from the perspective of adulthood, they may have grown larger than life.

If the Posey family endured hard times in those early years, the experience was lost on Alex. He enjoyed endless days at play with the companion of all his boyhood days, Tom Sulphur, a full-blood orphaned Creek child whom Hence and Nancy adopted. Alex preferred running through the woods with his two dogs to playing with the usual toys, and of the latter, according to Nancy, he chose bows and arrows.[14] With Tom he explored the natural world of Tulledega, fished and swam in its streams, hunted for wild game in the woods, and chased the wild horses that ran loose there and on the nearby prairies. There were chores like carrying wood and water, weeding the garden, and caring for the livestock, but they faded from Alex's memory as he grew older.

Alex more frequently remembered the days of fun and laughter that he and Tom shared. Years later he could still laugh about the time Tom "accidentally exploded a big bunch of parlor matches in his pants pocket and groveled in fresh-plowed earth to put out the fire on himself." Sometimes the boys acted on impulse, as when they pulled the stoppers out of the two-gallon jugs another boy was using to keep himself afloat as he learned to swim.[15]

Other pranks were more elaborate, taking time and careful planning. While Hoyt, the farmhand Hence had hired, was asleep, they put eggs in his gumboots. They watched old Chalogee pass so frequently that they knew what time he came by, and they usually hid, afraid of his "evil influence." One day, however, they put a rattlesnake one of the farmhands had killed across Chalogee's path. Alex later remembered what happened when the old man stepped on the snake with his bare feet: "Eighty or ninety years were not a burden to him then. He jumped backward further than Tom could jump forward, hop, step and a leap, made a wide detour and plodded on in the same fashion as though nothing had happened, while Tom and I held our hands over our mouths and rolled over each other." Even Nancy was not immune to their elaborate schemes. Once they dug a pitfall in her path to the garden, covered it with sticks and dirt, and waited for her to fall into the hole.[16] The boys sometimes felt the sting of the switch, but minds clever enough to create such mischief were without doubt keen enough to recognize the justice of the discipline that followed. The childish pranks they engineered reflected in Alex the making of the humorist, the ability to read the character of his fellow human beings and find comedy in their attempts to deal with their predicaments.

In later years a romantically inclined Alex remembered the freedom of those "days of lost sunshine," symbolized by the loose garments Nancy made for him and Tom to wear in the summer. Their long shirts, or "sweeps," were "flowing garments, made on the order of a tunic but longer and more dignified." And he recalled nostalgically, "There was a vast freedom in these gowns; freedom for the wind to play in, and they were easily thrown aside at the 'old swimmin' hole.' We looked forward with regret to the time when we would have to discard them for jeans coats and trousers and copper-toed boots, though these were desirable to chase rabbits in on a snowy day. Those who have never worn 'sweeps' have never known half of the secrets whispered by the winds of boyhood."[17]

The world of his childhood, which Alex remembered as idyllic, had harsher realities that were lost on the child or that he later chose not to recall. His father's economic views were clearly Anglo directed. Reared a Creek from early childhood and fluent in the language, he was a member of Broken Arrow, a Lower Creek town. Unlike the Creeks on the Canadian, whom Nancy came from, the Lower Creeks had more members with Creek-European ancestry; they had moved far along the road toward acculturation in such matters as economic values before removal, and acculturation had been more rapid among them in the postremoval period. Hence's life was quite like that of the frontier farmer-rancher who tilled the soil to feed his family and supplement what the range provided in winter for his hogs, mules, horses, work oxen, and cattle.

The farmer-rancher of those days in the Creek Nation had a precarious existence. Ideal weather, flood, or drought made the difference between adequate and insufficient pasture or abundant and failed crops. The drought that began in 1879 lasted until May 1880, but later rains brought a surplus of grains and a large cotton crop. During those drought years, ranchers were forced to sell off their herds for lack of grazing. In 1881 a devastating drought caused nearly total failure of grain and vegetable crops, but in 1882 and 1883 the crops were the best in many years. The winter of 1883–84 was severe, however, and much livestock died of exposure. In such times the ranchers could only skin the carcasses and dry the hides for market. Businessmen could judge the year's prospects by how many of these "poverty hides" came in.[18] Herds that survived the ravages of the weather were subject to infection by sickness such as cattle fever, blackleg, and hoof-and-mouth disease. Such dramatic turns in fortune made the farmer-rancher's future both uncertain and unpredictable.

Though a "progressive" farmer, Hence sometimes fell back on his Creek upbringing in the lean years. Once, perhaps it was 1880, his prospects looked dismal. There had been a poor crop the year before, and the drought was shriveling the current crop so that it appeared there would be no corn. It was a commonly told story that he sought out Chalogee, the rainmaker, and offered him five salt barrels of corn, then worth $1.50 a bushel, if he could make it rain within twenty-four hours. Chalogee promised Hence a shower. Then he went to the pool where he kept his thunderbolts, stripped, waded in and stirred the water, and declared that his thunderbolts were good and it would rain. That afternoon there was thunder as a black cloud formed and came in from the west. But Chalogee had lost control, and out of the cloud came such a downpour that the creek flooded the pool and washed his thunderbolts away. The rain continued until the next day when, after a desperate search, Chalogee found his thunderbolts in a raft of driftwood near the mouth of Limbo Creek and brought them safely home.[19] But Hence could not always count on the prophets to succeed.

Sometime during the mid-1880s, he started a new ranch at Bald Hill and moved his family there.[20] The only heights for miles around, Bald Hill rises above the prairies about eight miles west of Eufaula. In the 1880s it was on a major travel route from the Choctaw Nation, northwest toward Okmulgee and the Lower Creek towns on the Arkansas River. Near Bald Hill, this trail joined one from Eufaula to the east. Surrounding Bald Hill were expanses of prairie that would provide good grazing for Hence's livestock and rich farmland that promised better crops. He established his headquarters on the north side of Bald Hill. There, by the late 1880s, he had built a large two-story ranch house to accommodate his growing family.

The Creek Nation their children were born into was vastly different from the one Hence and Nancy had grown up in, having evolved through twenty years of political turmoil and strife. The Creeks had emerged from the Civil War a deeply divided people, split over a number of issues besides Union and Confederate loyalties: progressive and conservative social views; division of tribal annuities and disbursement of tribal funds; Loyal Creek claims against the United States at the close of the war; encroachment of federal power in law enforcement; adoption of the freedmen, former slaves of the Creeks; the coming of the railroads, which brought the development of American-style frontier towns such as Wagoner, Muskogee, and Eufaula; and the resulting intrusion of whites and American blacks on Creek lands. Lines of loyalty regarding these issues often shifted, making Creek politics volatile, but there was always a core of conservative Creeks, with whom the freedmen often allied themselves, who were generally disaffected from the direction of Creek affairs.

Conflicting views and attitudes over the long-standing issues were aggravated by the establishment of constitutional government. The Southern and Loyal factions had nominally unified as a nation in 1867 under a written constitution. The Constitution of the Muskogee Nation established a government patterned somewhat after that of the United States. It established a two-house council, consisting of a House of Kings with a member from each tribal town and a House of Warriors in which each town was represented by one member plus an additional member for every two hundred people in the town. A principal and second chief and other officers were elected every four years. The judiciary consisted of a supreme court and six judicial districts with judges, prosecutors, and police known as lighthorse companies.

The most conservative Creeks soon became dissatisfied, having understood, they claimed, that the old Creek law from before the war would be reestablished under the constitution, not that the whites' law would be adopted. They had little understanding of the new election process or of legislative and court procedures. Thus for many years they persisted in attempting to elect their leaders by preconstitutional means and to execute laws in the old fashion. Led by Sands, then Lochar Harjo, and finally Isparhecher, they resisted the establishment of constitutional government for fifteen years. Armed resistance seemed imminent in 1869, 1871, and 1873. Yet these were only tremors leading to the eruption of the Green Peach War in 1882, in which anticonstitutional forces under Isparhecher were driven from the nation by national forces led by Pleasant Porter. With the amnesty that followed this civil upheaval in 1882 and 1883, the conservatives ceased their open armed resistance to constitutional government. The historical facts indicate what happened, but not why. The Green Peach War has been explained recently as another eruption of the old antagonism between the "pure" Muskogees and the non-Muskogees. This theory of ethnic duality also does much to explain the social and economic cleavage that developed in later decades between conservative Creeks, who were in large measure non-Muskogees, and the progressive Creeks.[21] Though they continued to resist changes they believed threatened them, the conservatives did not thereafter present a serious threat of armed rebellion. With the decline of civil strife after the Green Peach War, the Creek Nation seemed to face a brighter political and economic future.

In the years leading up to the Green Peach War, Hence Posey twice served as a member of the lighthorse police. The first time was before he and Nancy were married. Then in September 1881 he was elected captain of the lighthorse company for Eufaula District but served only a few months, resigning his office on February 22, 1882. Perhaps he had realized, as political tension grew on the eve of the Green Peach War, that he might be called on to enforce the laws against his neighbors who were at odds with the government. That the political turmoil had divided Eufaula District is certain. In 1881 Hence joined a group of citizens who opposed attempts to oust the district judge as well as Captain Dick Berryhill and the privates of the lighthorse company.[22]

Official status as a peace officer was not a prerequisite for Hence to go after criminals. In late August 1885, two young Creek freedmen, Jake and Joe Tobler, brutally murdered and robbed Frank H. Cass and A. P. Goodykoontz, well-known and respected traders at Muskogee and at Vinita. A few days later the Toblers were captured near Eufaula by Hence, with the assistance of Bob Gentry and Freeland McIntosh. They received a reward of $500. Because the crime occurred on the Sac and Fox reservation just west of the Creek border, the case fell under the jurisdiction of the federal court at Wichita, Kansas, and the following summer and twice thereafter, Hence went there to testify. The Toblers were convicted and were hanged on November 21, 1888. Sometimes when he was not chasing outlaws himself, Hence traveled around the Creek Nation soliciting funds to feed others who were.[23]

Hence had never been one who ran from violence. In his world survival depended in large measure on self-defense and physical prowess. It was a world of guns and whiskey and personal vendettas. These once came together in deadly combination when Hence went to buy whiskey from William Sewell. When Hence arrived at Sewell's house, he tied his horse at the front gate and went inside. But Sewell accused him of stealing whiskey, and a fight ensued. Hence wore his thick, black hair long in those days, and during the fight Mrs. Sewell grabbed it and pulled him down. He finally broke loose, threw her aside, and ran to the front gate, where he had left his gun. He had just reached it when Sewell came out of the house, gun in hand. Hence got off the first shot and killed him.[24] Perhaps such violent episodes were inescapable in that time and place for one as strong-willed and independent as Hence.

Ranchers like Hence were forced to maintain constant vigilance against rustlers, who found their range cattle and horses easy prey. In the days before barbed-wire fences in the Creek Nation, Hence's livestock, like that of other Creek ranchers, ran on the public domain, his ownership shown by a large **JP** branded on his animals' sides. In 1885 he joined the Muskogee and Seminole Livestock Association, made up of Creek men and women of mixed heritage, Creek freedmen, and tribally adopted white ranchers who organized for mutual assistance in roundups and for protection against rustlers and horse thieves. In the early spring of 1885, Hence joined Cub McIntosh and Dick Berryhill, captain of the lighthorse police, in tracking a herd of stolen horses north through Muskogee to Concharty Town on the Arkansas River. At the house of Jonas Bush, they confronted one of the thieves, Mitchell Collins, who came out of the house firing a gun with each hand. Hence, McIntosh, and Berryhill riddled Collins, wounded another of the thieves, and recovered the horses.[25]

As with Alex's memories of the Tulledegas, the harsh realities of the violence and Hence's struggle for physical and economic survival did not enter Alex's recollection of his childhood at Bald Hill. Life there was not as isolated as in Tulledega, and Alex encountered a diverse population. There were the white ranch hands such as Bill Barns and Ike that Hence hired to help with the ranch work. Because Bald Hill was near the trail from Eufaula to Okmulgee, the national capital, visitors were frequent. During political seasons men sought out Hence to discuss politics. East of Bald Hill were the headwaters of Coon Creek, where there was a large settlement of Creek freedmen, among them the Graysons—Uncle Will, Uncle Dick and his wife, Aunt Cook, and their children Richard and Moses—about whom Alex gathered over time a large repertoire of stories, both firsthand and at secondhand from Hence. The Posey family, as Alex recalled, enjoyed an easy relationship with their neighbors and hired hands.[26]

The move to Bald Hill had put the family in closer touch with Nancy's relatives. Only five miles to the south were the hills surrounding Tuskegee, where she was born and where her church was.

In those hills and on south and east toward the main branch of the Canadian River lived most of her closest relatives. Her mother, Thlee-sa-ho-he, had died in 1874.[27] Nancy and her brother Tecumseh Phillips were both married, but Thlee-sa-ho-he left four other children—Benjamin, Winey, Johnson, and Lewis—whose ages ranged from middle teens to less than two years. The task of caring for them fell to her sister, Lydia Tiger. Lydia was the only mother Lewis really knew, and he remained with her for the rest of his life. In the early 1880s Nancy's aging father, Pahosa Harjo Phillips, married Betsy Riley, the widow of Tchadahkey, sometimes known as Tchadahkey McIntosh. She brought into the family a son, Louis McIntosh. Pahosa Harjo Phillips and Betsy had three children: Louis, born in 1883; Taylor, born in 1885; and Abbie, born in 1888.[28] They made their home near Artussee about three and a half miles southeast of Tuskegee, but Nancy apparently had little to do with her half-siblings, who were the age of her own younger children and, according to the still viable clan practices, would have been considered little kin to her.

Though Lydia Tiger later took Lewis with her to Mounds, near Tulsa, Nancy's other full brothers and her sister remained near Tuskegee and Artussee. Tecumseh (Cumsey) had first married Wysie, a Tulmachussee by whom he had one son, John. After her death he married Coosie, the daughter of Coosie Harjo, who had a daughter, Jennie Grayson. In addition to Jennie, Cumsey and Coosie had a large family of their own. Benjamin Phillips married Sarah Scott and had seven children when he died on January 18, 1889. Winey Phillips married Robert M. Evans, a white native of the Indian Territory who had been adopted by the Creeks in 1866, and settled near Tuskegee; and Johnson Phillips married Hannah, the daughter of Tie-e-tah-kee. She died shortly thereafter, and he married Hettie Riley and settled near Artussee.[29]

Also in the Tuskegee and Artussee communities lived many of Nancy's relatives who were descended from her father's brothers, Tussekiah Hutke and Takosar Harjo. Tussekiah Hutke had died, apparently in the late 1870s, but his widow, Lilka, known also in later years as Lillie Kernel and Lillie Jessie, remained at Tuskegee, as did two of their children, Billie Jessie and Minkey Francis.[30] Takosar Harjo had died in 1878. His daughters Sallie and Milla married William McCombs and David McCombs, both of whom played significant roles in the social, political, and religious life of the Tuskegee community.

The church at Tuskegee formed the nucleus of religious and social life not only for Nancy but for many of her relatives as well. Pahosa Harjo Phillips had been pastor of the church since its founding. The significant roles his brothers had played in its history made the church a focal point for their descendants, especially those of Takosar Harjo. Though in some ways a typical means of setting aside the old Creek cultural practices, the church ensured the vitality of the Creek language. Sermons, prayers, and songs were in Creek, and the weekly gatherings offered family members an opportunity to maintain ties. Of special importance were the extended summer encampments at the church, which let people fellowship and worship together. Families had designated camping areas that encircled the church, where they visited with one another and shared hospitality.[31]

Nancy's extended family, the descendants of Eu-pock-lotte-kae and Tustenuggee Chupco, played prominent roles in Creek national affairs, participating broadly in the establishment of constitutional government. Tussekiah Hutke had served in the House of Warriors in 1869. Pahosa Harjo Phillips represented Tuskegee in the House of Kings in 1886 and 1887, and in 1888 he was elected to the House of Warriors and would represent Tuskegee there until the eve of his death in 1895. William McCombs was also well known in the Creek Nation, having served in the National Council, as national interpreter, and on the supreme court as well as in other capacities.[32]

The family also helped establish constitutional processes on the district level. After the nation had been divided into judicial districts under the constitution, a courthouse was established for Eufaula District, first known as North Fork, between Bald Hill and Tuskegee and somewhat to the west. Before that, court was held, among other places, at the Tuskegee church. There, as elsewhere in the nation, adjustment to new concepts of meting out justice did not come easily. In the early days, in the absence of legal maneuvering, court sessions in criminal cases, for instance, apparently consisted of gathering witnesses for both the prosecution and the defense, having them tell what they knew about the case, and asking the jury for a verdict. Pahosa Harjo Phillips, Tussekiah Hutke, Takosar Harjo, Hence Posey, and Ben and Cumsey Phillips appeared frequently as jurymen and as witnesses for the defense or the prosecution.[33]

The importance of Alex's relationship to these families is great. They were among the most highly respected members of Tuskegee and Artussee, with a long history of involvement in the social, political, and religious life of the communities. Among them were some of the most "progressive" of the Upper Creeks. As an adult, Alex never failed to recognize his family bonds to these people, and as politician, educator, journalist, agent for the Dawes Commission, and land dealer, he sought them out for information and assistance.

Surrounded as he was by family members who were politically active, it is not surprising that by his late teenage years Alex had already developed a deep interest in Creek politics. It was a common topic in the Posey home, for politics fascinated Hence. He was at one time offered the office of judge or attorney for Eufaula District, but he saw himself as a power broker rather than an office seeker. By virtue of his service in the Confederate army, his political alliance after the Civil War had been with the Southern faction, but over time his loyalties shifted as the constitutional system took hold. In the election of 1887, for instance, he supported the Independent party, which nominated John Moore and James Fife to head the ticket. In the wake of smoldering political resentment after the Green Peach War, the party stood for streamlining the government, law and order, and opposition to the sale of Creek interests in the Oklahoma lands to the west. Party officials called on Creek voters to forget the old divisions between Loyal and Southern factions and the racial distinctions of full and mixed blood. Hence apparently viewed himself as a local "party boss" who had hopes at least of delivering the votes of the Creek freedmen from Coon Creek, who ordinarily aligned themselves with the conservative faction. Hence's effectiveness as a political boss is debatable, however. More significant is the discussion of politics that went on in the Posey household. Men often stopped by to discuss political questions, and the Posey children became accustomed to overhearing their conversations on the front porch and learned very early to be seen and not heard on those occasions.[34]

Alex's childhood idyll at Bald Hill began to fade for him, he recalled, at about age twelve. At that time Hence assumed a more important role in his upbringing. Alex now had six siblings with whom he must share Nancy's attention: Melissa, born in 1875; William, born in 1877; Frank, born in 1879; John, born in 1881; Mattie, born in 1883; and Cornelius (Conny), born in 1885. Nancy was a devoted mother who saw that all her children were well fed and comforted them when they were ill; yet Alex occupied a special place in her life. Though Hence would thereafter have more to say about the specific direction of Alex's future, mother and son had established a loving bond that remained strong for the rest of his life.

By the late 1880s Hence had become convinced that he must do something for his children if they were to survive the rapid social changes sweeping their nation. That "something" was formal education. He himself had received only rudimentary schooling, and his experiences during the Civil War had caused him "to see the vast disadvantages of ignorance and illiteracy." He decided that if he survived, he would learn to read and acquire "general knowledge, especially history." By the time Alex was a teenager, Hence was well informed on local and United States national affairs and kept current by subscribing to magazines and newspapers.[35] As an adult Alex saw his father as a "self-educated man of uncommon intelligence, with a philosophical and scientific turn of mind." Time had taught Hence practical lessons, and he was full of common sense. He lectured his children and stressed to them the importance of adages like "one wild shoat will spoil a gang of tame ones."[36] But lecture them as he would, the self-education and common sense that had served him would not equip his children to face the social changes their lifetimes would bring to the Creek Nation.

His first attempt at educating Alex failed. He had "picked up" somewhere a man with "a bookish turn" and brought him home as a private tutor. Alex described him as "a dried-up, hard-up, weazen-faced, irritable little fellow" who was apparently a better eater than teacher and who succeeded in teaching Alex only to recite the alphabet and "to read short sentences."[37] Like Nancy, Alex understood English "fairly well," but "its construction was so entirely different from his native tongue that he feared to trust himself in the use of it."[38] Thus he made little progress in English education until age fourteen.

At that time, according to Alex, an incident occurred that changed the boy's life forever: Hence forced him to speak English. "One evening," Alex wrote, "when I blurted out in the best Creek I could command, and began telling him about a horse-hunt, he cut me off shortly." Hence threatened him with a whipping if he did not tell the story in English after supper. Though Alex enjoyed eating, he suddenly lost his appetite, left the table, and busied himself with chores—"brought water from the well, turned the cows into the pasture"—hoping that Hence would forget his threat. "My goodness, however," wrote Alex, "was without avail, for as soon as he came from the table he asked me in a gentle but firm voice to relate my horse-hunt. Well, he was so pleased with my English that he never afterward allowed me to speak Creek."[39] While this event was dramatic as Alex recalled it, it did not quite put the Creek culture behind him. Though Hence forbade it during his childhood, Alex spoke Creek fluently throughout his life. Nevertheless, his transition to the Anglo-oriented world of politics and formal education was now under way.

Not long after this episode, Hence sent Alex to Eufaula to attend the Creek national public school. What an abrupt change that must have been for the youth! Eufaula, which had sprung up after the railroad came in 1872, was approaching five hundred in population. Alex, like some of the other students, boarded at the Forest Hotel. There he was initiated into a new world of town dwellers—men with education, politicians, and shrewd businessmen looking for quick money. Except for brief periods, he would spend the rest of his life amid such hustle and bustle.

In November 1888 Hence bought the Creek House in Eufaula and renamed it the National Hotel. Besides Alex and Melissa, who attended the Presbyterian Mission School in Muskogee, he had other children to educate, and his family was growing. Horace had been born in 1887 and James Blaine in 1888. Now there were nine children besides Tom Sulphur, and the family income had to be supplemented.[40]

At first the ranch at Bald Hill had been successful. Hence had even found the means to indulge the love of horse racing he had retained since childhood. In the mid-1880s he was superintendent of the race track at the Indian International Fair at Muskogee, where races drew large crowds during the fair seasons. There he raced his blooded stallion Dick and his roan Indian pony against the horses of such opponents as Cherokee chief Dennis Bushyhead, and in other seasons he trained his horses for private races.[41] By the late 1880s, however, times had become so hard that on occasion Hence claimed to have gone into Eufaula "to get a cup of real coffee" because he had "nothing but parched corn coffee at home."[42] Thus he left the ranch in the care of Bean Wilson, a ranch hand from Arkansas, and moved his family to town.[43] Alex settled into a garret room in the hotel and continued his studies soon going as far in his education as the Eufaula school could take him.

Alex progressed so rapidly that he found himself with free time. After school hours and during holidays, he spent much of his time in the local newspaper office of Albert Wortham, editor of the *Indian Journal*, who taught him how to do printing and to write articles for the weekly paper. He learned so well that when Wortham became ill he left the boy in charge of the newspaper business, and Alex proved Wortham's judgment correct. He managed to publish the paper each week and to do a "very creditable" job of it.[44]

Alex's days of newspaper office routine must have formed a sharp contrast to the memory of his exploits with Tom in the woods and along the streams in Tulledega. But the days in Tulledega were just that—memory. The "winds of boyhood" had ceased blowing for Alex forever. In the years that followed, as he moved further away from that early life, he looked back wistfully, yearning to recover it in his literary works yet realizing that it was forever lost. It was time to move on to something else. By summer 1889 he had already tried his hand at rhyming. That and the work he had done for Wortham strongly pointed the directions he would go.

In addition to the sharp intellect that his rapid progress at Eufaula demonstrated, Alex had by then acquired other characteristics that would help him on his way. Nancy had fostered in him a fluency in, and love for, his native language, a sensitivity to, and reverence for, beauty in nature, and the ability to closely observe the world around him. From her and her extended family he acquired his sense of place in Tuskegee and therefore the Creek world. They also provided him with good examples of "progressive" Creeks. From Hence, for whom he had great admiration, he had gained the strong will, determination, and fun-loving spirit that, along with a keen sense of humor, made up Hence's character. Hence, known as "a jolly fellow" who took every opportunity to play a practical joke, loved humorous stories and delighted in telling them in dialect, and he passed his bent for fun on to his children. They inherited as well the Creek propensity for joking with one another, ensuring fun-filled days of childhood and youth and, especially for Alex, a love of humor in adulthood. Both parents exemplified the art of survival. During the next few years, in reading Charles Darwin, Robert Ingersoll, and others, Alex would discover a word for the key to that survival: *adaptation.*

Chapter 3   Discovery of a Literary Voice

· ·

One night in 1890, a young would-be writer named George Riley Hall arrived in Eufaula and sought a room at Hence Posey's National Hotel. A native of Missouri, Hall had come to the Indian Territory in 1888 with his brother Jefferson. This son of a mechanic and farmer rented land west of Eufaula but was finding farming a poor source of livelihood. Though he had attended school, as he often said, only to the Fifth McGuffey Reader, he was self-educated and had turned to teaching to make a living. The only way Hence Posey could accommodate him that night was for Hall to share an attic room with Alex, "a shy, slim youth" going on eighteen, then home on leave from college. Hall and Alex went up to the room, and there, on a homemade bookshelf, Hall saw a number of neatly arranged volumes, among them "several standard works." Hall later said, "He seemed a bit timid and asked if I liked to read, and if I liked poetry. That was the beginning. I did like poetry and I found myself liking the Indian boy. We read and chatted until the early hours of the morning."[1] From this meeting emerged a close friendship that not only lasted but grew in the years ahead.

On first meeting Alex, Hall was struck by the intellectual and literary development of such a young man. "I know," he said, "that Alex Posey had come under some benevolent influence that was a very strong influence before I knew him." In Hall's estimation, Alex had "a remarkable appreciation" of literary values as well as the "elements of greatness in point of humanity and a remarkable mind, which if properly trained would make him a brilliant literary man."[2] In later years Alex would attribute this literary bent in part to his childhood freedom and experiences with nature, the nurturing and rich cultural heritage passed on to him by Nancy, and the formal education that Hence had insisted on. By the time Hall met him, it had been enhanced by Alex's studies at the Indian University at Bacone, where he was a student when they met. During his remaining years at Bacone, Alex set a lifelong pattern of reading and writing. In those formative years he established a literary voice that would stand him in good stead as a prose writer. Yet the tastes in poetry he developed at Bacone and the poetic models he chose to imitate led him to a style that would ultimately bar his way to greatness as a poet.

When Alex entered the Indian University in November 1889, he was barely sixteen. One of ten students selected by the Creek board of education, he had qualified for the second academic class, equivalent to a high-school freshman. The purpose of the academy was to continue the work of the elementary grades and prepare students for collegiate standing through the study of Latin, the sciences, modern language and literature, geography, mathematics, physical economy, English, civil government, music, and art. Because the school had been founded by Baptists and continued to be directed by them as a mission, the curriculum also had a strong emphasis on natural and moral philosophy and Bible studies.[3]

Alex found his first year at Bacone exciting, and he was sad when it was over. He had been successful in his studies and had enjoyed good rapport with his classmates from the Indian Territory and surrounding states. Alex had developed a warm affection for Miss Anna Lewis, a young woman from Litchfield, Illinois, who had come to Bacone with a strong sense of missionary duty to teach the Indians. Miss Lewis, Alex, and the other students felt especially close during the last four days of the school year. Together they had attended the "closing exercises": the Sunday sermon and the Sunday evening entertainment by the Christian societies of the college; the Monday evening cantata and lecture; the Tuesday evening entertainment by the academic department; and the Wednesday morning commencement exercises. On that Wednesday afternoon, June 18, 1890, they had walked together to the station, where the students boarded trains bound for their homes. Their parting so saddened young Alex that the "low desending [*sic*] sun seemed to weep as it sank out of sight."[4] This quick emotional attachment to Miss Lewis and his classmates is early evidence of his lifelong tendency to surround himself with a select circle of family and friends to whom he looked for comfort as well as intellectual stimulation and praise.

Alex returned to Eufaula that Wednesday evening imbued with the idealism of adolescence. Perhaps he was caught up in the theme of the cantata that had been part of the closing exercises. In "The Flower Queen," the flowers meet in a secluded forest valley to select a queen. There they encounter a discontented person who has retired from the cares and disappointments of the world. They instruct him in love and duty, teaching him that happiness results from filling well the position that Providence allots one. Thus taught, he returns to a useful life among humankind. The juvenile Alex who had left for Bacone returned to Eufaula a sad, thoughtful, romantic teenager. At home on the day after his return, he was so lonely for his schoolmates and teachers that when his sister Melissa began to play the familiar strains of "Home Sweet Home" he almost cried. Instead he wrote a letter to Miss Lewis, who was leaving Bacone that summer, having finished her tour of missionary duty. He told her, with some resignation, "But there must at last come a time in life when we have to part with the ones we love best, either by death or separation here on earth where sorrow forever predominates."[5]

Hardly two weeks later, he wrote to Miss Lewis again. Everything seemed "in harmony with nature," but he was out of tune: "Everything is so dull here that I hardly know what to do with myself. I have wished many times that I was back at B.I.U. . . . I wish school would begin again for it seems more like home than here." Still missing his school friends, he wrote:

When shall we meet again?
In God's presence where sorrow and woe is all unknown, where happiness dwells forever and ever. It can not be that earth

is our only abiding place. It can not be that our life is a mere bubble cast up by eternity to float a moment on the waves and sink into nothingness. Else why is it that the glorious aspirations which leap like angels from the temple of our hearts are forever wandering unsatisfied?

Why is it that the stars that hold their festival around the midnight throne are set above the grasp of our limited facilities, forever mocking us with their unapproachable glory?[6]

The flair for metaphor and simile is obvious, despite the adolescent effusiveness. Alex's love-struck attitude toward Miss Lewis and his enthusiasm for Christian ideals would wane during the next few months, but not the urge to practice his composition skills.

Although at the beginning of summer Alex was eager to return to Bacone, he apparently did not report for the fall term. He had vowed to Miss Lewis, "I am going until I graduate, and when I accomplish that I will be at the height of my ambition."[7] In late October, however, he was still at Eufaula, just recovering from sickness that he said had confined him "in bed for several weeks."[8]

Alex had matured a great deal since the start of the summer, for by fall he was exploring new ideas and new directions in thought that would become important to him as a writer. He began corresponding with George J. Remsburg, a Kansas collector and later newspaper man who asked Alex to put together a collection of Creek relics for him. How Remsburg selected Alex for the task is less important than that Alex agreed to undertake it. "I have no Indian relics of any kind," Alex said, "but will send you the best modern collection I can get. There is only one genuine relic I know of in this country," he continued, "and it is a tomahawk used in the famous battle of Tohopeka or Horseshoe Bend on the Tallapoosa River Alabama in 1813, it is in splendid state of preservation and used daily by an old Indian Chief as a 'pipe of peace.' I have often heard him say, 'Only a dollar and I'd be a millionaire for every wound this hatchet has inflicted in mortal flesh.'"[9] The "old Indian Chief" was Yadeka Harjo, whose father, from Kialigee Town, had served with Andrew Jackson during the War of 1812.[10] Alex would later immortalize the owner of the tomahawk pipe in his well-known poem "Hotgun on the Death of Yadeka Harjo."

Alex immediately set about collecting the artifacts, thinking the task would be easy. He soon acquired a few items, but as he later told Remsburg, "I have discovered . . . the collection of Indian relics I vowed to make . . . to be the hardest thing I ever undertook." The difficulty, he thought, stemmed from cultural changes occurring among the Creeks: "Civilization has become so very popular among the Indians that it is a hard matter to even glean a legend from the lowest ranks—let alone the more cultured. Old fashions and ways of living are fast becoming extinct."[11] It probably did not occur to the youth, well indoctrinated by then in the Euro-American view of such matters as "civilization" and "culture," that the opposite might have been true, that his fellow Creeks might have been reluctant to give up their "relics" because they *were* links to "old fashions and ways of living." And if he inquired among his relatives at Tuskegee, "old fashions" were indeed on the decline. Having met with little success himself, Alex made an agreement with a "certain Indian" who had claimed to know where relics could be found and who would work as his agent. But two years later, his agent had managed to search only his own town, and Alex had only "a small but a nice collection," which he described as follows: "Two arrows (old style), one bow, two ball clubs, a crown, a flap, and a puma's tail, more properly the skin of a puma's tail. This the warriors esteem equally as much as they do an eagle plume, which is sacred. The crown is of silver and was made by the Indians themselves; it is supposed to be beyond a century in age. Tho' traditions trace it back to time imemorial [*sic*]. The rest have no historic significance."[12]

Although it is doubtful that Alex delivered the collection to Remsburg, the importance of his efforts on Remsburg's behalf is inestimable. His inquiries about relics had brought him into close contact with his fellow Creeks and had caused him to draw conclusions concerning social change. Although he may have overestimated how rapidly Creek culture was dying, the result of his search was an interest in Creek social practices and in the legends and other oral traditions of his people. As his early writings demonstrate, his knowledge of traditional culture was limited. His attempts on Remsburg's behalf began a long process of learning about his people's past. Undoubtedly, the stories Nancy had told him now began to take on a richer cultural context. His growing insights into Creek history and traditional culture were grist for a maturing writer's mill. From these experiences there sprang as well a lifelong interest in the material culture of the Creeks. The pieces he found for Remsburg were

probably the basis of his own well-known collection of artifacts.

Exactly when Alex returned to Bacone is uncertain. Although he
apparently did not go back in fall 1890, he was a student in spring
1891, and he graduated from the academic to the collegiate department on June 17.[13]

Alex spent summer 1891 at Bald Hill. The previous February,
Hence had given up the National Hotel and moved back to the
ranch.[14] There, no doubt, Alex continued his reading and followed
the diversions ranch life had to offer: horseback rides, rambles
among the Tulledega Hills and along the Oktahutche, and occasional
trips into Eufaula with Hence.

The 1891–92 school year was consumed by his freshman collegiate studies. A full year of algebra and Latin and a semester each
of ancient history, modern history, psychology, and natural philosophy greatly broadened the base of his intellectual development and
of his reading.[15]

It was at that time that Alex began to write with some intensity.
He was surrounded by books and other forms of the printed word.
Besides reading for his courses of study, he also served as librarian
on Sundays and, after class during the week, set type for the *B.I.U.
Instructor*, a monthly promotional newsletter published by the faculty to advertise the good work of the university.[16] The *Instructor*
provided Alex not only with additional practical newspaper experience that would prove useful to him years later as a journalist but
also, and immediately, with an outlet for his first literary efforts.

In them he drew upon a resource he had been amassing since
early childhood: his knowledge of Creek traditional culture and history. In his search for relics for Remsburg, he apparently had been
interested, but had had difficulty, in extracting legends from the
more traditional Creeks. In early fall 1892 he wrote to Remsburg,
"The Indians have some very beautiful legends, and which if written, would certainly make an interesting book." Six weeks later he
reported that he had written "a few Creek legends," two of which he
enclosed.[17] These were probably copies of works Alex had published
in the *B.I.U. Instructor* during his freshman year, for by the time that
year had ended his submissions to the *Instructor* had gained local
attention.

Although the exact identity of the works he sent Remsburg is uncertain, one was probably "The Origin of Music according to the Creek Medicine-Men."[18] The overblown style, describing "melodious cataracts and scenes sublime" and "sable pinions" of darkness, marks it as the work of an immature writer. Despite his rapid intellectual development, the Baptist influence of his childhood and of his present surroundings was evident. The Christian dichotomy of heaven and hell and the appearance of Satan in the tale make it almost certainly one of Alex's freshman efforts. Thus for modern readers, his preface is more interesting than the narrative itself. Although his view had by that time been unalterably shaped by the Anglo-American educational objectives of Bacone, he recognized the richness of the Creek oral traditions when he said that "no doubt, in the remote periods of the Redman's existence, vast libraries of immense value were stored away on the invisible shelves of an uncultured brain, which has at the present time with the march of civilization dwindled almost to the verge of insignificance." Nearly all contemporary Creeks, he said, neglected the habit of transmitting the traditions orally, except those commonly styled the "medicine men," who at the annual busks prepared the medicine to purge town members of the past year's impurities, named the children, and told the legends to youths between eighteen and twenty years of age. In the years ahead Alex developed a growing respect for these old men, whom he considered unfortunate leftovers from an earlier time in Creek history and who figured prominently in his writing.

Alex contributed other pieces to the *B.I.U. Instructor* during his freshman year. Although their titles are not known because so little of the *Instructor* has survived, they were numerous enough to catch the attention of the editor of the *Indian Journal*, who in June 1892 described Alex as having "literary tastes and inclinations above the average man of maturer years" and described his works in the *Instructor* as "sensible, well constructed, strong articles that promise well for his future" and as "the most interesting feature of the paper."[19]

The work that drew the notice of his fellow Creeks was his freshman oration—"The Indian: What of Him?"—delivered at the commencement exercises in June 1892. The address argued that the stereotypes of the Indian as unprogressive, ignorant, wandering, and shiftless were falsehoods refuted by science and history. "Although it is possible," Alex said, "for one tribe to become a superior race, it is also possible for another, notwithstanding the degradation it may have undergone, in the process of time, to rival its superior." He predicted a future when Indian and white would be equals and would "go hand in hand through the fields of science and human progress." And he asked, "Can the people who have produced such men as McIntosh and Boudinot, who have entertained presidents and been the admiration of statesmen, be an unprogressive people? Can the people who have books and periodicals published in their native tongue be an unprogressive people? Can such men as Sequoyah, inventing alphabets, be unprogressive men? Do these give indications of degeneracy? I answer in the negative; and the man who strives to disparage them is rather the degenerate being." The oration, published in the *Indian Journal*, also appeared in pamphlet form, probably in late 1892, and may have been set in type by Alex himself.[20] Beyond the immediate public attention it brought, the oration was evidence that he had embraced the idea of progress at an early age. Although many ideas that had their roots in youthful idealism gave way over time, he never lost his belief in the Indians' need to bow to the demands of progress in the social, political, and economic contexts of late nineteenth-century America.

The address, as it was published in the *Indian Journal*, attracted the attention of the aged D. N. McIntosh. Perhaps it was Alex's allusion to McIntosh that caught the old man's eye. Perhaps he remembered how Alex's father had joined the Lower Creeks in the Confederate army, in which McIntosh had figured so prominently. Or perhaps it was that the Poseys were his near neighbors. For whatever reason, the address appealed to him, and McIntosh praised it and took its theme as his own in a political speech he gave at a barbecue at Brush Hill two weeks after the address was published. In his introductory remarks he said of Alex, "I am impressed that the producer of the article, young Posey, is a genius, and I am so constructed that if there is a shrine at which I can bow and worship it is at the shrine of genius."[21] How such praise from one of the Creeks' eldest statesmen must have impressed the eighteen-year-old! His reading in the romantics had bolstered his youthful idealism and introduced him to their fascination with the "great" men in history. In like fashion, he found great men in Indian history. Given as he was to hero worship, he had elevated McIntosh to high stature along with Boudinot and Sequoyah, where he remained. A few years later, at McIntosh's death, Alex delivered an address at the graveside and inscribed "Verses Written at the Grave of McIntosh" to his memory.[22] It was this admiration for great men, in part, that caused Alex to develop over the years a rapport with many elder statesmen of his nation, regardless of their political persuasion: Hotulke Emarthla, Isparhecher, Pleasant Porter, G. W. Grayson, Yadeka Harjo, and others.

After his basking in the limelight, it is difficult to say how well Alex adjusted to life during the summer in the Creek lands west of Eufaula, which to say the least was much different from campus life and the intellectual pursuits of the student. John H. Phillips, Alex's full-blood cousin, the son of Tecumseh Phillips, was another student who, like Alex, had to adjust. Though John was the same age as Alex and had entered Bacone at the same time, he was several grades behind him. A letter from him, written in his best English to Anna Lewis in summer 1892, gives insight into the events students could look forward to during the summer: "I am lonesome every day I dont what the matter with me. Just peaches getting ripe down here now but. Its not very much like we had it last summer because to much rain in Spring time. I wish it soon be school begin I'm tird to stay at home. . . . There will be fish killing next Wednesday I mean fish fry close to where I live. just in time for water mellon now. just as warm weather up now."[23] Besides the ripening peaches, watermelons, fish kills, and hot weather, there were also the usual mad-dog scares, a four-day camp meeting at the Tuskegee church, and cattle shipments from the stockyards at Eufaula. Such was summer life at Bald Hill and Mellette, where John lived, in the Creek lands between Eufaula and the Tulledega Hills. By then Alex had begun to look at the Bald Hill ranch as a quiet retreat from the workaday world and may not have felt boredom so acutely. Unlike John, Alex could fill his time reading, which had become habitual for him.

As George Riley Hall noted, Alex's reading ranged widely and had intensified during 1891 and 1892. In local and United States newspapers such as the *Indian Journal* and the St. Louis *Globe-Dispatch* he found reprinted the works of poets Rudyard Kipling, Thomas Bailey Aldrich, George Eliot, Joaquin Miller, and others of greater or less popularity. He was particularly interested in the dialect poems of Paul Laurence Dunbar, James Whitcomb Riley, and others. He read articles about Tennyson, Swinburne, and Burns and collected

portraits of Cooper, Harte, Emerson, Alice and Phoebe Cary, Haw-
thorne, Lowell, Holmes, Whittier, Longfellow, and others. By then
he had more than seventy books in his personal library.[24] Alex's
academic work had led him to a more systematic study of English
writers of the eighteenth and nineteenth centuries, including Pope,
Gay, Burns, Percy, Sheridan, Swift, Addison and Steele, Smollett,
Sterne, Defoe, Gibbon, Johnson, Boswell, Gray, and Scott.[25] Some
of these readings would prove most influential in his writings during his years at Bacone and, in good measure but in some ways
unfortunately, after that.

By the time Alex began his sophomore year in fall 1892, he had
grown considerably in his intellectual pursuits. The effects of his
reading were clear. Besides the "standard" writers, he had read the
works of religious skeptics, especially Thomas Paine and Robert
Ingersoll, "the great agnostic," whom he very much admired. Alex
had read and collected both poems and essays by Ingersoll and
articles about him.[26] He believed Ingersoll would have been a better
choice than Harriet Monroe to write a poetic commemoration for
the upcoming Chicago Columbian Exposition. With his admiration
growing for the advancement of American civilization, he considered her "Columbian Ode," read to a large gathering in Chicago on
October 21, 1892, unworthy of what he called "the greatest event in
human history." It deserved better. "Ingersoll," he said, "is a pretty
good hand at rhyming and could perhaps, had he been chosen, have
made better poetry without so much ambiguity and on a broader
plan. The latter is better known and could have, I think, excited
more universal interest." [27] Besides being known for his lectures on
religious topics, Ingersoll was also noted for his lectures on such
writers as Shakespeare, Voltaire, Burns, and Paine. Alex already
admired Thomas Paine, but after reading Ingersoll's article on the
eighteenth-century revolutionary in the *North American Review*, he
found a deeper "veneration for the great Revolutionary patriot."
This new respect inspired Alex to write a lengthy poem in his praise,
which read in part:

> And old or new, can records find
> A nobler man in book or scroll,
> Than he who taught a nation's mind
> To love the freedom of the soul? [28]

The ideas of these skeptics quickly made inroads into Alex's thinking. Bacone Indian University no longer seemed the haven for orthodox Christian idealism that it had been to him his first year there. In a letter to Remsburg, he called the university "one of the best institutions of this Country; tho' controlled by a religious denomination, to which I pay but little attention. A *freethinker* can enjoy the freedom of thought anywhere, and under all circumstances—'mid faggots or at the guilotine [*sic*]. So I enjoy mine and preach my views."[29] Alex had chosen to look elsewhere for a religious philosophy. Though he made no public statement on the matter, his friends in later years admitted there was "a more or less well founded belief" that Alex was skeptical regarding orthodox religion.[30] He had been so as early as his sophomore year at Bacone.

In Alex's sophomore year the academic schedule was more rigorous than before. He had daily studies in geometry, Latin, and Greek during the entire school year. He also studied rhetoric and civil government during the fall term and trigonometry, logic, and English literature during the spring.[31]

Nevertheless, he found time to continue writing for the *B.I.U. Instructor*, of which, unfortunately, no copies from this period have been found. In the October 1892 issue there appeared "The Comet's Tale," a long poem containing the legend of a great comet that appeared just before whites arrived in the New World. In the December issue there appeared "The Sea God," another legend in verse, as well as his oration from the closing exercises of the previous spring, "The Indian: What of Him?" It was probably at this time, too, that the latter work was printed as a pamphlet.[32]

Perhaps the most significant works of this period were a series of tales featuring the humorist Chinnubbie Harjo, "a notorious wit and drone," who possessed "every trait common to man, with a strong unnatural leaning to traits characteristic of neither man nor beast." He was a carefree poet and liar, given to whims of kindness or violence.[33] The first of these tales was apparently "Chinnubbie Harjo, the Evil Genius of the Creeks," of which no copy has been found. It was followed by "Chinnubbie and the Owl," in which Chinnubbie wins a storytelling contest by reciting an elaborate lie about how he tricked an owl into turning its head around and around until it twisted off. The third tale was "Chinnubbie Scalps the Squaws," which appeared in the May 1893 issue of the *Instructor*. In it Chin-

nubbie kills and scalps the women in the household of the chief of
a rival tribe and robs the chief of prized possessions, thereby win-
ning the admiration of his own tribesmen. The final tale was "Chinnubbie's Courtship," of which, again, no copy has been found.[34]
Although Chinnubbie was prone to violence and cruelty as well as
humor, it was his lighter side that appealed to Alex. In the succeeding
months, after he had firmly established the identity of this mythical
hero-wit in the minds of his readers, Alex usurped his name as a
nom de plume.

Though works like these continued to enhance Alex's budding literary reputation, the crowning achievement of his sophomore year
was his commencement oration. Publication of his works in the *Instructor* had placed his name before patrons of the school, but the
oration found a much wider public. Alex delivered it on the night of
June 21, 1893, during the commencement program that culminated
the four days of closing exercises. His topic was Sequoyah, creator of
the Cherokee syllabary. The Cherokee genius, Alex argued, should
be ranked with "the apostles of science and civilization, and with
the benefactors of mankind," for genius is not confined to any rank
or race but occurs among the lettered and unlettered alike. His description of Sequoyah's mind as one "tutored in the university of
nature" might well have been an expression of what posterity would
say about Alex himself: "His text books were the mountains, the
rivers, the forests, and the heaven. His soul was the soul of a philosopher, that thirst for mental gain and ceased never to investigate."
In rhythms and cadences achieved by repetition and other oratorical devices, Alex told how Sequoyah overcame ridicule, ostracism,
and addiction to strong drink, pursued his dream, and by his in-
vention earned a place in history that deserved recognition.[35] The
oration was highly praised by the local newspaper editor. A copy of it
appeared a month later in the *Cherokee Advocate*, the official newspaper of the Cherokee Nation, and in the *Red Man*, published at
the Indian Industrial School at Carlisle, Pennsylvania. At least one
Oklahoma Territory newspaper, the *Daily Oklahoma State Capital*,
picked it up.[36]

In fall 1893 Alex began his last year at Bacone. The curriculum
for the junior year consisted of an entire year of Latin and Greek as
well as surveying, astronomy, and the history of civilization during
the fall term and chemistry, zoology, and botany during the spring.[37]

In addition to pursuing these studies, he put even more energy than before into writing for the *B.I.U. Instructor*. One work was a long article titled "The Alabama Prophet," concerning an old Creek medicine man who had died in June 1892. The old man had been a natural genius, "praised and admired by all classes of men as a man of unusual intellectual ability." A rainmaker, medicine man, and prophet, he was attributed superhuman powers by his full-blood constituents because of his shrewdness. He never called on his thunderbolts to bring rain "unless his observations of external indications assured success." If a patient died, it was due to "the violation of natural laws, the lack of physical perfection and knowledge, and to the parental inheritance of sin." To prolong life, "he advocated decency, regularity, temperance in every thing and due obedience to natural laws." There was little to argue with in that. Indeed, wrote Alex, "the foundation of his greatness was constructed in that which he took care to glean away from the scenes of every-day-life, —from reason and the unerring teachings of Nature."

To say that Alex gave his central figure a touch of nobility would be an understatement. The Alabama Prophet is saved from being a true noble savage by the absence of criticism of the artificialities of "civilization." The piece reflects another romantic idea—the Indian as a vanishing species. The Alabama Prophet was clearly a relic of an older Creek world that had survived into Alex's childhood and youth. Yet he was to be admired, and through him the power of nature as teacher is clear: "How many such men could one find, whose minds have been exiled from the schoolroom and college hall, endowed with such talents and versed in such thoughts and maxims?" When Alex published the piece as a pamphlet, he attached a long elegiac poem titled "The Burial of the Alabama Prophet."[38]

The January 1894 issue of the *Instructor* contained his heroicomic poem "Death of a Window Plant."[39] It reads in part,

> The air was chill,
> The leaves were hushed,
>   The moon in grandeur
> Climbed the spangled
> Walls of heaven,
>   When the angel came
> That whispers death;

Unseen, unheard,
    To lisp that word, and
Leave my window
Sad when night should
Blossom into day.[40]

The plant is dead, and the poet's heart can find no solace in the "serene" light of the sun, the birds' songs, or the splendor of the sky. Like Poe's distraught lover in "The Raven," he says, "I mourned, and all / Was dark and drear / Within my chamber, / Lorn and bare, where / Sweetness was and / Beauty for a day." Thus he "grandly" entombs his "window-friend" within the "deep core" of his soul. Its death brings a chilling thought: "Should all thy race / Thus disappear, / In death forsake the / Soil in which you / Grew, the world would / Then be sad as I." Alex could hardly raise such an inconsequential subject to a higher plane, but he would write better verse. In the March issue of the *Instructor* there appeared "The River Strange," described as "a poem of some merit," and "Fixico Yoholo's Revenge," described as "the story of a warrior who assumed the form of a bear." [41] Unfortunately, no copies of these works have been found.

Alex published a number of other poems, apparently during this same period. A lyrical poem called "Twilight" appeared in pamphlet form. Though interesting for its obvious experimentation with verse form and metrics, its intended description remains too abstract. Shorter poems included "The Red Man's Pledge of Peace," "Death of the Poets," and "Happy Times for Me an' Sal." The first two appeared in the *Instructor*. The last one appeared elsewhere, perhaps in the Psi Delta Society's *Oracle*, and it is significant not because of its theme of rustic farm life at harvesttime but because it is Alex's first dialect poem. "The Red Man's Pledge of Peace" contains nearly three times as many stanzas as the version published after his death. It is a play on the whites' pledge that the Indians should enjoy their lands in the Indian Territory as long as the grass grew and the waters flowed. Unlike the whites' pledge, which at that time was being broken by the establishment of the Dawes Commission, the Indians' pledge was a "sacred treaty" that "Indian tribes of time unborn" would never break. "Death of the Poets" is interesting because it reflects Alex's assessment of the status of American

poetry. With Lowell, Whitman, and Whittier dead, who was to follow them? Oliver Wendell Holmes? "Then, alas! the space and sky
their / Genius lit must darken to its stars! / . . . Yes, the poetic sky
is scant of suns, / and only by its minor beacons graced."[42] It was
perhaps this assessment of the sad state of American poetry that
caused Alex to look consistently to earlier literary periods for his
poetic models.

Throughout the 1893–94 academic year, Alex also served as the
Bacone reporter for the weekly Eufaula *Indian Journal*. For the most
part, his column consisted of chatty reports about students, faculty,
visitors to the university, and campus events such as the activities
of the Psi Delta Society. Occasionally Alex's literary urge interfered
with his reporting "hard" news and he prefaced his reports with
statements like "Bird-songs, sunshine, poems of coming spring" and
"Those delightful showers Tuesday occasioned joy."[43] In some ways
these reports were the most important of his writing during his college career.

The most significant feature of his reporting was his continuation
of the comic voice he had found in "Death of a Window Plant,"
this time through his persona Chinnubbie, who signed each report.
Like his legendary namesake, the contemporary wit looked at campus and Creek national life with humor and often expressed his
opinion tongue in cheek. Those expressions took various forms: a
statement of the land allotment issue in a parody of Hamlet's soliloquy; doggerel about the end of school in "The picnic's comming"
[*sic*] and "The whippowill [*sic*] has come"; or rhymed couplets urging
Demosthenes to return to life to hear the would-be campus ora-
tors mock him with their efforts. One week Chinnubbie reported
that spring had come; students and professors were quoting poets
and writing "delicious rhymes" about her. "Do not be surprised,"
he wrote, "if you should see a book issued by the B.I.U. press ere
long, entitled 'Spring and Other Poems.'" But the weather turned
sharply, as it could easily do in the Indian Territory, and Chinnubbie
included some humorous verse about the devastation wrought by
the cold weather—like that which had blasted the window plant—
concluding: "And daisy lying drooped and dead, / The poet lorn sur-
veys / The sylvan scene where late he said, / 'O, Spring, 'tis thee I
praise!'"[44]

The success of Alex's humor depended on Chinnubbie's perspec-

tive as the witty, casual outside observer whom Alex carefully constructed. Chinnubbie referred to himself in the third person. "The
B.I.U. was represented at the international council at Checotah by
W. Micco and Chinnubbie," he once wrote. Another time, after listing faculty and students who were on the sick list, he wrote, "Chinnubbie is not feeling so very well himself." And after describing the
BIU picnic on the banks of the Arkansas River, he concluded, "Chinnubbie sat quietly in the shade meditating about the weather and
the prospects of the farmer."[45] Perhaps this detached observer contained the germ of Hotgun's detached listeners, Wolf Warrior and
Kono Harjo, in Alex's Fus Fixico letters a decade later.

As the end of the school term approached, Alex began to think
about his commencement oration. Several of his weekly news reports made lighthearted fun of his fellow collegiates' preparation of
their addresses.[46] As for himself, he had won wide praise with his
freshman and sophomore orations, especially the one on Sequoyah.
Perhaps a year later he felt it was important to match or surpass that
performance.

Alex probably enjoyed the exercises that brought his junior year
to a close more than any in former years, for there were fewer religious overtones. Instead of a commencement sermon, the Reverend
J. S. Morrow, longtime Baptist missionary among the Choctaws,
lectured on his recent travels in the East, and the Reverend A. J.
Essex's address to the collegiate Christian societies was on "Usefulness." The commencement program was an interesting mix of piano
arrangements of "Midsummer's Night's Dream," "Oberon," and
"Annie Laurie"; a vocal rendition of "Beyond the Sunset Gates";
and humorous sketches, melodramatic tales, and orations. Among
the latter were "Our Indian Heritage" by Freeland G. Alex and "The
Creeks, Past and Present" by John Phillips, Alex's cousin, who outlined the early characteristics of their people and compared their
ancient lifeways with those of contemporary Creeks. But it was Alex's
oration that the audience looked forward to. Those who had heard
his sophomore address expected much of him now.[47]

They apparently got what they expected to hear. Alex titled his
oration "Room at the Top," and it demonstrates the heights to which
his youthful idealism had risen. Using Daniel Webster's statement
as a point of departure, he argued that success came to the one who
could shake off misfortune and who was magnanimous and willing

to begin work at whatever level was necessary to start the climb to
the top. "Like the tree, he strikes root, grows, puts forth his leaves
and becomes the giant of his surrounding before the world is aware,"
said Alex. Echoing Thoreau, he told his audience, "Fashion and luxury foster the germ that makes physical and mental dwarfs of men
and women, and banishes every attribute of magnanimity from a
nation."[48]

In concluding his address, he applied his comments to the leaders
of the Creeks, Cherokees, Choctaws, Chickasaws, and Seminoles:
"We need such men in these five nations. If the Hebrews became
a mighty nation in Egypt, there is no reason why the Indians of
this territory cannot become a great nation in America. It is not impossible, and the truth demands perservering, top-destined, upright
men, with minds as broad as the sky above them, who can by dent
[sic] of reason and justice thwart even the measures of the United
States, and make the existence of an Indian commonwealth known
to the world!"[49]

In terms of composition, this oration was not as impressive as the
one on Sequoyah, but Alex's oratorical skills impressed his listeners.
One of them wrote that friends of the university "everywhere" knew
about Alex and admired his "brilliant mind and strong, manly character" and that his works were "among the brightest and best productions in the literature of this country." The writer concluded, "Of
a commanding presence and possessing a magnetism that at once
holds the attention of his auditors, he is a finished orator. His oration
was a masterpiece of English, rhetoric and eloquence."[50] These comments as well as the oration itself were reprinted in the *Indian Journal*. The reviewer probably overpraised the speech, but the praise
reflects the widespread recognition Alex had already achieved in the
Indian Territory.

During summer 1894, Alex wrote for the *Indian Journal*. On July
13 it contained Chinnubbie's prose piece "Uncle Dick and Uncle
Will," a narrative about cousins Dick and Will Grayson, Creek freedmen, former slaves of the Creeks. They lived in a freedmen's settlement on Coon Creek just east of Bald Hill, a sequestered, fertile,
healthful region. The two old men were unlike in looks, one tall and
lanky and the other short and rather fat, and in demeanor they were
different "as an acorn is unlike a banana." Uncle Dick was talkative
and Uncle Will was retiring. The narrative concludes with an amus-

ing anecdote about a "fight" between the two old men that erupts after Will chops off the nose of Dick's rowdy sow that is rooting up the sweet potato patch.[51] Alex had listened carefully to the speech patterns of the Creeks, Creek freedmen, and whites around him, and in this piece, for the first time, he wrote in the dialect of the freedmen. As time passed, dialect would become more and more a vehicle for humor in his prose and would be the mark of his most successful works.

On the day the story of Uncle Dick and Uncle Will appeared, Alex left Eufaula for Fort Gibson, Cherokee Nation, to report on the per capita payment then in progress among the Cherokees.[52] The Cherokee Treasury was distributing the $7 million that the Cherokees had received for sale of the Cherokee Strip, that vast outlet to the west that lay along the northern border of the Indian Territory from the Osage Nation to No Man's Land. Each Cherokee citizen was to receive $265. The payments had begun at Tahlequah, the Cherokee national capital, and subsequent payments had been made at Vinita and Claremore. Now the treasurer had moved to Fort Gibson, where over $1 million in cash was to be doled out.

The articles Alex sent back to the *Indian Journal* contained little "hard" news of Cherokee affairs or the per capita payment. His inclination then and thereafter was to go after the human interest story. He therefore described the carnival atmosphere that typified per capita payments in the Indian Territory. The buildings at the abandoned fort had been transformed into "hotels, banks, saloons and gambling resorts; and on all the vacant lots around them [were] the tents of venders of every possible description." Every fashion of human being was there, most to prey on the Indians who received their payments: "Schemers, robbers, gamblers and drunkards are here, and thriving well." It was unsafe to walk alone or to sleep with money in one's pockets. Law officers were kept busy spilling whiskey and spiked cider, and theaters, minstrel shows, and merry-go-rounds operated lucratively. Fakirs, horse traders, operators of "catch penny devices," and merchants were on hand to separate payment recipients from their cash. Some merchants who had sold goods on credit at exorbitant prices in anticipation of the payment now set up shop near the payroll office to catch debtors as they came out. Alex saw one Cherokee going from merchant to merchant with his hat full of money, allowing them to take what they claimed he owed them. After Fort Gibson the payment was moved to Webbers Falls, where the spectacle was repeated.[53] Alex returned to Eufaula from Webbers Falls on August 2, the day before his twenty-first birthday.

Despite his youthful promise to Anna Lewis that he would stay at Bacone until he graduated, Alex did not return to the university that fall. In his reports from Bacone during spring 1894, Chinnubbie had from time to time referred to students who had left the university, including one who felt he was too old for student life. Perhaps that was how Alex felt. Perhaps the campus regulations were too confining. Along with requirements concerning punctual payment of debts, cleanliness, and other matters were rules aimed at the students' behavior. They were required to attend the regular religious exercises and meetings at the university. Use of tobacco and alcohol and gambling were strictly forbidden. Work, amusement, and unnecessary exercise were prohibited on the Sabbath. English was to be spoken as much as possible and always at table and in the presence of teachers. The students' movements were also strictly controlled. Unless on duty assignment or in classes, the young men and women were restricted to their own parts of the buildings. Outside, they were not allowed to walk or ride in company and could meet only during their regular school duties or at university meetings. They could not go to town or far off the campus without permission. They could not send any correspondence unless approved by a teacher. And the young men could not take outdoor walks or exercise except under the direction of a lady teacher.[54]

These strict rules of conduct may have been too much for the "free-thinking" and fun-loving Alex. That his attitude toward student activities at Bacone was less than reverent is clear in Chinnubbie's reports to the *Indian Journal*, and he admitted being diverted from his studies at times. Marginal notes in his college textbooks suggest he spent some class or study time passing notes and that he enjoyed teasing, cutting corners in disciplinary routines, and "putting one over" on the professor. Near the campus, he reminisced, lived a "most amiable old Scotch lady" who sold pies to the students. Among her best customers were Alex and his Delaware classmate Henry B. Sarcoxie (pronounced *Cy-coxie*). "We . . . used to scribble doggerel verses to each other during study hours," Alex wrote, "instead of preparing our lessons. Sarcoxie rhymed beautifully with

FOXY; and 'Old Cy' eating pie rhymed beautifully also. . . . It was our nightly custom, after study hour, to go down Pie Avenue to Scotch Square and fill up on mince and rhubarb pies."[55] The prospect of a grueling senior year of French and German and Greek Testament and a term each of geology, physical geography, mental philosophy, political economy, moral philosophy, and a course called Evidences of Christianity may have been more than Chinnubbie could tolerate.

For whatever reason, Alex did not return to Bacone. He was certainly not the same person who had written earlier, "Education, like the sculptor, takes man, a stone, rude and unpolished, and makes him a model to be admired, a better being, with more influence and better equipped to set better examples and give higher thoughts to others."[56] Of course the youthful writer meant *formal* education, which he had had enough of by summer 1894. He was now ready to do something else with his life. The literary sensibility his friend George Riley Hall found in him at their first meeting had been cultivated during his years at Bacone. "His taste was surprisingly correct," wrote Hall, "even in his school days. The old masters in English and American literature crowded each other on his bookshelves."[57] As time would prove, his choice of the "old masters" as models placed some unfortunate limits on him as a poet. And he never broke himself of the habit of writing doggerel, though it served him well in later years as a political writer. But it was not as a poet that Alex would achieve his greatest literary success. He had discovered the comic voice that would be important to his prose writing, learned the usefulness of a persona, and acquired a pen name to go with it. He emerged from Bacone a voracious reader and a self-styled free-thinking skeptic, ready for the practical education that the life of a writer and man of public affairs could give him.

Nancy Posey, Alex Posey's mother, in 1928. Archives and Manuscripts Division of the Oklahoma Historical Society.

Tuskegee Indian Baptist Church, second structure, built in 1878. Courtesy of Daniel F. Littlefield, Jr.

Lewis Henderson (Hence) Posey, Alex Posey's father. Archives and Manuscripts Division of the Oklahoma Historical Society.

Alex Posey about 1880. Archives and Manuscripts Division of the Oklahoma Historical Society.

The Posey ranch, with Bald Hill in the background. Archives and Manuscripts Division of the Oklahoma Historical Society.

Lydia Tiger, Nancy Posey's aunt (seated); Lewis Phillips, Nancy's youngest brother; and perhaps his wife, Nicy (standing). Archives and Manuscripts Division of the Oklahoma Historical Society.

Betsy Riley Phillips, second wife of Nancy Posey's father (seated). The children have not been identified. Archives and Manuscripts Division of the Oklahoma Historical Society.

Alex Posey, age twelve. Archives and Manuscripts Division of the Oklahoma Historical Society.

*Bacone students and teachers. Anna Lewis, Alex Posey's favorite teacher
(seated, with book). Archives and Manuscripts Division of the Oklahoma
Historical Society.*

*Alex Posey, probably in a college skit. Archives and Manuscripts Division of
the Oklahoma Historical Society.*

Chapter 4. Politics and Poetry

· ·

On February 25, 1895, the *Indian Journal* carried a brief local item announcing that "Mr. A. L. Posey, the hermit poet, philosopher and scholar of Bald Hill" had spent the previous day in Eufaula. The description, intended to be humorous, accurately reflected the relative obscurity Alex had slipped into after the summer of 1894. For nearly a year he published very little and all but dropped from public view. But it was a year of preparation for life in the political arena.

In early October 1894 Alex had taken a position as a salesman in the large Brown Brothers mercantile house at Sasakwa in the extreme southern part of the Seminole Nation.[1] Owned by the Seminole governor John F. Brown and his brother, this business establishment was the largest in the Seminole Nation. Although Alex grew up on a ranch that employed white hands and had observed firsthand the white renters who lived along the Canadian River, he had not experienced the types of whites he saw at the intersection of Indian Territory life in the southern Seminole Nation. The frontier-minded whites who had made the land rush into the Potawatomi

lands to the west, the intruding Texas ranch hands in the Chickasaw
country to the south, and the ragtag elements passing through to seek their fortunes in the Oklahoma Territory were a rough sort of humanity whose crowing and bragging amused Chinnubbie. They spoke a different language that he tried to capture in "Wildcat Bill":

> Whoop a time er two fer me!
>   Turn me loose an' let me be!
> I'm Wildcat Bill,
>   From Grizzle Hill,
> A border ranger; never down'd;
>   A western hero all around;
> A gam'ler, scalper; born a scout;
>   A tough; the man ye read about,
> From no man's lan';
>   Kin rope a bear an' ride a buck;
> Git full on booze an' run amuck;
>   Afeard o' nothin'; hard to beat;
> Kin die with boots upon my feet—
>   An' like a man![2]

Life at Sasakwa did not agree with Alex, who throughout his life never stayed away long from the familiar scenes of the Creek Nation. In early December he resigned his position and returned to Bald Hill. His quick return to the Creek Nation may have surprised his friends, who had thought his success in the mercantile business was ensured by "the vim with which he always tackles things in general." He spent the rest of the winter and the following spring at the Posey ranch, making occasional trips to Eufaula to visit friends, transact business, or attend lectures.[3]

Among his friends was George Riley Hall, who had often visited Hence Posey's family since their first meeting. Hence welcomed him and treated him like one of his own sons, whom he lectured "constantly," according to Hall. In fall 1894 Hall was teaching in the Arbeka community, some ten miles northwest of Bald Hill. On weekends he visited the ranch, or Alex rode over to spend the weekend at Arbeka. On one of these trips, when Alex rode up he found Hall engaged in an Arbekan fish kill, just coming out of the river carrying his bow and arrows. "He was immaculate. Always went that way," Hall wrote. "He did not greet me formally, but sat on his horse and looked down on me with a severe sort of fixed gaze. Finally he blurted out: 'Hall, I thought you were a white man; but here I find you out among these full-bloods, wet, draggled and with a bow and arrow—just like the Indians.' He then drew me aside and produced a small flask in which there was enough whiskey for a drink apiece." They then joined the Arbekas, feasted on fried fish, and enjoyed the conversation, which was punctuated with "much levity." In recounting the episode, Hall wrote, "Some folks think the Indian has no sense of humor, but that is far from true. The trouble is that the Indian has his own way of making fun, and other people simply do not understand. I am a witness that Indian humor is keen—at times simply devastating. But you miss it unless you understand the language." During these weekend meetings between Alex and Hall, there were also serious moments. "We talked poetry, read poetry and wrote poetry," Hall wrote. "Perhaps that was one of the sweetest of years that constitute the old days."[4]

In spring 1895 Alex once more came to public notice. In April he attended the funeral of D. N. McIntosh, one of his national heroes, in whose memory he made an eloquent statement that highly pleased the McIntosh family.[5] Alex called McIntosh a man ahead of his time, a model for the "coming"—that is, progressive—Indian. He was the epitome of the man of reason described by Thomas Paine, whose *Age of Reason* plainly shaped Alex's language and ideas. McIntosh, he wrote,

> was an investigator—a seeker of the truth. He was not afraid to reason—not afraid to doubt. He built his religion on facts. His mind was too great and of too broad a sweep to accept as true what Nature contradicted. To him hearsay was not a revelation. He was above superstition—above bending his knee to a Deity he knew nothing about. He could not believe the man-written book, to which the world hangs in its ignorance, as inspired and sacred. He found nothing in Nature, and in what reason taught him, to substantiate its preposterous claims. He could not believe in the religion that slew with famine, sword, and pestilence. He chose rather to be a devotee of mental freedom—of the eternal march of cause and effect—of truth, liberty, brotherhood, sympathy and love. He knew that intelligence is ruled by reason, ignorance by fear.[6]

Alex concluded, "McIntosh lived for this world, if there be another,
he will live for that. He did what he could for the destruction of
fear—the destruction of the imaginary monster who rewards the
few in heaven—who tortures the many in perdition." Though these
statements were said to have been made extemporaneously, they
suggest careful, thoughtful composition.

By the time Alex made these statements, he had apparently decided to stand for election as a representative from Tuskegee to the
House of Warriors. His venture into politics received full support
from Hence, who not only encouraged him but may have been the
force behind his decision. Although Hence had taken the side of
the Lower Creeks during the Civil War, he subsequently developed
political views more in line with those of the conservative Upper
Creeks. In the election of 1895, he gave his support in the race for
principal chief to Isparhecher, the former leader of the anticonstitutional forces during the Green Peach War.[7] Beyond Hence's encouragement, Alex's good image, established while a student at Bacone,
and his extended connections with the Phillips and McCombs families of Tuskegee contributed to his decision to run for office.

In 1895 the Creeks were facing what Alex had called an "imminent peril." Although they and the rest of the Five Civilized Tribes
had been exempted from provisions of the General Allotment Act of
1887, it was soon evident that they must face the possibility of allotment of their lands in severalty and the dissolution of their tribal
titles. Bureaucrats, land grabbers, "boosters," and even reformers
charged that tribal governments were corrupt and inefficient. The
Indian Territory was being overrun by white and black intruders, as
illegal residents from the United States were called, and the popular press charged that lawlessness prevailed. To some degree it did,
but the Indians charged that it was largely due to the intruders, over
whom they had no legal jurisdiction. On March 3, 1893, Congress
established a commission to negotiate with the Creeks and other
tribes and authorized it to secure the abrogation of the treaties,
dissolve the tribal titles, liquidate tribal assets, and allot lands in
severalty. Before the Dawes Commission arrived in the Indian Territory, the Creek National Council had gone on record as opposing
such changes in their affairs.[8]

On February 19, 1894, an intertribal council convened at Checotah, in the Creek Nation, to hear from the Dawes commissioners and

discuss the tribes' situation. The Creeks were represented by some of their best-known men, including D. N. McIntosh, Roley McIntosh, Pleasant Porter, Hotulke Emarthla, Concharte Micco, Isparhecher, and G. W. Grayson. Well-known representatives of other tribes included Cherokees E. C. Boudinot, L. B. Bell, and Samuel Mayes and Green McCurtain of the Choctaws. To these and the other representatives assembled, Senator Henry L. Dawes of Massachusetts asserted that conditions had changed so much since the treaties were negotiated that they must be abrogated. The tribes had outgrown tribal governments, he argued. They were surrounded and could not hold out much longer against the tide of whites that would flood the nations and force them off their lands. Only the Dawes Commission, he said, stood between them and disaster, because the tribes had no choice. Congress had decided that change must come to the Indian Territory. If the tribes did not change voluntarily Congress would force them to. Dawes repeated the commonly stated argument that landholders, mainly Indians of mixed heritage, who had fenced off large tracts under tribal law formed the major opposition to allotment, and he asked that the council delegates accept the inevitable and repudiate the treaties.[9]

They refused on both counts. On February 21 the delegates resolved that Congress had been misinformed about the moral, political, educational, and economic conditions of the Indians through misrepresentations in the press. After a more "accurate" review of the conditions of the tribes, they asked Congress to allow them to remain in their "prosperous condition" until they were ready for statehood. Change at present would work to the advantage of the educated Indians but would mean fiscal ruin, moral degradation, and annihilation for the uneducated and conservative Indians. The delegates wrote:

> As Indians who love our country and one another, we say to the United States, "If you will not listen to our protests, if to our assertions, though so well founded in absolute truth as to be unanswerable, you simply reply that it costs too much money to allow our people to remain as we are, we as Indians possessing the common instincts of humanity, reply, then if the die is cast, you must do these things yourselves and not ask and expect us

to aid you in reducing ourselves to homeless, wandering pau-
pers; . . . and if the United States, having put the Indian here to
prepare himself for the duties and responsibilities of Territorial
government and ultimate Statehood, and out of mere impatience and to satisfy the clamor of the boomers, cuts the Indian
off when he is coming to the state of civilization when he will
be ready for Statehood, it will be in the eyes of every lover of
common justice, guilty of common robbery." [10]

Alex and Waetcah Micco, then students at the Indian University,
had attended this council, and as a result Alex had given his persona Chinnubbie a political voice. As he watched the proceedings at
Checotah, he was greatly impressed by the assembly of well-known
Indian leaders. Yet Chinnubbie seemed more impressed by the arguments of Dawes and the other commissioners and concluded that
the Indians were wrong to oppose change. "Indians," he wrote a
few days later, "if you ignore the opportunity which has presented
itself to you in the shadow of an imminent peril, and which if you
should accept, would place you where all that pertains to your welfare would have you, you will be guilty of wrongs and grievances to
your posterity." Thinking people, he argued, realized that the Dawes
Commission had the Indians' best interests at heart and wished to
see them "in harmony with advancement of the world." Congress
would not be so kind, he predicted, and he urged the Indians not to
allow the commissioners to return to Washington without accepting
the plan they had submitted for the tribes to consider.[11]
During the subsequent weeks, Chinnubbie pressed the issue with
his readers. Though it was a serious matter, he could not always
treat it seriously. He presented the allotment question as a parody
of Hamlet's soliloquy: "To allot, or not to allot; that is the / Question; whether 'tis nobler in the mind to / Suffer the country to lie
in common as it is, / Or to divide it up and give each man / His
share pro rata, and by dividing / End this sea of troubles? To allot,
divide / Perchance to end in statehood; / Ah, there's the rub!" [12] And
at the end of his commencement oration that year, Alex appealed to
Indian leaders to step forward, take the lead, and establish an Indian
commonwealth within the United States. Thereafter Alex, like many
of his "progressive" fellow Creeks, never wavered in his belief that,

under the circumstances, allotment was the best route for the Indians, though he would often take issue with the processes by which allotment policy was carried out.

These views seemed not to have posed a problem for him in the election of 1895, though the Creek Nation was obviously in a mood to refuse negotiation with the Dawes Commission and resist efforts to dissolve the common title. The first campaign rally for the principal chief's race was a barbecue on June 5 at the Eufaula District courthouse, not far from Bald Hill. This was a huge gathering of whites and Indians from all parts of the Creek Nation, to whom announced or unannounced candidates or their representatives put forth their views. Speakers were Isparhecher, Thomas Yohola, Second Chief Hotulke Emarthla, William McCombs, Ellis Childers, Ben Wadsworth, and Alex. All spoke in Creek except the last two, whose speeches had to be translated to the crowd.

As usual, Alex was effective. He praised the beauty and resources of the Creek Nation, which he said were coveted by the boomers, speculators, newspapermen, and lawyers who, out of avaricious intent, agitated before Congress for statehood for the Indian Territory. But it was for the Creeks, not Congress, to determine their "national destiny." "I wonder," he said, "that such a grand and potent government as the United States, boasting of equity, of humanity and of the blessings of liberty, would listen to and entertain the wishes of those who want to lord it over this country, and, with one tyranic wrench, dispossess it of its dearest heritage, which is liberty." The history of Indian-white relations was "a history of broken treaties and unfulfilled promises," and there was no "vestige of assurance" that any agreement with the Dawes Commission would be honored: "Can we be blamed for not wanting to treat with this Commission? Can you continue to trust the man who has never kept his promise with you? . . . The crisis, nay, the time that tries men's souls is upon us." Alex concluded, "Hold on to this country, is my watchword. Trust to the honesty of the United States and stand by the man who will protect and guard the interests of the people— Such a man is Isparhecher, the patriot, statesman and warrior." [13]

The speech clearly indicates that Alex had the makings of a politician. He had praised Isparhecher without really endorsing him. He had pointed out the pitfalls of negotiating with the Dawes Commission without telling his listeners that the Creeks should not negotiate

or that negotiation was inevitable. And he had told them that the
United States had been dishonest in its past dealings with the Indians but that they must trust to its honesty in the future. Alex was
becoming a master of the English language, and in public he no
doubt felt more confident with English than with Creek. Could he
have avoided committing himself in Creek? His references to the
Arabs' folding their tents and stealing away and the significance of
the words he borrowed from Thomas Paine would certainly have
lost some meaning in translation. The conservative Isparhecher may
not have comprehended the subtle inconsistencies of Alex's speech
or may have simply dismissed them as political rhetoric, for he and
other veteran politicians began to open political doors for Alex.

Convinced as he was that change must come to the Indian Territory and that the most intelligent and best-educated Creeks should
step forward to meet the national crisis, Alex must have felt out of
place among his fellow delegates to the intertribal council that met
in Eufaula later that month. Isparhecher was a veteran statesman,
but illiterate in both Creek and English. Roley McIntosh was an
able but uneducated leader, and John R. Goat was an uneducated
Creek from Wewoka District. All except Alex were strongly opposed
to negotiating with the Dawes Commission, yet as a national delegate Alex was obligated to represent the wishes of his people, and
of course it was politically expedient that he not argue the opposite
point. The pessimistic tone that had characterized the proceedings
of the Checotah council nearly a year and a half earlier also prevailed at this one, for which Alex served as secretary. The council
achieved little except to pass a resolution on June 27 endorsing and
reaffirming the Checotah resolutions of 1894.[14] Alex had been educated at national expense, and it had long been the practice to use
such persons as record keepers in public affairs. His education had
something to do with his selection as national delegate, certainly, but
the presence of such a young man among the older delegates suggests that the Creek leaders had recognized his intellectual abilities
and that a place had opened for him in Creek politics if he wanted
it. His initiation continued during summer 1895 and went beyond
the political campaign.

A crisis had arisen in the national administration that unfortunately seemed to confirm Dawes Commission claims that tribal
governments were inefficient and corrupt. National treasurer Sam

Grayson had been accused of disbursing funds without proper authority. Angry mobs drove him and Chief Legus C. Perryman from Okmulgee, the national capital, and the chief's duties were assumed by Second Chief Hotulke Emarthla, also known as Edward Bullette, a revered leader from Okchiye Town. A special council convened, and the House of Warriors, the representative body of the National Council, impeached Grayson and Perryman and installed Hotulke Emarthla as chief. The council also established a special committee, headed by E. H. Lerblance, to call in and investigate all outstanding warrants against the national treasury and to approve payment of those it found valid. At this special council session Alex served as clerk in the House of Warriors. Hotulke Emarthla appointed N. B. Moore as treasurer, and on July 25 he appointed Alex to the Lerblance committee, which was also to oversee the transfer of funds from Grayson to Moore.[15]

The transition, however, was not a smooth one. The appointments of Hotulke Emarthla and Moore were opposed by Dew M. Wisdom, the United States Indian agent at Muskogee, who was backed by white traders in the Creek Nation. Before the crisis, Grayson had been preparing to make per capita payments to Creek citizens from a part of the funds received by the Creeks for the sale of their interest in the Oklahoma lands, opened to settlement in 1889. Many of the Creeks were indebted, and Grayson had promised to pay funds due the debtors directly to the traders to whom they owed money. Moore, on the other hand, had vowed to pay the Creeks, who would be responsible for their own affairs. Wisdom accused Hotulke Emarthla and his backers of staging a revolution and threatened to call out federal forces to put it down. How far he would have gone is uncertain, for the traders relented. Thus early in September Grayson resigned, and Moore was officially appointed treasurer.[16]

Meanwhile the political campaign had continued, and the election occurred on September 3. Isparhecher was elected principal chief and Roley McIntosh second chief, their administration to begin in early December. Alex won his seat in the House of Warriors as representative from Tuskegee, which his grandfather, Pahosa Harjo Phillips, also represented in the same body.[17]

The last three months of the Perryman administration were fraught with controversy. Both Perryman and Hotulke Emarthla claimed the chieftaincy. Each had his following, and they dupli-

cated each other's work. On September 8, in the wake of Grayson's
resignation, Hotulke Emarthla appointed Alex and Roley McIntosh as a committee to escort the treasurer and to investigate and audit the treasury, and later that month he authorized them to collect money due the Creek Nation from the former treasurer, Sam Grayson. When the council met in the first part of its split session in October, Perryman was absent. Lerblance's committee, which Alex had served on, reported the discovery of fraudulent warrants against the treasury. As a result, the House of Kings followed the lead of the House of Warriors and convicted Grayson and Perryman of the offenses for which the lower house had impeached them. By the time Perryman was convicted on November 25, only nine days remained in his administration. Two days later, with the power of his office unchallenged, Hotulke Emarthla appointed Alex to a two-year term as superintendent of the Creek Orphan Asylum near Okmulgee.[18]

It appears that Alex had sought this or some other post. Decades later George Riley Hall asserted, mistakenly, that the position was political patronage from Isparhecher because Hence had been instrumental in his election. Hence had indeed worked for Isparhecher, and the appointment was patronage, but it probably came at Hotulke Emarthla's suggestion. During the last months of the Perryman administration, Alex had served Hotulke Emarthla in several ways, including copying the census rolls, serving on committees, and perhaps most important, serving as escort for the treasurer. The per capita payment that had caused the crisis in Creek government amounted to only $14.46 for each citizen. When the payment began in late September, Alex went to Muskogee for bags of nickels, dimes, and quarters to make change. The carnival atmosphere, replete with confidence men, gamblers, merry-go-rounds, and collectors, reminded him of the Cherokee payment he had reported on in 1894. The wild scene and the political tension that surrounded the payment put Alex under pressure. Hall thought that the fiscal responsibilities involved were too great for a twenty-two-year-old. When Hall arrived at the payment, there were Alex and other officials, surrounded by heavily armed guards, disbursing funds to the Creeks. "Posey looked pale," Hall wrote. "I stood as near as the situation would warrant, and caught his eye. He greeted me with what seemed to me to be a wan, feeble sort of smile." Alex's work with the national treasury did not appeal to his "literary side," according to Hall: "Alex was a poet, not a juggler of cash." With Hall's encouragement, it seems, Alex asked his father to help him find a position in education.[19]

In addition to Alex's dislike for the job in the treasury, there were probably other reasons he sought a change. Alex was more pragmatic than Isparhecher and those the incoming chief surrounded himself with, and unlike them, Alex believed nothing could be gained by "stonewalling" the Dawes Commission. In the first few days of October, the political friends of Isparhecher met in the House of Kings to draft a document officially forming the National party. They made overtures to the Union party friends of Ellis B. Childers, a follower of Perryman and an unsuccessful candidate for principal chief in the recent election. The purpose of the meetings was to form a coalition and, apparently, to decide major issues of political patronage. Alex served as recorder at these sessions, at which his grandfather, Pahosa Harjo Phillips, was present. The coalition nominated Alex for superintendent of the orphan asylum.[20] His appointment in the last days of the Perryman–Hotulke Emarthla administration suggests that he might not have expected any favors from the incoming chief, though there is no evidence that Isparhecher opposed the appointment, since he allowed it to stand for the full two years. It may be simply that Alex foresaw the end of an independent Creek tribal government after watching it work from the inside. Though politics continued to be of extreme interest to him, he would ultimately find his niche as a commentator rather than a participant.

By the time Isparhecher took office on December 5, the Creek Nation as an autonomous political entity was doomed. The crisis surrounding the executive branch in the summer and fall of 1895 seemed to substantiate federal claims that tribal governments were inefficient. Intruding whites and blacks were overrunning the Creek country, and the Bureau of Indian Affairs and the federal courts had abetted the intrusion through inaction. The Creeks themselves had abetted it by intermarrying with noncitizens, obtaining permits to hire them as laborers, and selling them illegal long-term agricultural leases. In October 1895 the council had taken such steps as taxing traders and empowering the chief to seek removal of intruders through the courts as well as to take legal action against Creek citizens who sold long-term leases. These efforts proved ineffective because the Creeks received no support from the federal

courts or the Indian Office. In fact, the courts had encouraged the
influx of non-Indians by ruling, in fall 1895, that towns in the Indian Territory could establish municipal governments. The result was a frenzy of speculation in town lots in places like Wagoner, Muskogee, and Eufaula. Speculators were also encouraged by an 1895 congressional act that provided for the survey of Creek lands. Only a few months after Isparhecher's inauguration, Congress required the Creeks to prepare a roll of their citizens, the first step toward allotment. Within a year after the inauguration, the Creek National Council would create a commission of its own to negotiate with the Dawes Commission.[21] By the time these latter events occurred, Alex was settled in his administrative duties at Okmulgee.

Holding his position as superintendent of the Creek Orphan Asylum through patronage, a practice clearly common in Creek politics, Alex himself was given to the practice. He surrounded himself with trusted friends and family members he loved. Alex was only twenty-two and inexperienced, and Hence insisted he ask George Riley Hall to assist him. This good friend, who was eight years Alex's senior and had been dealing with Creek school officials for five years, was teaching at the Artussee neighborhood school, six miles west of Eufaula, in fall 1895. Alex asked Hall to hire a substitute for that position and join him at Okmulgee on December 5, and Hall did so. Alex's "accomplished" and "comely" sister Melissa, who had completed her studies at the Eufaula high school in spring 1895, became his girls' matron. Alex's teaching staff, in addition to Hall, consisted at first of Miss Lillie Lee from Booneville, Arkansas, formerly a teacher at the Coweta Mission School; J. C. Tiger, one of his former classmates at Bacone; and John E. Emery, an Arkansan who served as principal.[22]

The school Alex had taken charge of was a recently constructed boarding school for orphaned Creek children of elementary school age. Its imposing two-story brick building stood on the high prairie about a mile east of the national council house at Okmulgee. There were about one hundred students, almost evenly divided between the sexes. Orphans between ages eight and eighteen were admitted. Their guardians could have them at home during vacation if they were needed to work or could take them out to enroll them in a higher school. Otherwise, they were under the superintendent's supervision until age twenty-one.[23] Alex was responsible not only for providing an education but for feeding, clothing, and caring for them.

What appeared to be an ideal situation for Alex was almost immediately fouled by a problem. John Emery, described as a "bright young man" and a good teacher who "had nice front, dressed well and made an excellent appearance," fell in love with Melissa and she with him. Alex was infuriated. Hall urged him to let the matter take its course, but he responded, "Why, Hall, that fellow has no sense. His mind is like the Canadian river—four hundred yards wide and an inch deep. And besides, he is a damned Arkansawyer." Alex considered beating up Emery, but Hall said, "I advised against that. Posey was [a] small man, a scholar, a poet and a philosopher but in my opinion he was in no sense a warrior. I felt that the athletic Emery would come off the victor in such a set-to, and so dissuaded the irate Posey." In an attempt to end the relationship, Alex fired Melissa and took her back to Bald Hill, where Hence and Nancy forbade her to see Emery again. But young love was not to be denied: the couple eloped. Emery left the school, and Alex promoted Hall temporarily to the principal's position.[24]

Alex had to find a matron quickly to take care of the nearly fifty girls at the school. His thoughts turned to Minnie Harris, a young woman from Farmington, Arkansas, whom he had met the previous summer when he had breakfast at a Eufaula hotel with John Thornton, an Alabaman who had recently become editor of the *Indian Journal*. Miss Harris was stopping at the hotel with a group of other teachers who were to take the stage to Okmulgee, where they would be examined by Creek officials to qualify to teach in the Creek Nation. Though their meeting was brief, Alex found her striking. "The beauty of the young schoolteacher thoroughly charmed me," he later wrote, "and, though I saw her frequently, I could not sufficiently overcome my Indian nature to talk with her. I thought of her constantly; would sometimes grow anxious to declare my love by letter," he wrote.[25] But he did not. Miss Harris returned to the Creek Nation in the fall, to teach at the Hillabee neighborhood school and Alex had found time during his political work to ride past the schoolhouse and back again in order to catch a glimpse of her. Though he had fallen more deeply in love with her, he had not pursued a relationship. Both Alex and Minnie said they met again by chance at Eufaula one night in January 1896, but Hall claimed that Alex inquired after her and sought her out. Thus it could be that the "chance" meeting was arranged. At any rate, Alex offered her the job as matron at the orphan asylum, and she accepted. According to Hall, "No seer or soothsayer was needed to forecast the future." Minnie later confessed that it was "love at first sight" for both of them.[26]

During spring 1896, Alex courted Minnie as only a poet could do. He called her Lowena, the name by which he tenderly addressed her for the rest of his life. He wrote birthday verse for her and signed it "Chinnubbie":

> The lark,
> From dawn
> Till dark,
> Has drawn,
> On fence and post and tree,
>   In meadow, brown and sere,
> From out its heart, so free,
> So full of mirth and glee,
> Sweet songs of ecstasy,
>   To hail the glad new year
>   That makes you twenty-three![27]

"He would read to me," she wrote, "and he asked my opinion of all that he wrote. He also was fond of having me read to him, or him to me, evenings, discussing the things we read,—mostly poems. Mr. Posey spent most of the forenoons in his study, but often in the afternoons he would ask me to accompany him in his walks and drives. I think he admired me for my practical ways. I saved him much bother and vexation over details in looking after the school." Thus, as Alex wrote a few months later, "when summer was come again, 'two hearts beat as one.'" They were married at Checotah on May 9, 1896. Hall could not help laughing at his young friend's marrying an "Arkansawyer" after having listed Emery's greatest fault, next to being a "nit-wit," as being from Arkansas. The marriage took other friends and family by surprise. Although Nancy would have good relations with her daughter-in-law, Hence had difficulty accepting her, always referring to her as "the madam."[28]

After a brief honeymoon, during which Hall took charge of the school, Alex and Lowena returned to Okmulgee. It was common practice for boarding school superintendents and teaching staff to live at the schools all summer at national expense. Of course the children who had no place to go remained at the orphan asylum during the summer and had to be cared for, but relief from administrative duties gave Alex time to devote to his two loves: Lowena and poetry. Hall later wrote, "The summer of 1896 was unquestionably one of the happiest periods of his life. The long hot months of vacation enabled him to do much literary work, and the whole world was in tune for him. Successful and happy, he dreamed of a future devoted entirely to literature. He was a model lover, a model bridegroom and a model husband."[29] By the time school began again that fall, Alex had developed a rather relaxed attitude toward his administrative duties.

As superintendent, Alex had few academic responsibilities. He sometimes visited the classrooms to listen to recitations or lecture the students. When teachers were absent, he heard their students' recitations and taught classes, noting after one such experience, "I think I missed my calling in not becoming a teacher."[30] He apparently delegated many details of daily routine to Lowena, leaving himself free to manage the larger affairs of the institution.

He faced minor crises at the asylum calmly and, in retrospect, often found humor in them. When Joe Tompkins, the cook, disappeared without notice, Alex simply observed that Joe "was a bird of passage." If supplies ran low and the freighters from Checotah got lost, were held up by bad weather, or bogged down in bad roads, he simply reduced the number of daily meals and waited. If incorrigible boys ran away from the school and took "good" boys with them, he considered it good riddance and did not send out search parties. If a runaway came back drenched, cold, and penitent, faced up to his mistake, and apologized before the entire school, Alex welcomed him back. "This will do him more good than a year's schooling," Alex wrote about one such boy. "I hope it will be the making of him. Experience never intends her lessons to be forgotten. Her precepts come like the white men into the Indian country—to stay." If runaways did not return, there were other orphans who needed a home and who would appreciate the opportunities the asylum had to offer. So Alex picked up orphans on the streets of Okmulgee and took others in if they showed up at the door.[31]

Alex maintained an air of familiarity with laborers and other

workers around the asylum and sometimes accompanied them on
their errands. The strong sense of humor he had inherited from
Hence and from his Tuskegee relatives surfaced frequently. He joked
with his cousin John Phillips, whom he had hired as a handyman.
"Knowing him to be fond of jokes and much given to laughter, I
tried to split his sides open," Alex wrote after one full morning spent
in John's room. Determined to break a habit of sleeping late that he
had acquired at Bacone, Alex was not satisfied with a new regimen
of getting up early himself. He rousted out John and Tompkins, the
cook, as well and amused himself with their sluggishness and grum-
bling. Once he got up before daylight and scared the cook witless. "I
got a white sheet," he wrote, "and made uncouth noise out side the
kitchen, letting the wind flap the sheet against the window where
Joe was preparing his dough. He hollered 'Whose dat?' and made
distance, dropping lard in all directions." In later years Hall called
Alex "a peculiar character" who, though "reserved" and "very dignified," was driven "to perpetrate practical jokes." Though he knew
well that Indians had a strong sense of humor, Hall said, "He had
enough Indian blood to make him taciturn, enough Irish to give him
a keen sense of humor; he was a practical joker, but his jokes never
extended beyond close circles." Despite the good humor and familiarity, Alex mentally drew a line that his workers could not step over.
He fired his cousin John. "I was sorry to be compelled to turn him
off," Alex wrote, "but he got too independent, and I cannot put up
with independence in a servant even tho he be my relative."[32]

As superintendent, Alex was responsible for welcoming guests
who dropped in for meals or who spent the night or several days at
the asylum. There were some he would rather not have seen, like
root and herb doctors and like Benjamin W. Wadsworth, who had
a nasty habit of using other people's toothbrushes and hairbrushes.
Besides having to guard his toilet articles, Alex found that Wadsworth "never misses an occasion to be where he is least needed."
Other guests, such as preachers, Alex virtually ignored. These men
gave the students the only religious instruction the asylum offered
under Alex's administration. He did not attend the preaching himself, on one occasion saying, "I rather preferred to be entertained by
Plutarch's accounts of the justice and the glorious conduct of Aris-
tides, the Athenian." Alex was sometimes even unaware that it was
Sunday. "One day is as holy to me as another," he said. Most guests,

however, were heartily welcomed. Politicians such as John Goat, the chief justice of the Creeks with whom Alex had served as an international delegate, and Samuel Benton Callahan, Isparhecher's private secretary, brought news of Creek affairs. Because the asylum was near Okmulgee, the seat of the Creek government, and on the road between the capital and Muskogee, visits like these became more frequent when the National Council was in session. Other guests were relatives of the faculty and staff, including Hall's brother Jeff and members of Alex's family.[33]

On most days, Alex read sometimes all morning when his duties as superintendent did not interrupt. The beauty of language intrigued him, and literature inspired him. He read not only for pleasure but to learn about human existence, and he read rapaciously.

His tastes ranged widely. During January and the first days of February 1897, for instance, he read among other works Plutarch's *Lives*, which fascinated him. In the biographies of the ancients he found lessons that applied to modern times. Alex wrote, "Plutarch has impressed me that in Greece and Rome one's greatness was determined by banishment," and "Plutarch is certainly a master of his wit. He is as much a philosopher as a biographer."[34] During that same month, he also read James William Buel's *Heroes of the Dark Continent*. He was deeply interested in the rivalry and jealously among the explorers who searched for the source of the Nile. But Buel's language was "high sounding," and Alex was disappointed in the author. His final assessment of the book reflected his concern about a tendency he found among contemporary writers—writing for the market at the expense of quality: "From a literary standpoint, the book is a failure, and not as complete as it might be as a history. The author seems to be in too great a hurry to be done with it; which gives one the impression that his main object was to put the book on the market and as quickly as possible enjoy the proceeds thereof." Buel had "carelessly used" his "rich material," which in the hands of Washington Irving, one of Alex's favorite authors, would have taken on "a structure of wonderous beauty." After Buel, Alex read *The Iliad*, Irving's *A Tour on the Prairies* and *Life and Voyages of Christopher Columbus*, the poems of Robert Burns, Shakespeare's *Othello*, Charles Dudley Warner's *Washington Irving*, Emily Dickinson's poems, the *Arabian Nights' Entertainments*, and *Dream Life* by Ik Marvel (Donald Grant Mitchell).[35]

During this period, as throughout his life, Alex also read many current newspapers and magazines as well as whatever back issues he could get, devoting several hours each week to this pastime. Besides the *Muskogee Phoenix* and the Eufaula *Indian Journal*, he regularly read newspapers such as the Kansas City *Star* and the Little Rock *Arkansas Gazette*. Among the magazines he read were William Cowper Brann's *Iconoclast, Puck, Truth, Judge, Up to Date, Current Literature, Review of Reviews, Midland*, and *Cosmopolitan*.[36]

In general, Alex read with enthusiasm and rarely voiced disappointment with literary works. His enthusiasm for Plutarch is obvious in his journal. He returned to the works of Robert Burns again and again. "I get some new pleasure, some new thought, some new beauty heretofore unseen," he wrote, "every time I read the 'Ayrshire Plowman.' His warm heart, his broad and independent mind 'glint' like the daisy in the 'histie stibble field' in every song he caroled." Alex wanted to share his enthusiasm for Burns with Hall, who thought Burns's dialect was "horrid" and therefore could not enjoy the poetry. Alex rendered "To a Mountain Daisy" in "good English" in order "to throw Hall into better love with the poet." But, he wrote, "In doing so, I fear I have spoiled the poem; for it is in his dialect that Burns is sweetest." Alex also returned again and again to the works of Irving, whom he counted as one of his favorite authors. And the works of Ik Marvel, he believed, could not be surpassed "in sweetness of fancy and purity of language," and he called Marvel's prose "first class poetry."[37]

He also liked much of what he found in contemporary periodicals. At first he could not understand why Brann's *Iconoclast* had enjoyed such "wide-spread notoriety." He read the December 1896 issue "for two solid hours . . . without stumbling onto so much as the slightest suspicion of a new idea or a decent attempt at witticism," but in the next issue he found Brann "cleanly witty" and saying "some right good things—at least in one or two articles." At other times he found Brann amusing enough to read aloud to Hall. Alex collected aphorisms from *Puck*. He enjoyed *Truth, Judge*, and *Up to Date* for their humor, calling certain issues "side splitters." He liked *Up to Date*'s sharp "thrusts at high life," and he found poems he liked in magazines and newspapers.[38]

Though he found much he liked, Alex also found much to criticize in the periodical literature. At times he was disgusted because magazines published the works of writers like Rudyard Kipling and Hall Caine, who wrote, he believed, simply because it paid. "It is not the material in the story or the poem the magazines want," he wrote, "but the name attached thereto." He was sometimes critical of a writer's style. Of a critique of Albert Pike's "Every Year," which Alex called "a poem of much beauty," he said, "The writer of the critique is too much like Dr. Hornbook. The way he slings his rhetorical terms about is simply dumbfounding." He added by way of parody, "The most inexcusable thing in a writer is the ostentatious display of acquirements." Alex disliked some literary forms altogether: "The serial stories I pay no attention to—be they Conan Doyle's, Kipling's or others' who write because it takes and pays. I have but little use for fiction at best and no use whatever for the kind of fiction we are offered by the magazines. I want facts—truths elegantly dressed— interpretations of nature—something to build on and to broaden my views—something to give me a deeper understanding in all that pertains to life." [39]

The periodicals fed the mild interest Alex displayed in international politics. Because his political concerns rarely ranged beyond the Indian Territory, he noted without enthusiasm the changes in administration in Washington. He concluded that arbitration was the best way of settling international disputes but that conflict benefited some nations. His example was England, which would "rot and fall to pieces without something of the kind." [40] He was most interested in the struggles of oppressed peoples, such as those of the Armenians against the Turks and the Cubans against the Spanish. On more than one occasion he called for a free and independent Cuba. Always seeing the parallels between such peoples and the Indians, Alex found irony in the fact that Senator George Vest, a free-silver populist, made strong appeals on behalf of Cuban rights after he had been instrumental in establishing the Dawes Commission through gross misrepresentation of conditions in the Indian Territory. [41]

Alex's reading did much to inspire his writing. In December 1896 the *Muskogee Phoenix* published his exclamatory poem "Cuba Libre," which encouraged the Cuban patriots and condemned General Valeriano Weyler as the Spanish "beast" and "butcher," as well as "The Indian's Past Olympic," a long narrative poem in heroic couplets describing the pageantry and excitement of the traditional Creek ball game. The latter is an attempt at the heroic, certainly, but "heaven's bliss," lions in "the shepherd's pen," typhoons, "straying zephyrs," jackals, and "luna-orbs" seem inappropriate to the subject. The form, the language, and the theme of the Indians' past golden age suggest that the poem may have been written during his college days. Also, the poem was published under "A. L. Posey," a name he had not used on his published works since he left Bacone.[42]

During the first five months of 1897, Alex produced a number of other poems. "The Conquerers," inspired by his reading of Plutarch, is about the violent ends some of the ancient conquerers met. "An Arbekan Episode," a poem about one of Hall's courtships, has not survived. "Lines to Hall" is little more than doggerel about Hall's growing dissatisfaction with life at Okmulgee. "Callie," on the subject of boyhood bashfulness, is a free-verse experiment about a renter's daughter whom Alex knew as a child. "The Two Clouds," a short lyric, treats the clash of weather fronts that often brought tornadoes in the Indian Territory. And "Daisy" was a verse tribute to a dog that belonged to Alex's little brother Darwin. The last two poems were published, apparently in the *Checotah Enquirer*, and "Lines to Hall" probably appeared in the *Indian Journal*. Throughout the spring Alex also worked on "a series of boyhood stories entitled 'Tom and Abe and I,'" as he said, "just simply to amuse myself and at the same time preserve in black and white those youthful recollections which I may not always remember." The sketches were destined to become works later titled "Jes 'Bout a Mid'lin', Sah," "Two Famous Prophets," and perhaps "Uncle Dick's Sow" and "Mose and Richard." Alex also produced a collection of "short sayings" titled "Shells from Limbo," which may survive as "Epigrams," and began a "book of experiences," apparently different from the boyhood sketches.[43]

For the most part, Alex relegated his reading and writing to a morning routine. At times, however, if he was not well or was resting after one of his frequent trips, he read all day. Sometimes he read far into the night and suffered for it the next day. On one occasion he wrote: "To burn the midnight oil is to wear one's self out and be fit for nothing on the morrow. It is as necessary to avoid taxing your mind and body too much as it is to avoid over-drawing your bank account."[44]

Unconcerned to any great degree about the day-to-day details of managing the orphan asylum, Alex found time to devote to Lowena as well as to his literary interests. To him, his love affair with her was the stuff of romance. During their years at the orphan asylum, he took her picnicking in the Cussetah Creek bottoms or driving to Okmulgee in the buggy behind his team Maud and Fanny, through the "dull gray winter woods," across the Cussetah onto the prairies beyond, or down to the Deep Fork to watch it in flood. Winter did not prevent their outings. Accompanied by their black dog, Mingo, they took the children to the frozen pond where, Alex said, "I skated to my heart's content, to the great amusement of the girls, this being the first time they ever saw anyone on skates. I am no expert skater but I can sometimes wind my legs up and stand on my head." Lowena did her part to please him by taking on many of the routine duties of running the asylum and by learning to make sofky—pounded corn cooked to a gruel in lye water—his favorite food. And please him she did! "I must compliment my wife," he wrote, "on the sofky she made today—this being her first effort. She, by some hook or crook, contrived to give it just the proper flavor." Love and his stomach turned him into a sophist: "No one but an Indian can make sofky; Lowena can make sofky; therefore Lowena is an Indian!" When her first pregnancy limited her activities, he gathered bouquets of wildflowers for her, and they read poems together. "He could read beautifully," wrote Hall. "His voice was low-pitched and musical. His enunciation was faultless. He did not allow himself the luxury of omitting his Rs, in conformity with his environment. His soul was attuned to the sublime. He loved sonorous sounds and musical cadences. If his sophomoric tendencies smacked of the bombastic at that time, it is distinctly to his credit than otherwise."[45]

On March 29, 1897, their first child—a son—was born. On the following day Alex wrote, "I am not in a mood yet to tell how it feels to be a father. The baby has cried enough to make me walk the floor at night. I am sorry to have to say that it looks very much like its father." They named the baby Yohola, which could mean "echo" or "one who makes a loud cry or whoop." The yoholas, or criers, had traditionally been associated with the white clans, to which Alex belonged, and had performed important functions in presiding over the busk. To this traditional name Alex added one from his reading. Since he was reading Washington Irving's *Life and Voyages of Christopher Columbus* at the time, they gave the baby the second name Irving. Yohola Irving Posey was not a healthy baby, and the young parents had several anxious moments during his first few weeks of life. By summer he was well, however, and Alex had learned to do his share in caressing and caring for the child, whom he called "the brightest and sweetest young one in the world." [46]

If anything was lacking to make these days of reading, writing, and being in love a halcyon time for Alex, it was supplied by the congenial group of people with whom he had surrounded Lowena and himself. In addition to his original faculty and staff, in 1896 he hired Rosa Lee, Lillie's sister, as a teacher. Lillie assumed the duties of principal, and Hall simply taught. In August 1896 Lowena had gone back to Arkansas to visit her family and had returned with her sister Catharine, familiarly known as Kittie, whom Alex hired as assistant matron. When Kittie left the group in early 1897, he hired Miss Ollie Wilson to replace her for the rest of the year. At various times Alex also hired his brother Bill and Hall's brother Jeff as hands.[47]

Free afternoons were filled with group picnics, walks in the fields and woods, buggy rides, excursions into Okmulgee, and croquet games. Although Alex enjoyed most games, croquet pleased him very much, and he took special delight in what he called "skunking" or "whitewashing" the ladies, though he was gentleman enough not to brag about it in public.[48]

In the evenings the group read to one another or held musical recitals where Hall played the violin and Rosa Lee sang and played the organ. Hall had a local reputation as a fiddler and in earlier years had been in demand at dances and parties, but he also played the violin seriously, sometimes accompanied by Rosa Lee at the piano. He played with what Alex called "considerable skill," though he could not "slide his fingers down the strings and make them shriek like a north wester through a rail fence." Alex once said of Hall, "To hear him attempt new pieces of music and strike a celestial note now and then is like looking at the sky on a cloudy night and once in a while seeing a star." Alex liked the violin well enough to try to learn to play, but he soon became convinced that he was the exception to the adage "No excellence without labor" and would have been satisfied to play only two tunes: "Swanee River" and "Evelena." In reality he preferred fiddle music, especially Arkansas breakdowns, and if Hall's violin renditions became too "highbrow" for him, he called them "dancy."[49] Fortunately the special rapport between Alex and Hall was deeply cherished by each man.

Hall, who was nearly a decade older, was generally more serious in demeanor than Alex and thus endured a great deal of teasing from his younger friend. Alex teased him about his courtships, the pistol he carried, his violin playing, his inability to learn to ice skate, his spying the nose of the man in the moon during an eclipse of the sun, and his fear of centipedes. But it was Hall's hunting that gave Alex the most opportunity to tease. He expected Hall to return from his excursions empty-handed and delighted in the hunter's excuses. "To hear him tell it," Alex once said, "he came within an ace of bagging a fine buck, just the other side of that little sandy place in the road between here and the lake." On another occasion he said, "I am under obligation to pay half the expense of the transportation of the game. I would that all my obligations were so safely made!" And when Hall returned, Alex said, "Hall came back as he went— without game. He almost got game, though—to hear him tell it. He made the water fly up right under a big white duck and can't understand why the duck flew away alive." Even Hall's successes came under attack. On one occasion, "Hall shot so much lead into a poor mud duck down on the pond that it sank!" Hall apparently took this relentless teasing in the same good-natured spirit in which it was given.[50]

Besides the fun that Alex and Hall enjoyed, there was a more serious side to their relationship. They walked together to Okmulgee for exercise or to see the sights and talk to the townspeople and visitors. They hunted and fished together or took walks in the surrounding countryside, sometimes accompanied by the children, digging wild onions, gathering flowers, and making notes on nature. Frequently during these outings their conversations turned to literary topics. During one excursion into the hills behind the orphanage farm, they sat on opposite sides of a waterfall and extemporaneously composed alternating lines of verse. No one bolstered Alex's literary energies or brought them into focus as Hall did, and he often gave vent to his creative urges after an exchange with Hall. He submitted his efforts for Hall's criticism and approval. He read aloud to him the works of his favorite poets as well as interesting periodical articles, and when Hall was ill Alex sat by his bed and read to the Poet, as he called his friend.[51]

The relationship between the two men was a remarkable one. From the time they met their friendship had grown, and it would only become stronger in the years ahead. They were absolutely loyal to one another not only in their friendship but in encouraging one another in literary, political, or business affairs. It is not surprising that, even within the close circle of friends that constituted their day-to-day world at Okmulgee, Alex and Hall, both lovers of literature, should turn to one another.

The very closeness of their circle, however, may have worked against Alex's development as an artist. Hall's influence at a time when Alex's literary urge was at one of its peaks reinforced earlier reading and writing habits that limited the range of his poetic achievement. When Hall said Alex's literary tastes were "correct," he meant that they agreed with his own preference for the American and British romantic poets of the early nineteenth century and their imitators in later decades, such as Bret Harte, Thomas Bailey Aldrich, Joaquin Miller, and James Whitcomb Riley. Although Hall's influence was strong and the months at Okmulgee proved productive for Alex, his most significant poetic expression would occur later in another setting.

In a literary sense, Alex gained far more from this relationship than Hall did. At first Hall had found life at Okmulgee inspiring. The summer of 1896 had "glided by in a sort of reverie" for him. Relief from teaching duties left him free to write, and during that summer he produced some lyrics as well as "Grave of the Bandit Queen" and "Belle Starr's Last Ride," two narrative poems that were frequently reprinted in the Indian Territory. By spring 1897, however, Hall wrote poetry only occasionally. By the end of 1896 he had grown restless at Okmulgee. He spent Christmas holidays that year with his brother Jeff near Senora, southeast of present-day Henryetta, "hunting, making inroads into Dog Town and having a good time generally." He fell in love with the countryside around Senora, and in early spring 1897 his visits there became more and more frequent. Despite the possibility of losing the day-to-day camaraderie he enjoyed with Hall, Alex urged his friend to give up his work at the orphan asylum and go to Senora.[52] On March 9 he wrote "Lines to Hall," which said, in part,

> You cannot sing in walls of brick,
>   George Hall; go get thee to a hut
> Along some Tulledegan crick.

High life ill suits thy muse. Go put

Her up an altar on the moor,

And keep the robins company.[53]

He went on to urge Hall to find an obscure place quickly "and carol as a brown thrush may," writing out the themes he knew well.

Alex understood his friend's feelings, for he too was growing tired of Okmulgee. As a member of the House of Warriors in 1896, he was necessarily involved in the political affairs of the Creek Nation. During sessions of the National Council the town was lively; as he said, "You can walk out almost any morning then and find a man for breakfast." At other times it was dull, and when Alex walked or rode his horse Cricket to town, he was less interested in the political scene than in amusing himself by listening to stories and tall tales in the offices and on the streets or engaging someone in conversation about boxing, schemes of some of the Creeks to emigrate to South America, or the nouveau riche, "who accumulate fortune by peddling books and rat-traps and cap the climax by allying their families with foreign nobility." Although he visited Isparhecher on occasion, it was less for political reasons than out of friendship. When the council met in special session in March 1897, he did not go: "I have not been down to inform myself of the proceedings and shall not go at all, unless I am called there for some other purpose than to find out what is happening. My business is here, not there. I despise to see a man hang around where he has no business."[54] By spring 1897 Alex had apparently decided to leave not only politics but Okmulgee as well. His growing discontent found expression in more frequent trips to Bald Hill during that spring.

He always looked forward to these trips. The all-day journey gave him an opportunity to observe nature and reflect. The trail went southeast from Okmulgee, skirting the eastern side of the Deep Fork of the Canadian to Wildcat, turned southeast from there, across the North Fork of the Canadian at Limbo Carr Ferry southeast of Burney, and continued the last six miles to Bald Hill. "The drive thro' the Senora and Tulledega countries is highly pleasant," he once wrote. "The recent rains have made the streams look like naughty children after crying—Deep Fork and Wolf Creek in particular." He took the difficulties of the journey in stride. He had to tie the buggy wheels during his descent of Tulledega Mountain to prevent a runaway. If minor streams were over their banks, he had to go miles out of his way to skirt the headwaters or find a ferry. Sometimes the ferryman was absent, and Alex had to wait hours for his return. Ferry crossings could be dangerous; on one crossing, his team spooked and fell into the stream. Alex narrowly escaped drowning, and though he managed to save his buggy and harness, his team drowned. In the face of such adversity, however, he could look forward to a good meal no matter what time he reached Bald Hill. When he finally arrived at the ranch after losing his team, he said, "Misfortune does not effect [*sic*] my appetite." Alex, like Ichabod Crane, was "a huge feeder." He loved to eat. He always ate "big" meals, and to him there was something special about meals at Bald Hill: "I enjoy eating nowhere as much as at home."[55]

During these visits he spent a good deal of time with Hence. He admired his father and saw him as a wellspring of common sense. He loved to hear Hence trade stories with old-timers about the days before the Civil War, and he considered some of the stories worth writing down. He enjoyed Hence's dialect narratives about Uncle Dick and Uncle Will Grayson and their descendants on Coon Creek. And Alex was amused when the politically minded Hence became agitated about "organizations and combinations, political, religious and otherwise." Alex and Hence rode around the ranch together or put on false faces and scared "the renters into fits," chasing them out of their houses and cotton patches. At times they drove to Eufaula to do business. On those occasions Alex dined with his friend J. N. Thornton, and he sometimes went to Eufaula alone just to have dinner and attend a concert with Thornton.[56]

These visits to Bald Hill apparently brought Alex much joy. There were good times with his siblings. Three more had been born since he went to Bacone: Darwin in 1890, Ella in 1891, and Mendum in 1893. Alex discussed crops with Frank and John and talked to John about school. He played croquet with Frank, Bill, and John and beat Frank at checkers, rubbing "a few diamonds off his championship belt." He was delighted by the younger children: Darwin, whom Alex described as "the boy of cute sayings," and the inquisitive Conny, a veritable "interrogation point" who told "improbable yarns." Their brother, in turn, delighted them by bringing them apples, candy, and nuts from Eufaula.[57] Alex also found quiet at Bald Hill. After the children had gone to bed and Hence had turned in early, he sat up late, read, played with the puppy, or chatted with Mattie and Nancy.[58]

Although these visits were symptoms of a growing dissatisfaction with his position at Okmulgee, they also reflect one of Alex's basic characteristics. He liked the security and intimacy of a small, tightly knit group of family or friends. The stories of his childhood he had recently written and statements he would later make to the press show that he looked back fondly on his early days in the Tulledegas and at Bald Hill as particularly happy. He had found some of the same security in his classmates at Bacone, and at Okmulgee his close circle of friends in their rather isolated world had made him very happy. Also, Alex liked people, especially women, to "do" for him. As Nancy had "done" for him as a child, so Lowena now took away much of the burden of running the school to leave him time for reading and writing. At Bald Hill he could count on Nancy and Mattie to care for him. It is perhaps not coincidental that his visits to Bald Hill became more frequent, like Hall's visits to Senora. Hall's desire for a change meant that the little group at Okmulgee would soon break up, but life changed little at Bald Hill.

The visits to Bald Hill seemed to feed both his discontent with his position at Okmulgee and his desire to pursue literature. In 1895 he had staked off a farm in the public domain at Possum Flat near Bald Hill, and in 1897 it was rented to a man named Cowin. Alex wanted to get back to the farm. "I am restless," he wrote early that spring. "I want to get away from this place. I feel that I am not free. I want to go to my farm, and, by the gods, I am going. I will throw me up a shack, buy a couple of Possum Flat razor back sows and a cow and let public life go down the country—and political friends with it." Later he wrote, "What an inactive life I am leading here! I want a change of air, of place and habits of life."[59]

The message he had stated in "Lines to Hall" applied just as much to him. During one of Jeff Hall's visits to the asylum, he, Alex, and Hall discussed their plans for the future. Alex described his part of the conversation as follows: "I build air castles. Plan a home in a Bald Hill valley. Remark that if I cannot build the kind of house I want I will content myself with a shack." Alex was not the first poet to yearn for the country cottage and the bucolic life, nor would he be the last. As the end of the school term approached, he said, "I want to get out of brick walls—out of politics and be a common citizen.

No more do I intend to be a government servant, and will not be a servant for any individual."[60]

More than fantasy was at work here. There was, among other things, a rejection of the public life of the politician. After his election to the House of Warriors in 1895, Alex never again sought political office, and there is no evidence that he even seriously considered doing so. Here also is an apparent early state of his rejection of certain types of publicity. He was quite willing for his name to be placed before the public—through his writing, his editorial voice, or his statements to the press—but he became more and more reluctant to address an audience directly. In fact, his address at the opening rally for the election was the last public speech he is known to have made. He would attend numerous political gatherings and conventions in subsequent years, but always as an onlooker, a delegate, or a secretary, never as the keynote speaker, chairman, or president, whose duties would put him on the speakers' platform. On the literary front there was reason for Alex to believe he had a future in literature. His level of inspiration was high, and he certainly must have known that his recent works were different in theme and content from the abstract and extremely sentimental writings of his college days. Such inspiration, bolstered by the energy of youth, could make any goal seem within reach.

Chapter **5** Return to Possum Flat

· ·

On the last day of the school term in 1897 Alex
wrote, "Our work is ended and our large family broken up." Alex
had more than six months remaining in his job as superintendent,
according to his appointment, so he would remain. But changes
were in the offing for other members of his little circle. Lillie Lee
would transfer to the Coweta Mission School and be replaced as
principal by Johnson Tiger; Rosa Lee would transfer to the Euchee
Boarding School, and Miss Belle Wright, a teacher from Eufaula,
would replace her. In the fall, however, Kittie Harris would return
as assistant matron.[1] The halcyon spring days of personal happiness,
camaraderie, and literary intensity were at an end. Alex might have
acknowledged the change more sadly had he not known that, despite his urging Hall to resign, the Poet would be back with him in
the fall as a teacher. Also, and more immediately, the leisure of the
summer would give Alex time to continue his reading and writing
and to lay plans for his departure from Okmulgee and return to Possum Flat, where he hoped to take up the life of a poet-farmer when
his term as superintendent expired.

The summer got off to a bad start, and the first few weeks of vacation proved hectic and unsettling. Twice during May Alex was called to Muskogee on legal business. Then he and Lowena took baby Yohola on his first trip to see his grandparents. After four days at Bald Hill, they took the train to Arkansas to see Lowena's parents. Alex reached there disgruntled, irritated among other things by cabmen contending for his business along the way. Lowena, of course, was happy to be back at the family farm at Farmington, but for Alex it was different. Though he enjoyed the beauty of the Boston Mountains from the train window, little else pleased him. His dissatisfaction grew, and he quickly became bored by sightseeing with his father-in-law, Milton Harris. After one day he boarded a train alone, "despite Lowena's pleading," and went back to the orphan asylum and to "fresh breezes and contentment," as he said. But the contentment did not last. After two days he was lonely. When a letter arrived from Lowena, he hitched up his team, Cayenne and Pepper, drove to Checotah where he caught a train, and arrived unannounced at Farmington at night. "Lowena is expecting me," he wrote, "and is not surprised."[2]

The impatience that displayed itself in his petulance and impetuous behavior resulted not only from the breakup of his circle of friends but also, in part, from his desire to return permanently to Bald Hill. That April he and Hence had driven around Bald Hill and selected a place for a pasture. He had also had carpenters come down from Checotah and had showed them where he contemplated building a home on his farm at Possum Flat. During his visit to Bald Hill with Lowena on their way to Arkansas, he found that Thomas Boone, a neighbor, had laid claim to the pasture he had staked off in April. After a conference with Boone that failed to resolve the issue, Alex took three of Hence's wagons and half a dozen of his hands and staked off a mile-square pasture that completely surrounded Boone. "I pay Boone back in his own coin and in some of my own," Alex said.[3]

As the summer progressed, Alex fell into a more settled routine at the orphan asylum. Hall occasionally visited him, or Alex traveled to Senora where Hall and his brother Jeff were farming. Alex, Lowena, Hall, Belle Wright, and the students who remained at the school found time for picnics, horseback riding, watermelon parties, freshwater pearl hunting along the Deep Fork, and buggy races that pitted Hall's Dolly and Fay against Alex's Cayenne and Pepper.[4]

Between trips and outings, Alex read. His summer reading included the poems of Shelley, Walt Whitman, and Bret Harte; Donald G. Mitchell's *My Farm of Edgewood* and *Wet Days at Edgewood*; Joaquin Miller's *The Building of the City Beautiful*; and *Aesop's Fables*. These readings offered him a temporary escape from the "blues." Of Mitchell's *My Farm of Edgewood* he said, "The first chapter has lifted my face to the blue skies, with here and there a white cloud dreamily drifting; has taken me to the mountain top overlooking cozy New England hamlets, arms of the sea and glimpses of the lordly Hudson in the distance." The impression stayed with him throughout the book: "Donald Mitchell, like Irving, never tires me. Can beautiful language, faultless and pure, delightful descriptions of nature, so true that you can hear the rustling of the poplar leaves, and philosophical excursions ever tire?"[5]

Not only Mitchell's works but all of Alex's reading of this period continued to reinforce his romanticism, and if he needed literary sanction for his desire to move to his farm, he found it in Mitchell. In his Edgewood books, mostly written some thirty years earlier, Mitchell described how he retreated from the hustle and bustle of life and established his farm to pursue agriculture, which he called "an experimental art." On days too wet to work outside, he delved into his vast library of "farm-writers" from the classical period to the early nineteenth century. In romantic fashion, he viewed as more important than agricultural science these writers' and his own observations and practical experience in farming. The life described in the Edgewood books is, to say the least, idealized.

In late July restlessness seized Alex again. This time he took a train to Galveston, Texas, checked into the expensive Brock Hotel, and spent a day and a half going out into the Gulf on a steamer, watching the young lovers, "taking in the sights and turning somersaults in the Mexican wave," and gathering impressions what would become poems such as "Sea Shells."[6] Like several of his visits to Bald Hill during the past spring, the excursion to Galveston was undertaken on impulse. If Lowena had not already become accustomed to his sudden trips and his frequent absence from home, she would soon do so, for by summer 1897 he had established a pattern that he would follow for the rest of his life.

The remaining weeks of vacation and the beginning of the fall school term of 1897 were uneventful. In late summer Alex once more lapsed into his settled routine with Lowena, Hall, and Miss

Wright. In early September he was visited by Nancy, on the "first long trip" she had taken "in years." Accompanied by Bill, Frank, Jim, and Mendum, she stopped at the asylum on her way to and from Nuyaka, where she visited her mother's sister, Lydia Tiger. About this same time, Johnson Tiger assumed his duties as principal. Alex apparently left the everyday routine of running the school to Tiger, for in October he moved his family to Stidham, where their new home had been completed about a mile and a half northeast of the Posey ranch. He nevertheless remained officially the superintendent of the orphan asylum until his tenure ended in December. Then, Hall wrote, "We left that place together as we had gone there together—Posey and I." Hall joined Jeff, who had rented a farm about five miles east of present-day Henryetta.[7]

Despite the move to Stidham, Alex's plan to become the full-time poet-farmer was put in abeyance for several months. After his appointment at the orphan asylum ended in early December, Isparhecher appointed him superintendent of public instruction for the Creek Nation, his term to run until the National Council convened the following October. Alex had not been first choice. Isparhecher had preferred J. H. Land, superintendent of the Euchee Boarding School, but Land, who had taught at Tuskegee in 1885 and knew the Poseys, had declined in favor of Alex.[8] As superintendent, Alex oversaw the operation of all neighborhood and boarding schools in the Creek Nation. He was responsible for not only fiscal but personnel matters. He could examine teachers and appoint them to the neighborhood schools, and he could appoint superintendents of the boarding schools, who, as Alex had done at Okmulgee, could appoint their own staffs.

Although Alex was no doubt pleased to be near Bald Hill, there was at least one disadvantage. Hence found it convenient to give him advice and was responsible for one of Alex's first and most unfortunate official decisions. Hence took advantage of Alex's appointive power to secure a position for his second son, Frank, who had passed the age of twenty-one. Alex appointed his brother superintendent of the Coweta boarding school. Though Hence knew that Frank's education and age did not qualify him to be superintendent of a boarding school, he wanted to do something for him. Thus Hence and Alex prevailed upon Hall to go to Coweta with Frank and help him run the school.[9] Such blatant patronage, though a fact of Creek political life, was inexcusable and, played out on a national level, made the Creek government vulnerable to criticism by outside groups such as the Dawes Commission and the United States Congress, who had vested interests in abrogating treaties and nullifying tribal titles. But patronage was only one practice that the Creeks under constitutional government had learned from white politicians. It was not the Creeks, after all, who had coined the phrase "the spoils of office." Yet if Alex did not have misgivings about appointing Frank, he should have.

The first salvo came from a surprising quarter. A. G. W. Sango and W. A. Rentie, influential Creek freedmen from Muskogee, went before Henry C. Reed, the black judge of Muskogee District, and charged Alex with taking a bribe. Their charge grew out of the appointment of Mrs. P. A. Triggs, wife of a Muskogee hotelkeeper, as a teacher at the freedmen's boarding school at Pecan Creek. According to Sango and Rentie, Alex had visited the Muskogee newspaper office of W. H. Twine, the prominent black editor of the *Cimeter*, and had read a letter from Mrs. Triggs offering money in return for an appointment. Though Alex had told Twine he would have nothing to do with Mrs. Triggs, she was appointed to the Pecan Creek school, and Sango and Rentie concluded that Alex had accepted the money. To build a case for Alex's corruption, they cited the Posey family plan to appoint Frank and Hall at Coweta. Alex had discussed the appointment with them, they claimed, at the Posey ranch in December.[10] The attack from Rentie probably surprised Alex. In 1895 Rentie had prosecuted Sam Grayson at his impeachment trial before the Creek National Council. The Isparhecher-Childers coalition, which had nominated Alex for the Okmulgee superintendency, had nominated Rentie for the superintendency at Pecan Creek and Reed for the judge's bench in Muskogee District. Rentie and Sango had gone to the Posey home soon after Alex was appointed superintendent of public instruction, probably hoping for a share of political patronage. Apparently failing in their objective, they brought the charges.

Alex's response to the bribery charge was simple: under Creek law he could not appoint teachers to the boarding schools. He had examined Mrs. Triggs to see if she was qualified to teach, but she had been appointed by the freedman superintendent at Pecan Creek,

J. P. Davidson. Of course Alex had the authority to remove Davidson

or to retain him in his position. Still, charges made by a man like
Rentie, a leader in the Afro-American League in the Indian Territory, carried weight with Isparhecher. Alex had not been his first
choice for the position, and the chief attempted to fire him. But Alex
obtained an injunction against Isparhecher and managed to retain
his position.[11]

Alex also had to defend Frank's appointment. Frank and Hall
had taken charge of the Coweta school by the time the charges
were filed, replacing H. Marcey Harjo, whom Alex had suspended.
Harjo immediately filed suit before the Creek supreme court, asking to retain his position, but the court affirmed Alex's authority.
Harjo also failed in his appeal to the United States district court
at Muskogee. In Alex's favor, too, was that long before his own appointment as superintendent of public instruction, the citizens in
the Coweta community were dissatisfied with Harjo's administration of the school and had complained about him to Isparhecher.[12]
With the legal issues of Frank's and Alex's appointments settled,
there remained only the matter of Alex and Hall's guiding Frank
and compensating for his deficiencies as superintendent. They did
well during the spring term, but during summer 1898 Hall, as usual,
did not remain at the school, leaving Frank to his own devices.

When Hall returned in the fall, he faced a disagreeable situation.
Frank had married Emma, the daughter of Judge Joseph Mingo,
an upstanding member of the Coweta community. But young Posey
had fallen under the influence of Mitchell Wadsworth and Robert
Mingo, Emma's brother, and had begun to drink. Hall was awakened at night by drinking parties on the school grounds, and Frank
refused to listen to his advice to behave and be mindful of his reputation. As long as Alex was in a position to protect Frank, his job was
secure. But Alex had been appointed to serve only until the October
term of the National Council, and he was not reappointed. Alex filed
suit to block the appointment of his successor, Alex McIntosh, but the
courts affirmed Isparhecher's appointment. With the authority of his
office secure, McIntosh undertook an official inquiry of the Coweta
school, and Frank was suspended just before Christmas 1898. Hall
left of his own accord shortly thereafter.[13]

Although he had delayed his plan to become a full-time poet-
farmer, Alex had not given it up. Despite his duties as superinten-

dent, he managed to find time to write, just as he had at Okmulgee. From his home he could see Bald Hill rising high above the prairies. It was close enough that he could visit the ranch at will, make excursions into the Tulledegas, which more and more attracted him, and oversee the work that renters were doing on his farm. He was among familiar scenes and drew inspiration from them for his poetry. All these pursuits led him closer to his dream of a life devoted to literature, and he contemplated what it meant to be a poet:

> The poet sings but fragments of
> A high-born melody—
> A few stray notes and castaways
> Of perfect harmony
> That come to him like murmurs from
> The sea of mystery.[14]

His desire to return to Possum Flat had fed his urge to write during the latter half of 1897. Despite his restlessness during his last months at Okmulgee, Alex had managed to produce a surprising number of literary works. During the vacation months of 1897 he revised the chapters he had written for his book about his boyhood.[15] His concern to record his early experiences for posterity reflects his growing image of himself as a writer. Poets are rare enough in any society, but they were even rarer in those days of the Creek Nation. While there was no doubt some of the posturing of the poet in these autobiographical works, there was more to them than that. Alex's idealized pictures of life in Tulledega and at Bald Hill, taken with statements he would make to the press in the next few years, reflected how far he believed—or wanted the public to think—that his literary bent had its roots in his boyhood freedom and closeness to nature. In the years to come he would have his readers believe that, as external pressure for social change was placed on the Creeks, his childhood years constituted the last "palmy" days of Creek society and that he was qualified to write about them.

Alex also wrote a number of poems during his vacation months in 1897. These included the lyrics "June" and "To a Humming Bird" and the free-verse pieces "The Idle Breeze," "To the Century Plant," "Sea Shells," "In Vain," and "The Boston Mountains."[16] The last is a sarcastic statement of his impressions of the mountains, jaded by his unhappy experiences during his visit to Fayetteville. Though the poems are marked by the sentimentality, halting lines, and weak endings that typify much of his verse, they also display the striking, sometimes brilliant images he was capable of: he compares the bird to "some frenzied poet's thought, / That God embodied and forgot," the plant's blossom to a truth that is uttered by one persecuted in an earlier age and takes on glorious meaning in a later one, and the breeze to a shepherd boy herding clouds, which stray and disappear while he idles away his time on earth. Also from this period is "My Fancy," destined to become one of his most frequently reprinted and, though sentimental, successful lyrics.[17] These poems reflect a shift from the political and occasional poems of earlier months to the themes of nature that would henceforth dominate his work. A notable exception is "Verses Written at the Grave of McIntosh," an elegiac poem in which he borrows the caroling thrush from Whitman and, like the poet in "When Lilacs Last in the Dooryard Bloom'd," finds consolation in the return of life and love in April and in the oaks that stand sentinel at the grave of his friend and "Indian brother."[18] Of these poems, only the hummingbird poem and those on the seashells and the Boston Mountains were published during this period.

In fall 1897, with the onset of a new school year at Okmulgee and the move to Stidham in October, Alex had continued to write, but at a slower pace. He had produced only a handful of poems, including "To a Cloud," "Autumn," and "To the Crow."[19] Though the last is undistinguished, the others are interesting. "To a Cloud," no doubt inspired by his summer's reading of Shelley, is a lyrical tribute to the British poet in which Alex asks if Shelley's spirit rose "up from the cruel sea" to the cloud that bears it over the world. "Autumn" is free verse filled with good descriptive images.[20]

Quite settled at Stidham, early in 1898 Alex entered a period of intense literary production. During his tenure as superintendent of public instruction he wrote at least thirty poems, and perhaps as many as fifty. His subjects ranged widely. There were occasional pieces for Yohola and Lowena and attempts at humor such as "The Athlete and the Philosopher," "To an Over-stylish Miss," and "Kate and Lou." By far the dominant subject is nature, however, but nature in the larger sense—earth, sky, prairies, fields, hills, and streams and the wildlife they contain. Many of the pieces are sentimental and didactic, as usual, but there is evidence of metrical experiments. His free verse, for example, was not always entirely "free" but included unrhymed metrics in which he created an unusual effect with the unaccented end of one line and the accented beginning of the next. Other poems appear to be merely experiments in rhyming, and a few contain the powerful, sometimes brilliant images he was capable of creating.[21] In terms of volume he wrote more during the first nine months of 1898 than ever before or after, but not much of it was very good. Alex apparently realized that, for he sent little of it to be published.[22]

Relieved of his bureaucratic duties as superintendent in fall 1898, Alex was free to pursue his literary goals full time. The home he had built at Stidham for Lowena, Yohola, and himself was a modest square bungalow with a portico on each side. There, for nearly a year, he passed what has been called the "golden era" of his life.[23] As he had done at Okmulgee, he established a routine of reading and writing in the mornings and rambling about the farm in the afternoons, observing nature and absorbing images that would find their way into his poems. He kept a number of pets, including squirrels, dogs, and a turkey. A lover of flowers, he cared for those that grew in profusion around the house. Practically every day he talked to white renters and the elderly Creeks in the neighborhood.[24] He watched their expressions, listened to the rhythms of their speech, and absorbed their ideas, filing them away in his mind. He had more time for Hence, whose health had begun to fail, and for Nancy, who doted on him and appeared, to onlookers at least, to have selected him as her favorite. According to his family, he read and translated his poems for her and looked to her for approval.[25]

Perhaps he believed he had found what he sought:

> I ask no more of life than sunset's gold;
>   A cottage hid in songbird's neighborhood,
>   Where I may sing and do a little good
>   For love and pleasant memories when I'm old.[26]

In his "cottage hid in songbird's neighborhood," he found time to contemplate what he wanted to achieve in the poetic process:

> What mountain glens afar
>   And woodland valleys are
>   To echoes in the air,

My soul would be
To harmony.[27]

Here at his "hermitage" he felt, like Walt Whitman, "apart from the pulling and hauling":

> Between me and noise of strife,
> The walls of mountains set with pine;
> The dusty care-strewn paths of life
> Lead not to this retreat of mine.[28]

Here, as he had always done, he shared his poetic efforts with close friends, especially Hall and Thornton. Though Hall's visits were less frequent than formerly, Thornton was often at the Posey home, and he and Alex read the poems to each other.[29]

Much of Alex's inspiration came from those nearby "walls of mountains," the Tulledega Hills. There he could let what Hall called his "dreamy side" come into play. There, in that "wild and indescribably beautiful" place, he and Hall had wandered and loitered without conversation. "He was in tune with the beautiful in nature," Hall said. "It thrilled him. He responded instantly to such influences. No wonder there was little conversation. We needed little." Hall could often tell how Alex felt by simply looking at his face. He had never known a human countenance "more expressive" and "could almost always tell when he got a happy thought." Hall said of his friend, "He loved the shining reaches of Limbo creek that winds its way through the Tulledega hills, but above all he loved to lie under the whispering pines of the mountains and listen, in rapt silence, to the crooning melody of the forest. To him the sighing branches told tales of wonderous mystery. They touched his poet-soul with the magic of the wild, and lingered in his memory forever."[30]

Alex took every opportunity "to spend a day in the hills," according to Lowena. When she could, she often rode horseback with him all day as he interpreted nature, telling her the Creek names for birds, flowers, and trees. He had "the Indian's natural love of solitude," as she called it. "I nearly always accompanied him on his rambles," she said, "but there were times when he liked to walk alone." But, Hall said, Alex "never felt alone when out in the pathless forest or seated on a boulder, feasting his eyes on the long stretches of yellow sand and limpid water of North Canadian. He was a child of nature, and had a soul attuned to all the sweet and varied harmonies of the universe." Alex struck Hall as one who "was always reaching for something that was just beyond his reach. He was reaching for ideals, expressions and thoughts and there was about him a certain wistfulness, a certain yearning, a sort of spirit-something that was hard to define."[31]

These retrospective impressions of Alex and his attitudes during this period led to the belief that he remained detached from the workaday world. There was certainly an element of that. The leisure time he required for thinking and writing was made possible by an economic practice that had become firmly rooted in the Creek Nation during the preceding decade. Farming had developed rapidly then in the wedge of land between the north and main branches of the Canadian River. Under Creek law, Creek citizens could stake off and fence as much land as they could improve, so long as it did not encroach on another citizen's claim. Huge tracts had been staked, mainly by Creeks of mixed heritage, for ranching and agriculture. Many Creeks did little of the physical labor themselves; controlling the land, they simply hired laborers or rented out small tracts to farmers, mainly whites and blacks who had come into the Creek country from the United States. Alex followed this practice when he staked off several hundred acres at Possum Flat. The sharp decline in the amount of productive land available for claiming inevitably led to conflicts, like the one between Alex and Boone in summer 1897. Alex did not work the land himself. Several tenants occupied his claim, and he collected rents. But Lowena relieved him of even that chore and of otherwise having to deal with the tenants. She managed the farm and protected him from disturbances while he was reading and writing.[32]

Such was Lowena's habit then and thereafter. Though Alex was too modest to allow her to use the word, she considered him a genius, whom she defined as "one that has the ability and patience to sit and produce for us what we common mortals cannot produce for ourselves, but so much enjoy." Thus she sheltered him from interruption while he worked, and as she later said, "Those who came during Mr. Posey's work hours had good reason to believe that I did my work well, for unless their business was very important, they transacted it with me or came again." In after years, she would consider the two years at Stidham a most happy time that was "all too

short."[33] Ironically, the economic practice that made Alex's leisure
possible was a major reason that opponents of tribal government cited for dissolution of the common title. It was a system that was doomed. For Alex and Lowena, the "golden age" lasted only until late summer 1899.

During the preceding year, relations between the Creek Nation and the United States had taken a dramatic turn. Although the Dawes Commission was created in 1893, it had little success in getting the large tribes of the Indian Territory to agree to abrogate their common titles and disband their nations. The Cherokees had refused altogether to treat with the commissioners. Whether to stall, mollify the commissioners, or make the best of a bad bargain, the Creeks, Choctaws, Chickasaws, and Seminoles had created commissions to conduct negotiations, and the Seminoles had gone so far as to sign and ratify an agreement to dissolve their nation and accept allotment of land in severalty. Frustrated in its attempts to appease land-hungry Americans by opening the Indian Territory, on June 18, 1898, Congress passed what was generally known as the Curtis Act. It provided for dissolution of the common titles and allotment of lands in severalty without tribal consent. Provisions of this act forced the tribes to negotiate for the best terms possible in the circumstances. During the next few years allotment would be carried out under various congressional acts and agreements arrived at between the individual tribes and the United States.[34] The process was irreversible. The prediction Chinnubbie had made to his fellow Creeks during his last year at Bacone had become reality, and as a mature poet Alex wrote,

> What does the white man say to you?
>> Thus speaketh he to you: "You've got to cast
>> Your laws as relics to an empty past.
> You've got to change and mend your ways at last.
>> I am your keeper and
> Your guardian, in the judgment of mankind,
>> And 'tis mine to command
> You in the way that leaves your savage self behind."[35]

In the summer of 1899 Alex was asked to assist in the process.

Despite the Curtis Act, in education as in other areas of Creek affairs, the old practice of political patronage died hard. While the process of allotment went forward, the Interior Department increasingly assumed control of fiscal matters and other affairs of the tribes. In education as elsewhere, there were local attempts to forestall, thwart, or sabotage the transition to federal control. John D. Benedict, who was appointed United States supervisor of schools in the Indian Territory, had the task of overseeing the transition in education. He met stubborn resistance from Alex McIntosh, who had succeeded Alex as superintendent of public instruction for the Creek Nation.

In summer 1899 Benedict and McIntosh agreed to consult one another in appointing teachers for the next school year. To Benedict the agreement meant that McIntosh must have his approval for all appointments; to McIntosh it apparently meant little. The newspapers reported that when the time came for teacher examinations, McIntosh collected a dollar fee from each applicant, pocketed the money, and left the examinations to Benedict. Then McIntosh appointed the teachers for the coming year without consulting Benedict. When William McCombs resigned as superintendent of the Eufaula boarding school, McIntosh replaced him with his uncle Luke G. McIntosh, who moved his family into the school building before McCombs had moved out. Benedict learned that in former years the elder McIntosh had badly managed the Coweta and Wetumka schools. The source of this information may have been Alex Posey, whom Benedict wanted to replace McCombs. With the school term fast approaching, the McCombs and McIntosh families still occupied the school. Benedict had turned down all the teachers' appointments made by Alex McIntosh, appointed Alex Posey as superintendent of the school, and refused to sanction Luke McIntosh's appointment or to pay him. Alex McIntosh, in turn, had refused to recognize Benedict's authority to make appointments.[36]

It took months to resolve the issue. To McIntosh, it was a matter of blatant interference in Creek affairs by the United States. Of course there was also the matter of his own pocketbook and the grudge he bore Alex for attempting to stop his appointment as superintendent of public instruction. Although Alex finally got possession of the school and the Department of the Interior reaffirmed Benedict's authority to review and approve appointments, McIntosh still refused to sign any requisitions for services or contracts to maintain the Eufaula school, and he refused to recommend any appropriation of funds for the scholastic year. By way of compromise, he

asked Benedict to withdraw Alex's name and agree to another appointee, but Benedict stood firm. Although Alex administered the school from the beginning of the fall term, it was not until December that McIntosh relented and signed his official appointment as superintendent for the rest of the year. The irony of Alex's triumph over those who had defeated him a year earlier was not lost on the editors of territorial newspapers, who approved of his appointment and called him "not only a well-educated young man in the ordinary acceptance of the term, but . . . a thinker as well." [37]

Although it is not certain why Alex decided to take this position, there are several possible reasons. First, allotment, which appeared to be inevitable, would bring a redistribution of the land, with each Creek citizen receiving title to 160 acres. The selection process had begun. The large agricultural tracts would be broken up, so adjustments would be necessary in the tenant farmer system. Second, a deep personal sadness may have contributed to Alex's decision to move from the Bald Hill area. In late 1898 death had broken for the first time the tightly knit circle of the Posey family. On December 9, his ten-year-old brother James Blaine Posey had died of jaundice. As the oldest child, Alex had doted on his brothers and sisters. "Standing by the bier of that handsome little fellow," Hall later wrote, "he realized for the first time the pangs of parting which death imposes." [38] Jim's death was a heavy weight on Alex, as his later writing revealed. Finally, during spring and summer 1899 Alex had probably found it necessary to assume Lowena's duties in managing the farm, for on March 5 their second son, Pachina, was born. Unlike Yohola, Pachina was fair skinned and had light eyes and hair. Alex gave him the second name Kipling, after the British poet and fiction writer Rudyard Kipling. Pachina's birth brought added personal and financial responsibilities.

In addition to these reasons, Alex must have realized that his experiment at being a poet-farmer had been less than successful. He had continued writing during the first half of 1899, but his works had been no more successful than those of the previous year. In the past there had usually been only a short time between composition and publication of his poems. Because of a lack of extant publications for that period, it is difficult to date some of his published works with certainty. Of those poems written from fall 1897 until summer

1898, only three or four were published during that time and perhaps no more than ten appeared during his lifetime. Compared with newspaper verse in the Indian Territory at the time, his did not lack quality. He simply must not have sent it in. Perhaps he had begun to reconsider himself as a poet. Descriptions of his attitudes and actions during his time at Stidham suggest something of a pose, a heightened awareness of being a poet. His poems suggest that he looked at nature as he thought a romantic poet should, abstractly and sentimentally, in its largeness. The terms "mystery" and "harmony" appeared more frequently as time passed, and only seldom did he render nature concretely. As events of the succeeding months would show, he was on the verge of reevaluating his work and, after that, of ceasing to be a serious writer of poetry. This process had probably already begun by summer 1899.

Young Jim's death, Alex's growing family, and the imminent shift in land tenure were all indications that life at Possum Flat and Bald Hill had entered a new phase. Someone so well read and with such a literary sense must also have concluded that his failure to write much that he was willing to send to publishers showed the need for change in his literary career as well. Alex's accepting the position at Eufaula suggested that, for whatever reason, he had put aside, at least for the time being, the life of the poet-farmer that he had yearned for so desperately two years earlier.

As he was prone to do, Alex added relatives to his staff at the Eufaula High School. He had apparently healed the rift with his brother-in-law, John E. Emery, and despite his earlier belief that Emery was shallow minded, he hired him as principal. That arrangement did not last long, however; ironically, Emery became principal at the orphan asylum, where he and Alex had first met. Alex also hired Lowena as matron and her sister Kittie as assistant. It is doubtful that Alex hoped to recreate the atmosphere surrounding his days at Okmulgee. For one thing, Hall was teaching at the Hutche Chuppa neighborhood school north of the North Canadian so that he could be near his and Jeff's farm near Senora.[39]

Even had Hall been able to join Alex, the idyll could be no more. Too much had happened to dull the youthful enthusiasm of earlier days. Besides Jim, death had claimed Rosa Lee, their much loved and admired friend at Okmulgee.[40] Taking stock of the changes that had occurred in their lives since their days at the orphan asylum,

Alex put his sense of loss into lines inscribed to Hall, concluding:

> Tho' far apart we've drifted, Hall,
>> 'Tween you and me there's but a single river
> And but a single mountain wall—
>> 'Tween Rose and Jim and us, the vast Forever.[41]

This, then, was a turning point for Alex. He sensed it, and the next two years would make the idea a reality.

For the camaraderie that seemed a necessity for him, Alex turned to the Informal Club. With its membership limited to Alex, Hall, John N. Thornton, and George W. Grayson, the club had simple rules: a new member could be added only if one of the four died, and "a member must have something to say worth hearing before calling a meeting." Although the three Eufaula residents met on occasion, the club almost always convened when Hall was in town. In late December 1899, Hall called a meeting to tell the members that he would not live in town under any circumstances, saying in part, "Men who live in town, on account of having to follow some business for a livelihood, become sort of automatic machines for the accumulation of pennies."[42]

Besides reflecting his need for the small circle of friends, Alex's membership in the Informal Club demonstrated his tendency to seek out older men for friendship and intellectual companionship. All the other members were older than he. Grayson, for instance, one of the most prominent business and political figures in the Creek Nation, having held several public offices, was the age of Alex's father. But in intellectual matters, age had never been important to Alex. The group served as an outlet for discussing his political, economic, literary, cultural, and social ideas. In Grayson, Alex found one of the most knowledgeable of his fellow Creeks in matters relating to Creek culture and history. A native speaker from childhood, in summer 1885 Grayson had done extensive study and analysis of his language for John Wesley Powell of the Bureau of American Ethnology. As a public official, he had been out among the people and often served as an interpreter.[43] In subsequent years Alex would be able to count among his friends—all much older than he—others of the most influential Creeks and, among those, some of the most knowledgeable about Creek politics, history, and culture. He would also demonstrate an ability to establish rapport with older, unlettered members of the Creek Nation.

Not all of the Informal Club's business was serious. The members also enjoyed each other's humor and lighthearted fellowship and teasing. Thornton, for instance, preferred charges against Grayson for having become "unduly intoxicated" and having "reviled" him at an earlier meeting, but because Grayson was absent and could not defend himself, the club took no action. Thornton and Alex complained about the smell of Hall's cheap cigars—"two fors," as Alex called them—which nearly broke up the meeting. For years Alex had made it a practice to meet with Thornton to dine. The club afforded an opportunity to continue that practice. On Christmas Day 1899, the club had dinner at the Posey ranch at Bald Hill. "We may not look upon such a dinner again," said Alex. "My father's hospitality is as boundless as his common sense."[44]

The proximity of Bald Hill to Eufaula made it possible for Alex to stay in close touch with his family and with scenes familiar to him. Not only did he visit the ranch, but Conny, John, Horace, and Mattie were enrolled in the Eufaula school so that Alex could supervise their education. Perhaps the distance from Bald Hill and the surrounding countryside was enough to make him reflect and render their wildlife into poems such as "The Mockingbird," "The Blue Jay," and "Bob White" and their natural scenes into poems such as "Where the Rivers Meet," "Limbo," "Spring in Tulwa Thlocco," and "Song of the Oktahutche," one of his best-known poems.[45]

Late in 1899 he began to receive attention as a poet outside the Indian Territory. Six of his short lyrical poems—"Shelter," "An Outcast," "A Creek Fable," "To a Daffodil," "To a Morning Warbler," and "Nightfall"—appeared in the century edition of the *Muskogee Phoenix* on November 2. A St. Louis *Republic* correspondent who saw the century edition sent in the poems and a biographical sketch of Alex, and with the exception of "Shelter," the *Republic* published them a few weeks later. His "Ode to Sequoyah" had appeared in the April 1899 issue of the *Twin Territories*, published at Muskogee and circulated nationally, and in November the magazine began, with "Pohalton Lake," to publish his works steadily. During the next two and a half years it would print many of his poems and prose pieces.

Throughout this period, Alex also continued to publish in the *Indian Journal.*[46]

In early January 1900 one of his poems that had appeared in the *Journal*, perhaps "Pohalton Lake," caught the attention of Elaine Goodale Eastman, wife of the celebrated Santee Sioux physician and writer Charles A. Eastman. Mrs. Eastman, who was in charge of *The Red Man* at the Indian Industrial School at Carlisle, Pennsylvania, wrote to Alex requesting an original poem for her publication, which circulated nationally to alumni, federal bureaucrats, libraries, and patrons of the school. He sent her "My Hermitage," which describes the poet's rural retreat from the "noise and strife" of the world. It appeared in the February issue of *The Red Man* and was followed in April by "The Decree," a rather conventional poem that expresses the whites' decree that the Indians must give up their culture and follow the whites' ways. Mrs. Eastman informed Alex that "My Hermitage" had "attracted some little attention" because it had been "copied in several periodicals and favorably commented upon." One of those reprinting it was the *Indian's Friend*, the organ of the Women's National Indian Association, which sent its publication to thousands of members of reform and friends-of-the-Indian organizations. The poem was also reprinted in part in newspapers such as the Nashville, Tennessee, *Daily American*, which also carried a brief story listing Alex as one of the "good" emerging Indian writers, along with Simon Pokagon, a Potawatomi, and Zitkala-Sa, a Yankton Sioux. According to the editor of the *Twin Territories*, "critics and persons" with "prominent positions in American literature" had written to Alex, "complimenting him and urging him to devote more time" to his writing.[47] Thus, as the school term closed at Eufaula in spring 1900, it appeared that all was going well for Alex in his personal life and literary career.

Alex was also doing well as an educator. Interior Department officials perceived him as an important figure in the transition of power in education from the Creek Nation to the United States. Benedict had undertaken a campaign to correct certain fiscal abuses in the school systems. He instituted procedures for auditing accounts and inventorying and accounting for Creek national property. Alex's appointment had apparently been part of Benedict's campaign to improve the administration of the Eufaula school. He approved of

Alex's work, and in late spring 1900 he prevailed on him to take charge of the Wetumka National School for a year.[48]

Less than a week after Alex had been appointed at Wetumka, death once more broke the Posey family circle. Baby Pachina, who had been a delight to Alex and Lowena, became severely ill on June 16. A physician was called from Checotah to consult with local doctors, but in the early hours of June 17 the bright, laughing, spritely Pachina died. The devastated parents buried their son not in the family plot at Bald Hill, but in the cemetery at Eufaula.[49] Late in the summer, they and three-year-old Yohola sadly moved to Wetumka.

At Wetumka, more than forty miles west of Eufaula, Alex was farther away from friends, family, and familiar landscapes than he had been since his stay at Sasakwa in 1894. Much smaller than Eufaula, Wetumka lacked both the economic bustle and the potential for intellectual or artistic stimulation and outlet that Eufaula had offered. The rolling blackjack-covered hills around Wetumka did not appeal to him like the prairie ranges and farmlands around Bald Hill and the more rugged Tulledegas. He no doubt felt estranged, though he returned to Eufaula on occasion to visit or to buy supplies for the school. With the onset of spring in 1901, his spirits revived somewhat. The season was dry and cold, and he watched the slow awakening of the landscape with interest during his rambles through the woods and fields, his rowing excursions on nearby Wewoka Creek, or his buggy rides behind his team, Joaquin and Shelley. In Thoreau-like fashion, he kept detailed and insightful notes on trees, wildflowers, birds, insects, and other wildlife.[50]

During his stay at Wetumka, Alex had continued to receive press notice as a poet. Throughout 1900 his work had continued to appear in the *Indian Journal* and *Twin Territories*, often reprints of poems he had published earlier. But there had been new works, too, like "Song of the Oktahutche," "To a Robin," and "Bob White." He also continued to supply poetry to *The Red Man and Helper* at the Carlisle Indian School, where his sonnet "The Blue Jay" appeared in September. These publications, particularly the last, brought Alex to the attention of the American reading public once more. An article about him, containing five of his poems, appeared in the *Kansas City Journal* on September 26, 1900, and caught the attention of William R. Draper, correspondent for the St. Louis *Republic*. Draper

asked for a photograph and information so he could do a similar feature for his paper. In early October E. Leslie Gilliams, a freelance
writer, also asked Alex to supply information for a news story about
him and his work.[51]

The result of this last request was an expanded version of an
autobiographical statement Alex had published in *Twin Territories*
earlier that year. That statement, which appeared in the May issue
and was repeated in the *Kansas City Journal*, no doubt added to the
aura that surrounded him as a poet. For the first time, he told the
now familiar story of his childhood in the Tulledegas and at Bald
Hill: the boyhood freedom he enjoyed with Tom Sulphur, his first
"dried-up" teacher, Hence's forcing him to speak English, and his
education at Eufaula and Bacone.[52]

This narrative was expanded and, as it appeared in the Philadelphia *Press* on November 4, 1900, became his best-known statement
about the Indian as a literary artist. He said, in part, "If they could
be translated into English without losing their characteristic flavor
and beauty, many of the Indian songs and poems would rank among
the greatest poetic productions of all time." He continued,

Some of them are masterpieces. They have splendid dignity,
gorgeous word pictures, and reproduce with magic effect every
phase of life in the forests—the glint of the fading sunshine falling on the leaves, the faint stirring of the wind, the whirring
of the insects. No detail is too small to escape observation and
the most fleeting and evanescent of impressions are caught and
recorded in the most exquisite language. The Indian talks in
poetry; poetry is his vernacular, not necessarily the stilted poetry
of books, but the free and untrammeled poetry of nature, the
poetry of the fields, the sky, the river, the sun and the stars. In
his own tongue it is not difficult for the Indian to compose, he
does it instinctively; but in attempting to write in English he is
handicapped. Words seem hard, form mechanical, and it is to
these things that I attribute the failure of the civilized Indian to
win fame in poetry.[53]

This statement's curious reflection of belief in the "noble savage"
and the Emersonian concepts of the figurative quality of "savage"
language and of the purity of language rooted in nature indicates
the thoroughly romantic base of Alex's thinking regarding poetry.

Besides these comments about the Indian as poet, Alex also made some revealing remarks about his own literary ambitions. He had not attracted a wider reading audience because he had not sought one. His first poem to draw any attention, he said, was "Ode to Oblivion," which included local references to Indian legislation passed in Washington. The poem had appeared as "O, Oblivion!" in the *Checotah Enquirer*, probably in 1895. It is a humorous poem in which Chinnubbie Harjo tells how politicians like Charles Curtis or Dennis Flynn or Henry Teller come out of oblivion and make a name for themselves by introducing bills to do away with the Indian governments. The poem was reprinted by other newspapers in the territory. Its success caused him to write more poetry of the "local" type, he said. Because of the local quality of his work, Alex expressed doubts like those of James Russell Lowell, who believed that his "Yankee rhymes" would be "cashiered" outside New England. Thus Alex said, "I write exclusively of the West, of home scenes and places, and fearing that my local allusions might not be appreciated elsewhere, I have never made any attempt to get a hearing in the East."[54]

Whether or not he sought "a hearing in the East," he got one. The *Press* had printed a photograph of Alex and four of his poems: "A Vision of June," a sonnet he had written at Bacone and revised over the years; "Twilight" and "To a Morning Warbler," lyrics published earlier; and "Memories (Inscribed to George Riley Hall)." This last poem, which dealt with the deaths of his brother James and Rosa Lee, was a personal expression of the grief he and Hall shared, and his submitting it with his statements about his poetry seemed to underscore his comments on the "local" quality of his work. Nevertheless, the article or versions of it along with poems appeared in the Kansas City *Star*, the New York *Evening Sun*, and a weekly Boston paper, and Alex began to receive inquiries about whether his poems had appeared in book form as well as requests for photographs and autographed poems.[55]

Draper's article on Alex appeared in the St. Louis *Republic* in late November. It contained a brief biographical sketch and reprinted two of his short lyrics: "All the While" and "Moonlight." After it appeared, Draper asked Alex for information on Indians for an article for *McClure's* and invited him to write an article on the Snake faction of Creeks, who were causing excitement in the Indian Territory at the time by resisting the breakup of the tribal government.[56]

Such reactions to Alex and his work seemed to refute his belief that audiences outside the region would not appreciate his work. Many of his poems, he claimed, had been "scribbled off" on the spot, "when he was riding alone in the woods, sitting beside a stream, or paddling his canoe." Those who knew him best said he was always modest about these "scribblings," placed little value on them, and apologized for some of them. Alex insisted, "I write entirely for my own pleasure and am entirely indifferent to reward or criticism. I am content with being called the sweet singer of my tribe and with having an opportunity to praise the glories of the landscape I love so well." [57] Editors found it difficult to understand why he was reluctant to send them his work and to seek a wider audience, concluding that the promise of fame meant nothing to him. He sometimes failed to respond to written requests. He promised to send something to an Oklahoma editor but failed to do so, which triggered a racist response from the editor: "Thus he revealed his Indian instincts and habits, for with an experience with a dozen Indian writers in Oklahoma, especially in the eastern side, I have never found one that will stick to anything, not even his promise. Not that I think any of them deliberately break their promises, but they procrastinate." [58]

Alex's concern that eastern readers would not appreciate his work seemed to belie his indifference to "reward or criticism." He knew, too, that other Indian writers such as Simon Pokagon and Zitkala-Sa had successfully presented local materials to eastern readers. A good example, too, is Charles A. Eastman. In late summer, when Alex sent Elaine Goodale Eastman his sonnet "The Blue Jay" for *The Red Man*, he also sent to Dr. Eastman, through her, his comments on Eastman's article "The Story of the Little Big Horn," which had appeared in the July issue of *Chautauquan*. Eastman was "gratified" by Alex's comments, for he planned to do more writing of the same type, his wife said. "He has made a careful study of the history of the Sioux people," Mrs. Eastman wrote, "and finds much that has not so far been brought to light." [59] A voracious reader of periodicals, Alex must have known that the American reading public was at that time much drawn to Indians and Indian subjects.

Despite the flurry of interest that had attended the publication of his poems in the East, Alex for some reason failed to take advantage of the wider market for his writing. Instead he remained at Wetumka until his appointment expired at the end of the spring term in 1901, writing very little but continuing to submit his works for publication in the *Indian Journal* and *Twin Territories*. Alex had apparently finished for the time being with his dream to live as a poet-farmer at Possum Flat or Bald Hill. Before he had left Eufaula he had written,

> I'm tired of the gloom
> In a four-walled room;
> Heart weary, I sigh
> For the open sky
> And the solitude
> Of the greening wood.[60]

But something had changed. Alex's most important poetry was behind him.

It is significant that at the time Alex received his greatest notice as a poet, he had almost stopped writing verse. Only one manuscript can be attributed with any certainty to his year at Wetumka. His distance from familiar landscapes and his close circle of friends as well as the emptiness left by Pachina's death no doubt contributed to his malaise. Although his deprecation of his work during this period might be viewed as typical false modesty, it seems he was undergoing dramatic changes in his perception of himself as a writer.

The change had begun some months earlier. In late 1898 or early 1899, Alex had collected a large number of his poems, but for what purpose is uncertain. Some poems he copied unchanged from earlier manuscript or published versions; others underwent minor revisions; others still contained major changes. To the old poems he added several new ones, some poetic renderings of former brief prose works. Few of these new works found their way into print during his lifetime. Alex either could not or did not intend to distinguish between his best and worst verse, for the collection contains both, ranging from his earliest to his most recent works.[61]

Surely he realized that his poetry rarely succeeded. By then he must have begun to recognize that the kind of verse he wrote resulted in large measure from his isolation from other poets and from his having taken as models such poets as Burns, Shelley, Bryant, Longfellow, Lowell, Whittier, and the late nineteenth-century regional romantics like Harte, Miller, and Riley. In 1903, when he had practically ceased writing poetry, he wrote to a friend,

Old Walt Whitman has wound himself into my affections as
thoroughly as "Bobbie" Burns. He celebrates any old thing regardless of how it sounds and jars the over-sensitive and civilized nature of man and maid. But his "yawps" are interwoven
with finely spun sentiment and philosophy and there is in him
on the whole more gold than dross. Gold without alloy is of no
value as a medium of exchange and this is also true of ideas.
Were it not otherwise, Oscar Wilde's quintessence of thinking
would find wider appreciation than Whitman's "yawps." Walt
Whitman and Henry Thoreau are, I believe, the two most original characters in American literature.[62]

A writer of Alex's poetic sensibility who had arrived at this understanding of Whitman's achievement could not have failed to see the
weaknesses in his own poetry. In contrast to Whitman's concrete depictions of cities, landscapes, people, and occupations, Alex's poems
had remained for the most part abstract. Unlike the Good Gray Poet,
who had attempted to adapt language to his subject, Alex imagined
moors in a land of prairies, wolds in a land of woods and thickets,
rills and brooks where there were creeks, and dells where there were
hollows. Whether Alex had arrived at his conclusions by 1900 is uncertain. If he had, they no doubt contributed to the decline in his
poetic output.

There were other causes, however. The exuberance of youth was
on the wane. He was, after all, approaching thirty. His enthusiasm
for love and the mysteries of life was giving way to a concern for
the social, political, and economic realities of the Creek Nation.
He also viewed nature less abstractly than in his period of intense
poetic production. As his notes indicate, he looked at it more closely,
after the fashion of Thoreau. In 1903, in addition to calling Thoreau
one of "the two most original characters in American literature,"
he admitted to "constantly" carrying a copy of *Walden* in his jeans,
"mainly just to have it near me," he said. He also expressed a fond-
ness for the naturalist John Burroughs. "His poetic and classic dic-
tion," Alex said, "captivates me entirely."[63]

By 1900 Alex was also turning to prose in his writing and would
in time find in it his greatest literary achievement. That year, besides his autobiographical statement, he published five prose pieces
in the *Twin Territories*: "Uncle Dick's Sow," "Jes 'Bout a Mid'lin',

Sah," "Two Famous Prophets," "A Creek Fable," and "Mose and
Richard." Some of these were the sketches of his childhood that he
had begun at Okmulgee, and others were about the Creek freedmen
of Coon Creek east of Bald Hill. Taken together, these works paint
a picture of Creek society much different from the realities of the
Creek Nation in 1900. It was those realities that Alex was now on
the verge of confronting in a new way.

Soon after school closed at Wetumka in spring 1901, Alex and
John Thornton fulfilled a longtime dream: to take an extended float
trip down the Oktahutche in a rowboat. While Alex's notes reflect
a lingering enthusiasm for the grandeur of the landscape, they also
reflect a close observation of nature on a small scale. It is significant that the only known literary result of this journey took the
form of prose. Their craft was the "Hithy Mahta," or *Good Martha*.
With Doc Williams, whom Alex described as "a good-natured Creek
full blood," as their oarsman, they launched the *Good Martha* near
Wetumka in the early afternoon of June 10, beginning a journey of
several days that would take them past Wewoka ("Barking Water")
Creek, the Alabama Rapids, Piney Creek, and the Tulledega Hills
to Eufaula. The distance overland from Wetumka to Eufaula was
slightly over forty miles, but the twists and turns of the Oktahutche
would carry them perhaps twice that far.

The river was "on a slight boom," thus requiring little effort at
rowing and leaving them free to enjoy the scenery and follow their
inclinations. As they floated along, "eavesdropping on Nature," Alex
carefully observed the wide variety of trees that grew along the
banks: willows, cedars, walnuts, oaks, sycamores, and cottonwoods.
He recorded his sightings of catbirds, downy and pileated wood-
peckers, flickers, cardinals, crows, buzzards, and other birds. Near
homesteads along the river they watched Creek fishermen, Creek
women at their washing and cooking, and white renters who watched
them in return. Thornton and Alex named the islands they came to,
and Alex named the largest and most beautiful for Yohola. At one
quiet moment Doc called Alex's "attention to a strange whistle way
out in the mountains" and said it was "the wood spirits." Alex wrote,
"The old Creeks tell of Cha-cha-nah, who whips trees. He is tall,
heard only at night, and seen only when the sun looks small in a
mist. Whoever sees him straightway becomes a good hunter."

They rowed ashore whenever they pleased. Doc fished, and Thorn-

ton hunted. Not content with that, Thornton seemed inclined to fire
at practically anything that moved: fish hawks, water moccasins, or
tarantulas. In later years it was claimed that Alex revered all life and
would not harm the least of nature's creatures, but his journal of this
trip does not bear out that claim. He hunted deer and wild turkeys,
and at one point he wrote, "I cut a moccasin in two with my rifle."

There were quiet times in camp. Alex and Thornton read from the
Greek Anthology, Doyle's *White Company*, the Kansas City *Star*, and
current issues of *Current Literature*, *World's Work*, and *Review of
Reviews*. Near the mouth of Piney Creek, Alex and Doc climbed tall
pine trees and, looking east, saw Lenna Prairie and Bald Hill on the
south side of the river and Checotah Prairie on the north. Beyond
Bald Hill, of course, was Eufaula, the end of their river journey. In
all, it was a memorable experience, marred only by mosquitoes and
by fleas they had brought with them in their bedrolls.[64]

That summer Alex and his family returned to Stidham. Family affairs drew him back, and he had his own farm to look after. In 1899
he had enrolled Yohola, Pachina, and himself with the Dawes Commission and had made allotment selections that adjoined, on the
southwest, those of Hence, Nancy, John, Conny, Darwin, Horace,
Mattie, Ella, and Mendum, whose allotment selections took in Bald
Hill and its immediate surroundings. Bill, Melissa, and Frank had
selected allotments near Wagoner. Hence's health had continued to
fail, and he was less able to attend to his farming and ranching. Accompanied by John, he had spent part of October and November
1900 at Hot Springs, Arkansas, taking mineral bath treatments.[65]
With the eldest of Alex's younger brothers gone from home, Alex
probably found it necessary to look after some matters concerning
the Bald Hill ranch as well as his own farm. Whatever his plans were
when he left Wetumka, they included no enterprises that would take
him, at least in the near future, far from Bald Hill and Possum Flat.

During fall and early winter Alex continued his rambles in the
neighborhood of Bald Hill, sometimes taking Conny and Horace
with him and occasionally keeping detailed notes on his observations
of nature.[66] By Christmas he was contemplating a new direction in
his career.

Creek Orphan Asylum faculty in 1896. On the porch (left to right), *Lowena and probably the Lee sisters; in the foreground, Alex Posey and George Riley Hall. Archives and Manuscripts Division of the Oklahoma Historical Society.*

A family scene at the Bald Hill ranch. Archives and Manuscripts Division of the Oklahoma Historical Society.

Bill Posey, Alex Posey's brother, born 1877. Western History Collections, University of Oklahoma Library.

Frank Posey, Alex Posey's brother, born 1879. Western History Collections, University of Oklahoma Library.

Horace Posey, Alex Posey's brother, born 1887. Western History Collections, University of Oklahoma Library.

Mendum Posey, Alex Posey's brother, born 1893. Western History Collections, University of Oklahoma Library.

Mattie Posey Howe, Alex Posey's sister, born 1883. Courtesy of Elliott Howe.

Posey family picnic on top of Bald Hill. Archives and Manuscripts Division
of the Oklahoma Historical Society.

Alex and Yohola Posey at their Stidham home. Archives and Manuscripts Division of the Oklahoma Historical Society.

James Blaine Posey (1888–98), Alex Posey's brother, whose death inspired his writing. Western History Collections, University of Oklahoma Library.

Pachina (born 1899), Lowena, and Yohola Posey (born 1897). Courtesy of Daniel F. Littlefield, Jr.

George Riley Hall, Alex Posey's longtime friend and brother-in-law, about 1902. Archives and Manuscripts Division of the Oklahoma Historical Society.

Chapter 6 Journalism and Progress

If Alex still harbored any hope of returning permanently to Bald Hill, the first few weeks of 1902 erased it. When the new year began, Hence lay gravely ill at the ranch. His illness during the past three or four years had gotten steadily worse, and now the family could only watch and wait. He died on January 17. A large crowd assembled at the ranch for his funeral, and he was buried beside his son James in the family plot on the slope of Bald Hill, about a hundred yards behind the house.[1] Hence's death caused Alex to reflect on the passing of a generation of Creek citizens and on the significant changes in lifeways that were occurring in the Creek country. A few weeks later he wrote of William Fisher, a long-time friend of his father, "He is one of the very few living Creeks belonging to that old school of strong friendship and generous hospitality of which Col. John F. Simpson, Col. D. N. McIntosh, Capt. L. H. Posey and the Crabtrees were noted members."[2]

Just as Hence's death marked the end of an era, it marked the beginning of a new stage in Alex's development as a thinker and writer. He gave up poetry for prose, a better form for expressing his belief that it was time to put aside nostalgia and Indian citizenship and to set out in new directions. Thus he entered the field of journalism, through which he would gain national recognition. Out of his journalism would grow his greatest literary achievement: the Fus Fixico letters. These in turn would bring him national notice as a political commentator and dialect humorist. But Fus Fixico came after he had established himself as a journalist, raising a strong voice in favor of social, economic, and political progress in the Creek Nation.

Within days of Hence's death there occurred three other events that were significant for Alex. The bitter sorrow at the loss of one of his heroes was offset to some extent by two joyous events. The first was the marriage of George Riley Hall, his old friend, to Lowena's sister Kittie. The strong friendship Alex had enjoyed with the Poet for over a decade was now made even stronger by family bonds. The second event was the birth of a daughter on February 9, and in keeping with his penchant for literary names, Alex called her Wynema Torrans Posey. The first name was that of the well-known Modoc interpreter whose story was the subject of a play popular in the late 1870s and early 1880s. More recently, and closer to home, Wynema was also the heroine of an 1891 novel by the young Creek teacher and writer Sophia Alice Callahan, daughter of S. B. Callahan, who was Isparhecher's private secretary and who had on occasion visited Alex at Okmulgee. The second name was for John Beauregard Torrans, a Texas poet of some local note and Alex's longtime friend at Muskogee.[3] Shortly before these two events, Alex had bought the Indian Journal Printing Company from his friend J. N. Thornton. At about the time of Hence's death, he settled in as editor of the *Indian Journal.*

Although the life of a small-town newspaper editor was new to Alex, he seemed to take up the work without much difficulty, perhaps because of his brief newspaper experience as a student. Being editor provided him an excellent context for literary expression. Well known as he was throughout the Creek Nation, visitors to Eufaula sought him out. He was always happy to converse with Creek citizens—whether Creeks or freedmen—from the most highly educated to the least schooled, "progressive" or "pull back" conservative, friends, relatives, or strangers. He was constantly on the streets, talking, watching, and gathering news to put in the *Indian Journal.*

Alex considered the *Journal* a strictly local newspaper and aimed at serving the needs of Eufaula and its immediate region. He gave much space to local news items, and within six months he had moved them to the front page.[4] "We are more concerned about what is going on here at home than we are in what is going on thousands of miles away," he wrote; "we had rather chronicle a visit of Farmer Jones in town on Saturday than bore our readers with a long-winded account of some French nobleman and his party doing New York City." He concluded, "We are more interested in a short scrap than we are in a 22 calibre insurrection down in South America. . . . Our interests and sympathies are bound up in home affairs and home people. The rest of the world can go to grass."[5]

To underscore his local mission, hardly a "Farmer Jones" visited Eufaula without the visit's making its way into the local news columns. Having grown up west of Eufaula and having traveled widely in the Creek Nation in recent years, he knew the people for miles around, the names of their horses, and what kinds of dogs they had. He often observed their comings and goings with the eye of the humorist. He reported a fight between two women that was "veiled in mystery and a fog of hair" and drew humor out of events such as someone's selling fish: "Grant Harris brought in a lot of buffalo fish Saturday and sold them before you could say, 'Are you a Buffalo?' He also had some catfish and they went like scat." When the Kansas City *Star* picked up his report that a local gardener had grown a radish that looked like the Venus de Milo, he responded, "There is nothing impossible to the soil and climate of Eufaula." Just to make certain no one missed his point, three weeks later he reported a radish that looked like a catfish.[6]

Contrary to expectations, Alex did not write editorials. As a public school administrator, he had demonstrated a tendency to be impulsive, opinionated, and stubborn on issues he felt strongly about. Yet throughout spring and summer 1902, he refused to write editorials because, he said, the *Journal* was "a newspaper and not an essay." His readers had editorials of their own, as varied as their number. To write editorials would simply be to add his opinion to theirs. At first he reprinted brief editorial comments from other territorial newspapers, but he insisted that his paper was unbiased and fair. He bristled if anyone suggested the *Journal* was partial to any person or party, and he flatly denied reports that others besides him had financial or political interests in the newspaper.[7] For as long as

he owned the *Journal*, a full-fledged editorial was rare in its pages,
but as time wore on editorial statements from a sentence to a paragraph long became common. He may have begun with the aim of being independent and impartial, but it soon became apparent that he was not.

The *Journal* was, in fact, an instrument through which Alex promoted the idea of social, political, and economic progress in the Indian Territory, particularly the Creek Nation. He had embraced the idea as early as his college days, when he had called the Columbian Exposition the greatest event in human history. He had become convinced during that same period that, under the circumstances, the best route for the Indians of the territory to take was to accept allotment and join the march of progress. The alternatives were too impractical or potentially disastrous to consider. Though he had at times bitterly denounced the way the United States carried out its policies, there is no evidence that he wavered in accepting the inevitable, and he had enrolled himself and his children for allotments as soon as the books opened. By 1902 the drift toward allotment and statehood for Indian Territory was assuming a clearer direction. Alex used the pages of his newspaper to espouse the idea that the outcome would be good for the Indian Territory and to demonstrate that, if not the Creek Nation, certainly Eufaula District was prepared to make the transition.

Alex's first priority was to secure the patronage of the local populace by boosting Eufaula and its immediate region. In his brief editorial statements he argued for civic improvement, urging that the town build better roads, construct sidewalks and waterworks, improve telephone service, and employ a night watchman. He promoted town pride, pushing for a livestock law to keep animals off the streets. He complained about hogs rooting up the streets and about the "town cow" that wandered around. He urged citizens to pick up their trash and cut the weeds, keeping his readers up to date on the current crop of dog fennel growing in the alleys. Alex promoted the economic growth of Eufaula. He supported the efforts of the Commercial Club and urged readers to patronize local merchants. He encouraged the building of tenement houses and a dairy. After the Creek Townsite Commission had appraised lots according to regulations issued by the Department of the Interior, he promoted the sale of town lots.[8] "We can pull a big load if we stick together," he wrote; "but if we get to kicking over the traces of the car of progress, we will only succeed in sticking up in the mud."[9]

He characterized Eufaula as a "coming city." With statehood, county lines would be drawn and seats of government established. On the MK&T Railroad between McAlester to the south and Muskogee to the north, only two towns—Eufaula and Checotah—were large enough to qualify as the county seat. Although in 1902 no statehood bill had been passed and no county lines had been drawn, Alex rightly assumed that a contest for county seat lay in Eufaula's future. One of his few full-length editorials dealt with the relative merits of the two towns. When in early 1903 the United States court at Eufaula was made a court of record, Alex believed the county seat question was settled. But he was relentless in his attacks on Checotah, making much of the fact that the Katy Flyer stopped at Eufaula but not at Checotah, fifteen miles to the north.[10]

By summer 1902, Alex had firmly established the *Journal* as the booster voice of Eufaula. He had bought a paper that consisted of four pages of local and regional news and four pages of fillers. In June 1902 he bought the *Eufaula Gazette* and merged it with the *Journal*. The combined circulation and advertising patronage allowed him to go to all home print. He told his readers that he would be fair and avoid controversy: "We shall be satisfied to extend fair treatment to all, to publish the news and to go to our length in the up-building of Eufaula, to us the only town in the wide world." A regular part of the *Journal* had been weekly news columns from outlying communities such as Bald Hill, Stidham, Fame, Lenna, and Canadian. He now gave more space to such news.[11]

The *Journal*, then, promoted Eufaula as exemplary of the progress Alex espoused. In early 1903, in one of his rare editorials, he surveyed the history of the newspaper, which had begun in 1876 in the "palmy" days when the Indian Territory "was truly the land of the red man" and "the Indian politician was boss with an emphatic B." Then gradual change had become swift in "modern times" with the creation of the Dawes Commission, the allotment issue, and the "indisposition of the government at Washington to keep its treaties with the Indian sacred." Now "the strenuous life" was "staring the red man in the face," his land "rapidly slipping from beneath his feet." Now "he must needs dig in his toes deep in the soil and bow his back to stay in the land which the Lord God has preserved

unto him." The *Journal*, Alex said, would as always be the Indian's
friend, "espousing always the cause which it believes will redound to his betterment." [12] That cause was progress. The Indian's survival and adjustment to the "strenuous life" depended on giving up old habits and adopting new ones. A week later, Alex wrote, "The Indian that falls in line with progressive movements and manifests a cooperative disposition will not fail of recognition in the councils of his white brethren. But the pull-back Indian, as well as the unregenerate white man, will not survive the sentiments and traditions which have been outgrown." [13]

As he did with Eufaula, Alex promoted the rural communities of Eufaula District as exemplary of the progress that the Creeks in general were making. The news columns in 1902 and 1903 from outlying communities such as Stidham, Fame, Lenna, Bald Hill, Tuskegee, Artussee, and Mellette form a verbal mosaic of life in the wedge of land between the branches of the Canadian River west of Eufaula. They chronicled the rapidly changing lives of the people in such matters as modern farming practices, regular mail service, and expanding business. Not only the people but the very face of the land was being transformed. Towns sprang up, and the more ambitious and affluent citizens built farms and places of business. Ancient traces and historic trails were cut by fences as the public domain disappeared and Creeks fenced the allotments they had claimed.[14] New roads were cut, conforming to the geometric regularity of section lines.

No better examples of progressive citizens could be found in the district than Alex's own family. The ranch at Bald Hill remained the hub of the immediate family. Nancy, as matriarch, presided there, leaving only to attend church and, sometimes, to visit Eufaula to sell her farm produce, shop, or see about the Loyal Creek claim that had remained unsettled since her mother had filed it in 1870. She also made an occasional trip to Coweta to see Frank and his family. Mattie and the younger children remained at home. Conny alternated between going to school and working the ranch. Bill, who had been working for the Dawes Commission, had returned to the ranch, but John managed the farm and ranch, working not only his own allotment but those of Nancy and Hence as well. Melissa and her husband returned to Bald Hill from Wagoner in fall 1902, and near the end of that year they moved to Lenna, where Emery had built them a new home.[15] The Bald Hill news columns chronicled the doings of the Posey family and their neighbors, presenting a picture of a thriving farm community.

In like manner, the Artussee and Mellette columns provide insights into the daily lives of the Phillips family, Nancy's relatives. They record a trip by Betsy, widow of Pahosa Harjo Phillips, into Eufaula to sell wild blackberries; the death of her son Louis McIntosh from pneumonia; the marriage of Cumsey's daughter Sarah; a trip by Johnson Phillips and his wife to see Nancy at Bald Hill. Alex delighted in reporting the activities of his uncle Johnson, pastor of the Artussee Baptist Church: his "tying the knot" for young couples, guests who drank sofky at his house, his aspirations to open a store and post office at Artussee, his bagging five ducks one day and a duck and five quail the next, his church activities, and his achievements in growing cabbages and sweet potatoes. But Alex's cousin John Phillips, with whom he had had frequent contact since their days at Bacone, seemed to be Alex's favorite member of the Phillips family. He delighted in reporting on John's pursuits: his mail deliveries between Eufaula and Mellette, his business trips to Eufaula, his farming, his hunting and fishing trips, and his church work.[16]

The Tuskegee community, where other relatives lived, received as much attention as Bald Hill. One of Alex's favorites there was Bob Evans, who had married Nancy's sister Winey. Alex loved Evans's home place, known locally as Evans Spring for the natural water source that spouted a stream as thick as a man's arm. In summer 1902 Winey nearly died from a snakebite while working in her vegetable garden, prompting Evans to tell Alex stories about outsized snakes. Alex was always amused at such stories, and he enjoyed his uncle's visits to town. Once, when Evans brought him a sack of apples, Alex thanked him in the local news column and concluded, "May his shadow never grow less." Alex also reported on the families of David and William McCombs, who had married Nancy's cousins, the daughters of Takosar Harjo. He especially admired William McCombs, a Baptist minister, as an orator, an educator, a Creek legislator, and a national translator.[17]

Ostensibly Tuskegee, like Bald Hill, Stidham, and other communities of the district, was a barometer of rural progress in the Indian Territory. It included the substantial farmers—Alex's relatives not least among them—who served as a bulwark of economic develop-

ment by farming, tending their livestock, modernizing, investing in
the future, and assuming responsibility for their own financial affairs. The news columns painted a pastoral scene peopled by honest,
law-abiding citizens, replete with harvest views, domestic vignettes,
and courtships of wholesome rural lads and maids.

But Alex was well aware that not all citizens of the district were
as progressive as his relatives and their kind. When he reported, for
example, on the annual busk held by the Eufaulas, he called it a
"jollification" presided over by Folopa as "master of ceremonies."
There were no wholesome rural lads and maids on the busk grounds;
rather, he referred to the participants as "squaws" and "bucks."[18]
The tone of his report did not stem from cultural aversion. Although
his own town had not held a busk since the end of the Civil War,
Alex was interested in the ceremony and understood its significance
very well. It was simply that he saw such events as "pull back" activities, obstacles blocking some Creeks' path to the progress they
must accept if they were to survive the changes taking place in land
tenure and economics. The busk belonged with the "palmy days
of Indian rule," now at an end. This belief was epitomized in his
statement about Isparhecher, who died in late 1902: "He stood for
what was best for the fullbloods and the old regime and he passed
away with it."[19] Those who did not accept the passing of "the old
regime" were unfortunate victims of history. Nowhere are Alex's
views clearer than in his reporting and commentary on the so-called
Snake faction of Creeks, who stood at opposite poles from Alex's
Bald Hill and Tuskegee relatives in social, political, and economic
perspectives.

With Chitto Harjo, whom the whites commonly called Crazy
Snake, as their spiritual and political leader, the Snakes had two
basic goals: recognition and strict enforcement of the Treaty of 1832
and a return to tribal government. In fall 1900 they had established
their own government. Chief Pleasant Porter had called upon the
United States marshals to break up their gathering, but they assembled again early in 1901 at their council at Hickory Ground,
northwest across the Oktahutche from Bald Hill. This time they sent
out their lighthorse policemen to whip Creeks who signed up for
allotments, rented land to whites, or hired white laborers. And this
time a troop of cavalry was ordered out, so that nearly a hundred
Snakes, including Chitto Harjo, were captured and taken to Mus-

kogee, where over two-thirds of them languished in jail for several weeks awaiting trial. They were finally handed long prison sentences, which were suspended, and "paroled" on their promise of good behavior. Thus ended the "Snake Uprising."

After several quiet months, the Snakes again assembled at Hickory Ground in the early days of 1902. Long allied publicly with the "progressive" Creeks, Alex argued that no matter how desirable it might be to continue the Creek Nation of the old days, that course was not practicable in twentieth-century America. Allotment, statehood, and American citizenship were the only workable course. Yet because the former *was* desirable, because he often gave in to nostalgia for the Creek Nation of his youth, he was sympathetic to the Snakes, who, he said, were "too numerous for councilors and too few for war." In his poem "On the Capture and Imprisonment of Crazy Snake," Alex romanticized the famous leader, presenting him as a noble savage as he had been prone to do with the Alabama Prophet and other "relics" of earlier Creek times. He called Chitto Harjo "The last true Creek, perhaps the last / To dare declare, 'You have wronged me!' " Call him, Alex said, "A traitor, outlaw, —what you will, / He is the noble red man still." [20] There was, after all, much truth in what the Snakes said: they had not agreed to allotment, and a majority of their tribesmen had not wanted to dissolve the Creek Nation. Those who had agreed did so for the most part because they had no other choice. Only circumstance allowed one to see the inevitability of the Nation's demise. That point came home to Alex when he was visited in 1902 by Tom Sulphur, his adopted brother and boyhood companion. After reminiscing about their childhood exploits, Alex wrote ironically: "Alas! Tom is but a poor, misguided Snake Indian now, while we are a big rich country editor." [21] To be able to view history as simply as the Snakes did might indeed have been bliss.

In 1902 as before, the Snakes were perhaps "misguided," but not dangerous to the public peace. When they gathered at Hickory Ground in February, the residents in the Senora neighborhood became alarmed, however, and even threatened to raise a private army to rout them. Alex dismissed the possibility of danger, describing them as simply snakes crawling out of their dens to sun themselves. One reputedly very dangerous Snake was Jackson Tiger, about whom Alex wrote, "Now the last time we talked to this Snake

—about two months ago—he was nearly dead with consumption."
The cause of their current discontent was a poor growing season in
1901. They had little corn and therefore little sofky, their staple food.
"They are the most ignorant among the Indians," Alex wrote, "and,
like the most ignorant among the white people, they believe the party
in power makes good or bad crops at pleasure." It might appear that
they had gone back on the conditions of their parole of the year before, but as Alex pointed out, the terms of parole had not said what
was to be done if the crop failed and there was no sofky. Although
the Snakes were only "pestering the serenity," Chitto Harjo and a
number of his followers were arrested and sentenced to jail terms
"for not behaving themselves." Alex concluded his report of the sen-
tencing with sarcasm: "This ought to be a warning to all Indians to
be good." [22]

Chitto Harjo had created quite a spectacle when he and eleven of
his followers were brought through Eufaula on the way to the federal
jail at Muskogee. They had been arrested by United States marshals
without incident and had behaved themselves on the overland journey to Eufaula. A large crowd of the curious gathered at the depot
to catch a glimpse of the "renegade," who sat, seeming to ignore
them, with "a black slouch hat pulled down over his eyes." Alex's
description of him contains images strikingly similar to the romantic
view expressed in his poem about the Snake leader. To Alex, he was
"a typical Indian," with "the coarse black hair and piercing eye, the
high nose and cheek bones, the arrow-straight carriage and the reserved dignity peculiar to the true Indian." Alex overheard him say
of the spectators, "I wonder what kind of animal they think I am?"
Shortly thereafter, Alex reported, Chitto Harjo said:

> I don't know why we have been arrested and taken from our
> families at a time when our families can least spare us. We'll not
> suffer, perhaps, but they will. Food is scarce, and how are women
> to get it? We were peaceably assembled counseling among our-
> selves for our own good. We meant nobody harm. Why should
> we be taken to jail for this? We have not laid waste nor plun-
> dered. No home is vacant and no field lying untilled because
> of our mischief. Rather our homes are vacant and our fields
> are lying untilled. We believe that if the United States officials
> understood our wants and needs as we understand them, we

would not be regarded as outlaws, but as friends to be helped and pitied.[23]

Alex kept up his news coverage of the Snakes during the succeeding weeks as federal officials continued to round them up. Marshals discovered documents showing that the Creek Snakes still considered their own government viable, with Lah-tah Micco as chief. Evidence was also clear that the disaffected members of the other large tribes were working with the Creeks for restoration of the former treaties under the leadership of Yaha Hocochie of the Seminoles, Soletawa of the Cherokees, Samuel Yokes of the Chickasaws, and Daniel Bell of the Choctaws. By early March, all these leaders were in custody except Lah-tah Micco, who had been captured but had escaped. In jail they were "fumigated," as Alex said, and their long hair was cut.[24] Alex expressed no outrage at such indignities. When Washington Riley, Hotgun, and other Snakes were released after two months in jail, he was bemused at Hotgun's threats to sue the United States government for false imprisonment and "loss of his long black locks."[25] He did, however, recognize the absurdity of allowing the remaining Snakes to languish in jail. Echoing the words he had attributed to Chitto Harjo, he said, "Meanwhile, their sofky patches are lying untilled at home. When they are finally released they will either have to starve or rebel again and get back in jail."[26]

During the next year, Alex kept his readers informed about the Snakes. More were captured and jailed in summer 1902. After a quiet fall and winter, they became active again in spring 1903. Members of the Ahlincha faction were duped by a Washington attorney who convinced them he could get the allotment agreements overturned for $500. At the same time the Cherokee Keetoowahs were gathering, and during the summer delegations of Choctaw and Creek Snakes passed through Eufaula on their way to confer with them about "up-rising and removal to Old Mexico," according to Alex's report. When President Porfirio Diaz passed through the Indian Territory on his way to St. Louis, a group of the Creeks met with him at the Eufaula depot to discuss their possible settlement in Mexico. When Chitto Harjo visited Eufaula to do business, so quiet and modest in his actions that he went practically unobserved, Alex spoke with him and reported on his activities.[27]

Despite his obvious regard and apparent admiration for Chitto

Harjo and his sympathy for the Snakes in their plight, Alex looked
on them as unfortunate social relics of times past. He referred to
them as "has beens" and "pullbacks" or simply "Indians," a term
that took on more racial and social meanings for him as time passed.
Underscoring the contrasts between these Creek citizens and their
more progressive neighbors were the reports Alex published concerning Wacache, one of Chitto Harjo's followers who lived near
Lenna. Wacache, a full-blood, had been a farmer, more prosperous
than most, until allotment selections began. He refused to enroll for
an allotment, and when the land his home sat on was selected by
someone else, he burned his house piece by piece, along with most of
his possessions. He kept a fire burning there constantly, held dances,
became a "prophet," and acquired a great following among not only
the Creek Snakes but those of the Choctaw Nation as well, whom
Alex labeled "ignorant" and "credulous." These actions, which Alex
reported throughout his editorship, formed a sharp contrast not only
to what Wacache once was himself but to the enterprising pursuits Alex reported among the white renters and progressive Creek
farmers in the Lenna community.[28]

Alex's attitude toward the Snakes is perhaps clearest in a story
he published in early March 1903. He went out into the street one
day looking for "anything odd that might turn up." He found it
in the form of an old Snake, whose hair, "though long and flowing," Alex wrote, "was not over abundant and its thinness reminded
us of the tail of a scrub pony from which the cockle burs had just
been removed." The Creek had a pair of saddlebags thrown over
his shoulder. "The long hair and the saddlebags seemed strangely
out of place in this age of Creek deeds and statehood agitation,"
Alex wrote. "Then it occurred to us," he continued, "that the long
haired Snake Indian, with his old time saddlebags, was only one
of the many discordant notes in the grand march of our westward
civilization."[29]

Until recently, the deeds Alex mentioned in this report had also
been, in his view, an impediment to progress. The allotment agreement with the United States, ratified by the Creeks on May 25, 1901,
had required the secretary of the interior to supply the Creek chief
with blank deeds immediately after ratification. When the deeds
were completed, they were to be returned to the secretary for his
approval. By the end of 1901, the failure of Chief Pleasant Porter to

issue any deeds had become the subject of frequent news stories and editorials in Creek Nation newspapers. The bureaucratic process was slow, but Porter was also in no hurry to issue the deeds. He and other Creek officials realized that, under their agreement with the United States, any lands not allotted or reserved would be opened to sale to non-Creeks as the surplus lands of the Oklahoma tribes had been. Thus they sought passage of a supplemental agreement to remedy oversights in the original agreement, including the assurance that all allotable lands would be divided equally among the Creeks according to the standard of 160 acres with the value of $6.50 per acre as the basis for equalization. To sign the deeds before the question of allotments was finally settled would create confusion and result in litigation. When in May 1902 no deeds had been issued, Alex wrote, "We are beginning to believe that the Creek supplemental treaty was hatched for the purpose of delaying the issuance of deeds indefinitely, or until such time as the big land companies operating in the Creek nation gobble up all the lands."[30] And shortly thereafter he wrote, "The country is not going to develop until the Indians get their deeds. Delay of deeds means delay of progress."[31]

Chief Porter and others remained steadfast in their position despite such criticism. In late May it was reported that five thousand deeds were at the Dawes Commission office in Muskogee awaiting only Porter's signature. Despite growing dissatisfaction among the freedmen and progressive Creeks, including Alex, Porter refused to sign them, saying he would sign only after passage of the supplemental agreement unless directed to do so by the secretary of the interior.[32]

Porter had his defenders, not the least of whom was G. W. Grayson, Alex's good friend and fellow member of the Informal Club. Grayson had been a member of the commission that had appraised the Creek allotments and was therefore deeply involved in the allotment process. In his autobiography, Grayson wrote that the idea of allotment for a time "paralyzed" the Creeks. "Here we," he wrote, "a people who had been a self-governing people for hundreds and possibly a thousand years, who had a government and administered its affairs ages before such an entity as the United States was ever dreamed of, are asked and admonished that we must give up all idea of local government, change our system of land holding to that which we confidently believed had pauperized thousands of white

people." [33] Although time bore out their belief that allotment was a
scheme to dispossess the Creeks of their land, Grayson had come
to believe, as had other Creeks like Alex, that under the circumstances the change in land tenure was best. But Grayson wanted
the Creeks to salvage as much as possible during what he called the
"approaching wreck" of the Creek Nation.

While the existing agreement had some good points, such as for-
bidding the sale of allotments for five years, prohibiting attachment
of deeds for prior debt, and limiting leases to one year, Grayson
believed any additional safeguards that could be obtained in the
supplemental agreement should be in place before the deeds were
issued. Land companies were already dealing in Creek allotments,
openly advertising in newspapers. They obtained agreements to sell
under the guise of "leases." Though illegal, such agreements would
be sufficient to cloud the title, and the land companies believed
they could later use their influence with Congress to approve the
sales. It was the eight thousand full-bloods, the freedmen, and other
"unthinking" Creeks who needed protection from the white land
buyers. They were not the ones, Grayson argued, who were clamor-
ing for deeds. They had always had as much land as they wanted,
and most could not see the need for a change in tenure and therefore the necessity of deeds. It was the whites and Creeks of mixed
heritage who were "chafing." Grayson had some pointed words for
Alex: "You, dear editor, myself, and a possible hundred other Creeks,
may wish that title would issue so that we might go into the real
estate business at once; but the 13900 other Creeks and negroes
who constitute our nation proper, are entering no complaints about
their deeds." Grayson realized that his ideas were not popular in
some circles and might not be "good" for the *Journal* because they
were considered "anti-progress," but to Alex's credit, he published
Grayson's letters anyway. [34]

Porter prevailed. Congress approved the supplemental agreement
on June 30, 1902, the Creeks ratified it on July 26, and the president proclaimed it on August 8. In addition to restrictions placed on
the sale of allotments in the earlier agreement, this one added or
amended a number of provisions regarding additions to the tribal
rolls, inheritance, and allotment. Among the provisions was one that
made allotments inalienable for twenty-one years in order to secure
each citizen a homestead. Although Porter had said he would issue

deeds as soon as the agreement was ratified, it was not until the beginning of 1903 that the Creeks began to receive them.[35] It was shortly thereafter that Alex published his statement that in the "age of Creek deeds and statehood agitation" the Snake Indian was out of place "in the grand march of our westward civilization."

Individual ownership of land and statehood were inextricable issues. One was a necessary precursor of the other. The Republicans in Congress, in the McKinley and Roosevelt administrations, and in Oklahoma Territory had dragged their feet on the statehood question for years because they believed that new states in the Southwest would likely be Democratic.[36] The inevitability of statehood had been accepted long ago by most citizens of the Indian Territory. Though the reality was still some years away, by 1902 lines of debate had begun to form. Central to the debate was whether the Indian Territory would constitute a separate state or would be combined with Oklahoma Territory as a single state. At issue was which form of statehood would be better suited to the development and progress of the Indian Territory. Many Indian leaders favored separate statehood, envisioning a new state whose political destiny within the United States would be determined by Indians. At first Alex espoused the opposite view.

One of the Indian leaders who first worked publicly for an "Indian" state was Creek Chief Pleasant Porter. In fall 1902 he called for a meeting of members of the Five Civilized Tribes to organize to work for separate statehood, but when the meeting convened at South McAlester, in the Choctaw Nation, only the Creeks and Seminoles attended. Alex had predicted that the meeting would fail. "The more the people of the Five tribes think the more they will favor union and statehood with Oklahoma," he wrote in one of his brief editorial statements. "It is the plain, logical common sense of destiny and the sooner the chiefs of the Five tribes make up their minds to conform the less time they will waste in vain resolutions and futile regrets." Convinced that separate statehood was the only way to retain a political voice, Porter called another meeting for late October. That too failed.[37]

As this meeting approached, Alex argued that Porter's scheme not only was unwise for the territory but was doomed to fail. He was convinced that it was not to the Indians' benefit to remain organized as a "separate class" but that they should be like other citizens of

the United States, like other races that contributed to forming the
"great American people." Those who argued to the contrary meant well, he said, but the idea of a separate state was doomed, a lost cause based in sentiment. "The old days are gone," he wrote, "and they were dear to the memory of the old people. The new order is here and the new Indian must meet the new condition not as an Indian, but as an American citizen and work out his own salvation as an individual depending on no fellow citizen but upon himself." He argued that it was the "progressive," not the "pull back" Indian who would receive recognition from the whites, for the "pull back" would not "survive the sentiments and traditions which have been outgrown."[38] In another brief statement he said, "When the Choctaws unite in politics and quit their monkey business; when all the old feuds in Kentucky and the Creek nation have been wiped out; when the Indian gets the deed to his land and fools it away; when every town in the new western district is dry as punk; when the Five Tribes find out that they can't stick together in a one horse state; when Democrats cease breaking their necks in pursuit of false gods; when Indian Territory is hooked to Oklahoma, this will be a pretty decent country to live in, after all."[39]

Though the second meeting failed, the chiefs came closer to agreeing that a separate statehood movement could succeed. A third call to convention was issued, this time by the Choctaw chief Green McCurtain. The Indian Territory was like a dog chasing its tail, Alex said. He predicted that the Eufaula meeting then planned would be "a futility following on the heels of futile effort." The separate statehood question was dead, he argued: "Governor Porter and his confederate governors are clinging to a lost cause. The cause was never a logical one, but one of sentiment. It will die with the adjournment of the governor's convention at Eufaula." The meeting, however, was successful. Delegates convened in late November and drafted resolutions asking Congress not to annex the Indian Territory to Oklahoma but to admit two states.[40]

Shortly after the Eufaula convention, proponents of single statehood for Oklahoma and the Indian Territory began a strong countermovement. In the Indian Territory it was led mainly by white businessmen and entrepreneurs whose future plans did not include Indian control of local politics. In early December 1902 they were encouraged when a United States Senate subcommittee on territo-

ries reported a bill for admitting one state under the name Oklahoma. Alex used his pen in the cause through brief commentary in
the *Journal*. "Fall in line gentlemen; single statehood is inevitable,"
and "Every Indian will work out his own salvation that is not too
lazy," he wrote. About the growing momentum for single statehood
he wrote, "They are all making goo goo eyes at single statehood now
except South McAlester. Poor town, she's Moon-eyed."[41]

A single statehood convention was called to meet in Oklahoma
City on January 6, 1903, and a few days before that a convention met
at Eufaula to elect Indian Territory delegates. Resolutions adopted
by the convention expressed the delegates' concern that the omnibus
bill then before Congress menaced the Indian Territory by merging
it with an organized territory. They feared being left with little or no
voice in framing the constitution. They favored single statehood, but
only under conditions that guaranteed their equal participation with
Oklahoma in forming the new state. Alex publicly denied rumors
that he was responsible for the Eufaula meeting, which had been
called by the Commercial Club. However, he was a conspicuous
presence among the Eufaula delegates who went to Oklahoma City.
He was the only Indian; the rest were white businessmen, members of the Commercial Club. The convention adopted resolutions
that allayed the fears of the Eufaula delegates and others. Thus, on
his return Alex reported proudly that the Indians had been given
"the place of honor" at the convention. During the several weeks
that followed, Alex espoused the single statehood cause and attacked the proponents of separate statehood for the Indian Territory.
When in late March Chief McCurtain called for another convention
at Eufaula, Alex predicted failure for the "scheme," as he had for
earlier meetings.[42]

Two months later, however, Alex had changed sides in the debate.
He may have been persuaded by Pleasant Porter, whose leadership
was receiving more respect from Alex. In early May, Secretary of the
Interior Ethan Allen Hitchcock planned a trip to the Indian Territory. Porter asked G. W. Grayson and Alex to meet the secretary at
Muskogee and ride with him in his special railroad car to Okmulgee, where they accompanied him around town and to a reception
at the council house. The ride to Okmulgee gave them an opportunity to talk freely to the secretary, and they found him at least giving
lip service to concerns about questionable practices in the leasing

of Indian allotments and expressing some interest in protecting the
Indians' rights.[43] He was for rapid development of the Indian Territory, which in his view, as he had said a few days earlier, depended
on attracting a good class of farmers. Hitchcock's visit was a turning
point; Alex sharply curtailed his criticism of Porter.

Alex was also encouraged by other developments. One, it seems,
was the makeup of the convention McCurtain called at Eufaula
on May 20; white residents of the Indian Territory were invited.
Alex had argued from the first that separate statehood could not be
worked out without their help. Also, during recent weeks the single
statehood movement had cooled while the separate statehood effort
had gained momentum, and Alex did not like to be a political outsider. For whatever reasons, he switched sides, and he now described
McCurtain as a "wise and far seeing statesman," who would be a
hero if the single statehood movement succeeded.[44]

Alex also believed that if success occurred, the Eufaula meeting
would "go down in history as the inauguration of a great movement." The Choctaws were there, of course, led by McCurtain. Chief
T. M. Buffington represented the Cherokees. The Seminoles were
represented by Chief Halputta Micco and Thomas Little, an orator and statesman. The Creeks were represented by Porter, Cheesie
McIntosh, Lawyer Deere, and Alex, whom Porter had appointed.
The convention organized a permanent statehood committee, with
McCurtain as its chairman, and laid plans for calling a constitutional convention. Each national council of the five tribes was to call
a special election on the statehood issue. If the voters approved the
separate statehood concept, a constitutional convention of delegates
from the tribes would meet to draft a constitution. Then a convention
of non-Indian residents would meet to amend the Indian constitution, after which a conference committee of ten from each group
would meet to adjust differences. The Eufaula convention drafted
resolutions calling for separate statehood and asking Congress to
prohibit intoxicants in the new state. Even the single statehood proponents granted that the prohibition stand would bring great support for the separate statehood movement. McCurtain urged Alex to
use his "editorial pen vigorously" on behalf of separate statehood,
calling the people of the Indian Territory "a reading and thinking
people" who were "largely influenced by the country press." He said,
"You have the ability to handle this sentiment with much force, and I

hope to see you take hold of the matter and present it to your readers in the attractive form with which you are capable."[45]

Alex now seemed fully committed to the separate statehood movement. He had written to McCurtain, "The double statehood sentiment is getting very popular. The plans outlined by the convention appear to be just what the people of the Territory have long wanted. Success is bound to come if the proper methods are employed and we 'keep at it.' " As secretary of the Eufaula convention, he sent a draft of the resolutions to President Theodore Roosevelt and to the secretary of the interior. In return, he received assurance through Secretary Hitchcock that the resolutions would be "duly considered." Meanwhile, he turned his pen to supporting the movement in brief editorial comments attacking the single statehood efforts. In July, Porter appointed him as the Creek representative on the Executive Committee for Independent Statehood of the Five Civilized Tribes, and he worked behind the scenes with the other members for the success of the movement.[46] Debate on the statehood issue ebbed and flowed with the debate in Congress, however. During summer 1903 it entered one of its lulls.

The quieting debate on the long-term issue of statehood was overshadowed in the local press by the immediacy of the Creek national election. Ever since drafting their constitution over thirty years earlier, the Creeks had taken their elections seriously. This one was no exception, for it would be the last time the Creeks would choose their own chief executive, whose job it would be to oversee the last stages of settling the tribal estate and bring Creek national affairs to a close.

Although other candidates were discussed and some entered the race, only two viable candidates for principal chief emerged from the political maneuvering that took place in late spring 1903: Legus Perryman for the Union party and Pleasant Porter for the National party, which had elected him in 1899. Though Alex at first was reluctant to support Porter, he bitterly opposed Perryman. Perryman had been impeached the year Alex first entered Creek politics, and there were undoubtedly some bitter political memories associated with those difficult months during the summer and fall of 1895.

His support for Porter had not come easily. The National party had named Porter its candidate in December 1902, much earlier than the Creeks usually nominated. "But the old order changeth," said

Alex. At the time of the nomination, Alex was attacking Porter for his
separate statehood efforts and his refusal to issue deeds to allottees. Throughout spring 1903, Alex's news stories and editorial commentary were slanted in favor of Charles Gibson, his longtime friend and a contributor to the *Journal*, now an announced candidate for chief. He said that the Creeks admired Porter "for his ability and for the power he can wield in the councils of the Great White Father at Washington"; but they loved Gibson "for his nearness to them and for his absolute honesty and sound manhood." Alex, of course, was looking for a progressive candidate like Gibson. Though his relations with Porter had improved in the late spring, he supported the incumbent chief only as a last resort. When Gibson withdrew from the race in July and threw his support to Porter, Alex wrote: "The *Journal* has no choice left but to do the same thing—and we might do worse."[47] By then the Union party had nominated Perryman, and for Alex both that alternative and Chitto Harjo, the other candidate left in the field, were unthinkable. Alex's endorsement of Porter was important. Clarence Douglas, editor of the *Muskogee Phoenix*, said of it, "Here is an influence worth more than the first reading might suggest. Alex Posey's position in the race means much."[48]

Alex could be merciless toward those he disliked. He was short-tempered and could not stand to be criticized publicly. Those who would attack an editor should think twice, he once wrote, because an editor knows more than he tells. What would happen, he asked, if an editor chose to hold up his critics' faults to public scrutiny in the newspaper? In August 1903 he called the editor of the *Checotah Times* a Simple Simon. "Climb out of the cess-pool in which you delight to wallow," he wrote; "shake the slime from your garments and take an injection of carbolic acid and brace up."[49] This same vitriol he turned on Perryman in summer 1903.

There was something about Perryman that brought out in Alex the worst form of bigotry, to which he had always been prone. Some of that tendency had been inherited from Hence. In his dialect stories, Hence had painted the Creek freedmen, particularly those who lived on Coon Creek, as chicken and hog thieves and had taken a patronizing stance toward them, finding humor in their ignorance and simple ways. Alex had displayed the same patronizing attitude, common among whites and among many Indian groups, in his dialect stories and articles about the freedmen and in news items, especially about the Graysons from Coon Creek. But that attitude had never been ugly or displayed itself as wanton meanness or viciousness.

But it was a different matter when it came to political power for blacks. Despite his statements that the *Journal* favored no party, he was fiercely Democratic. He urged his readers to support the Democratic ticket in city elections over the Citizen or Republican tickets. He followed United States politics, praising Democrats and attacking Republicans. He characterized Theodore Roosevelt as a windbag who talked incessantly. He argued that Republican success depended on courting the black vote. In response to a Kansas City *Star* editorial on how Missouri could achieve a Republican victory, he wrote, "The only way to obtain that result is to import a portion of the population of Hayti to Missouri." He believed the fifteenth amendment had been a mistake. As if anticipating the ugly debate over race that would attend Oklahoma statehood, he attacked Republican editors. "The Checotah Times is a Republican paper," he wrote, "and has appreciative readers in Africa." When the *South McAlester Capital* called the editor of the *Muskogee Phoenix* a "dark horse" in the race for Republican national committeeman and said that he hung on "to things black," Alex reprinted the story and added, "Yes, and he has just been elected captain of the Muskogee military company, and we are prepared to hear of him rallying his 'soger boys' and start on the much talked about invasion of Hayti any day." To Alex, progress did not include either political power or social equality for blacks. When a white Indianapolis chambermaid refused to make up a bed that Booker T. Washington had slept in, Alex said she was "too intelligent looking for a hotel chambermaid. Let her come south and live with her friends."[50]

His pen was likewise unrestrained in his racist attacks on Perryman, whose ancestry, Alex alleged, included a person of African descent. When news came that Perryman had been nominated, Alex wrote: "Our command of Creek is fluent and we are more or less familiar with English and Choctaw, to say nothing of our meagre knowledge of stock quotations in Greek and Latin, but language fails us when we attempt to express our disappointment of the choice of the Union party for the next chief of the Creek people. All that we are able to say is that he is a nigger and a bad one at that."[51] Later Alex wrote: "Legus Perryman will address the negro citizens of Eufaula in the near future. Legus sticks to his own people."[52] Still

later, Alex reminded his readers that Perryman was the same man
who had been impeached eight years earlier. "He hasn't changed a
bit," Alex added; "he has the same kind of pigment under his skin
that doesn't fade." Perryman was not really running for chief, Alex
said, but had developed a formula "to take the kinks out of wool"
and was "only seeking a little free advertising."[53]

Alex was relentless on the racial issue as the campaign wore on.
He reported that, at a barbecue at Flat Rock on behalf of Porter,
Abe Kite would sell lemonade and "operate a nigger doll rack for
the benefit of those that desire to throw it into Legus Perryman." He
continued his attacks up to election day, reminding voters on that
day to "drop a black pellet into the ballot box for Legus." There was
apparently more than race at issue here, for Pleasant Porter, who
defeated Perryman and whom Alex now strongly supported, could
also count an African among his ancestors. Porter's contemporaries
claimed he "had a decided strain of negro blood" that came to him
from his maternal grandfather, Tulope Tustenuggee. Porter apparently viewed Alex's racial attacks on Perryman as political rhetoric
rather than personal conviction, for upon his election he thanked
Alex for his help and promised to repay him in any way he could.[54]

By the time of the election, Alex had apparently decided to sell
the *Indian Journal*. His journalism had received widespread attention during the summer, and in the midst of the campaign there
had been rumors that he was leaving the *Journal* and going to the
East. He had firmly denied these rumors, saying that he was still
pulling for Eufaula's prosperity and Porter's reelection. Reports that
he had sold the *Journal* caused one editor to call him "one of the
brightest lights in the literary field of the Southwest," who would
be hard to replace. Despite his earlier claims that he was through
with politics, Alex told a fellow editor that he had left the field of
education to continue "his game of politics" as a journalist. He had
made some powerful political friends during his years as editor, particularly during the election just past. Despite his love for Eufaula
and his best efforts at boosting it, Alex must have realized that in
the rapid advance of progress he had so strongly espoused, his town
could aspire to little more than being a county seat on the Katy Railroad. Muskogee, however, had been undergoing a great economic
boom in recent years. With a population approaching ten thousand,
it was the headquarters of the politically and economically ambi-

tious. By 1903 it was obvious that Muskogee was the undisputed center of political activity in the Indian Territory. There were located the Indian agency, the offices of the Dawes Commission, and the federal courts. Alex had called Muskogee "the fountain head where flows the deep still waters of Indian affairs." [55]

If one aspired to engage in politics, that was the place to be. Muskogee was the place where news was to be made in the transition to statehood. Thus in October Alex sold the *Journal* and entered a joint venture with Ira Reeves, a promoter and builder, to publish the daily *Muskogee Times*, of which Alex became city editor. He had made the *Journal* a strong voice for economic, political, and social progress, which he most likely continued to espouse as editor of the *Times*.

Because no copies of the *Times* are extant for his editorship, it is impossible to say what views he held day to day, but he made his opinions on progress and development in the Creek Nation amply clear in a deposition in early January 1904. Alex's ideas were similar to those of others who favored rapid development in the Indian Territory. Among their common arguments was the belief that the regulations regarding leases and restrictions on the sale of all but the homestead allotments prevented "corporate interests" from investing wisely and farmers from developing the croplands. During summer 1903 a strong movement had begun to seek removal of the restrictions.[56] This movement continued during the succeeding months. During early January 1904, the Chamber of Commerce at Muskogee appointed a special committee to canvass the Indian Territory and determine the people's sentiment concerning the issue, and they forwarded the findings to Secretary Hitchcock.

Alex was among the first to give his deposition to the committee. In it he expressed his belief that the Indians were "as competent to take care of their own affairs as any other people." There were no more incompetents among them than among any other class of people in the United States. Alex's statements included one that echoed an argument used to justify allotment: that the Indians would benefit by having prosperous white farmers settled among them as models. Secretary Hitchcock had used this reasoning in opposing the allotment of all Creek lands because he believed that selling the unallotted lands to whites would "cause the rapid settlement of the surplus lands by a fine class of farmers, and place the territory in a position for development and government." Alex now argued that restrictions on sales and leases kept out "the sort of farming class of people that we want in this country" and produced "a very inferior class of tenants." Red tape led to speculation and complication of legal affairs. To remove restrictions, he said, "would result in the immediate growth and development of the country and the betterment of the allottee, and would enhance the value of the homestead." He continued, "It would also result in the building of schools, churches, roads, bridges, and other improvements, that would be to the benefit of the Indian allottee and the settlers, and in my opinion is the only way to prepare the allottee for self-government."[57]

From the time he bought the *Indian Journal*, Alex had used his pen in the cause of progress. His views on Creek competence in fiscal matters had been shaped in large measure by the progressive, prosperous Creeks and tenant farmers and ranchers in the rural communities west of Eufaula. He realized, however, that not all Creeks were so progressive, and he did not believe all that came with progress was good. To the ethnologist who claimed that the Indian was becoming extinct, he replied, "We fear the ethnologist has been going about looking for wigwams, arrowheads and the like and not coming across many such relics, has concluded that the Indian is fast going the way of the dodo." There would be no "blanket" Indians in sixty years, he predicted, but there would be plenty of them "wearing overalls and loving firewater."[58]

These, then, were Alex's views near the end of his career in journalism. The *Muskogee Times* was not a successful business venture. Alex left it at the end of March 1904 and went to work for the Indian Office and, later, for the Dawes Commission to do his part to carry the allotment process forward and bring tribal affairs to a close.

7 Fus Fixico and Literary Acclaim

· ·

When Alex traded his editor's desk for the office of a federal bureaucrat in spring 1904, he could look back on his career in journalism with some satisfaction. He had been a success in several ways. He had proved himself an able newspaperman and stylist who had earned the respect of his fellow journalists; he had published what became widely known as the Fus Fixico letters, which proved his greatest literary achievement; and through the letters he had established himself as a political commentator whose views were eagerly sought by the reading public.

As soon as Alex became editor of the *Indian Journal* in early 1902, the other editors with whom he exchanged issues noted a remarkable difference in the newspaper. Here was something different, and they liked what they read. Alex quickly won considerable praise from editors throughout the Indian Territory as well as in Oklahoma Territory and Texas. They used such language as "one of the best writers"; "unique style in Journalism, in which individuality is marked by terse and quaint expressions"; and "terse style of injecting humor into two or three line personals." But the term most

commonly applied to his style was *originality*. One editor attributed
the appeal of Alex's style to its reflecting the "charm of his own delightful personality."[1] In none of his writings is the way Alex looked
at the world, especially his fellowman, so evident as in his writing
for the *Journal.*

161

Fus

Fixico

and

Literary

Acclaim

He could find humor where others might miss it. He could make
laughable his reports of events as far ranging as a man's attempt to
load his team on a ferry, a battle between two colonies of red ants in
downtown Eufaula, or the meeting of the city council, whose members he always called the "city dads."[2] He often reduced the serious
business of politics to absurdity.

That he was an avid Democrat himself did not prevent him from
turning humor on his own party members. A good example is his
lengthy account of a meeting of Democrats to select a Eufaula city
ticket in March 1903. At the start of the meeting, local attorney A. L.
Kean moved that the session be resolved into a citizens' mass meeting. "Then the fun commenced and fur did fly," Alex reported. He
described what followed:

> J. N. Thornton bounced upon a chair like a jumping jack thrown
> from a catapult, and moved as an amendment that the conven-
> tion adjourn until next week. Cries of "no," "no," "no," "Sit
> Down! Get off the perch!"
>
> Kean vigorously protesting; Republicans mad; cheers and cat
> calls. Meanwhile the house divided against itself, and Thorn-
> ton's amendment got it where the chicken got the ax. More
> protesting; more enthusiasm.[3]

In a style that was a curious cross between a sports announcer calling a boxing match and stage directions for a drama, Alex continued
his blow-by-blow description. As the evening wore on, it was more
of the same: "J. T. Crane moves to adjourn until next Tuesday night.
Cat calls, cheers, protests, Thornton on the floor making spasmodic
efforts to catch the chairman's eye on the rebound." The meeting
went on past midnight: "Then comes attorney Owen to do or die
for the lost cause—and he dies. He says: 'Fellow citizens, I—' then
20 brass bands with a saw-mill thrown in for good measure would
not be in it." At 12:30, "Lots more doing. W. T. Fears moves that an
executive committee be appointed. Roll call. Motion killed dead as
Hector." When the meeting finally adjourned just before 2:30 A.M.,

162

Fus

Fixico

and

Literary

Acclaim

the assembly was congratulated "upon the harmonious manner in which the business before it had been conducted."[4]

Much of the humor in Alex's reports sprang from his way of closing an ostensibly serious story with a humorous or understated conclusion. When only one candidate announced for the position of mayor and local politicians were looking for another, Alex ended the report as follows: "We would suggest fly paper or a lasso, and if that fails to bring one, try a shot gun, for a mayor we must have." He reported once that Dick Greenwood, a full-blood Creek, was sunning himself against the end of a caboose in the railyard, when a sudden coupling of cars jolted the caboose and sent Greenwood jumping for his life: "When he struck the ground he said, 'Holwox!' which is Creek for almost anything you might want to say in English." Alex concluded a story about Creek evangelist Charley Williams with the following: "When he fails to stir 'em up to the shouting point, they are beyond redemption and lost world without end." The children of one of his Creek pressmen, he reported, had found a dryland terrapin climbing a tree. The story ended, " 'No limbs, straight up,' said the Indian." Finally, Alex wrote of one of his fellow editors, "The editor of the Checotah Times compliments us on the size of our head. We regret that we can't return the compliment."[5] When one grows accustomed to this style of delivery, one reads Alex's stories with the anticipation of someone listening to a joke and waiting for the punch line.

Alex was a master of understatement. He said of Secretary Hitchcock, notorious in the Indian Territory for the number of regulations he issued, that the secretary had "failed to issue 'rules and regulations' pertaining to the Indian land in the Territory for several days." About the discovery of a huge turtle's skull on the river he said, "In life the turtle must have been as large as the bay window of a modern cottage and a worthy rival of the dodo in the matter of physical beauty." When a young drunk resisted the city marshal's attempts to arrest him, he "never knew anything more until he saw the gray dawn peeping through the bars of the calaboose Sunday morning."[6]

In avoiding the formalities of journalistic prose, Alex gave originality to his style in a number of other ways. His columns were rife with literary allusions, often striking in their context. He reported, for instance, on Witty Hope of Possum Flat, who went around the neighborhood catching geese, wringing their necks, and carrying the "silly heads" in his pockets: "He runs into a flock of geese as

163

Fus

Fixico

and

Literary

Acclaim

Don Quixote ran into sheep folds and few ganders escape decapitation." In another report he said that the new electric streetlights in Eufaula blazed "in a path of glory through 'the dark Plutonian shadows.' " He stated his complaint about weeds growing in Eufaula as follows: "Behold the dog fennels of the alley; they toil not, neither do they spin. Verily, we say unto you. Solomon, in all his glory, was not arrayed like one of these." [7]

Alex also had a tendency to choose the unusual expression. Marriage licenses were "knot papers." Checotah's record in raising funds looked like "a Mexican coin with a hole in it." During a thunderstorm "the heavens seemed full of Numidian lions." A skunk that raided a henhouse was "Sir Mephitis Americana." He once wrote that there was "no danger at this writing of Eufaula going to the eternal bowwows under the present city administration." Of Secretary Hitchcock's insensitivity to criticism he said, "Hitchcock has a hide on him like a rhinoceros and a quart of 'high' wouldn't phase [*sic*] him. He cares no more for editorial grape shot than a dry land terrapin does for hail stones." Finally, his report of a local baseball game would rival the jargon of any late twentieth-century sportswriter in his attempt to vary the descriptions of how players performed at the plate and in the field through nine innings of play.[8]

Alex's columns were also liberally sprinkled with slang, western local expressions, and coined words. A Mahara's Minstrels performance was "bum." Of the rising tensions between Japan and Russia he wrote, "It's dollars to doughnuts that the little Jap makes the Big Bear look like thirty cents before the third round is called." In a report on wild horses that had been killed by severe cold weather, he said that "only the real hardened range pestle-tails were able to survive it." And of a progressive little town in the western part of the Creek country he wrote, "Paden is not sucking the hind teat because she is the westmost town in the Creek nation." Finally, he reported a local rainfall as follows: "The biggest, the finest, the longest, the pouringest, the ground soakingest and gully-washingest rain that has fallen in twelve months fell in Eufaula Tuesday. Now, the biggest, the finest, the sellingest and good-times-makingest crops are expected." [9]

In numerous ways, then, Alex brought a freshness to his news reporting that won the respect of his fellow journalists. He used his literary skill to make seemingly insignificant events and local news

164
Fus
Fixico
and
Literary
Acclaim both interesting and entertaining. He was a member of the Indian
Territory Press Association, which in spring 1903 created the office
of poet laureate especially for him. On June 15 of that year, because
of the success of his newspaper, he established the *Daily Indian
Journal*, which appeared in the afternoon. He continued to publish
the weekly *Journal* on Fridays as well. An Arkansas editor wrote
that Alex's journalism had "the distinct merit of originality" and
that no other territory publication compared in the way "he mingled
humor and philosophy so admirably that what he wrote was read-
able, agreeable and digestable. All of it smacked of the time and
the place, it was a growth of the soil and conditions." The editor of
the *Daily Muskogee Phoenix* summed it up nicely: "There is a freshness, a crispness, a novelty with each issue that is delightful and
entertaining!" [10]

Alex's editorship of the *Indian Journal* firmly established him as
not only a journalist but a humorist. Had he left nothing but his news
columns, he would have qualified as the greatest Indian humorist before Will Rogers. Fortunately, he left much more. During his
last year as editor of the *Journal*, he published thirty-three of his
seventy-two Fus Fixico letters, which won him brief national notice
as a writer and humorist. The letters seem to have grown out of his
aversion to writing extended political editorials. By fall 1902 it was
apparent to him that he must find an editorial voice. The imminent
demise of the Creek Nation as an autonomous entity, the approach
of statehood, the controversy over the Creek deeds, and the election
of principal chief in 1903 would demand attention.

Alex cast about for a means of getting his point across. He settled
on Fus Fixico, or "heartless bird" as the whites translated it, a fic-
titious full-blood Creek who wrote to the local editor concerning
his domestic affairs or, more frequently as time passed, reported the
monologues of Hotgun, whom Fus Fixico overheard as he talked to
his listeners Tookpafka Micco, Kono Harjo, and Wolf Warrior. Also,
Hotgun became more concerned with political developments in the
Indian Territory as tribal affairs wound to a close and statehood approached. The political and economic realities that forced the conservative Creeks to the margins of society in the movement toward
statehood gave Hotgun the advantage of distance as a political observer. His often bemused observations on grafters, bureaucrats, and
office seekers and his innocent yet incisive questioning and analysis

of political events, presented in the English dialect spoken by the 165
Fus
Fixico
and
Literary
Acclaim

full-blood, cut to the heart of matters and delighted his readers.

Fus Fixico, who first appeared on October 24, 1902, had a number of antecedents in Alex's writing. As early as his days at Bacone, he had discovered the usefulness of a persona. After leaving school he had published only one poem under his own name but had written as Chinnubbie or Chinnubbie Harjo. While at college he had found the persona of Chinnubbie useful in reporting campus news and viewing events with a humorous eye. Now as editor of the *Journal*, he sought in various ways to find the right voice for his opinions. First, in summer 1902 he published a series of "street interviews," in which Creeks like Billy Barnett and Luke McIntosh expressed their views on Creek affairs. The topics were usually the conservative Creeks, their difficulties in adjusting to legalities such as land deeds and marriage licenses, or the debate between "progressive" and conservative Creeks over the direction of tribal affairs. It is not surprising that the views expressed in these interviews usually coincided with Alex's. Apparently dissatisfied with the street interviews, Alex dropped that column and sought a different means of getting his views across.[11] In the summer and early fall of 1902 there appeared letters by and about one Joe Harjo. With a common English given name and a common Creek warrior-class designation as his surname, Joe Harjo was a kind of Everyman of the Creek/Seminole full blood world, who reported through letters the everyday events of his community. Though Joe was the kind of character Alex sought, he was not quite right. In Joe, however, Alex found the dialect voice he wanted.

That voice, like the persona of Fus Fixico, evolved over a period of months. Alex had written in dialect since his college days. He had attempted rural white dialect in his poem "Happy Times fer Me an' Sal," and in 1894 he had written "Wildcat Bill" in cowboy "lingo" and the first of his Uncle Dick and Uncle Will Grayson stories in black dialect. He had published three narratives in black dialect in the *Twin Territories* in 1900, but he had done nothing in the dialect of the Creek full-blood until summer 1902. In his street interviews with Billy Barnett, Alex reported part of the conversation in the dialect and made fun of Tams Bixby, chairman of the Dawes Commission and one of Hotgun's favorite targets, calling Bixby's distinctive signature "hieroglyphics." Although the dialect of that

166

Fus
Fixico
and
Literary
Acclaim

interview bears little similarity to that of Fus Fixico, the style of the Joe Harjo letters is unmistakably that of the Fus Fixico letters. One letter read: "Please I sent you news, I was down at Sunday night stomp dance and somebody was stole my winchester and coat and three dollars in money. I aint find him yet. So I will close." [12] The next letter read, "I will sent you put in news. Mr. Joe Harjo and his brother Johnson Harjo and some friends he have been to Santa Rosa city of Mexico, buying cattle. Mr. Harjo said four car load of cattle be here at Seminole country this week. Sometime Joe Harjo was life stock in Seminole country. Him and his brother and friends return north bound train. Joe Harjo of Thurman and brother of Sasakwa. That's all I got news." Two weeks later, the first of the Fus Fixico letters appeared in the *Indian Journal*.[13]

Alex's problem, however, was not simply to find a dialect voice, but to give that voice a credible character. In his search for such a character, he capitalized on the current activities of the Snakes. When Fus Fixico finally appeared on the scene, privy to conversations among the followers of Chitto Harjo and reporting on their doings, he provided the character Alex had worked toward for many months.

Even Fus Fixico seemed tentative at his initial appearance, though. The first two letters were printed on October 24 and October 31; then there were no more until November 21. In the interim, Alex experimented with presenting the local news in the dialect of the full-blood. His "Artussee News Notes" for November 7 read as follows:

> I will sent you a few words for news.
> Well, last Sunday evening while the sun was hang about 4 o'clock high, Louis Colbert was marry Sarah Phillips at Artusse [sic] church house. The wedlock was join by Rev. Johnson J. Phillips, and many people was be present and see it.
> That Sunday morning Rev. Watson Washington was preach from Luke, 15:4, about one sheep what the man was lost in his woods. Watson preach big sermon.
> We had good times and lots good things to eat.[14]

After late November, the Fus Fixico letters appeared more or less regularly until Alex sold the *Journal* nearly a year later.

Alex continued to experiment with the central characters of the
letters. The first dozen letters focus on Fus Fixico himself as he reports on events in the conservative Creek communities. Two characters appear frequently—Choela and Hotgun—but there is no hint of reported conversations like those between Hotgun and Took-pafka Micco, which later became the hallmark of the letters and the source of most of the pointed commentary. In these early letters Choela, a blacksmith turned medicine man who specializes in gunshot wounds, is a far more significant figure than Hotgun. He might have become the focus of the letters, but in the letter of March 20, 1903, Fus Fixico announced Choela's death: "Well, so I was tell you bad news about my old friend Choela. He was gone to be good Injin, like white man say when Injin die. It was look like all old Injins die now and make good Injin that way. Maybe so pretty soon Fus Fixico was make good Injin, too." [15]

That letter appears to be a turning point. After that Hotgun grew increasingly prominent until he became the central figure in the letters. Alex later described Hotgun as "an Indian tinkerer of great fame," whose "inventive genius" allowed him to "make anything": "He was a philosopher, carpenter, blacksmith, fiddler, clockmaker, worker in metals and a maker of medicines." [16] In 1902 Alex had interviewed this exceptional follower of Chitto Harjo when he returned from jail in Muskogee, where he had had his hair cut and had been held for several weeks without trial.

At the time Hotgun became the central figure of the Fus Fixico letters, their content and tone changed. Though somewhat political in content, the early letters had not made such pointed commentary on Creek-federal relations. Among Fus Fixico's reports on his health, the climate, and crops, there was running commentary on Chitto Harjo and the Snakes. "Well," he wrote, "Chitto Harjo and his friend, was all come back from jail, and was had some councils in the woods already. They was made lots big speeches about old times. I think maybe so if they don't quit their monkey business the white men will round them up and put them back in jail for about ten years next time." [17] For years the Snakes had discussed in their councils various plans to emigrate to Mexico or South America and reestablish the old tribal government. Fus Fixico made light of such schemes. When the rains came so that a flood seemed imminent, Hotgun told Fus Fixico that he could show him how to build a better

168

Fus

Fixico

and

Literary

Acclaim

ark than Noah's: "Maybe so Hotgun thinks he can get in and go to Mexico easy this way, but he was had to look out himself like me." When the weather turned terribly cold, Hotgun became more convinced that going to South America, where it was warm, was a good idea.[18]

The early letters also contained frequent references to Wacache, the follower of Chitto Harjo who had quit farming and turned prophet. Fus Fixico wrote, "Wacache he says he was had a talk with God and knows lots of things like wise mens of old times in the Bible. He says the Creeks was not live right now like before Columbus and Dawes commission. So God was tell him to make medicine for Creeks, and make them wash off in the branch, too, and rub lots sand on their hides, and dance stomp dance and play ball game. This way they was get strong and quit renting land to white folks and let the country get wild and have lots game like long time ago." When the cold weather came, Choela blamed a blizzard on Wacache's attempts to make it rain in wintertime. And Hotgun decided that "maybe so there be lots a drought next summer 'cause he think Wacache's thunder bullet was freeze up and bust everywhere like firecracker as was no 'count any more for nothing."[19]

His most pointed, though still mild, political commentary in the early letters concerned Pleasant Porter's failure to deliver allotment deeds to the Creeks. His opening salvo was as follows: "Well, one thing I like to know is if Porter was quit trying to issue them deeds. I guess maybe so he was had so many deeds to sign up he was just give out of breath and quit. I think the Creek council ought to elect some white man to fix them up for us anyhow. It's too much work for one Injin."[20]

Unlike Choela and Hotgun, who would rather have a ticket to Mexico, he said, Fus Fixico wanted his deed. Without it, the white land speculators would lend him money, using his allotment as collateral, at a rate of only fifteen cents an acre. He worried that he would have nothing to drink at Christmas except sour sofky because he could not borrow any money. He was afraid his deed had been returned to Porter or sent to the dead-letter office. He hung up his "socks" hoping that Santa Claus would bring the deed, but to no avail: "Well, so I was had bad luck Christmas times. I was fly out of bed soon about daylight and look in my socks, but I was see nothing

in there but big holes. Maybe so, my deed was fall out in the fire,
or, maybe so, Old Santa Claus think I was not want my deed, like
Chitto Harjo and Hotgun."[21] Then he wondered if perhaps he had
said too much, and he announced he was going to stop talking about
the deeds. "Maybe so Porter was get mad," he wrote, "and say he
wont issue deeds soon if I was not shut up tight like terrapins. Maybe
so he don't give me no office neither, like delegates to Washington
and superintendent of public instructions. So I was stop bothering
him about the deeds." When he finally received his deed, he could
not read the signatures: "They was one name signed to it," he wrote,
"that was look like a thousand-leg that was froze to death in winter
time. I was show it to some lawyers in Eufaula and they say, maybe
so, Tams Bixby was sign his name that way."[22]

To this point, in early spring 1903, the letters had dealt almost
exclusively with Creek matters. Now their scope became wider to
include Indian Territory and United States national issues. There
had been only an occasional play on names. Theodore Roosevelt was
called President Rooster Feather, and Gid Morgan, the Cherokee
politician, was Kid Morgan. Now the practice, for which the letters ultimately were famous, became common. With the character of
Fus Fixico and the format of the letters established, Alex embarked
on a more systematic commentary on political affairs in the Indian
Territory.

One issue that received much attention was whether the Indian
Territory should enter the Union as a separate state or join Oklahoma Territory in forming a single state. Alex at first favored joint
statehood with Oklahoma, and shortly after he attended the joint
statehood convention in Oklahoma City in early January 1903, he
turned to Fus Fixico to lend support to the movement. Fus Fixico
wrote, "The Bible say it is no good to live alone by yourself, and
maybe so that's what Injin Territory and Oklahoma say last week
when they was had big council." One major point of opposition to
a merger with Oklahoma was that the Indians opposed the sale of
intoxicants, which Oklahoma residents favored. In typical fashion,
Alex turned attention away from the constitutional question at hand
and focused on a secondary issue—an emotional one in this case—
as the source of his humor. Fus Fixico said, "I sure vote for single
statehoods quick, too, so next times I go to Keokuk Fall or Shawnee,

170

Fus
Fixico
and
Literary
Acclaim

I was bought red-eye and don't be afraid to go home with it neither, like Christmas times when my old filly was fall down in the night close to John Dutchman's and bust my jug up bad." [23]

In late March, when Choctaw chief Green McCurtain called for a separate statehood convention to meet at Eufaula in May, Alex attacked the plan through Fus Fixico. He called it a scheme to "make a big statehood" out of the Indian Territory, "like Rhode Island." The conservative Creeks were not interested in such doings. "So, I was not worry about being delegate to statehood council 'cause they was nothing to it no how," he wrote. He accused those involved of self-aggrandizement: "So, I think big man in statehood council was just want office, like governor, or, maybe so, send him to Washington, and make big promise like old Handy Jackson and lie like everything like a yaller dog and no squirrel in the tree." As late as early May, Fus Fixico was still chiding those who persisted in their stand for separate statehood. They reminded him of "a poker player that was stood pat on two dueces [sic] and nothing to nigger with." [24]

But on the eve of the Eufaula separate statehood meeting later that month, Alex did an abrupt turnabout. It may have been the result of the waning of the single statehood movement, Secretary Hitchcock's visit to the Indian Territory, or Chief Porter's appointing him a convention delegate. Whatever the cause, he now supported the movement as vigorously as he had opposed it in earlier letters. At first Hotgun and Tookpafka Micco, whose conversations were more and more becoming the content of the letters, were wary because of the prospect of prohibition in the new state if the Indians had their way. Hotgun said that "if they didn't had no saloons in double statehood he was druther be tacked onto Oklahoma so he wouldn't had to drink busthead and get put in the calaboose for being sick on the street. And Tookpafka Micco he say if they was made a double statehood out of Injin Territory they had better had Bud Wiser than Choctaw beer or maybe so Old Crow than Peruna." [25] But Hotgun and Tookpafka Micco soon changed their minds and argued for double statehood because "they was too much long-tailed cyclones out in Oklahoma and people was had to live right close to a hole in the ground like prairie dogs to keep out a they way" and because "out in Oklahoma they was had a drought in the summer time and hard times in the fall, 'sides blizzards in the winter time and cyclones with long tails in the spring." Hotgun concluded that no one in the

Indian Territory was for single statehood now except a few newspapers that had no circulation. He admitted he had been "for single
statehood long time, 'cause he didn't see no other straw to grab at.
But now, Hotgun he say, Secretary It's Cocked and Chief Make Certain was made a good raft to ride on and prospects was bright like a
new tin pan for double statehood."[26]

By midsummer, debate on the statehood issue had subsided. When
the single staters convened one last time in Shawnee in late June,
Hotgun and Tookpafka Micco made fun of their lack of unity and
concluded that the leaders must be carpetbaggers and fence sitters,
waffling as the political sentiment appeared to be shifting toward
separate statehood.[27] In reality the issue was of less current concern
because Congress had failed to enact statehood legislation during
the spring; as it usually did, the statehood question became secondary to more immediate issues between sessions of Congress. Thus
Alex turned his attention to other matters, among the most pressing
being the election campaign for Creek principal chief, which heated
up in summer 1903.

Because of its importance, the Creek election had become a more
frequent topic of discussion by Fus Fixico and his friends during
the spring. The way tribal affairs were brought to a close during
the next few years would depend in large measure on who was the
last to occupy the executive office of the Creek Nation. The election in September would determine who that person was. Early in
the year Fus Fixico made casual reference to the likelihood that the
incumbent, Pleasant Porter, would be a candidate. Roley McIntosh,
Isparhecher's second chief, was also discussed, but he had publicly
announced that he did not wish to run. Although Porter looked like
the only viable candidate in the field, he was not Fus Fixico's choice.
The chief's refusal to issue deeds had been a sore point, and it had
been a general criticism that Porter spent too much time away from
the executive office. Fus Fixico said, "Porter was stay too much in
Muskogee and St. Louis and Washington and places like that to
make good chief. Injins not like that. Porter he was send deed by
express like he was not want Injins to have it; or, maybe so, he make
you come after it to Muskogee. Injins was not like that neither." He
accused Porter and John Goat, the Creek delegate, of wasting their
time in Washington and complained that the Creeks were becoming
apathetic about politics, virtually ensuring Porter's reelection. "Well,

172

Fus

Fixico

and

Literary

Acclaim

so," he wrote, "they was not much talk about next chief, and it was look like Creek Injins was lost they grip and they suspenders couldn't hold up they breeches. If Chief Porter was not talk good, maybe so he was had a black filly run over him like at a horse round-up." If Porter was to get Fus Fixico's vote, the chief would have to hold a big barbecue and give Fus Fixico a political office like superintendent of public "destruction." [28]

The potential "black filly," or dark horse, that Fus Fixico warned about appeared in the form of Charles Gibson. In late March this well-known figure, Alex's good friend and the contributor of a regular column in the *Journal* on Creek history, lore, and current events, announced his candidacy, which Alex endorsed. Fus Fixico described the event as taking exercise before a foot race: "Maybe so he was make Porter look like he was stand still in the big road same as elm stump so wagon was had to go around him." In April, when Porter's party could not agree on a running mate for him, Fus Fixico predicted that Porter "was done had his day in Creek politics." He said that "it's look like Chief Porter was lose ground bad like coyote when grey hounds was after him on the prairie." Perhaps that was just as well; Porter could run for the United States Senate after Chief McCurtain succeeded in making a state out of the Indian Territory. Gibson, on the other hand, "was run like a deer in the lane for chief. Everybody was want him for next chief," Fus Fixico wrote, "except some that want to be chief theyselves." [29]

The race became more complicated when a number of others expressed interest in seeking the chief's office, including former chief Legus Perryman and Alex's old friend G. W. Grayson, whom Fus Fixico called Yaha Tustanugga, or Wolf Warrior. "But I think it was laid between Yaha and Charley," he wrote, " 'cause they get all the Injin votes and was left nothing for Pleas and Legus but niggers to vote for them and maybe so a few half breeds that was hungry for pie." When the Union party met in convention at Okmulgee in June to nominate its candidate, the contest was between Perryman and Grayson. Fus Fixico described it in terms of dogs scrapping over a bone. When Perryman won, Tookpafka Micco observed that " 'good men like Wolf Warrior don't all time get in office' " and that " 'it was laid between Chief Porter and Charley Gibson to scratch up the bone.' " [30] But in early July Gibson withdrew from the race. Although Chitto Harjo was the candidate of the Snake faction, he was generally discounted as a potential winner. That left Porter and Perryman in the race.

173
Fus
Fixico
and
Literary
Acclaim

Alex now turned the Fus Fixico letters to supporting Porter and attacking Perryman. He had steadfastly supported Gibson and only reluctantly turned to Porter. Hotgun and his friends felt like the children of Israel in Egypt, looking for a Moses. When all candidates were weighed, they decided Porter was the one with brains enough to lead the Creeks in concluding their tribal affairs. Alex went to greater lengths to attack Perryman than to support Porter. Hotgun reminded his friends of the fiscal scandals that had dominated Perryman's former administration. Alex's editorial attacks on Perryman's African heritage were reflected in the letters. Hotgun " 'was mighty sorry old Legus got nominated, 'cause he aint a full-blood Injin.' " Fus Fixico called Perryman "a sly old coon," and Hotgun believed he would make a good janitor and described him as " 'sweating like a nigger at a 'lection.' " And after Porter had soundly defeated Perryman, Fus Fixico observed that "Legus Perryman could do the cake walk but he couldn't scorch fast enough to be chief."[31]

With the election behind him, Alex turned the letters toward a scandal that had been brewing during the summer concerning federal officials involved in fraudulent land deals in the Indian Territory. The scandal brought to public attention some questionable practices in land transactions that the Indians had complained about ever since the allotment process began. Buyers and land speculators had already begun to take options to purchase land and otherwise to maneuver for legal challenges to titles when allotments were finally made. Assaults on the Creek titles were made on numerous fronts. Although restrictions were placed on the sale of their own allotments, the Creeks could make deals involving the allotments of relatives who had died since filing for their lands. Some Creeks learned early that money was to be made dealing in the allotments of dead relatives. On any Saturday they could be seen on the streets of Eufaula, "talking deeds and dead kin folks." Alex wrote early in 1902, "We don't know how it is, but it seems many Indians have died while filing on the best lands, leaving their relatives with more real estate than they know what to do with." There had also been widespread speculation in town lots for years. That continued, and large land companies had been formed to speculate in allotments.

174

Fus
Fixico
and
Literary
Acclaim

Concerted efforts had also begun to have Congress remove restrictions on the sale and lease of Creek lands. Meanwhile, speculators encumbered prospective titles by advancing money to allottees in return for leases for the land.[32]

During spring and summer 1902, these manipulations had been spotlighted in the debate over what was known as the Creek supplemental agreement, which amended the original allotment agreement with the United States. The land companies that G. W. Grayson had complained about in letters to the *Indian Journal* lobbied against provisions calling for allotment of the surplus land that remained after the homestead allotments had been made. They also opposed requiring the secretary of the interior's signature on leases. Grayson, Porter, and others argued that such provisions were necessary to protect the ignorant and needy Creeks who were the primary prey of land speculators. It was estimated that the titles to hundreds of thousands of acres of Creek land had been encumbered by land buyers through leasing and other questionable methods. Ratification of the supplemental agreement, however, had failed to check these practices, which continued unabated through the early months of 1903 despite regulations issued by the Interior Department. The Muskogee papers abetted the speculators by publishing the names of allottees to whom deeds had been delivered.[33]

In the early Fus Fixico letters, Alex had attacked the leases. One complaint made by Grayson and others was that the ignorant Creeks knew they could lease their allotments for cash but did not realize the legal implications of the transaction. Fus Fixico, however, implied that the Creeks might have been taking advantage of the whites. In the first letter he wrote, "I was go to Muskogee last week and buy heap stuff on my land. Them white mens was good to me. Next time I go to Checotah, or maybe Eufaula, and buy stuff the same way." Just before Christmas 1902, he wrote that after one trip he had come home in a wagon that he had "got for Christmas present on my land in Checotah. When I go to Eufaula, maybe so, I was got big fine buggy for Christmas present, too, on my land."[34]

In a series of letters to the *Journal* in early 1903, G. W. Grayson continued to press for the allotment of all Creek lands in order to eliminate any surplus that could be sold to speculators. He and Creek writers like Gibson urged that any surplus lands be allotted to children born since the rolls had closed. Grayson accused "capi-

talists" of lobbying against such allotment because they knew where 175
Fus
Fixico
and
Literary
Acclaim
mineral deposits were and wanted them. He called for a second
supplemental agreement to protect the rights of newborns. Grayson
considered allotment a social experiment by the United States; thus
it behooved the Creeks to protect the rights of their posterity while
they were "still sufficiently recognized as a nation." He attacked
the press—and his comments apparently included the *Journal*—for
lauding allotment, "showing everything on the surface beautiful and
altogether lovely." The press was full of praise for "progress" and
"development," which were "all well enough if pursued on conservative and just lines and not to the injury of the Indians who own
the land." [35] Though such criticism must have hit Alex hard because
of his stand for progress, he published Grayson's letters.

In fact, he found much he could agree with in what Grayson said.
He was for progress, but not at the expense of the Creeks. Fus Fixico
wrote in late February, "Well, I was like to read what Yaha Tustanugga say in Journal last week 'bout surplus land what the white
man was had his eye on long time. They is lots a good land like that
and Injins ought a grab it theyselves stead a letting government sell
it cheap for spot cash like storekeeper that think he was going get
busted." Echoing Grayson, he wrote in April, "Well, so we hear lots
a talk about big progress in Creek nation and read about it in the
newspaper before breakfast time. They was good news all time about
long stride and development and things like that till you can't make
a crop and get out of the hole if you was try to hear all of it." The
public did not hear about the full-blood Indians whose homes had
been filed on by someone else, he said. "But we hear all time about
some fellow that was find a coal mine with a post auger, or maybe so
some other fellow that was strike oil that was shoot up like a squirrel
gun soon as he touch it." [36]

By summer 1903 there was growing evidence that federal officials, including members of the Dawes Commission, were involved
in the rampant land speculation on a large scale. Muskogee had
more people on the federal payroll than any city in the United States
except Washington, D.C. It is not surprising, with the economic
changes allotment would bring, that some would be tempted to vio-
late the ethics of office in return for cash or land options. A year
earlier, in the pages of the *Journal*, Grayson had called for an investigation of land transactions to find whether "combinations of

176

Fus

Fixico

and

Literary

Acclaim

persons" were at work in the nation. Calls for an investigation now became common. Alex added his editorial voice. An investigation should have occurred long ago, he argued. "Turn the rascals out— when you find them guilty, Mr. Secretary," he wrote.[37] Charges of graft and fraud were ultimately leveled at a number of people, including members of the Dawes Commission and lesser officials. Charges ranged from influence peddling to padding the tribal rolls to silent partnerships in land companies.

Hotgun and Tookpafka Micco found the situation amusing. They mulled over the rumors that federal officials were padding the Creek census rolls and buying interests in large land trust companies. Perhaps Hitchcock would take action to make the grafters "quit running up good hands for theyselves instead of giving the Injin a square deal and a chance to shuffle the deck after 'em." They described Hitchcock's rumored investigation in terms of smoking out game. They predicted he would go after top officials such as Tams Bixby, chairman of the Dawes Commission, and J. Blair Shoenfelt, Indian agent at the Union Agency. Hitchcock had fired Clarence B. Douglas, editor of the *Muskogee Phoenix*, from his position as clerk in charge of the land division of the Indian agency under a cloud of suspicion of influence peddling. The secretary had flushed only a rabbit, Tookpafka Micco said. Next time, Hotgun predicted, he might smoke out a fox.[38]

But for several weeks it was uncertain whether there would be an investigation. It was rumored that Chief Porter opposed it for fear it would hurt his chances for reelection. Charges named more and more officials. "What the ganderleg dudes in Washington, who presume to run our affairs, need," Alex wrote, "is hickory poles instead of twine strings for backbone." Secretary Hitchcock claimed to have limited powers to investigate and issued more regulations, which he claimed would prevent fraud. William Mellette, United States attorney for the Western District of the Indian Territory, refused to convene a special grand jury. Whether he was speaking of the weather or the political nature of the controversy, Mellette said it was too hot to call such a jury.[39] That statement was too much for Alex, who wrote:

> He hates to sweat
> Does Bill Mellette.

He'll wait till frost, no doubt;

It's too hot yet

For Bill Mellette

To turn the rascals out.[40]

177

Fus

Fixico

and

Literary

Acclaim

Meanwhile, S. M. Brosius of the Indian Rights Association had conducted his own investigation and in mid-August made public charges of graft against Pliny Soper, the United States attorney for the Northern District, all members of the Dawes Commission except one, and other officials. Brosius charged that "a more systematic monopoly" by trust companies and their agents existed in the Creek Nation than elsewhere. Among their tactics were contracts for sale at the end of the lease without additional compensation, leases for twenty-five to seventy-five cents an acre and subleases to farmers for one to two dollars an acre, and use of the Indians' lease money to pay for improvements made by renters.[41]

Brosius singled out a number of trust companies for criticism. The Tribal Development Company of Tishomingo, organized March 25, 1903, had as its largest stockholder Guy P. Cobb, then internal revenue inspector for the Indian Territory. Its vice president and a substantial stockholder was Pliny Soper. Officers of the Muskogee Title and Trust Company, organized February 24, included Tams Bixby, who was also a large stockholder and vice president, and J. George Wright, United States Indian inspector, who was a director. Bixby was also a stockholder and president of the Canadian Valley Trust Company of Muskogee. G. W. Hopkins, formerly chief clerk of the Dawes Commission, and P. G. Reuter, former clerk in charge of the commission's land office, had resigned those positions and joined this company. Thomas B. Needles, Dawes commissioner, was vice president and a director of the International Banking Trust Company of Vinita. Charles A. Davidson, clerk of the United States court at Vinita, was a director; James H. Huckleberry, assistant United States attorney for the Northern District of the Indian Territory, was attorney for the company, and James H. Huckleberry, Jr., was a stockholder. Besides these questionable associations, Brosius reported that Dawes commissioner C. R. Breckenridge was a stockholder in the Eufaula Trust Company, that Bixby owned real estate at Fort Gibson, Tahlequah, Tishomingo, Sulphur Springs, and other points in the Indian Territory, and that Soper was a stockholder in,

178

Fus
Fixico
and
Literary
Acclaim

and attorney for, the Cherokee Oil and Gas Company, chartered in Arkansas but operating in the Indian Territory, as well as general counsel in Indian Territory for the St. Louis and San Francisco Railroad. In the wake of these accusations, Alex wrote, "If the officials accused of corruption are guilty, throw them in the 'bull pen' the same as other rascals." He reported that Hitchcock was angry with Brosius for "flushing his game" before he could get his own investigator into the field.[42]

Alex was relentless with Fus Fixico's criticism of Hitchcock and the grafters. From the beginning, the secretary's inaction or ineptness in protecting the Indians' rights had been reflected in the name Fus Fixico gave him. He was like the cocked pistol, always ready but never fired. Thus he became Secretary It's Cocked. For the officials involved in carving up the Indian Territory and getting their share of the "pie," he created names that reflected their avarice. Tams Bixby, Thomas B. Needles, and Clifton R. Breckenridge of the Dawes Commission became Tams or Dam Big Pie, Tom Needs It, and Break in Rich. Pliny Soper became Plenty So Far, and J. George Wright, the Indian inspector, became J. Gouge Right. J. Blair Shoenfelt, the Indian agent, became J. Bear Sho' Am Fat. According to Hotgun, President Roosevelt had ordered the secretary to investigate the game Brosius had treed in the Indian Territory, but the secretary was too busy "fixing up rules and setting down on skin games to climb up in the tree to see what's up there." If he had followed the president's orders, he would have found "old raccoons" like Bixby, Wright, Needles, and Soper, who had been chased out of the "Injin's sofky patch" they had been robbing.[43]

Under increasing scrutiny by journalists, federal bureaucrats began to distance themselves from land transactions. Bixby publicly denied that he or the companies he was affiliated with had ever bought an acre of Indian land. Soper and Benjamin Colbert, United States marshal, withdrew from the Tribal Development Company. Joseph McCoy, assistant district attorney for the Western District of the Indian Territory, resigned on September 1. It was reported that he was an attorney in the leasing operations of Bixby's Canadian Valley Trust Company and that he watched over the territory business interests of his Kansas City business and political friends. Hotgun and Tookpafka Micco saw McCoy's resignation as a sign the grafters were like quail that "was flushing so Secretary It's Cocked

couldn't get a pot shot." The Brosius investigation had charged that
all the members of the Dawes Commission had connections with
trust companies except W. E. Stanley, but it now became known that
he was vice president of the Tishomingo Trust Company, though he
claimed he owned no stock.[44]

Other revelations appeared in print. The trust company of which
Tams Bixby was president had offices in the same building as the
Dawes Commission. United States marshal Benjamin H. Colbert,
whose name had been associated with the Tribal Development Company, was accused by Chickasaw editor Finis Fox of taking prisoners
out of jail and forcing them to vote as he directed. It was also revealed that not only was Dawes commissioner Breckenridge a stockholder in the Eufaula Trust Company, but his family owned $27,000
in stock. Other stockholders included Commissioner Needles and
Creek chief Pleasant Porter. In addition to earlier revelations, it tran-
spired that James H. Huckleberry was a director of both the Verdigris Oil and Gas Company of Vinita and the Midland Oil and Gas
Company of Claremore. Finally it came out that a number of lesser
officials of the Interior Department and Justice Department were
stockholders or officials in the Welch Gas and Oil Company and the
Jefferson Trust Company. More allegations about the trust companies' methods appeared in the press. A special matter of concern was
what were called "cut-throat" five-year leases, which the companies
acquired for cents an acre and rented to farmers for dollars. According to government policy, renters were required to improve the
property, and these improvements were to go to the Indian owner at
the end of the lease. However, the companies told ignorant Indians
that they had to pay for houses, barns, fences, and other improvements, that making improvements was optional, or that the owner
must buy the improvements at the end of the lease. The companies
hired special agents known as "rustlers" who traveled throughout
the territory, rounding up Indians who had not been "branded" by
others.[45]

The Dawes commissioners now went on the offensive, asking
Hitchcock to investigate so as to prevent "fanatical reports and questionable journalism" from undoing "the result of years of unremit-
ting toil" by the commission. Admitting that he was connected to the
trusts, Tams Bixby publicly asked his attackers what they were going
to do about it. Bixby said that the Canadian Valley Trust Company

180

Fus
Fixico
and
Literary
Acclaim

had been organized before Hitchcock's visit to the Indian Territory and that he had told Hitchcock about it. He also argued that he had a right to engage in "private business," and Alex agreed with respect to Bixby the private citizen. But as chairman of the Dawes Commission it was another matter: "His knowledge of real estate values in Indian Territory gives him too great advantage over the legitimate investor, and his 'private business' is of such a character as would tend to swerve his official judgment in matters that conflict with his personal interests."[46]

Other bureaucrats followed Bixby's lead in thumbing their noses at accusers. Pliny Soper shrugged off implications of wrongdoing by saying that his actions were acceptable because the Tribal Development Company was not in his district. Alex responded editorially, "Pliny Soper admits that he is into it, but not in his own district. Maybe he thinks the department of justice can't extradite him." Later he wrote, "The Kansas City Journal intimates that Pliny Soper is part Indian. Maybe Pliny was grafted. Anyhow, he's a peach." In early September, John D. Benedict, United States supervisor of education for the Five Civilized Tribes, resigned as director of the Bradley Real Estate Company of Muskogee. C. M. Bradley, president of the company, was notorious for his dealings in Creek lands and admitted that he was nothing but a grafter who found the Indians and freedmen easy prey as a result of the secretary's administration of the allotment process. He told the press that the allottee was like a bucking bronco that falls under its rider: "Every time the secretary of the interior changes his rules and regulations he throws the allottee to the ground and he rises firmer in the grasp of the grafter and is a little weaker than before." Bradley claimed he held over four hundred leases.[47]

As the weeks wore on and no official investigation had begun, Alex continued his editorial criticism of the alleged grafters: "If wrongdoing has existed it exists now and will continue to exist so long as the proposed investigation of territorial affairs is confined to mere threats from headquarters." By early September the Justice Department had begun to investigate its officials, but Hitchcock delayed an investigation of Interior Department officials because he claimed he could not find a man honest or competent enough to conduct one. Hotgun said that Hitchcock was like Diogenes looking for an honest man, in this case one "that didn't had his breadhooks hung up under his coat tail for boodle." But honest men were scarce: "They was put near all extinct in politics and they was hardly 'nough left in the republican party for seed." Finally, on September 15, Charles J. Bonaparte was appointed, apparently with instructions to conduct an investigation of limited scope.[48]

181
Fus
Fixico
and
Literary
Acclaim

There were reasons to entertain suspicions about Hitchcock's delay. Brosius claimed he had informed the secretary of the dealings of Bixby and other high officials months before the scandal broke. There had also been accusations that proceeds from town lot sales by the Dawes Commission had been deposited in the banks of Hitchcock's friends in St. Louis, accusations that he denied and Roosevelt declared untrue. Alex was skeptical about the outcome of any investigation. Before Bonaparte's appointment he had asked, "After the investigation, then what? Why whitewash to be sure." When announcement of the appointment came, he wrote, "Give us a bona fide investigation, Mr. Bonaparte." But as Hotgun and Tookpafka Micco tried to second-guess what Bonaparte would do, Tookpafka Micco concluded, "Well, maybe so it was all come out in the whitewash." For a month Bonaparte tried to conduct the investigation from afar, receiving complaints through correspondence. It then became clear that on-site investigation was needed. Clinton Rogers Woodruff was hired as Bonaparte's assistant in late October and was sent to the Indian Territory, arriving in late November. Bonaparte himself did not arrive in Muskogee until December. From the beginning, Hotgun predicted that the investigation would be "the biggest republican whitewash that was ever come down the pike." He and Tookpafka Micco claimed that "Boney Parts" holed up in the Katy Hotel, got out among the people very little, and formed a kind of exclusive secret society with Bixby, Breckenridge, Shoenfelt, Soper, and others as members. Alex's emphasis on Bonaparte's conducting his investigation behind closed doors may have referred to the fact that these men and others involved in the scandal were members of the exclusive Town and Country Club at Fort Gibson or the Wauhillau Outing Club in the eastern part of the Cherokee Nation. After he had been there a week, Bonaparte issued a public statement saying essentially that the investigation was over, that he had heard all citizens who wished to complain. As if anticipating criticism of his final report, he said that Secretary Hitchcock was not responsible for the actions of the investigators.[49]

182

Fus
Fixico
and
Literary
Acclaim

Apparently few local officials, including Pleasant Porter, had wanted a thorough investigation. During his campaign the preceding summer, Porter had been implicated in the scandal but denied that an investigation would damage his chances for reelection. He had also become displeased with A. P. Murphy, the attorney for the Creek Nation, for charging irregularities in the handling of Creek allotments by Clarence B. Douglas, editor of the *Muskogee Phoenix* and clerk of the land division of the Indian agent's office. At the time of his appointment the previous winter, Murphy charged that Porter had tried to get him to be the attorney of record, to remain in Missouri, and to let a Muskogee attorney, J. W. Zeveley, handle affairs in his name. There was "something back of it," Murphy told Secretary Hitchcock. Murphy had gone to the Creek Nation and was despised, one editor said, because he had insisted on being independent. In an interview with the *St. Louis Post-Dispatch* after his reelection, Porter defended the public officials in the Indian Territory, saying that the Indians had not been hurt much. When Bonaparte arrived in Muskogee, Murphy charged, he refused to pursue allegations or subpoena witnesses that Murphy had named. Bonaparte did look into the matter, but his report dismissed Murphy's charges as having been made without authority. Murphy's suspicions of Porter may have had merit. Four years later Porter, Bixby, and others would be sued by the Creek Nation for the return of town lots that they allegedly held beyond the number allowed by law.[50]

By the time Bonaparte and Woodruff reached Muskogee, Alex had been city editor of the *Muskogee Evening Times* for several weeks. Between selling the *Indian Journal* and assuming his duties at Muskogee, he had continued the Fus Fixico letters in the *Fort Smith Times*, keeping his readers abreast of developments in the scandal. His letters in the *Muskogee Evening Times* show that he believed the Bonaparte investigation would go nowhere, so by the end of 1903 he had dropped the issue from the letters.

The report of the investigation, which was not filed until March 1904, did what Hotgun and Tookpafka Micco had predicted. Although ample evidence had been produced during the preceding months that federal officials were involved in land speculation, the investigation failed to bring any of them to account. The Bonaparte report admitted the truth of Brosius's allegations concerning public officials' connection to the land companies but stopped short of

charging the companies with illegal dealings. The report criticized 183
Fus
Fixico
and
Literary
Acclaim Bixby, Needles, Breckenridge, and some minor officials and recommended abolition of the Dawes Commission and delegation of its
duties to other agencies. According to the *Muskogee Times*, Alex's
paper, Bonaparte and Woodruff reported "glittering generalities"
concerning matters of insignificance and "less than minor interest" and "after inadequate investigation passed adverse judgment
on Chairman Bixby and his fellow members of the Dawes Commission." Alex had predicted the outcome of the investigation in part,
no doubt, because he accepted the corporate development of Indian
Territory as a fact. In boosting Eufaula, he had not questioned the
source of capital for economic development. The first major corporate incursion in the Indian Territory had been the building of the
railroads before his birth. Throughout his life, companies had done
nothing but expand their investments. Historian H. Craig Miner has
concluded that in the process of "corporate intrusion and the decline in Indian sovereignty" in the Indian Territory, no Indian nation
demonstrated a "consistent, unified opposition to development of its
land by white corporations." Only the full-bloods, he argues, whom
Alex viewed as a stumbling block to progress, were steadfast.[51] Alex
must have realized, as others did, the complicity of tribal leaders and
Indian citizens in establishing the corporations' hold on the territory.
Like them, he must also have understood that the relationship between the federal bureaucrats and the corporations was not as easily
sorted out as journalists and reformers might have liked.

When the Bonaparte report was published, Alex was close to the
end of his career as a journalist. Because he would devote his time
to other matters, his literary production would decrease. The Fus
Fixico letters had appeared irregularly while he was editor of the
Times, and only three appeared between the first of the year and
his resignation at the end of March 1904. By that time he had written more than half of his seventy-two Fus Fixico letters. He would
not produce them again regularly until the few weeks preceding
his death. Yet the first thirty-seven letters had brought him literary
acclaim and established him as a political humorist.

The appearance of the *Daily Indian Journal* during summer 1903
had caught the attention of the journalism world. The first major
newspaper to print a story about the Creek Indian editor and his
daily was the *Kansas City Journal*. Then Alex was beseiged by re-

184

Fus
Fixico
and
Literary
Acclaim

quests for information about himself from writers for the *St. Louis Post-Dispatch*, the *New York Herald*, and the *New York Tribune*. Requests also came from several free-lance writers as well as from the Gilliams Press Syndicate and the Union Bureau of News. Articles about him appeared in newspapers and magazines as far flung as the Colorado Springs *Evening Telegraph*, the Philadelphia *Public Ledger*, the *Pittsburgh Leader*, the *Indian's Friend*, the *New York Times*, and the *Boston Transcript*. Letters came from newspaper editors and individuals throughout the Indian Territory and in Oklahoma, Iowa, Georgia, Hawaii, Kansas, Indiana, New York, Missouri, Tennessee, Massachusetts, Ontario, and England, requesting copies of the daily, his autograph, or biographical information. The editorial department of the *Kansas City Journal* asked for an account of his life "to be used when need arises." [52]

This widespread publicity, combined with the national focus on the statehood issue and the graft scandal, brought popular interest in the Fus Fixico letters. Local and regional attention had been immediate on their first appearance in fall 1902. Alex was compared to other dialect voices: "We have philosophers in all kinds of dialect. The Irish, Mr. Dooley; the Negro, Uncle Remus; the slang of George Ade; the Dutch, Jacob Undervider; and even the Norwegian or Swede in Ole Oleson or Yonny Yonson. Not last of all, yet oldest of all, we have the Indian and the latest disciple is Fus Fixico of Eufaula." He was referred to as "the William Allen White of Indian Territory." He had been noted in the Texas papers and, by spring 1903, was mentioned regularly in the Kansas City *Star* and the Kansas City *Times*, the latter calling Fus Fixico "the Dooley of Indian Territory politics." [53]

The article in the *Kansas City Journal* that had brought Alex's daily newspaper to national attention also created publicity for the Fus Fixico letters. They were picked up by other newspapers, Alex was asked for information about how the persona had evolved, and J. Ojijatekha Brant-Sera, a Mohawk, wanted him to take his humor on the stage by joining a program of lectures that Brant-Sera was arranging for Indians from various parts of the country. Alex received requests for regular contributions of the letters from newspapers in New York, Philadelphia, and St. Louis.[54]

But Alex expressed the same doubts about seeking a wider audience that he had expressed in earlier years about his poetry. He told the editor of the *South McAlester Capital*, "Heretofore I have always made my letters of territorial importance only, using characters and incidents that all of our people are familiar with. I fear that eastern people would not understand me." He apparently rejected the editor's suggestion "that he deal with national characters and national incidents for the eastern press, giving the Indian idea of the American politician, financier and soldier." Perhaps he rejected it because, despite his success and the national attention it had brought, he was by that time thinking of selling the *Indian Journal*.[55] As subsequent events demonstrated, his production of the letters diminished greatly after he sold the *Journal*, and they never again appeared with such frequency.

185

Fus

Fixico

and

Literary

Acclaim

Alex's comments also reflect the modesty he always exhibited concerning his own work. He had not hesitated, however, to use the *Indian Journal* to praise and encourage the literary activity of other Indian writers in the Indian Territory. In addition to publishing the regular "Gibson's Rifle Shots" by Charles Gibson, Alex printed articles and comments about Gibson's work, praising it highly.[56] He also published letters and essays by George Grayson. He had nothing but praise for Ora V. Eddleman, Cherokee editor of the *Twin Territories* magazine at Muskogee. He commented on individual issues, urged people to subscribe, and printed articles about Eddleman and her work. He published articles and notes about the literary accomplishments of other Cherokees: DeWitt Clinton Duncan (Too-qua-stee), linguist, poet, political essayist, and short-story writer, and William Eubanks, linguist and essayist. To Alex's credit, except for the Fus Fixico letters and a few other pieces, for the most part unsigned, he did not use the *Journal* to push his own literary career. As the editor of the *Holdenville Times* wrote, Alex knew enough "not to burden his paper with poems, but use them purely as literary sauce." Several of his poems appeared in the *Twin Territories* during 1902 and 1903, all published before. Yet there remained an interest in his poetry outside the Indian Territory. One writer apparently worked on a story about him and Ora Eddleman for *Success*, and a major article about him appeared in the *Criterion* in September 1902.[57]

Despite the continued interest in him as a poet, it was the Fus Fixico letters that were his crowning literary achievement. They were the perfect vehicle through which Alex could express his political views. Since his exit from politics, he had avoided the public spot-

186

Fus
Fixico
and
Literary
Acclaim

light. He liked something between him personally and the public: a poet's voice, a newspaper column, or a persona. As the latter, Fus Fixico was his most brilliant success. In the letters Alex had found the effective combination of style and subject matter that he had not found in his poetry. They were commentary on the dramatic unfolding of events in the Creek Nation and the Indian Territory, presented in the language and cadence of one deeply concerned. In establishing a voice he could call on as he needed, Alex had fixed his literary reputation for generations to come.

Chapter **8** In Search of the Lost Creeks

. . . .

In early October 1904 Alex attended the meet-
ing of the Creek National Council at Okmulgee, not as a member or
a curious onlooker, but as official interpreter for the Dawes Commission. He accompanied J. J. Beavers, chief clerk of the Creek enrolling division, and stenographer Drennen Skaggs, whose task it was
to secure additional evidence concerning outstanding applications
for enrollment in the Creek citizenship lists. Although the applications had been filed before the prescribed date of May 25, 1901,
they lacked the corroborating evidence required for enrollment and
the issuing of allotment certificates. Because Okmulgee would be
crowded with representatives from the tribal towns and others who
had business before the council, the occasion seemed a good opportunity to obtain reliable testimony and to clear many of the cases
from the files. This trip was the first of many Alex would take during
the next two and a half years in search of Creeks whose names, for
various reasons, did not appear on the official tribal rolls or appeared
without verification. During this period Alex wrote little compared
with his usual output. As he put aside his personal literary goals and

expended his energy enrolling his conservative tribesmen, his opinions about them mellowed somewhat and began to take new shape.

During spring and summer 1904, while he worked as interpreter
for the Office of Indian Affairs, Alex had more time for his family
than he had had since they left Wetumka in 1901. Regular trains in
all directions made it convenient for them to travel to Fayetteville to
visit Lowena's family or go to Eufaula to visit his. And it was just
as convenient for Alex's relatives to visit him and Lowena in their
home on South Cherokee Street. Relieved of the long hours of the
newspaper editor, Alex found time to cultivate friendships with local
politicians, businessmen, and newspaper correspondents from the
states and to walk over nearby prehistoric encampment sites looking
for artifacts.[1] This leisure time with family and friends came to an
end in October, when he was assigned as interpreter for the Dawes
Commission's Creek enrolling division, taking testimony during the
National Council session. He would not have such freedom again.
Why would a loving husband and devoted father want to give it up?

The Fus Fixico letters he wrote during his tenure as translator
might fairly gauge what Alex was thinking during those months. He
produced fewer than a dozen letters in 1904; all appeared before he
went to work for the Dawes Commission, and all but three were published between the time he left the *Times* and early summer. That
they appeared first in the *Muskogee Phoenix*, a Republican paper,
reflects the way their content transcends issues of partisan politics.
The perennial issue of statehood revived, but the most revealing letters focus on the removal of restrictions on the sale of allotments.
The question was not on whether restrictions should be removed;
Alex had already taken a stand in the affirmative. It was what would
happen to the conservative Creeks afterward.

Hotgun, Tookpafka Micco, and their listeners Kono Harjo and
Wolf Warrior found themselves—and the conservatives in general
—swept along by the tide of social, economic, and technological
change. On New Year's Day 1904 they shared dinner at Kono Harjo's
house at Weogufky, where they feasted on sour bread, sak-ko-nip-
kee, blue dumplings, and hickory nut sofky. The occasion made
Hotgun "lonesome for olden times put near twenty-five years ago,"
which Alex had often referred to fondly in his writing. Those days
stood in stark contrast to the present, the age of modern towns where
customs differed so greatly from those of the little trading towns

in the earlier time. Then the visitor to Muskogee could hear the
howling of coyotes, which stole young pigs from the site where the
town now contemplated building an opera house. Now one could
not find one's way around without asking a policeman and could no
longer eat in a "shack restaurant" without being entertained by a
string band. Tookpafka Micco added to Hotgun's observations that
in " 'them days the store keeper and hod carrier didn't eat dinner at
supper time and jackasses didn't try to be elks.' "[2]

With the failure of the Bonaparte investigation, Hotgun and the
others became resigned to graft as an everyday part of the new age.
Though officials had distanced themselves from the land companies
and a recent Indian appropriations act had prohibited their dealing
in land, it was generally conceded that most continued in various
nefarious ways. Shortly after he and Bonaparte filed their report,
Woodruff wrote that the land companies were back in business as
usual.[3] After all, " 'the grafter he been here a long time and was a
pioneer, like the Dawes Commission,' " Hotgun said. He came first
in the form of the salesman of lightning rods and then of kitchen
ranges too large to fit into the Indians' cabins, almanac clocks, Gale
harrows that were too heavy to use in small sofky patches, and buggies. " 'So everywhere you go now,' " Hotgun said, " 'you find lightning rod for clothes line and steel range cook stoves for the children's
play house, and calendar clocks for ornament over the fire place and
Gale harrows for scrap iron and old buggies for curiosity.' " After this
long history of being "taken," the Indian " 'was still good picking' "
for the land grafter, " 'ready to bite like a bass when you was used
grasshopper for bait.' " Convinced that Hotgun was right, Tookpafka
Micco vowed that when he sold his land he would take good care
of the money and stay away from " 'the walled-up streets in Muskogee.' " But Kono Harjo was not persuaded; he told Hotgun, " 'Well,
so come see me and, maybe so, I was took you out to drive in my
new buggy and leave colt at home.' "[4]

To Hotgun, history was repeating itself. He said, " 'The Injin he
sell his land in the old country (Alabama) and he sell his land in
Injin Territory and was had a good time out here like back there in
olden times. But back in the old country he was live different, 'cause
he was sit on a long chair like a fence rail.' " Now he sat on a chair
with four legs and a soft cushion. He had become "civilized": " 'He
wear a white shirt now and black clothes and shoes that was look like

a ripe mush melon. Then he was buy bon bons for his papoose and drop-stitch stocking for his squaw and part his name in the middle, J. Little Bear.' " The white man convinced the Indian that his wagon was out of fashion and sold him a new buggy. Of course all these material goods were paid for with money from the sale or lease of land. What would happen when the money ran out? " 'Well, maybe so about three years from now,' " Hotgun said, " 'the starch was go out a the Injin's white shirt and make it limber like a dish rag, and his black suit was fade like the last rose of summer and his breeches was get slack like a gunny sack, and his big toe was stick through his tan shoes like a snag in Deep Fork, and his fine buggy was tied together with baling wire and his old fillies was made crow bait pulling the fine buggy to stomp dances.' " Perhaps then the Indian would be " 'awakened up to his sense a duty and earn his bread by the sweat a his brow like a good republican or maybe so a democrat.' " [5]

The Indians had to face up to the realities of the times. As Hotgun said, " 'The Injin was had to go up against it to learn and, maybe so, after while he catch on, same like the white man and go to Mexico and bunco the greaser.' " [6] A preview of events to come occurred on April 21, when Congress removed the restrictions from the surplus allotments of adult non-Indians and gave the secretary of the interior discretionary power to remove restrictions from the allotments of adult Indians who applied. The act made eligible for sale over half a million acres of land belonging to the freedmen and white adopted citizens of the Creek Nation. As a result, Hotgun said, " 'the niggers could squander they land for a blue suit of clothes and rubber-tired buggy and make room for progress, while the Injin he look on and learn a good object lesson.' " As he predicted, much of the freedmen's land was rapidly transferred to white owners. In the face of historical events, even Chitto Harjo, who had been quiet of late, was giving in, according to Hotgun. He reported that the Snake leader had called his people together and told them that they were without hope or "provisions," so they might as well, like the Chinese, become "reconciled." He said,

> " 'The United States was break treaty and break treaty, and the white man he has come from Arkansas and come from Arkansas and stay and write back to his kinfolks and say this was the garden spot a the earth and you better come out here before it's

all gone. So that way the country was settled up and settled up, and they was no game left but swamp rabbits. We couldn't had any fish fry and stomp dance like in olden time. The white man he was make town and make town and build railroad and build railroad and appoint federal judge and appoint federal judge to say it was all right and we couldn't help it. So if we was had a council to talk it over, the marshal and soldiers was arrest us for trying to kill the president and put us in jail to catch consumption and maybe so lice. So I was make a motion to give it up and see what become of us anyhow.' " [7]

The conservatives, then, viewed the future with uncertainty as they realized the sharp contrasts between their values and those of the emerging American-dominated society. The relaxed, sociable atmosphere that Hotgun and his friends enjoyed at Weogufky Square differed greatly from that of the incorporated town where there was " 'a policeman standing on the corner with a big six-shooter to throw down on you for being absent from Sunday school.' " [8]

The white's world was duplicitous, hypocritical, avaricious, grasping, and Christianity ridden, according to Hotgun and his friends. He could " 'graft hard all week and, maybe so, think a heap a Jesus on Sunday.' " On Sunday the Indian could " 'go off down towards the creek and enjoy the sunshine and scenery,' " while the white Christians sat on hard benches in musty churches, remembering " 'the Lord once a week to be in style.' " But to Hotgun " 'the best place . . . to be sorry for grafting and to get close to the Great Spirit was out in the woods, where you couldn't had any temptation except to feel like swearing when something was stole your bait, or maybe so when a seed tick try to strike up acquaintance with you. That way you could catch mudcat and bass, or maybe so pluck a boquet, and live and enjoy life.' " The Indian " 'could turn the old work filley out on the grass Sunday morning,' " while " 'the family horse was had to stand up in the stable and eat dry hay so he could take the Christians sight seeing.' " The white-dominated society was driven by "policy," while common sense went by the board. The storekeeper, politician, or deacon " 'was compelled to had a good stock a policy to stay at business. You couldn't let your light so shine, or maybe so show your hand, 'cause policy was the key to prosperity.' " What if the business, political, and religious leaders sacrificed personal integrity for the dollar? " 'If you was laid up a big roll a greenback in the bank, or maybe so a fine suit in the clothes press,' " Hotgun said, " 'you needn't need 'em in your business when you was dead and your tombstone was leaning to one side.' " [9]

How was the conservative to compete in a world where the watchword was material prosperity at whatever cost? Hotgun had advised his companions on New Year's Day to eat heartily, for " 'if the restrictions aint removed it's the only chance we was had to get a belly full in Nineteen Hundred and Four.' " [10] Removal of restrictions was only a temporary solution. Indians must earn money in order to find their place in the new social order. Thus in late spring 1904 Hotgun was contemplating becoming " 'a country editor, with five thousand readers in some town that was had a good future and put near two hundred souls in it.' " The country editor had high status in the community and was the recipient of "lots a compliments," produce from the local farmers, bouquets from "the ladies' aid society," and ingratiating visits from office seekers. He could boost the town and be toastmaster for the Indian Territory Press Association. Tookpafka Micco said he would rather get free rail passes " 'like a flunkey a the federal court, or maybe so a roustabout for the Dawes Commission or Injin agent. So, when the conductor was come 'round and holler, "tickets?" all I had to do was flash the paste board and keep my eye on the landscape like I was had a deed to it.' " To this Hotgun replied, " 'Well, so, anyhow I was druther had my name to the head a the column and lots a snap shots hanging under it than a pass on the railroad and privilege to bog up when I want to in the palace car carpet and no votes to make me sanitary policeman.' " [11]

These words have more implications for Alex than for the Snake characters who uttered them. The possibility that a Snake like Hotgun could become a country editor or in any other way join the mainstream booster society was remote. The life Hotgun envisioned was basically the life Alex had led at Eufaula. The occupation to which Tookpafka Micco aspired was basically the one Alex chose after he left the *Times*. While in reality Hotgun and Tookpafka Micco had no choice of occupation, Alex did. The Fus Fixico letters from spring 1904 have a strong antiurban theme. Perhaps the "walled streets" of Muskogee had gotten to him as the "four walled rooms" of the Creek Orphan Asylum and the Eufaula Boarding School had gotten to him in earlier years. Perhaps he was ready to abandon the "metropolis" of the Indian Territory and get back to the rural areas,

which a position as interpreter for the Dawes Commission enrolling parties would allow him to do. One point is certain: the letters of this period present the conservative Creeks in a new light. The Hotgun of a year previous, who with his friend Choela had refused his deed, was now anticipating removal of restrictions from the sale of his land. The formerly "misguided" Snakes were now contemplating with uncertainty their imminent entry into a society they little liked or understood. If these letters reflect in any way Alex's own views at the time, he entered his fieldwork for the Dawes Commission if not with a more sympathetic view of the Snakes, at least with a patience that would allow him to deal with the conservatives.

The enrolling party that Alex accompanied to Okmulgee in October 1904 was more successful than it could have hoped. Besides the council session, disbursement of funds to Loyal Creek claimants, whose claims had finally been settled after nearly four decades, was taking place at Okmulgee. The payment attracted large numbers of conservatives, who accounted for not only the largest number of claimants but also the largest number of unfinished enrollment cases. Within three weeks the party had investigated more than 150 cases. Among those who gave testimony was Chitto Harjo. Through Alex's diplomatic efforts the Snake leader, who had theretofore steadfastly refused to have anything to do with the Dawes Commission, gave evidence in several cases. But he also used the occasion to vindicate himself, saying that, despite popular opinion, he had never encouraged violence, that he was interested only in saving his people, that he remained against allotment, and that he would oppose any statehood plan that did not recognize the integrity of the lands of the Five Civilized Tribes. Perhaps he surprised his listeners by displaying a knowledge of international affairs when he sympathized with the Japanese in their current conflict with the Russians. The Russians, he said, were "white people." [12]

Apparently because of his success with Chitto Harjo, Alex was appointed clerk in charge of a Creek enrollment field party. With Drennen Skaggs as his notary public and stenographer, he was to travel about the Creek Nation and do the work that the Dawes Commission could not do at its offices in Muskogee: taking additional testimony for enrollment applications, enrolling "lost" Creeks, and attempting to conciliate the Snakes. Travel expenses were prohibitive for some witnesses for citizenship applications, so Alex was to go to them. The "lost" Creeks were simply names on the town rolls that had never been identified. If these people were not found, they would be excluded from a share in the Creek assets when the allotment process ended. The Snakes, who would not be reconciled to allotment, had been assigned land arbitrarily by the Dawes Commission. Alex's task was in part to lead them to accept the inevitable—to make them realize that failing to enroll meant choosing a destructive path. This was important work that the commission had given him—work, as he said, that "must be done on the roadside, at the hearthside and in the cotton patch." Between the first of November and the Christmas holidays, Alex and Skaggs were in the field, working out of Weleetka and Eufaula, returning to Muskogee between trips to catch up on their paperwork.[13] During the next year and a half, Alex and his stenographer would travel throughout the Creek Nation, concentrating their efforts on the remote areas of the southern and western sections where most of the conservatives lived.

The remoteness of most applicants' residences presented the greatest obstacle to the fieldwork. Alex and Skaggs would take the train from Muskogee to Eufaula, Okmulgee, Bristow, or some other town, where they rented a buggy from a local livery. They struggled with "pokey" teams, breakdowns in rough terrain, dust, and mud and were often caught in the open by sudden changes in weather. Sometimes they drove many miles over bad roads only to find the prospective witness or enrollee away from home, then returned to town over the same route, sometimes arriving late at night, knowing they had to make the journey again to secure the testimony. The accommodations they returned to were not always restful. Alex laughed sometimes at what passed for "hotels" in the small towns. At Hoffman he and a dozen others shared a room that reminded him of an open hospital ward: "The inmates cracked jokes, laughed and passed many a quip and crank. Some of them had been in jail, some were almost there, some were busted, but the entire crew were in Hoffman trying to retrieve fortunes lost in other lands than ours."[14] The two men took their meals where they could find them, in cafés, boardinghouses, or hotel dining halls, at picnics in the countryside, or in the homes of the Indians. About one of these homes Alex said, "That's where we got good eating. We had good old fashioned sorghum molasses and it was so cold that we had to jab our knives into

the pitcher and wind up a big batch of it until the knives looked
like Indian ball clubs. Skaggs would call for the 'fry' and with bis-cuits as big as turtles, and as good sinkers, we sho did fill up." They bought watermelons from farmers, and from housewives Alex bought apusky—pounded corn, browned in hot ashes, that he could later mix with water. He had a weakness for sofky and never passed the sofky pot at the threshold of a cabin without partaking.[15]

The work was tedious. One visit to a neighborhood was rarely enough. Witnesses were sometimes away from home, knew little, or refused to tell what they knew. In one case Alex went to the same house five times before he found the Indian at home, each time traveling twenty-eight miles for the expected interview. At times the evidence obtained was insufficient to establish a claim to citizenship or to clarify the rolls. Social patterns among the conservatives added to the tedium of the task. Under clan law, a man whose wife had younger sisters was entitled to marry them as well if he had done well in the first marriage. To Alex it seemed that some had taken as many wives as they wanted or believed they were entitled to, making it extremely difficult and time consuming to trace the lineage of the offspring of the polygamous marriages.[16] Thus the field party found it necessary to return to some communities again and again.

Alex and Skaggs found ways to relieve the boredom as they trav-eled around the countryside. Alex let Skaggs do much of the driv-ing while he read aloud humorous stories from current magazines. Skaggs entertained Alex by singing "ragtime." They took along a camera for snapshots. Alex, always the prankster, had fun at Skaggs's expense. Once, as he translated while they were bargaining for bas-kets, the old Creek basket maker asked Skaggs for twenty-five cents. Alex told her to ask for fifty; she did, Skaggs paid, and Alex said he should get his basket free for raising the price on Skaggs. He later told the story to reporters to have a laugh on Skaggs. They enjoyed the frequent humorous incidents that occurred during their travels, and after each excursion in the field they delighted in telling them to reporters in Muskogee, who expected their "usual quota of stories," some not "fit to print." One that was "fit" was their encounter with a white renter from Izard County, Arkansas. They were lost, and when they asked if he could tell them where they were, he replied, "Yes, sah, you are all standing at my front gate, I reckon." Wrote one reporter, "We have never been able to satisfy ourselves whether these stories are the real thing or whether Posey and Skaggs just 'trumped them up' while riding along lonely roads and conversation got slack." [17]

During his travels, Alex also enjoyed frequent visits with his relatives. When he and Skaggs worked near Bald Hill, they spent their nights at the ranch. At Artussee, Alex dropped in on his uncle Johnson Phillips and dined on "Indian dishes galore." Alex greatly admired Phillips, a successful farmer and pastor of the Artussee Indian Baptist Church who, in Alex's opinion, had been able to compete with the whites. "In him the Indian problem has been solved through sheer self-effort," Alex would later say of his uncle. At Mellette Alex visited his adopted brother Tom Sulphur, and at Okemah he took dinner with his cousin John Phillips. When he worked near Henryetta, he visited George Riley Hall, who had published the *Henryetta Free-Lance* since 1902, and Lowena sometimes joined him there to spend a few days with Kittie. [18]

Alex's work kept him away from Lowena and the children for days at a time. Because his efforts were concentrated in the south, soon after he went into the field they gave up the house at Muskogee and moved to the ranch at Bald Hill. His work in those first few months was often within driving distance of the ranch and he could come home at night. In July 1905 he and Lowena bought a house at 1124 Hartford in Muskogee, and the family moved back to town. Thereafter Alex came home on weekends as often as he could. The family made excursions to Hyde Park, the local amusement park, or he and Lowena spent a quiet day reading. They sometimes entertained family members from Bald Hill or Kittie Hall from Henryetta. When Alex's work took him back to the vicinity of Bald Hill, Lowena and the children sometimes spent a week at the ranch, and they all returned to Muskogee together on the weekend. Only when office work was necessary or bad weather made travel impossible did Alex get to spend full weeks with his family at Muskogee. [19]

During his long periods of absence from home, Alex and Lowena kept in touch by letter, addressing each other as Mamma and Papa. She told him about her excursions, and he wrote about what he was reading and sent the magazines home to her after he had finished them. But for the most part the letters were expressions of their love and loneliness for one another. If it was raining, he hoped it was bright where she was. Once he wrote, "I have dreamed of you once since I have been away. Have you of me? How I should like to be with you this beautiful day!" And he always signed his letters, "Good bye—love and kisses from Papa."[20]

Though Alex worked diligently in the field, the Snakes resisted his efforts. Near Senora in April 1905, Wileya ran away when he found out Alex's mission. He did not want the Dawes Commission to learn his name and record it on a piece of paper. When Alex approached John Kelly in his "sofky patch" and tried to convince him of the futility of insisting that the "old treaties" were valid, Kelly responded as follows: "The real Indian was not consulted as to allotment of lands; if he had been consulted he would have never consented to depart from the customs and traditions of his fathers." He continued, "Our tribal government was upset by the stroke of a pen, because a few cried 'change' and because we were helpless." Alex argued in return that "the tribal governments had fallen into decay," that "the country had been over-run by white people, out-numbering the Indians ten to one," and that "it was impossible for the United States to arrest progress" for the Indians' sake, but these arguments failed to convince Kelly. Said Alex, "The growth of towns, the building of railroads, the leasing and selling of land, the clearing of forests, the disappearance of game and hunting grounds and all the marvelous progress of the country cannot disturb his opinion. He will not vary. He stands pat."[21]

Snakes like Kelly were united in opinion with their leader Chitto Harjo, whom Alex and Skaggs visited at his home west of Burney in late September 1905. The old Snake greeted them civilly but coldly and told them, among other things, "I shall never hold up my right arm and swear that I take my allotment of land in good faith—not while the water flows and the grass grows. God in yon bright firmament is my witness." That same God was also witness to the agreement between the whites and the Creeks, guaranteeing the Indians' right to possess the lands as long as the grass grew and the waters flowed. "I notice that the grass is still growing, that the water in the North Canadian is still flowing toward the sea and that the leaves still appear upon the trees," he said. He could therefore see no reason for abrogating the treaty: "The civilization of the Indian has not changed very materially, he still tills his sofky patch, his color remains the same and he attends to his business and has asked no change." Chitto Harjo refused to give Alex and Skaggs the

information they were seeking, and though the women were preparing a meal, he did not ask them to eat with him, but let them go
away hungry.[22]

Despite Hotgun's 1904 prediction that Chitto Harjo would give
up, the Snakes' resistance had become stronger in the preceding
spring as a result of efforts to enroll "newborn" Creeks. On March 4
Congress provided for the enrollment of children who were born
after May 25, 1901, and before March 4, 1905, who were living on
the latter date, and whose parents were Creek citizens whose names
appeared on the approved rolls. The Dawes Commission was to take
applications for only sixty days, and after an approved roll was made,
the children were to be given allotments. Knowing that the Snakes
would not enroll their children, just as they had refused to enroll
themselves, the commission sent Alex back to the Snake communities to scour the countryside that he had already covered while
investigating older applications.[23] The sixty-day limit meant he must
suspend his other work and concentrate on what the bureaucrats
called "the newborns."

Alex encountered the same difficulties he had experienced during
the preceding months. He and Skaggs began their work at Paden,
Dustin, and Hanna, where they found that conservative parents, as
expected, refused to enroll their children. One man told Alex that
"he would rather knock the brains of his children out against a tree
than make applications for them." Another told him that the minute
land was allotted to the children, "they became slaves and were no
longer free." Other parents hid their children to prevent their enrollment. Despite this resistance, Alex worked diligently to make
applications for as many of the children as possible because, he said,
"I know that it will be a great wrong if they are not given their allotment because of the folly of their parents. When the parents refuse
to talk to me I find some neighbor who will tell me about them."
Thus the affidavits he filed contained the names of many children
about whom he got no information from the parents, but he listed
them in a last attempt to secure their rights.[24] Still, he knew that
some would be left out.

After the deadline for filing applications had passed, he faced
the task of verifying them. That meant covering the same territory
still again, obtaining two affidavits certifying the birth and parent-
age of each child. Once more Alex had trouble determining an-

cestry because of the polygamous practice of many of the Snakes.

He sometimes learned that a child existed but could not learn its
name, so he acted as "godfather" and gave it a name like Osceola
or Sappho. Sometimes witnesses were less than reliable. One Creek
freedwoman recorded the birth of the children in the neighborhood
by drawing a line through the date in her almanac to refresh her
memory. But alas, said Alex, "if anything else happens she does the
same thing." [25]

There were no signs that the Snakes were wavering in their resistance to the Dawes Commission's work. They had retained an
attorney in Washington who, in summer 1905, claimed to be preparing a bill for the restoration of the old tribal government. In the
Snake settlements throughout the Creek Nation, Alex saw their cooperative farms. Ten to fifteen men worked each little patch of cotton
to raise money for the legal fight against the government. [26]

Their arguments remained the same. In May 1906 Artus Hotiye
told Alex, echoing Chitto Harjo's words of the previous fall, "You
crossed the Wewoka creek this morning. It is spring and the water
runs; you see the green grass on the prairies; the grass still grows.
Our people have agreed that so long as water runs and grass grows
we shall not have our lands divided nor our government supplanted."
He refused to supply the information Alex sought about his daughter,
who was deceased; she was in the graveyard, the only allotment
she deserved, the only allotment God intended for him as well. The
Snake concluded his statement as follows: "The Great Father placed
the Pacific on one side and the Atlantic on the other, and the land
between he gave to the Indian. The white man came and he set corner stones and told the Indian that he must live between these. The
Indian cannot live so. He is being stifled by the white man, who has
disarmed him of his bow and arrow and driven him from the forests and game. The end of the Indian is near, but I am not ready to
contribute to hastening it." [27]

Thus Alex had to be innovative in obtaining evidence. Quite by
accident he and Skaggs came upon a "stomp dance" one night at the
home of Jim Bird near Weleetka. Skaggs felt out of place because
he was the only white person there, but Alex felt at home, especially
at the tables set with sofky, sour bread, apusky, blue dumplings,
and pounded dry beef. He succeeded in getting testimony from a
number of those present. At another dance he joined in playing

seven-up. All the money had been gambled away, and the players were betting chewing tobacco, hats, and other articles. Alex lost all the tobacco he had, but he got some information he sought. Near Senora, he found several of John Baker's neighbors plowing crops for Baker, who was ill, and took testimony from them in the field. At Ben Deere's place west of Eufaula, he approached the women who were in the field planting a crop, and he had succeeded in getting testimony about one child when Deere came and put a stop to the interview. Alex followed other witnesses into the woods where they were hunting squirrels. He caught people on street corners or at their washboards. He even took testimony from an informant who was sitting on his horse.[28]

The search for "lost" Creeks kept Alex in close personal contact with many of his conservative fellow Creeks for two and a half years and brought him a deeper understanding of a Creek culture that was disappearing, but perhaps not as rapidly as he had thought. As a young adult reminiscing about his childhood, he had claimed knowledge of traditional figures such as Chalogee and the Alabama Prophet. Though perhaps embellished or magnified by the romantic screen they were filtered through, those memories had represented his childhood as an idyllic time in Creek society, now long past. In the intervening years—during his school days, his tenure as an educator, his experiment in "farming" at Stidham, and his editorship—his main associations had been with the educated or farming, ranching, and business classes of Creeks.

During those years, however, especially during his first editorship, he had made some important and lasting friendships that contributed significantly to his knowledge of the old-time Creeks. His newspaper office had been a channel for information on Creek history, language, and lore. The men he associated with then and later— Gibson, Grayson, Porter, all men of his father's age—were knowledgeable in those subjects, and all served at one time or another as linguistic and ethnohistorical informants for fieldworkers of the Bureau of American Ethnology. From Gibson he learned about such matters as the revered copper plates, the legendary history of the Spokogees, old-time Creek buffalo hunts, and the economic life of thirty-five years before. Hardly an aged Creek who visited Eufaula left without an interview with Alex. Cussetah Yohola gave him his history of the Green Peach War, and Capeche Emarthla told him

about the old times before removal. Alex had interviewed Chitto
Harjo and his Snake followers at every opportunity. And he had frequently visited with Jackson Lewis, also an informant for the Bureau
of American Ethnology, described by Alex as "a capital humorist
and story teller."[29]

Now, in the field for the Dawes Commission, his understanding became fuller as he saw the deep-rooted strength of a culture that he, Gibson, and others had tended to write off as belonging to the bygone days of Creek society. At Council Hill, for instance, he drank from the spring "where members of the first Creek council quenched their burning thirsts" before the council was moved to Okmulgee. It was on the allotment of Temiye Kernels, who claimed its waters had curative properties. From abandoned and decaying log huts he retrieved rare specimens of pottery that the Creeks no longer made. Near Hickory Ground he found a sofky jar thought to be over a hundred years old, the abandoned property of Tustenuggee Thlocco, grandfather of Mele Thlocco of Hickory Ground. He kept some of the relics for his own collection and gave others to Tams Bixby and other Dawes Commission workers. Near Okemah, from an old Koa-sati woman, Alex and Skaggs bought a number of unusual baskets made of dogwood and naturally dyed.[30]

There was also less tangible evidence of lingering lifeways. Alex saw ancient town rivalries flare into modern violence in a ball game between the Arbekas and the Eufaulas, who met on the open prairie halfway between their town squares in early fall 1905. In the ball play, the ancient towns were divided into two divisions, the Spoko-gees and the Chief Towns, each side always referring to the other as "a person that always opposes him in playing ball." Eufaula was a Spokogee and Arbeka a Chief Town, and some 2,500 spectators watched what Alex called "perhaps the bloodiest game ever pulled off in Indian Territory." Betting was heavy, men and women stak-ing their valuables and articles of clothing. Only one ball was tossed up, and in the ensuing melee not one of the thirty-two players on each side escaped injury. One was shot or stabbed and seriously wounded. Peace officers fired pistols into the air in a vain attempt to stop the brawl. Alex also visited the homes of old Creeks like Yadeka Harjo, the blind medicine man at Hickory Ground, who had made the removal trek from Alabama nearly seventy years earlier. He smoked with the old man, heard his songs, and listened to his advice. The pipe they smoked was the famous tomahawk pipe that Yadeka Harjo's father had received after the battle of Horseshoe Bend, and he loved to smoke it and talk of the past. As he would tell his friends later, "he had passed through many days." Near Morris, Alex saw the huge, elaborate grave houses that Cinda had erected for her relatives, and near Wetumka, at the abandoned cabin of Joe Larney, a new grave and a more modest house with a bundle of clothes in it.[31]

Alex admired the creative energy of Cinda and other conservative Creeks. West of Henryetta he found the thirteen-year-old son of Little Fish, who had fashioned a fiddle from a long-necked gourd he had hollowed out. He had stretched a dried squirrel skin over the cavity and strung the instrument with threads of various thicknesses. Alex loved fiddle music and delighted in the boy's renditions of "Sugar in the Gourd," "Sally Johnston," "Billie in the Low Ground," "Gray Eagle," "Walk Along, John," and "The Devil's Dream."[32]

In all, he had gained a new perspective on the more conservative members of the Creek Nation. He had listened to the reasoned arguments of the old men like Chitto Harjo, Yadeka Harjo, Hotgun, and Chofolop Harjo. He was struck by the beauty and power of elderly Creek women like Fahnee, whose advice the men listened to and who had helped shape Snake policy for years; or the old Koasati basket maker; or the independent Cinda, who had built the striking grave houses with her own hands; or Toche, "who was reputed to be the best dancer and the handsomest woman ever known among the Alabamas." And Alex's heart was touched by the poverty and disease that wracked the present generation of Snakes. He recorded striking vignettes in his journal: an ill three-year-old girl, barefoot and "thinly dressed," falling asleep outside the cabin on a March day, or a young man, dying of consumption, lying in a tent in the yard because there was no room for him in the small cabin.[33]

Alex's journal entries have the tone of new insight or discovery, reflecting his growing concern for the gulf that existed between him, as a Creek, and them. As he read over his journal notes, he must have recognized the ample evidence that the Snakes viewed him— this educated young man, dressed in his white shirt and tie, who sought them out in their remote cabins—as different from them both racially and socially: John Kelly's reference to "real" Indians, Artus Hotiye's and Chitto Harjo's lectures on growing grass and flowing

water, and Chitto Harjo's failure to extend hospitality. Alex's journal account of his and Skaggs's interview with Chitto Harjo does
not reflect confrontation, but shortly after the event, Alex told Hall
that the Snake leader had read him the "riot act." Decades later,
when he recalled what Alex had told him, Hall could not vouch for
the exact language, but he was sure about the sentiment expressed:
Chitto Harjo called Alex a traitor who had tricked him into testi-
fying at Okmulgee the year before. Alex had seduced him with the
Creek tongue of his mother and betrayed him with the lying tongue
of his white father. He told Alex to leave, that he did not want to see
him again.[34]

The arguments that Chitto Harjo and the other conservatives
made to Alex did not represent a mindless resistance to the inevitable. Nor were they based in an emotional and cultural attachment
to the lands of their fathers, which lay east of the Mississippi. Instead, the arguments were basically legalistic, an insistence on rights
guaranteed by treaty. The Snakes had not acceded to the abrogation
of the Treaty of 1832 and insisted on the restoration of its provisions.
The matter seemed clear to them, and they had chosen to insist on
their rights. Alex recognized the futility of their stand and foresaw
its consequences. As a Creek, he too had made his choice: to bow to
the inevitable and make the best of a bad bargain. But he was now
more understanding of their position and more sympathetic about
their plight. His earlier defense of Creek readiness for statehood and
American citizenship had to be revised.

Part of this sympathy sprang from new perspectives on the economic development of the countryside, which was hailed throughout
the territory as "progress." The quiet persistence of the majority of
Snakes contrasted sharply with the rapid changes occurring outside
their communities. The Snake settlements were like Irving's Sleepy
Hollow—small eddies where the bubbles rode quietly on the surface while the swift current rushed by. In his search for the "lost"
Creeks, Alex had everywhere seen evidence of the negative effects of
economic development: the ragweed where the prairie sod had been
broken; the frame shacks with siderooms that renters had put up on
Indian allotments; the riffraff that came into the Creek Nation and
congregated in the new towns, looking for opportunities to make
their fortunes.[35] These towns, which as editor of the *Indian Journal*
he had hailed as evidence of progress, had a cheap, flimsy, unsub-

stantial look. Most had started as speculative ventures and would never thrive.

As time ran out on Alex's work, the Snakes' lack of preparation for the changes facing the conservative Creeks sank in. He worked steadily until March 4, 1906, when the tribal government was to cease. Alex now saw that as an event "fraught with grave consequences for the poor Indian unaccustomed to the requirements of a civilization so unlike his own, though it bring great and many blessings to those who are ready to receive them." It was "a deeply pathetic story" to him: "Yet who cares or pities? Not the press, catering to public sentiment. Not the politician expecting future honors. Not the president, not congress pursuing the lines of political expediency. 'Lo, the poor Indian!' Prophetic words indeed!"[36] Alex was convinced that the condition of the conservatives resulted in part from a lack of clear communication by the Creek government. The National Council had considered establishing a national newspaper in 1904 to keep them informed on rulings by the secretary of the interior, and it was rumored that Alex was to be its editor. By fall 1905 Alex was convinced that failing to publish a newspaper had been a mistake: "What a pity that there is no newspaper published in the Creek language for the benefit of the fullbloods! The lack of such a paper has been the cause of all the misunderstanding between government and ward."[37]

On April 26, 1906, Congress once more opened the Creek rolls to minor children of enrolled parents living on March 4. Tams Bixby appointed Alex to take applications, so he entered the field again on behalf of the Snakes, this time with James B. Myers as his stenographer. When the rolls were closed on July 25, he still believed there were children he had not found, though it was generally believed that he had succeeded in gathering more information about the Snakes than anyone else could have gotten.[38]

Considering the gulf between him and the conservative Creeks, why had Alex been so successful in this work? Despite the Snakes' steadfast refusal to cooperate with the Dawes Commission, how had he been able to find some who were willing to give him the information he sought? Certainly his fluency in Creek and his extensive knowledge of traditional etiquette and protocol were important. He knew how to listen patiently to his elders and to endure their scoldings, such as Chitto Harjo had given him. He knew what his duty was when Yadeka Harjo asked him to light his pipe "according to the

old fashion." Of importance also were Alex's town and clan. Tuskegee was a white or peace town; political power had shifted after the
Civil War from the red or war towns to the white towns. The Wind
Clan was one from which leaders were traditionally drawn, and it
was also a white clan.[39] Thus his clan and town commanded respect
and gave him entry into the most conservative communities. Alex
had undertaken his work with the best intentions: to prevent the
Snakes from being excluded from their share of the tribal assets.
Ironically, in doing so he appeared to some to have betrayed them.

The work had been time consuming, leaving him little freedom
for literary work. By the time the rolls closed to applications in July
1906, he had been in the field for over a year and a half. He had read
a little from current periodicals when he could find time on the road,
in hotel rooms during lulls in his work, or on weekends at Muskogee. In fall 1905 he had read extensively in Thoreau's journals. But
he had written very little. In March 1905 he published a series of
four letters from the field to Henry Hains, editor of the *Muskogee
Democrat*. These were a curious mixture of descriptions of nature,
humorous anecdotes, and satire against emerging towns like Paden,
Dustin, and Hanna. During 1905 and 1906 he published fewer than
twenty Fus Fixico letters, which had to do with political events in
the territory. By early 1906 he was also reported to be writing a
series of Creek fables and legends. But none of these seem to have
been published immediately, though he would continue to work at
that project over the ensuing months. In 1906 he also promised to
keep the press up to date on his travels through a series of sketches
called "Woods Notes," but they apparently were not written. Despite his small output, he still received some literary notice. A long
article about him appeared in the St. Louis *Globe-Democrat*, and
he received substantial treatment in an article in *Sturm's Oklahoma
Magazine*.[40]

But Alex was no longer the youth who, a decade earlier, had worshiped at the shrine of literary art. His work for the Dawes Commission had taken its toll on his creative energies, and he had seen more
clearly the harsh social realities of the closing days of the Creek
Nation. He faced the advent of statehood a changed man. As his
appreciation of the conservatives increased, his enthusiasm for what
he had called "marvelous progress" nevertheless had not become so

jaded that he was willing to slow it down. While he certainly looked back on the old days with nostalgia, he would not have argued for a return to them. While he understood more clearly how tragic the future was likely to be for the conservatives, he realized that history would not wait for them.

*The Posey home in Muskogee, 1905, with Yohola and Wynema in the yard.
Archives and Manuscripts Division of the Oklahoma Historical Society.*

Alex Posey in 1905, lighting Yadeka Harjo's pipe. Archives and Manuscripts Division of the Oklahoma Historical Society.

Chapter **9** Death of the Creek Nation

· ·

In early March 1906 Charles N. Haskell, who
was destined to become first governor of the state of Oklahoma, sent
Alex the first issue of the *New-State Tribune*, containing one of Alex's
Fus Fixico letters. Haskell was an Ohio attorney turned construction
magnate who had come to Muskogee in 1901. Since then he had
built, among other things, the Ozark and Cherokee Central Railroad, the Midland Valley Railroad, the Muskogee Union Railroad,
the Indianola Building, the Turner Hotel, and the Hinton Theatre.
He had developed grand schemes for navigation of the Arkansas
River and for damming the Grand to generate power for Muskogee.[1]
He was perhaps the most important figure at the Sequoyah constitutional convention in summer 1905, and in early 1906 he had great
political ambitions.

Haskell had established the newspaper as a mouthpiece for his
political views during the continuing debates concerning statehood.
He hoped to use Alex's pen to achieve his political goals. He thanked
Alex for the letter, asked for another, and said, "Remember that we
consider the Fus Fixico letter of more importance at this time than

getting full blood testimony." But at the moment Alex would not have agreed. The separate statehood movement had reached its peak with the Sequoyah convention in 1905, and though the statehood issue was still before Congress in early 1906, hope for a separate Indian-controlled state was dying, and with it, part of Alex's enthusiasm for statehood. Although he would be mentioned in 1906 as a potential candidate for Congress from the proposed new state, he also had lost much of his taste for politics.[2] He would make occasional commentary through the Fus Fixico letters, but his main concern in the months ahead was the fieldwork that remained regarding the Creek rolls. After that his ambitions would take him in directions that were in some ways surprising and, no doubt, troubling to those who knew him.

Alex had been a late convert to the separate statehood movement with its goal of an Indian-controlled state, a possibility that for years had captured the imagination of Indian leaders. After spring 1903 it captured his too and held it for a time. From the separate statehood convention in Eufaula in 1903 until summer 1905, Alex worked only sporadically for the realization of a separate state. In summer 1903 Pleasant Porter appointed him Creek representative to the Executive Committee for Independent Statehood of the Five Civilized Tribes. Other members were W. Henry Ansley of the Choctaw Nation, William H. Murray of the Chickasaw Nation, A. J. Brown of the Seminole Nation, and William Connell Rogers of the Cherokee Nation. Their task was to coordinate efforts toward separate statehood and to prepare for the convening of a constitutional convention.[3]

Alex served as treasurer of the executive committee, which set about drafting press releases and memorials that went to temperance and religious publications as well as to Congress. It attempted to rally the Women's Christian Temperance Union to the cause. But the committee was hampered by a lack of funds: only the Choctaws appropriated the full amount that the committee assessed the tribes. The Eufaula convention had recommended a convention date no later than February 1904. Despite the committee's work through fall 1903, no convention was called, and only the Choctaws called for a vote on holding one. By early 1904 Ansley concluded that the plan for a convention had failed because of inaction by the Indians themselves. The Choctaws had done their part "nobly," he said. The

Creeks had carried out the plans only partly, the Seminoles somewhat less, and the Cherokees and Chickasaws not at all. He warned
McCurtain that to call a convention would expose him to criticism by
single state newspapers because response to the call would likely be
poor. Interest in the separate statehood movement continued to flag
until fall 1904, when the issue was revived in the various national
councils.[4] During 1904 Alex's anti-Oklahoma feeling was apparent
in the Fus Fixico letters, but even for him separate statehood was
not a theme of first importance. However, six of the seven letters
published in 1905 addressed the issue in one fashion or another.

The first letter concerned practical matters rather than geographi-
cal or cultural differences between the two territories or the question of Indian autonomy. Hotgun began the year by predicting that
some congressional action would be forthcoming in 1905. Watching would-be office seekers maneuver to be in position when the
time came to campaign made him "homesick for old times." Since
the inevitable could not be ignored, he asked the practical question
of who would pay taxes in the new state, then answered it himself:
" 'The Injin couldn't 'cause the Big Man at Washington he say the
Injin didn't had enough sense to know what he was doing. The white
renter couldn't 'cause he didn't had nuthing but a mule blind in one
eye and a lot a children all about the same size to raise a mortgage
on. And the business man in town couldn't 'cause he was had to vote
bonds for Abe Lincoln school houses and George Washington parks
and things like that 'sides going down in his jeans for money to fight
tribal taxes with.' " Perhaps the Indian Territory was in too much of
a rush for statehood because the people did not know a good thing
when they had it: " 'The Government was looked after us and paid
all the bills now and all we had to do was to lay in the shade and
drink sofky and set on the jury. The government was appropriate
money for our children to go to school on when they wasn't picking
cotton. It was had deputy marshals to capture whisky peddlers and
judges to carry out Arkansas laws and take cases under advisement
for twelve months and maybe so longer than that. So what more we
want?' "[5]

Despite Congress's failure to act on their previous appeals and
memorials, the Indian leaders made one last brilliant effort to demonstrate not only their desire for single statehood but their ability
to manage political affairs. Chiefs McCurtain, Rogers, Porter, and

Brown decided to proceed with the plans for a constitutional convention that had languished since 1903. Chief Douglas H. Johnston
of the Chickasaws refused to cooperate. Having realized long before
that they could not achieve their goal without the cooperation of the
whites in the territory, the chiefs called on a number of influential
men for assistance, including William H. Murray, a Texan who had
married a Chickasaw and was close to Governor Johnston. Following a call issued in July, local conventions chose delegates to meet
at a constitutional convention in Muskogee on August 21.

Alex lent his own voice as well as that of Fus Fixico to help ensure that the convention would be a success. He did not expect to
be a candidate for delegate himself because his official duties as a
fieldworker for the Dawes Commission would prevent him from attending. He called for the election of the best men to the convention:
"It should be a deliberative, conservative body of men chosen for
their especial fitness for the important work in hand." He endorsed
J. Blair Shoenfelt, whom he had called J. Bear Sho'amfat in the Fus
Fixico letters, as delegate from the tenth recording district, which included Muskogee.[6] In the Fus Fixico letters, Hotgun and Tookpafka
Micco weighed the possibilities of the convention's success. Of the
defection by the Chickasaws, who had never figured prominently in
the separate statehood movement, Hotgun observed that Johnston
was beset by problems at home, including a fiscal scandal for which
he would soon be answering to a grand jury. " 'But all the same the
Chickasaw nation be represented,' " Hotgun said. " 'One swallow
don't make a summer.' " In the Indian Territory, single staters were
" 'getting as scarce as bald headed Injins,' " he said. " 'No one was
opposed to the move to have statehood separated from Oklahoma
but railroad lawyers and well-meaning but misguided country editors and cornfield statesmen with beehives in they hats.' " He sized
up the attitude of single staters in Oklahoma Territory, who had
convened earlier in the summer, as follows: " 'Well so the nigger
preacher bow his head and say, "O Lord, we was mighty thankful for
this feast. Please pass the possum." Same way Oklahoma was pray
to Congress, saying, "We was mighty thankful for statehood. Please
pass the Injin Territory." ' "[7]

On the eve of the Muskogee convention, Hotgun and his friends
gave the convention one last boost. Hotgun had not been elected a
delegate, but he offered the meeting his moral support: " 'Maybe so

the Injin Territory wouldn't make a big state by itself like Texas, but

you could put Rhode Island down in it twenty-five times and had
room left for the floating population of Arkansas.' "[8] When Tookpafka Micco asked him if the Indians were ready for statehood, Hotgun replied, " 'Good and ready. We was ready for the Government
to keep its promise and fence us off to ourselves. We was give up
all our bad habits, like wearing breech clouts and feathers on the
head. We wear hand-me-downs now all the time and live in box
shacks with a side room to it instead of log huts daubed with mud.
We was give up the simple life, and buy fine buggies and lightning
rods and calendar clocks and had our forefathers' pictures enlarged
and be civilized citizens instead common fullblood Injins. So we was
ready for statehood.' " As to what name the convention delegates
would give the new state, he said, " 'Well, so some say call it Terra-
india, the land of the Red Man; but maybe so they better name it
Ta-ra-boom-de-ay, the land of the boomer.' "[9]

Although the Indian leaders had encouraged participation in the
convention by non-Indian citizens of the territory, the latter in general took little interest in the proceedings. The convention was, on
the surface at least, an Indian affair. Pleasant Porter was elected
president, and each tribe was represented by a vice president, including Rogers of the Cherokees, Brown of the Seminoles, and
McCurtain of the Choctaws. The Chickasaws were represented by
William H. Murray. The Creek Nation was represented by Haskell,
who claimed to have underwritten much of the cost of the convention. Alex, who had not been chosen as one of the 167 delegates,
was nevertheless elected secretary. Proceedings were conducted in
English and in tribal languages, and four-fifths of the committee
charged with drafting the constitution were Indians.[10]

Alex recognized the propaganda value of the convention. Indian
leaders had sought separate statehood, in part, because they feared
political domination by Oklahoma if the two territories merged. Besides being an earnest attempt to achieve their goal, the convention
was also an opportunity to demonstrate that they had the political
know-how to address constitutional matters and conduct the affairs
of state. While the convention was in session, Alex underscored the
momentousness of the occasion in a letter from Fus Fixico. Hotgun
said of the Indian, " 'Long time ago he give a war whoop and go on
the warpath; this time he call a convention and go on record. Instead

a making medicine he make history; instead of chasing the pioneers with a tomahawk, he preside in convention and use the tomahawk for a gavel and call the pioneers to order; and instead a swearing vengeance against the pale face, he get up and make a big talk on how to make a state. The Injin is civilized and aint extinct no more than a rabbit. He's just beginning to feel his breakfast food.'" Hotgun continued, "'Well, so somebody was had to take the lead for separate statehood, and the Injin say "might as well be me." So he report for duty first and was immortalized himself. He wait put near a hundred years and opportunity didn't find him asleep in the wigwam. He was watch faithful at his post and make good when the time came.'" Finally, Hotgun said, "'The Injin was kicked out a his swaddling clothes a red tape and was ready to follow the flag and constitution without Oklahoma to give him encouragement with stimulants. The United States was bound by treaty and Christian duty to back the Injin up in the struggle for his rights.'"[11]

The convention, which had adjourned for two weeks while the drafting committee did its work, reconvened on September 5 to consider adoption of the Constitution of the State of Sequoyah. It was basically a populist document of some 35,000 words, containing a bill of rights consisting of thirty-one articles and reflecting a distrust of the legislative branch of government by, among other things, inserting detailed provisions that should more properly have been left for the state legislature to enact as laws.[12] Murray and Haskell played prominent roles in drafting the constitution and later took much credit for the document's final form. The credit was probably not undeserved, especially on Haskell's part. It was his motion that determined the timetable for the convention and the way votes were taken. He led the convention fight to name the state. As vice president of the convention, he was an ex officio member of committees. Haskell had such power, he claimed, because Porter needed his help. He had met with Porter, the chiefs of the Cherokees and Seminoles, and Murray, who represented the Chickasaws, in a Muskogee hotel and had promised to help them if they would agree to give up the separate statehood idea if the convention failed. They had agreed, he said, in writing.[13]

Although Murray later described Alex as a "very efficient" secretary, the role, if any, he played in drafting the constitution is uncertain, for he was in the field for the Dawes Commission during most of the time the drafting committee was at work as well as when the convention reconvened to vote on adoption. Because he was not an elected delegate, he served on none of the committees, nor was he on the committee assigned to redraft the constitution, a process Haskell directed.[14]

Though Alex is credited with the clarity and conciseness of the document's style, there is no manuscript evidence to support the claim. It might well be, however, that stylistic revision was his only role in the convention. It had been his tendency since he left politics to place some medium, such as the editorial column or the persona of Fus Fixico, between himself and the public at large.

The roster of vice presidents is significant. Those for the Cherokees, Chickasaws, and Seminoles were their former representatives on the executive committee created by the Eufaula convention in 1903. McCurtain of the Choctaws replaced Ansley, who had committed suicide earlier that year. Instead of Alex, who had served on the committee, the Creeks were represented by Haskell. Alex had attended the local convention that met in Muskogee in early August to elect delegates to the convention. Haskell, whom Porter had appointed as chairman of Muskogee's recording district, conducted the meeting, and the process of delegate selection looked cut and dried to the local press. Alex was called on to make a speech, but he refused "with the laconic observation of 'Wolf Warrior' that he would rather sit back listening and spit in the ashes than talk." [15] Alex was not among the delegates selected. Was Haskell elected delegate and later vice president because Porter had made overtures for his support, as Haskell later claimed, or had Alex simply bowed out of the spotlight once more? He had said from the start that his duties in the field would prevent his being a candidate, and once the convention began he kept away from the public sessions of the convention.

Although he was not active in shaping the constitution, Alex was accutely aware of the political motives that would be at work. Even before the election of delegates, Alex had recognized that large attendance would be ensured because the convention would take up such matters as senatorial and legislative districts and county boundaries in the proposed state. Being chosen county seat meant economic security for a town. Delegates would be on hand to influence county lines so as to give their own towns the best advantage with the least competition when county seats were determined. Hotgun said, " 'It was this way: If Okmulgee didn't want the county seat, Henryetta was take it off her hand like a duck catching a June bug; if Wagoner did not seek after a county seat Coweta was willing to relieve her a the burden; if South McAlester was indifferent, Haileyville was got busy; and if Eufaula didn't had her boundary lines on straight, maybe so Dustin was profit by it.' " [16] Alex was right. During the drafting of the constitution, Murray and Haskell used county seat location to cajole, persuade, or intimidate delegates to follow their lead in constitutional issues.[17]

The location of county seats was also important in the campaign for ratification of the constitution. Haskell and others made it prominent to stir interest and bring people to the polls. In a Fus Fixico letter that appeared a few days before the vote, Hotgun said that on November 7 " 'the Injins an' niggers an' white element could exercise they great American privilege an' pile up a staggerin' majority for separate state hood,' " after which " 'all Injins be constituents instead a wards a the big man at Washington.' " Tookpafka Micco had heard much talk about county seats and, uncertain, asked Hotgun what a county seat was. Hotgun described it as " 'kin' of a busk ground, only it was more assumin'.' " Every little hamlet wanted one, but there was a problem: " 'They was only forty-eight counties in the state of Sequoyah, but looks like they wasn't enough to go roun' an' they was heap a squabblin' between railroad flag stations an' star route postoffices an' back district neighborhoods.' " Hotgun and Tookpafka Micco believed the creation of the state of Sequoyah was possible. Hotgun found it hard to tell what Congress would do, but he believed that the " 'separate statehood prospects right now look so flatterin' they was a big howl goin' up over in the Short Grass country.' " And Tookpafka Micco said, " 'Well, so the language a the treaty was plain an' the honor a the United States was staked on it. So I vote for Sequoyah an' the nearest postoffice for county seat when the time come.' " [18]

The ratification vote said much about the sentiment of the general population concerning separate statehood. Although Hotgun had said that only a few " 'misguided county editors and cornfield statesmen' " opposed separate statehood, the opposition was much broader than that. There had indeed been much press opposition. In atypical fashion, Alex had taken some editors to task in a Fus Fixico letter, calling them by their real names rather than making some humorous

play on them as he usually did.[19] He had addressed the opposition in
another by having Hotgun say, " 'You could call the movement for
separate statehood bosh, or fiasco, or sentiment, and names like that
if you want to, but I was call it a declaration of independence that
was had its foundation on every hearthstone in Injin Territory.' "[20]
But sentiment was not that pervasive. Just before the ratification
vote, the Creek National Council passed a resolution stating that the
Sequoyah convention had not represented the Indians of the Creek
Nation.[21] When the votes were counted, the constitution was ratified
overwhelmingly, but fewer than half of the eligible voters went to
the polls, reflecting a general lack of enthusiasm for a separate state.

Despite its promise, the Sequoyah movement was doomed. That
winter, copies of the constitution were presented with a memorial
asking for admission of the state. The Sequoyah convention had
named a large committee to go to Washington for that purpose
and to lobby for the appeal. Once again Alex was not among the
group, though his signature as secretary appeared on the copy of the
constitution. Congress took no action on the appeal. In December,
President Roosevelt recommended admitting the two territories as a
single state. By early 1906 it was clear that the sentiment in Congress
was in favor of one state.[22] Politicians in the Indian Territory began
to work for the best possible deal for the territory when the merger
occurred, thus enhancing their chances of entering public office. It
was for these reasons that Haskell began publishing the *New-State
Tribune*, in which he expanded on provisions that the new state's
constitution, whenever it was written, should contain. Haskell called
on Alex for help. Alex, however, was not as enthusiastic about the
prospects of statehood as in earlier times, perhaps because by March
1906 he had traveled a year and a half among the poorer classes of
Creek citizens. Throughout spring 1906 he published only four Fus
Fixico letters in Haskell's newspaper.

Though the Indian governments were due to expire on March 4,
1906, it was evident that many affairs of the nations were not settled,
including the completion of the tribal rolls. Thus on March 2 Congress extended the tribal governments until the allotment process
was completed and the tribal assets were disbursed. Alex's first Fus
Fixico letter to the *New-State Tribune* was a response to this act.
In Hotgun's words, " 'Congress was take the extinction o' the Injin
under advisement an' order Secretary Its Cocked to fan the council

fire until further notice.' "[23] Fus Fixico reported that when Took-pafka Micco learned of the extension, he said, " 'Well, so then I go to lots o' trouble an' expense for nothin', gettin' ready to take up the white man's burden an' walk off with it.' " He had told his wife to stop gathering wild onions in the creek bottoms and attend the women's literary club to gather gossip, to stop pounding corn in her mortar and subscribe to the *Ladies' Home Journal,* and to hire a Creek freedman driver and go shopping in a fancy buggy. He had asked the Indian agent to remove the restrictions from his land so he could sell it and buy some tailor-made clothes. Then he had gone among the politicians and " 'help build a machine to swing the full blood vote when the time come.' " Hotgun responded, " 'Well, so you better countermand your orders an' stick to your sofky patch an' die a nat'ral death with the rest o' the Injins.' "[24]

The remaining three letters Alex published in Haskell's paper focused on the statehood debate in Congress during spring 1906. By mid-March, separate statehood was out of the question. As Hotgun said, " 'So it didn't take a first-class prophet to prophesy 'bout state-hood, an' you didn't had to put on your specs to see which way the wind was blowin' the straw.' "[25] In fact, political sentiment in Washington was mounting so steadily in favor of joint statehood that it appeared Congress might at last pass a statehood bill. Speaker of the House Joseph Cannon and other Republicans feared the strength of the Indian Territory Democrats in the new state's politics and sought to bolster the position of Republican Oklahoma Territory by asserting that it should take the lead in the statehood process because it had a territorial government already in place.

Alex, of course, knew how capable the people of the Indian Territory were of governing themselves. When senators praised the Oklahoma pioneers, especially the women, who they claimed had brought civilization to the wilderness, Hotgun said, " 'The injin was the only bona fide pioneer in this country, an' the Injin squaw was the woman that furnish the magic an' help overcome the wild animals an' carry civilization into the waste places with her sofky pestle an' mortar.' " Tookpafka Micco's response was "Well, so the Lord helps 'em that help 'emselves—except the Injin.' "[26] Would-be politicians from the Indian Territory were eager for statehood and instigated a campaign of telegrams to Congress in support of a bill, signing their messages as postmasters, lawyers, businessmen, edi-

tors, or vox populi, to give strength to their pleas. Hotgun believed
they all had ulterior motives: "The postmaster he want to keep on cancellin' stamps an' puttin' your mail in somebody else's box; the lawyer he want no end o' law suits over cloudy titles an' a chance to take the stump for office; the business man he want to exploit the Injin an' escape the tribal tax; the editor he want the county printin' an' anything else he could lay hands on.'" Tookpafka Micco said that the "common" Indians and white renters were not consulted about statehood, to which Hotgun replied, " 'Well, so, the common run o' Injins an' white people was more anxious for a good crop an' liftin' the mortgage off the ol' dun mule than a constitutional convention anyhow.' "[27] As the congressional debate wore on, Hotgun compared Oklahoma and Indian Territory to Chuffee the rabbit a "long time ago," when " 'all the animals was had a big powwow to settle the food question.' " When each animal was given a choice of foods, Chuffee chose the balls on the sycamore trees. He sat under the tree, waiting for the balls to ripen and fall, and nearly starved to death while he watched them dry up and blow away.[28]

The result of the congressional debate throughout spring 1906 was the Enabling Act, approved on June 16, that provided for the establishment of a single state from the two territories. Voters were to elect 112 delegates, 55 from each territory and 2 from the Osage Nation, to meet and draft a constitution, which was to be submitted to a vote of the people of the territories before admission to the Union could occur. Campaigning began for the election of delegates, to take place on November 6. At first Hotgun warned the Indians to remain neutral: " 'He don't want to be Democrat or Republican. Maybe so 'is hair was long enough for a Populist, but he better not. If he takes sides he won't 'mount to nothin' an' couldn't be dog pelter.' "[29] Tookpafka Micco readily admitted that he was a Democrat, but he refused, he said, to vote for a yellow dog just because it was yellow. Alex predicted political apathy among the Indians because they tended to view politics as "white man's business." However, he also predicted that those Indians who voted would overwhelmingly support the Democrats because Indians thought democratically and because the Democrats had made the effort to print campaign literature in the Indian languages.[30] An example was a booklet titled *Prominent Indians' Views of the Political Parties of the Day*, issued by the Oklahoma Democratic Committee. It contained statements by Choctaws Green McCurtain and D. C. McCurtain, Chickasaws L. L. Byrd and Charles D. Carter, Creek Pleasant Porter, and others. Selected sections of the booklet were translated for the Choctaws and Chickasaws. All laid out the evils of republicanism and espoused the virtues of democracy. When the votes were counted, 99 of the 112 delegates to the constitutional convention were Democrats, but only 10 of them were of Indian descent. The convention met at Guthrie, Oklahoma, on November 20 and began its work, which would take almost nine months to complete.

Throughout the months leading to the convention, Alex had continued his work on the Creek rolls. His task was to clear from the books those applications that had been filed within the prescribed time but had not been approved or rejected because the applicants had not filed sufficient evidence, because they had changed their names, or because their whereabouts were unknown. He spent fall 1906 in the field with his stenographer, James B. Myers. They traveled the Creek Nation as he and Skaggs had done throughout 1905 and early 1906. They even went west to Fort Cobb in search of the family of James H. Deer, who had gone to the Wichita Reservation shortly after the Civil War. Deer had joined the Wichitas and had taken an allotment with them, and he refused to return to the Creeks.[31]

Alex himself exhibited the political apathy he had predicted among the Indians in general. The public heard little from him regarding political issues after the series of Fus Fixico letters he wrote for Haskell in March. He had not published another letter until after the Enabling Act, and then there were no more until after the election for constitutional convention delegates. His letters reflect a growing suspicion of machine politics, especially after the failure of the Sequoyah movement. Part of this suspicion resulted, no doubt, from the Democrats' growing criticism of big business and big—especially Republican—government. Since the Fus Fixico letters of 1903, Alex had pointed out the connections between grafters and would-be Republican politicians and railroad interests. By 1906, however, the statements were more direct. In a March letter, Hotgun said, " 'They was n't any difference 'tween nineteen-ought-six, A. D. an' nineteen-ought-six, B.C., only Pharoah rode in a chariot an' Roosevelt busts the bronco; an' 'stead o' the pyramids, we got the Panama canal project; an' 'stead o' tyrants like Nero, we got phi-

lanthropists like John D. Rockyfeller; an' 'stead o' Solomon, we got
Senator Smoot; an' 'stead o' the Parthenon, we got Tammany Hall;
an' 'stead o' the Golden Age o' Pericles, we got the era o' the Big
Stick, an' life insurance graft, an' coal strikes, an' railroad rebates,
an' machine politics.' "[32]

There was more than party politics involved in his criticism. He
had witnessed the birth of Democratic machine politics in Oklahoma
in the tactics of Haskell and Murray at the Sequoyah convention.
Despite the public praise of the convention as a political achievement
by the Indians, the fact remained that in its final form the constitution was in large measure the work of those two white men. Haskell
had offered Alex a place in his machine when he invited him to
publish the Fus Fixico letters in his newspaper, but when it became
apparent that separate statehood was not possible, Alex severed the
relationship and submitted nothing to the *Tribune* after March.

By then Alex was apparently convinced that the Indians were incapable of coping with machine politics and would ultimately be
excluded from the political process. In the wake of the Enabling Act,
Hotgun summed up the state of affairs this way: " 'Well, so before
statehood they was too much sentiment mixed up in the Injin problem. The missionary he tell the Injin he must lay up treasures in
heaven, but he didn't show 'im how to keep body an' soul together
on earth an' lay by for the rainy day; an' the school teacher he learn
'im how to read an' shade 'is letters when he write, but didn't teach
'im how to make two blades o' grass grow out o' one; and the philan-
thropist remind 'im o' the century o' dishonor instead o' the future
individual responsibility; an' the government dish out beef an' an-
nuity to im' instead of a mule an' a plow. Everything like that make
the Injin no count, except give jobs to government clerks.' " To this
Tookpafka Micco replied, " 'Well, so the ol' order was passed away.
Maybe so now the politician tell Injin how to win salvation in the
Democratic party, or Republican party, an' party bosses teach 'im
how to put in two votes instead o' one.' "[33]

The Democratic landslide in the election of delegates to the Oklahoma constitutional convention verified Alex's belief that the Indians would be excluded from the political process. In the Fus Fixico
letter he wrote after the election, Hotgun's description of how the
Democrats delivered the Indian vote was presented as a parody of
the Twenty-third Psalm: " 'The new state politician was my shep-

herd an' I got all I want. He was tolled me off to one side an' had business with me for my local influence. He was cultivated my acquaintance for his party's sake. He was prepared a table before me in the presence o' the bartender an' hol' up two fingers an' call for a couple o' small ones. He was tell me, "Eat, drink an' be game, for, maybe so, to-morrow I want you to vote for me." ' " To Tookpafka Micco it was history repeating itself. In earlier times, through whiskey and treaty medals, the whites had bought everything the Indians had but their votes. In the recent election they had bought those too: " 'So he was tolled him off back in the alley, if it was in Muskogee, or to the corner saloon, if it was in Shawnee, an' set 'em up to him an' give him entertainment an' try to trade him out of it. The pale face was too cunning an' the red man was too easy. He sell his birthright for a nip.' " Those talked about in the press as potential elected officials of the new state were whites—wealthy entrepreneurs or professional politicians. But, Tookpafka Micco asked, " 'if you was listened right close to hear what my ol' time friend Nokos Elle an' my ol' time friend Hotulk Emartha was running for, you could heard a pin drop. The news gatherers wasn't lying in wait for ol' Cho Eka to interview him about his chances for congress, an' my ol' time friend Chepon Holata wasn't livin' in retirement like John D. Rockyfeller, an' dodgin' the kodak fiends an' stayin' out o' the lime-light.' " [34]

Alex's doubts about the role of Indians in state politics became more pronounced the longer he remained in the field for the Dawes Commission. He had gone out in March and remained in the field for most of 1906. His experiences in the remoter sections of the territory contrasted sharply with the world of political campaigns and constitutional debate in other sections of the territories. At Alabama Town, he found a sick and starving woman alone with a three-year-old child. At Hutche Chuppa he arrived at the home of Holathoye at mealtime and enjoyed sofky with her while he took her testimony. Near Wetumka he visited Artus Hotiye and found him as steadfast in his faith in the old treaties as he had been a year earlier. From him Alex bought a loom made of wild cane and reeds that the old Alabama's wife had used to weave the gay sashes for ball players. Alex took Christmas dinner with friends at Hickory Ground, the menu consisting of "sofky, sour bread, blue dumplings, sakkonipkee and new formula Peruna which, in Indian Territory, is the regulation border booze."[35] Meanwhile, the constitutional convention had begun its work at Guthrie, but its proceedings interested him so little that he wrote only one letter about it. That letter, which appeared in the early days of 1907, made fun of the delegates' concern with such matters as whether God should be mentioned in the preamble than in the contents of the constitution.[36] His lack of interest in political affairs in general is reflected in that he produced only one other Fus Fixico letter in 1907.

Alex worked steadily in the field during the first two months of 1907 because the tribal rolls were to be closed on March 4. Shortly after Christmas 1906, he was called in from Okemah, where he had been working, and sent on a new mission. Tams Bixby wanted to rush through the Creek citizenship cases that Alex had completed and have him investigate one area that had received no attention: Creeks who had lived in the Cherokee Nation since the Civil War. If they were to receive Creek allotments, they must be convinced to return and establish residency. Thus Alex was to go to Braggs, Sallisaw, and Stilwell to investigate a number of cases. Lowena and Wynema, who had been with him at Okemah, accompanied him, leaving Yohola at Bald Hill. On January 7, 1907, they found a room in Braggs at "a shack" that passed for the Commercial Hotel.[37]

The following day Alex, Lowena, and Wynema took a buggy into the rugged Greenleaf Mountain district of the Cherokee Nation to find the Creeks living there. They recognized Creek homes by the sofky mortars and pestles in the yards and the grave houses in the nearby cemeteries. When Alex called out to the householders in English he received no response, but when he called in Creek the people emerged. He interviewed several families but found only one person who was willing to return to the Creek Nation to take her allotment.[38]

The next day Alex moved to Illinois Station. Lowena and Wynema continued on the train to Fayetteville, where they spent a few days with the Harris family. Myers had gone ahead to Sallisaw, leaving Alex to scour the Greenleaf countryside near Illinois Station. Again the sofky patches and other evidence directed him to the Creeks, who asked him his town and seemed eager to hear a stranger who spoke their language. He became convinced that all the Indians in that part of the Cherokee Nation were Creeks but found that most of them were on the Cherokee rolls and had taken allotments where they were. He also found that they spoke Creek "with a Chero-kee accent," and he found none who were willing to return to the Creeks.[39]

At Sallisaw Alex met Myers, who accompanied him to Stilwell to see Itshas Harjo. The old Creek, who had been about fifteen when the Creeks were removed from Alabama, told Alex, "I have passed through many days and traveled a long way, the shadows have fallen about me and I can see but dimly, but my mind is clear and my memory has not failed me." What he remembered was that many Creeks who lingered in Alabama, reluctant to leave, were forcibly removed, and he told how his stepfather and stepmother had been shot down for refusing to go. He clearly recalled the hunger, dis-ease, and other hardships of the removal journey. After removal he and his brother Mewike, or John Killer, had settled in the Cherokee Nation and had never lived in the western Creek Nation, though he still recognized Arbeka Deep Fork as his town. Since then, Its-has Harjo wanted no dealings with the United States. He opposed allotment, had never filed for it, and had not been curious enough to ask if he had been allotted land with the Cherokees. "If my name appears on either the Creek or Cherokee roll, and I am to be hedged about with corner-stones," he told Alex, "I want it stricken from the roll." Alex was the first Creek to visit him at his home. "If I had met you out in the woods," he said, "I would have spoken Cherokee to you and you would not have known that I was a Creek Indian."[40]

After Stilwell, Alex and Myers returned to the Creek Nation to dispose of a few remaining cases. Alex was joined by Lowena and Wynema, who went with him back to Okemah. During the rest of January he worked at Okemah, Henryetta, and Dustin in the Creek Nation; Prague and Keokuk Falls in Oklahoma; and Wewoka in the Seminole Nation. They traveled from town to town by train, as usual, then rented buggies. When the weather and roads permitted, Alex took Lowena and Wynema with him into the countryside. Lowena took in stride the difficulties they met with in travel and lodging, but she was a little squeamish about the dirty restaurants. When it came to food, however, Alex was oblivious to dirt. Once, when they had been out all morning and were hungry, Lowena suggested they stop at a Creek home and have some sofky, but the place was so dirty that she could not get the sofky down. "A man is blind to dirt," she said, "except in his wife's kitchen so Mr. P. drank the sofky."[41]

These were good times for Alex and Lowena. Alex, as always, enjoyed talking with the conservative Creeks. Lowena especially liked
watching the Creek women at their cooking, washing, and quilting
and the men at their farming or cutting firewood. Together they enjoyed picnic lunches by the roadside, and Alex amused Wynema,
whom he called Weemie, by letting her drive the buggy.

These good days however, were near their end. Alex's work for
the Commission to the Five Civilized Tribes was nearly finished.
The tribal rolls were to be closed finally on March 4—hence the
last attempt in early 1907 to investigate as many outstanding cases
as possible. Alex remained in the field at least until the last days of
February.[42] He worked a few weeks longer taking care of unfinished
business, but for the most part his work for the Dawes Commission
was done.

The closing of the tribal rolls was a prelude to the final chapter of the history of the Creek Nation as an autonomous political
entity. Forces were now in motion to create the first chapter in the
history of the state of Oklahoma. Only a few days after the rolls
closed, the constitutional convention adjourned, having been in session since November under the leadership of William H. Murray
and Charles N. Haskell. The constitution that the convention had
drafted would be placed before the people for a ratification vote on
September 17. Of these events, however, Alex would take little public notice, and practically no literary notice. Instead, he directed his
energies to capitalist ventures that the advent of statehood made
possible.

Chapter **10** Land and Progress

· ·

The summer of 1907 was a heady time for the materially ambitious because of the potential for making fortunes in Indian land and from the oil and minerals that lay beneath it. There occurred an orgy of land speculation unlike any witnessed before. The five-year anniversary of the supplemental agreement under which Creek allotments were made was approaching. Surplus allotments had been restricted from sale for five years, and as the fifth anniversary approached, the speculators moved in on the Creeks, those listed on the rolls as full-bloods and others alike. There was some question about exactly which date constituted the anniversary: when the agreement was approved by Congress, when it was ratified by the Creeks, or when it was proclaimed by the president. There were questions, as well, about whether a Creek could sell lands or whether the homestead allotment was restricted from sale. In 1906 Congress had included in legislation what was known as the McCumber amendment, which restricted the sale of all lands belonging to those enrolled as full-bloods for twenty-five years unless permission to sell was granted by the secretary of the interior. But land speculators were confident that the amendment would be overturned, and during the days leading up to the anniversary of the supplemental agreement they prepared to do voluminous business. Much to the surprise and disappointment of some of his friends and acquaintances, Alex had joined their ranks. He may have had motives other than simply material gain in his venture into real estate. His literary life had lain dormant for many months, and he may have intended to revive it. His long-range plans will never be known, for he would not live to bring them to fruition.

From the time allotment began among the Creeks, there had been land dealings of all sorts in the Creek Nation. Though many were illegal, most conformed to the provisions of the various agreements between the Creeks and the United States and the regulations established by the Department of the Interior under congressional acts. Town lots had been sold for years, as had the allotments of deceased Creeks, with the sales overseen by the Dawes Commission and the secretary of the interior. The congressional act of 1904 had removed restrictions from the surplus allotments of enrolled whites and Creek freedmen and had authorized the Interior Department to consider individual applications for removal from adult Indians. The rapidity with which the freedmen sold their land after the 1904 act had only whetted buyers' appetites. The lobbying and agitation for removal of restrictions on other allotments had accelerated during the winter before the Indian national governments were due to expire. However, the act of 1906 that extended the tribal governments not only failed to remove restrictions but added to them for enrolled full-bloods by way of the McCumber amendment.[1]

The land speculators were undaunted. Through their system of "leases" and other means, they had legal claims on thousands of acres of land, believing correctly that it was simply a matter of time until most restrictions were removed and they could obtain titles. In November 1906 a select committee of the United States Senate visited the Indian Territory to hold public hearings on the question. The senators on the committee disliked Hitchcock's administration of land sales and leases and favored removal of restrictions. Although some conservative Indians drafted petitions and Creek leaders such as Chitto Harjo made impassioned speeches opposing removal of restrictions, the testimony consisted for the most part of statements by a parade of witnesses who agreed with the senators.

The arguments they advanced were that land sales were necessary to form a tax base for the new state to come, that restrictions should be determined by the local courts, and that restrictions impeded economic growth and created opportunities only for grafters while excluding honest real estate dealers. There was general sentiment in favor of protecting the allotments of minors and the homestead allotments of those enrolled as full-bloods, however. In the end, the senators recommended removing restrictions from all allotments of whites and blacks and from the surplus allotments of Indian adults.[2]

These hearings occurred during the same month when delegates were elected and the Oklahoma constitutional convention met. The issues of taxation and local control over land sales reflected the concerns of the convention, which presented to Congress a memorial that went further than the recommendations of the senate committee, calling for the removal of all restrictions on sales and leases except on the homesteads of enrolled full-bloods. But Congress took no action.[3] Thus in summer 1907 speculators turned their attention to the five-year anniversary of the supplemental agreement as a means of advancing their interests.

With potential fortunes on the line, speculators were willing to take chances. On July 1 and 2, the first two days following the fifth anniversary of congressional approval of the Creek allotment agreement, an estimated 100,000 acres of land allotted to enrolled full-bloods changed hands, despite the McCumber amendment. The constitutionality of the twenty-five-year restriction had been challenged by Daniel Gritts, leader of the Cherokee Night Hawk Keetoowahs. The case was then pending before the United States Supreme Court. Land speculators and lawyers believed the McCumber provision would be declared void. The speculators began to advertise that they would soon be able to provide clear title to Creek lands.[4] They protected themselves from huge losses by paying down only a small amount, however, usually one-tenth of the sale price. The Indians received contracts saying they would get the rest when they could provide clear title. The Indians kept possession of the land, and the speculators had no debt to pay interest on. How many frauds were perpetrated in such sales will never be known, but they were no doubt considerable. In a sales agreement between two people, the one who had a lifelong understanding of individual landownership and understood the legalities of contracts and deeds was at a decided advantage.⁵ Thus with little capital and less risk, an enterprising land dealer could obtain options on vast amounts of Indian land. On the last two days of June land buyers flocked to Eufaula, one of the six recording districts in the Creek Nation, ready to do business on July 1. Among them was Alex.⁶

Even before he resigned from federal service, he had announced that when he finished his work in the enrolling division he would become a real estate agent. People who knew him were surprised and sad that he would consider entering "the prosaic field of land grafting." One editor said, "The only explanation of his conduct lies in the fact that he may be wanting to get closer to nature." Had these people been able to get past the image of Alex as a literary man, they might not have found his venture into business so surprising. In 1903 G. W. Grayson had hinted at Alex's interest in real estate in one of his letters to the *Indian Journal*. Alex had long believed that the sale of Indian land was necessary for economic progress. Though his enthusiasm for progress had become somewhat dulled in recent years, he nevertheless considered himself a progressive and, like most of his fellow Creeks who were so called, realized that sales were necessary to establish a tax base for state and local governments. Whatever his specific motives, on resigning from his position with the Interior Department he went to work for the International Land Company.⁷

The association of his name with the International Land Company was unfortunate. The president of the company was C. M. Bradley, a white man married to a Creek. He had established the Bradley Real Estate Company in Muskogee in 1901 and had enjoyed phenomenal success dealing in town lots. Alex had known Bradley for some time. Bradley was director of the Bank of Commerce and was active in the Muskogee Chamber of Commerce, to which Alex belonged. In 1903 he had organized a real estate exchange, a group of men who argued that the regulations governing deeds to Indian lands discriminated against them, in an attempt to do something about the red tape. Since then he had strongly supported efforts to remove restrictions on the sale and lease of allotted lands. After restrictions were removed from the sale of whites' and freedmen's allotments in 1904, Bradley expanded his real estate business, dealing mainly in freedmen's lands. He was indicted for forgery and conspiracy involving freedmen's allotments, and though the charges were later dropped, his tactics became so notorious that in late 1906 Pleasant Porter called him the "king of grafters."[8]

Bradley had made the news in November 1906 when he told the Senate select committee, then holding hearings on the restrictions, that he was indeed a grafter whom the Interior Department's regulations abetted. He described in detail the methods that were all too familiar. The buyer made a small down payment, for which he received a warranty deed and the Indian got a promise to pay the rest of the agreed price as soon as clear title could be delivered. Though some contracts were written, many agreements were oral; the Indian held no mortgage. Contracts were immaterial anyway, Bradley argued, because many of his clients could not read. Bradley worked from the assumption that the Indians needed money just like anybody else. He bought land without seeing it. He often paid the Indian a little amount down and doled out small amounts over time, deducting them from the sale price. He counted on those he dealt with in this way to tell their friends about him and thus increase his trade.

The land dealers, he said, had tried to get around the restrictions any way they could, and he promised the senators that if the McCumber amendment was not repealed, the land companies would "go after it and bust it." Meanwhile, they were willing to speculate in lands with clouded titles. Bradley claimed to have dealt with over five hundred full-blood Indians, paying them as little as he could; his company, he said, had tied up more than 100,000 acres of Creek land, excluding freedmen's allotments. He admitted that his company did not have enough capital to cover all his contracts, but he claimed to have the backing of St. Louis banks. Bradley believed he was doing the territory a good deed by buying the land and reselling it to people who came there looking for farms. Despite ample testimony to the contrary, he argued that most of those enrolled as full-bloods wanted restrictions removed and that it was educated Indians, mainly of mixed heritage, who wanted them to remain. The Indians, he said, would make "good" Americans, but restrictions made them appear inferior. Bradley made a gushy appeal to the senators to relieve his wife and son, who were Creeks, of the stigma. Bradley's admission of grafting was picked up and printed widely by Creek Nation newspapers.[9] Thus, only months before Alex went to work for Bradley's company, its name had been publicly associated with graft.

Fortunately Alex's association with the International Land Company was short-lived. What his duties were is uncertain, but it is safe to assume that, as he would do for others and for himself in succeeding months, he acted as a purchasing agent, dealing specifically with the full-bloods. But though the association was brief, it was long enough to damage his reputation.

On May 8, 1907, with D. P. Thornton and M. G. Young, Alex established the Posey-Thornton Oil and Gas Company. Its articles of incorporation gave it sweeping powers to buy, sell, and lease real estate; to buy and sell personal property; to act as agents and trustee receivers; to deal in livestock; to engage in mercantile and manufacturing business; and to prospect for oil and gas and mine coal and other minerals.[10] Alex was now prepared to speculate in oil as well as land. It was simply a matter of time until restrictions would be removed from the sale of many allotments and land could be bought and sold without limits.

By the time the Creek surplus allotments went on the market that summer, Alex was probably acting as an agent for the Palo Alto Land Company, for he himself lacked operating capital. The main force behind this company was George W. Barnes, an oil man from Toledo, Ohio, who had been in Muskogee for several years. He was vice president of the board of the Commercial National Bank, which in 1903 had been designated United States depository in the Indian Territory. Barnes was an associate of Charles N. Haskell and later served as the personal representative of the governor in quasi-official capacities. Barnes's partner in the land company was H. H. Bell, formerly a director of the Bradley Real Estate Company. As the head of the Palo Alto Land Company, Barnes set as his goal during summer 1907 the purchase of 40,000 acres of Indian land. The land company was incorporated on July 1, with offices in Muskogee, and Alex's name was associated with it from the start. Although he was not a member of the corporation, he signed an agreement with Barnes and Bell to work for the company as an agent dealing with the full-bloods.[11]

The frenzy of land sales that began on July 1 continued for several weeks. July 26 was the fifth anniversary of the Creek approval of the allotment agreement, and July 27 brought a rise in sales. August 8 was the anniversary of the agreement's proclamation, and Charles J. Bonaparte, now attorney general of the United States, handed down a decision that, after that date, adult Indian citizens could sell all but their forty-acre homestead allotments without the consent of the secretary of the interior. Although some buyers would not deal in allotments of full-blood enrollees, others like Bradley worked in earnest, buying them despite the McCumber amendment. The Creek leaders sought to protect the full-bloods. Before sales began, the National Council had endorsed the McCumber amendment. Pleasant Porter died suddenly on September 3, and his successor, Moty Tiger, warned his fellow full-bloods that they could sell only land they had inherited and urged them not to sign sales agreements. The land men had organized an effort to prevent the Creek council from taking official action on the McCumber amendment, believing that the Supreme Court would refuse to review the pending test of its constitutionality if the Creeks did so.[12] Despite the council's action, the speculators were confident, and rightly so, that Congress and the courts would eventually remove more restrictions than they would preserve.

As an agent for the Palo Alto Land Company, Alex fell back into a familiar routine, and one he was good at: traveling the Creek Nation and dealing personally with the full-bloods. On each of the signal dates in July he was at Eufaula, location of the court for one of the recording districts for the Creek Nation. For the next several months he traveled frequently to Eufaula and went to other towns such as Dustin, Weleetka, and Okmulgee, working in the communities he knew best. His cousin John Phillips had a real estate office in Okemah, and his uncle Lewis Phillips traded in oil leases through an office in Sapulpa. Both had been in the land business as early as 1904. Alex's brother-in-law John E. Emery had been involved with the Dustin Townsite Company in town-site booming as early as 1903.[13] Whether Alex worked with these men in any way is uncertain.

Alex proved an effective land agent. Within a year the Palo Alto Land Company had bought or acquired options on eleven tracts of land in McIntosh County alone, most of them in the Bald Hill, Tuskegee, Artussee, and Mellette communities. The company also had extensive land dealings in Okfuskee County, including options on the surplus allotments of Betsy, the widow of Pahosa Harjo Phillips. Besides his, Yohola's, and Pachina's allotments, Alex himself obtained title to part of the Lucy Washington allotment near Tuskegee, part of the allotments of his brothers John and Conny, the Emma Posey allotment near Wagoner, part of the Mandy Bird Creek allotment near Weleetka, and the Bud Jameson allotment five miles north of Hanna. He also had power of attorney or guardianship for a number of allottees, and the Posey-Thornton Oil and Gas Company had oil and gas leases on fifteen tracts.[14] Most of these transactions had been completed by the first few weeks of 1908.

Although much land had been opened to sale, much remained restricted. The failure of Congress to act during the winter session of 1906–7 had not stifled debate on the issue. It heated up in summer 1907 as a result of the land buying frenzy and the campaign to ratify the Oklahoma constitution and elect Oklahoma's first state and local officials and members of Congress. During the campaign, both the Democratic and Republican parties endorsed removal of restrictions. The election was held on September 17, the constitution was ratified overwhelmingly, and Haskell was elected first governor of the state. Oklahoma was admitted to the Union as the forty-sixth state on November 16. All the elected senators and representatives favored removing restrictions and would work hard for legislation during the succeeding months.[15]

Throughout fall 1907 Alex was busy as a land agent. He gave no public evidence of whatever interest he may have taken in the political events during those months, not so much as a Fus Fixico letter concerning the campaign. His silence here, following his less than enthusiastic response to the constitutional convention of 1906, suggests the completion of his long withdrawal from politics. By this time he had in mind other plans whose success depended on the land base he had begun to acquire.

Alex's land buying ventures had kept him away from home much of the time, especially during the first few months of his affiliation with the Palo Alto Land Company. The summer of 1907 had been particularly lonely for Lowena, since ten-year-old Yohola was often at Bald Hill, leaving her and Wynema alone at Muskogee. During the Chautauqua season, she attended the lectures, musical performances, readings, and magic shows, or she read and sewed to pass the time. The nights were particularly difficult, for then she was afraid. Alex called her long distance, or she placed telephone calls to his hotels, simply to chat and to say good night. Failed connections disappointed her, and after they talked she hated to hang up. "He is so thoughtful of us when away," she told herself. "It brings him nearer to hear his voice & chat with him even over the phone." [16] Alex, in turn, recognized his neglect of her:

> I've seen the beauty of the rose;
> I've heard the music of the bird,
> And given voice to my delight;
> I've sought the shapes that come in dreams,
> I've reached my hands in eager quest,
> To fold them empty to my breast;
> ·While you, the whole of all I've sought—
> The love, the beauty, and the dreams—
> Have stood, thro' weal and woe, true at
> My side, silent at my neglect. [17]

He and Lowena did manage, however, to find a little time for one another. In August he stayed off work long enough for them to travel to the Jamestown Exposition, celebrating the three hundredth anniversary of the first successful English colony in the New World. When business kept Alex in Muskogee, he sometimes worked at his office in the Brown Building during the mornings and spent the afternoons with Lowena. On weekends and holidays they went on family outings or spent quiet days reading together. [18] The plans he was working on in fall 1907 would give him more time for his family.

Those plans included developing his property at Bald Hill. On October 26 he granted a lease to the Bald Knob Oil and Gas Company of Tulsa to drill exploratory wells on his, Yohola's, and his brother Conny's allotments. It was not until spring 1908, however, that the company began preparing to drill. During the first week of April, company agent Robert D. Howe, an attorney, announced at Eufaula that later that month the Bald Knob Oil Company would begin to put down four test wells at the site. [19] By that time, because of oil and real estate interests in McIntosh County, Alex had decided to move back to Eufaula.

Only a few days before Howe's announcement, it was reported that Alex and associates had bought the *Indian Journal* from George Raker, to whom Alex had sold it in 1903. The capital behind the Indian Journal Printing Company came from its president, I. H.

Nakdimen, a well-known banker and newspaper owner from Sallisaw, Oklahoma, who had recently acquired banking interests in Eufaula. Alex had very little financial investment in the company, owning only thirty-four shares of stock. His job was to edit the *Journal* and do "literary work." His fellow editors, who had been disappointed when he entered government service and, later, the real estate business, now expressed their pleasure that he had "gone back to his rightful calling after four years of battling with a vulgar commercial world."[20]

But Alex had not finished with the "vulgar commercial world." He maintained ties with the Palo Alto Land Company and also with the Barnes Investment Company of Muskogee, and exploration for oil was going forward at Bald Hill, no doubt a major consideration in his decision to return to Eufaula. In his opening edition of the *Journal* he wrote: "The people of Eufaula and McIntosh county have been my friends since I can remember, for I was born and brought up in these parts. There are no better people and I shall do my best to serve them as editor of the Journal and in any other manner that I may be of use to them." These words may have rung hollow to some of his readers, who harbored resentment about his land dealings. Others, among them some of his relatives at Tuskegee, felt he had betrayed the Creeks by trying so hard to enroll them for allotments and then going to work for the land companies.[21] Whether Alex was aware of their bitter feelings is uncertain.

Alex resumed editing the *Journal* at an opportune time for Eufaula. Eufaula had been named the county seat of McIntosh County, but the citizens of Checotah had successfully petitioned for a special election to put the question to a vote of the people. Eufaula needed Alex's pen as the election approached. Although Stidham and other small communities made a bid for selection, the real contest was between Eufaula and Checotah. As editor of the *Journal* in earlier years, Alex had boosted Eufaula and made good-natured verbal jabs at its rival to the north. Since then he had maintained a lighthearted antagonism toward Checotah. In 1905, when he learned that the Sequoyah Statehood Convention proposed to put both towns in the same county, he had said that the county was not big enough for both of them.[22] When the Oklahoma Statehood Convention said the same, the rivalry between the towns flared. More than town pride was at stake; being the county seat brought economic benefits.

Alex put forth his best editorial efforts on Eufaula's behalf. He boosted the advantages of Eufaula and made direct appeals to the voters, arguing that the merchants at Checotah overcharged, that the ginners charged the farmers more for processing their cotton than the Eufaula ginners did, and that the election would place an undue tax burden on the county. To bring in the Indian vote, he, Charles Gibson, G. W. Grayson, Jackson Lewis, and other prominent Creeks published an appeal in the Creek language for those who could not read English. He published an interview with Tookpafka Micco, who was in town on business: " 'Well, so,' " he said, " 'Eufaula was the Injin's old stomp ground, and all the Injins was feel good to be here. Eufaula was the Injin's first resting place when he come here from Alabama. So the Injin didn't want no new busk ground like Checotah.' " Alex filled empty spaces in his columns with one-liners such as "Checotah is an habitual loser." He put the case against Checotah in lyrics to be sung to the tune of "Tell 'Em No." [23] And he wrote limericks. One was aimed at Checotah's ginners:

> There was a small town, Checotah
> A very nice place to gotah,
>   'Till the farmers got skinned
>   On the cotton there ginned
> And rose in their might and smotah. [24]

Another attacked the editor of the *Hoffman Herald*, who had endorsed Checotah:

> There was an editor, O'Blenness,
> Subsequent cognomen, Dennis,
>   Who gave as his quota
>   One vote to Checotah,
> And his folks approached him with menace. [25]

Alex also enlisted the voice of Fus Fixico, who had been silent for nearly a year and a half. In reviving the letters, he literally resurrected Hotgun, who had died a few months earlier. Hotgun and Tookpafka Micco, unsure what a county seat was, compared it to a busk ground and found Checotah wanting in the necessities of shade and water. Hotgun said, " 'It was had abundance o' high winds an' horizontal zephyrs an' distant prospects, but things like that wasn't solid advantages.' " Alex also resurrected an old Fus Fixico letter.

Like Indian Territory waiting for statehood in earlier times, Checotah—expecting to be named the county seat—was like Chuffee the
rabbit, who nearly starved to death sitting under the sycamore tree
and waiting for the balls to fall.[26] In the election on May 23, Checotah polled more votes than Eufaula, but because of votes cast for
other communities, it failed to obtain the majority required by law
to relocate the county seat.

When the election occurred, the state of Oklahoma was only six
months old, yet old enough for Alex to have begun to assess editorially the results of the economic, political, and social progress he
embraced. By then it was clear that the events of 1906 and 1907
had demonstrated a significant fact: the Indians' land was necessary
for the success of the new state but their participation in the government was not. This fact applied particularly to the conservatives.
The rhetoric that had surrounded the Sequoyah convention in 1905
was heard no more. In an address to the people, issued during the
last stages of the drafting of the Sequoyah constitution, the principal chiefs of the Five Civilized Tribes—the Chickasaws excepted—
had expressed their hopes for the Indian peoples under statehood.
To them statehood was another step in a long process of acculturation, a process necessary for survival. Their people had striven to
learn English, they said, and had embraced Christianity, which had
taught them that out of death came life. From the death of their
separate nations, they argued, would emerge "a larger, better life
for all who live within the Indian Territory, a life of equal rights
and equal protection through the common citizenship thus established. . . . Through this transition," they said, "our present government shall not be annihilated but transformed into material for a
nobly builded state. Thus we shall have life, not death."[27]

In the wake of the failed Sequoyah movement, the rhetoric
changed. In the election of delegates to the Oklahoma constitutional convention in 1906, the progressive Indians became active,
and ten—most with more European than Indian ancestry—were
elected to the convention. The conservative Indians, however, had
little to do with it because the issues were foreign to them and they
were fearful of the process. Only a few of them voted, in sharp contrast with the Creek election of 1903, when they still took their politics seriously and participated actively. This turn of events prompted
Pleasant Porter to observe that the "real" Indian would have no

political role in the new state.[28] Alex had long since arrived at the same conclusion; in Hotgun and Tookpafka Micco, in the Fus Fixico letters of 1905 and 1906, he depicted a growing alienation from the changing state of affairs.

Like other progressive Indians, Alex believed that restrictions on allotments contributed to second-class citizenship and thwarted progress. Though they disagreed somewhat about which restrictions should be removed, the Oklahoma members of Congress worked during the session of 1907–8 to get a bill passed. Some favored continued protection of the Indians enrolled as full-bloods, but the part-Cherokee senator Robert L. Owen, who had referred to those Indians as "defectives" and "children," had no desire to protect them. Though Alex had a higher opinion of the full-bloods than Owen did, he had become convinced since 1904 that the restrictions on their allotments did them no good. "The law does not permit the Indian to sell his land," he wrote in the *Journal*, "nor does it allow him to lease it for agricultural purposes for a period longer than one year. Now, there is no range or game within the limits to which he has been restricted. What is Poor Lo to do?"[29] Alex was convinced that the full-blooded enrollees would not improve their allotments. In spring 1908 the Indian agency at Muskogee undertook a policy of hand delivering allotment deeds to the Snakes who had refused them. In editorials, Alex questioned the wisdom of the policy. It was simply another means "to withhold Indian lands from the white man, who is anxious to have them, willing to pay for them and swift to utilize them." He wrote, "This policy of the government causes curious people to speculate as to whether the government in forcing treaties upon the Five Tribes had in view the creation of a state of the union or a forest reserve."[30]

These "reserved" lands were not subject to taxation, which Alex considered the key to Oklahoma's prosperity. When it appeared in spring 1908 that Congress might remove all restrictions, Alex endorsed the idea. Removal of restrictions, he argued, "means everything in the way of schools, good roads, public buildings and other state institutions that statehood has made necessary. It means that all land in the new state will not only be subject to taxation but will be put in a way of cultivation at the earliest possible time and that the richest section of the southwest will be soon sending its rich harvests to the markets of the world."[31] Clearly, then, to Alex prosperity

depended on putting the land to agricultural use, which he believed
the full-bloods would not do.

While Alex was convinced that the full-bloods, as a rule, would not
prosper, there were exceptions whom he held up in the *Indian Journal*. One was March Thompson of Burney, a district judge, prose-
cuting attorney, and council member during the days of tribal rule
and, under the new order, a progressive, influential man in public
affairs. Thompson had amassed a considerable fortune in bank stock,
farming enterprises, livestock, and mercantile ventures, competing
with "white business talent of the highest order." He was interested
not in selling his land but in buying more. He owned thousands
of acres, most under cultivation, and was a successful farmer and
rancher. There were exceptions, Alex admitted, "to all rules characteristic of peoples and March Thompson is an exceptional fullblood
Indian." Alex found other examples in Thompson Colbert, who had
secured a lucrative oil lease on an inherited tract of land, and Johnson Phillips, Alex's uncle, who was a successful farmer. Colbert, he
said, demonstrated what an "unprotected"—that is, unrestricted—
Indian could do, and in Phillips, he said, "the Indian problem has
been solved through sheer self-effort." [32]

The condition of these enterprising Creeks stood in sharp contrast to that of the most conservative Creeks, the Snakes. They continued to cling tenaciously to their belief that what Alex called "the
as-long-as-grass-grows-and-water-flows treaty" would be restored. [33]
In spring 1908 rumors circulated among them that a black man
had been appointed Indian agent, whose purpose was to remove all
whites from Creek lands, and that Pleasant Porter was not really
dead but was in jail in Washington. The Snakes were advised by their
leaders to go to Hickory Ground and await removal of the whites. In
April many gathered at the old Eufaula town square in preparation
for the move. By late May, Snakes had gathered at Hanna and at
Hickory Ground, where the largest number to gather in years had
assembled. Among them were Creeks, Creek freedmen, Choctaws,
and Chickasaws. Some were armed, which alarmed local residents,
but Alex saw no danger. The Snakes had never harmed anyone and
would not start now, he said. What concerned him was that they had
sold or abandoned their property and left their sofky patches during
the planting season; with no corn, they were sure to be hungry in the
fall. He blamed the situation on the Snake leaders, who had deceived

their followers—"perhaps innocently," perhaps not. "In the beginning of the Snake movement," he wrote, "there is little or no doubt
that these leaders were sincere, but with the passage of years these
men have surely learned that the restoration of ancient customs and
methods of holding Creek lands are an impossibility, and the early
Snake patriotism seems to have degenerated into modern graft."[34]

Having traveled extensively among the Snakes as an agent for the
Dawes Commission, Alex understood well why they had come to
this point. Echoing what he had said in earlier Fus Fixico letters, he
described the Creek Nation of some twenty years before, when there
were few licensed traders and the Indian was happy with a cabin,
sofky patch, plentiful game, horses, and domestic herds. Then came
the lightning rod salesmen and the sewing machine salesman, followed by the "pasture man," who "corrupted his government, fenced
up his range, killed his game and drove off his unmarked yearlings."
Then came the calendar clock salesmen, Gale harrow salesmen,
family tree salesmen, and the steel kitchen range salesmen. Finally
came the Dawes Commission, who "grew into the carpetbagger,"
and the call for statehood, "the greatest good for the greatest number." Meanwhile, the conservative Creeks did not change. Echoing
what Chitto Harjo had told him in 1905, Alex wrote, "The Indian of
the late five civilized tribes is still the Indian of twenty years ago save
these wounds. He has an allotment but no farm. He has American
citizenship but he can neither use or dispose of the one or exercise
the other to any purpose. We speak thus of the real Indian, the full-
blood, and not those few of his tribe who have become to all intent
and purpose members of the white race. They are a thousand years
behind the civilization which has engulfed them. Regardless of the
fact that he has let the calendar clock run down, that he has let the
steel range cook stove that he could not get into his cabin rust under
the brush arbor and that he has let the Gale fall to pieces in the fence
corner, he is expected to take up the white man's burden and walk
off with it."[35]

Alex foresaw further social disintegration for some of these people.
When the Dawes Commission began receiving applications for allotments in April 1899, the Creek citizens with the least Indian blood,
he said, rushed in and filed on the "cream" of Creek land. When the
conservatives later began to file, only second- and third-grade land
remained. Remnant factions of the Creeks refused to file, and the

Dawes Commission arbitrarily filed for them, for the most part as-

signing allotments in the western part of the Creek Nation, twenty-
five to fifty miles from their home places along the North and South
Canadian rivers. In many cases those home places had been allotted
to others: it was only a question of time until the owners would evict
them and force them to move to their allotments, where they would
be strangers. "There are several hundred families of these Indians
thus situated," Alex wrote, "and they are the real Indians which the
United States Government has made so much talk and bother about
protecting. These people are totally unfitted to face the conditions
that now surround them in Oklahoma." In fact, he concluded, "in
Oklahoma the fullblood Indian is sure to become a burden on the
state and without hope for himself." For some time, large numbers
had been despondent and in dire need, without cash, having used
up their credit because of restrictions on their allotments.[36]

Those Snakes who had successfully resisted signing up for allotments had been excluded altogether. There was now some talk of
reopening the rolls to admit them. Alex strongly opposed that action.
It had taken the Dawes Commission ten years, he argued, to enroll
the members of the Five Civilized Tribes, using every method possible to induce them to cooperate and even enrolling many against
their will. "When the rolls were closed justice had been done the real
Indian as far as lay within the scope of human endeavor," he wrote.
Many claimants had been rejected, but hardly a case existed where a
"genuine" Indian had been refused admission to the rolls. The best
lands had been allotted, as had nearly all of the second- and third-
grade land. There remained insufficient land and funds to equalize
allotments of those who got short shrift in the division. Now some
of the previously "disaffected" appealed for a reopening of the rolls
and admission to a share of tribal lands. "The half breeds and others
not fullbloods got far the best of the first division," Alex wrote. "It
would work an injustice upon these Indians to reopen the rolls at
this day and take what little remaining land there is for equalization
purposes."[37]

If the Snakes did not fit into the new state and were burdensome
to it, what was to be done with them? The "more intelligent" and
"well-informed" Indians, Alex said, believed they would be better off
in Mexico, where land grants were available. Since removal, factions
of various tribes had considered Mexico a potential haven from the

whites. While he was at Okmulgee more than a decade earlier, Alex had discussed the emigration plans of the Cherokees and Creeks at length with Red Bird Harris, one of the leaders of the Cherokee conservatives. Harris, whose sons had attended Bacone with Alex, had wanted him to attend a mass meeting to be held in Okmulgee to help the conservatives draft resolutions urging Isparhecher to appropriate funds to find them a new home if negotiations with the Dawes Commission went forward.[38] Although ample evidence shows Alex believed emigration schemes were futile in the face of unfolding historical events, the openness and trust apparent in his dialogue with Harris and the confidence Harris placed in his abilities reflect the rapport he had then with very conservative Indians, among not only the Creeks but the Cherokees as well. In recent years the Snakes among the Creeks and the Keetoowahs among the Cherokees had considered migration at length. In spring 1908 organizers were among the Creeks, discussing Mexico once more.

Alex had scoffed at such plans in his Fus Fixico letters a few years earlier, but in 1908 he hoped the government would favor such a move and help develop a plan. He suggested creating a commission to help the Snakes find a home in Mexico in exchange for their allotments and share of the Creek national fund. In the last issue of the *Indian Journal* that appeared before his death, Alex published a letter responding to his article about the government's responsibility to help the Indians find a new home. The writer was a part-Cherokee promoter from Texas whose letter advertised his services in helping the Creeks relocate in South America.[39]

Any of Alex's readers who were surprised at his editorial position on the Snakes should not have been. During his college days he had enthusiastically embraced Western progress and had accepted the inevitability of allotment and individual land titles if the Creeks were to enjoy the fruits of that progress. On the eve of the twentieth century, in his poem "The Homestead of Empire," he had glorified the progress of Western civilization, which brought freedom to the world. He had concluded it thus:

> Move on, world of the Occident,
>   Move on! Thy footfalls thro' the globe
> Are heard as thou marchest
>   Into that larger day

Whose dawn lights up the armored front
In Cuba and the Philippines.[40]

As an editor in 1902 and 1903, he had viewed the conservative
Creeks as discordant notes in the grand march of progress. He believed they were misguided, but he understood their refusal or inability to adapt. During his work for the Dawes Commission, he had
helped protect their share in the tribal assets, even if against their
will, and he tried to convince them individually that it was useless to
resist allotment. Though he sympathized with them in their poverty
and demoralization, his long firsthand experience led him to con-
clude that they were a relic of a past civilization, one he had shared
during his childhood. Now, after the advent of statehood, it seemed
to him that their lot would get not better but worse and that they
would become an economic burden on the state. The best policy, he
concluded, was to remove them. Those impressed with the progress
of Western civilization during the youth of his grandfather, Pahosa
Harjo Phillips, had made the same arguments in Alabama.

We should not suppose that Alex's forecast of doom for the Snakes
meant he accepted the popular concept of his day that the Indians of the Five Civilized Tribes were vanishing.[41] In the future they
might be found wearing overalls and loving firewater, as he had said
earlier, but they would be Indians nevertheless. Survival depended
on change. Alex considered himself an example of the Indian's
ability to adapt and survive. The Creek Nation had been, after all,
an amalgam of peoples of diverse races, cultures, and ethnic identities, whose history since the sixteenth century had been marked
by changes in economics, social patterns, and material culture in
response to contact with Europeans and Africans. Accommodation
to cultural change began before removal and had accelerated in the
West. It has been argued that not only the Creeks but all the Five
Civilized Tribes were distinct from other groups in such accommodation and that change had been so rapid after removal that by the
time of allotment most of them looked at the land as an economic,
rather than a spiritual, resource. Thus, though they may have preferred a common title, they understood the concept of individual
titles to the land and the economics of personal property.[42]

A pointed expression of this idea came from Pleasant Porter.
In 1891 he wrote to his political opponent Isparhecher that en-

croachment by federal authority had long ago caused Creek self-government to cease. The Creeks had "advanced" so that they now lived by "the same means of industries as other peoples." By slow measures the Creeks had "unconsciously . . . passed over from a system of communism to that of individualism." Porter favored not allotment but limits on how much of the public domain an individual Creek could use.[43] Porter generalized, of course, and there were no doubt exceptions. However, in 1908 the most conservative Creeks were apparently further along the road of accommodation than Alex realized or was willing to admit. Their descendants now living in Oklahoma testify to the error in his judgment regarding them.

Considered in light of the diversity of the Creek peoples, Alex's acknowledgment of racial as well as cultural distance between him and the Snakes is not surprising. His casting his arguments in terms of "full-blood" and "not full-blood" or "real" Indians and those who had effectively joined the "white race" might grate on modern readers, but it would not have been so jolting to his contemporaries. When the Dawes Commission was established, leaders of the Five Tribes had refused to negotiate with the committee because they knew many of their nations' members were not prepared to accept the responsibilities of individual ownership of land and United States citizenship. When the allotment process began, it was generally conceded that the most culturally conservative members, most of whom were commonly classed as full-bloods, remained unprepared for a change in land tenure and therefore needed legal protection of their rights. The debate on removal of restrictions had also turned on racial lines. Bonaparte and Woodruff had accepted, for instance, the judgment of one witness who told them in 1904 that the "average full-blood Indian" was "about the equal, intellectually and morally, of a white child of 10." Bonaparte and Woodruff made careful distinctions between these "genuine" or "real" Indians, as they called them, and "nominal" Indians. The conclusion reached by policymakers after 1904 was that the former needed protection while the latter did not.[44] Such thinking was also pervasive among the population in the Indian Territory.

By 1908 Indians' rights to dispose of or lease their land depended on their recorded quantum of Indian blood. In fact, legislation that emerged from Congress in spring 1908 embodied these concepts. Passed on May 27, the day Alex died, it removed restrictions on sales

from allotments held by adopted whites, freedmen, or Indians of
less than one-half Indian blood. Those who had at least one-half but
less than three-fourths Indian blood could not sell their homestead
allotments but could sell their surplus lands. Those with more than
three-fourths Indian blood were restricted from all sales. Restrictions were to remain in effect until 1931 unless they were removed
individually by the secretary of the interior under a system of regulations he devised.[45]

As the allotment process went forward, it also became the accepted
notion that competence not only in legal affairs but in economic and
political affairs as well was related to the quantum of Indian blood.
By 1908 enough elections had been held to demonstrate that the
Indian citizens of mixed heritage could participate in the political
process—even be elected to office—while those commonly referred
to as full-bloods, whom Pleasant Porter had called the "real" Indians, could or would not. Thus agreements, regulations, and laws
regarding allotment had helped create social classes based on racial
definition.

Although some scholars now question the validity of labels such as
full-blood and mixed-blood, they had currency in Alex's day.[46] They
may have carried little cultural relevance, but they had profound
social, political, and economic implications for those they were applied to in the twilight years of the Indian Territory and the early
years of Oklahoma's statehood. Alex's language simply reflected the
social, political, and economic realities of the day.

How could Alex—fluent in Creek, once active in Creek politics
and the Creek bureaucracy, knowledgeable about Creek history and
culture, and critical of the allotment process—hold such views of a
whole class of his fellow Creeks? It has been argued that not only
the Creeks but members of all the Five Civilized Tribes saw themselves not as unified tribal peoples but as citizens of nations made
up of culturally and racially diverse groups who were bound, especially since removal, by a common history.[47] Allotment had been
another episode in that history. Though Alex was nostalgic about
the Creek Nation of his childhood, he had no desire for its return.
He did not look backward; he looked steadily forward with confidence. Such a perspective provided room for continued cultural
accommodation without the emotional struggle that accompanied
the assimilation process for other Indian writers of Alex's time, such

as Zitkala-Sa and Charles A. Eastman. It would permit some of the next generation of the Five Civilized Tribes to refer to themselves as supercivilized Indians.[48]

If Alex's self-concept is a problem for readers, the problem may be of the readers' own making.[49] It matters little which side of the cultural fence public or academic opinion places him on. Whether Alex wrote about "progressives" or "pull backs" or about "fullbloods" or "half breeds and others not fullbloods," he referred to Creeks. He was no less a Creek than the full-bloods. To him they were still nineteenth-century Creeks whereas he was a modern Creek, quite capable of competing in the technology-driven society of twentieth-century America. Although Alex's views on the full-bloods were perhaps not surprising to his contemporaries, they may have contributed to the undercurrent of resentment against him that still survives. When he wrote about them, his life was near its end. He did not live to see how true his predictions concerning all classes of his fellow Creeks might prove to be.

Chapter **11** "Gone Over to See"

. . . .

During April and May 1908 Alex devoted his attention
to editing the *Journal*. Work on the drilling project at Bald Hill had
gone slowly because of the weather. April was a rainy month, and
many roads were impassable, making it impossible to get heavy drilling equipment to well sites. By the first of May the Canadian and
its tributaries were at flood stage. No one knew then that the rains
would continue until the river reached its highest level in fifty years.
Because the floods made it impossible to get out into the countryside, Alex did little besides editorial work, which did not take all his
time, since he included much less local news than in former years.
He had not moved his family to Eufaula immediately on assuming
his editorial duties, and he soon found that the paper took so little
of his time that he could commute from Muskogee one or two days
a week and still get each issue out.[1]

There was nothing unusual, then, about his trip from Muskogee to
Eufaula on May 27. It was a routine he was accustomed to. Lowena
had taken the children to Fayetteville to visit her family, and he

and Robert D. Howe planned to execute lease agreements on his, Yohola's, and Pachina's allotments at Eufaula that day.[2]

When word came that Alex had died in the flood near Cathay, Lowena took the train to Muskogee. We can only imagine what went through her mind as she rode the train alone that night. She was not well, and the wire telling her of Alex's death had put her in a state of nervous shock.[3] It must have been hard to accept the idea that the Oktahutche, the river where Alex had swum and fished and boated, that he loved and praised in poetry, had claimed his life. Over a decade earlier he had written in a poem for baby Yohola:

> If I were dead, loved one,
>   So young and fair,
> If I were laid beneath
>   The grasses there,
> My face would haunt you for
>   Awhile—a day may be—
> And then you would forget
> And not remember me.[4]

But he was not under the "grasses there," and the forgetting could not begin until he was. Everything was different now. She was no longer Alex's beloved Lowena; she was Mrs. Minnie Posey, widow.

The coming days would be difficult. The newspapers would publish graphic eyewitness accounts of Alex's ordeal in the floodwaters, Howe's frantic efforts to get him help, the attempt to rescue him, and, despite that attempt, the horrifying spectacle of his death. There would be many expressions of sympathy and shock. Those who had been close to Alex did their best to comfort his widow. John Phillips, Alex's cousin, learned of his death while he was in the Southwest, where he had taken his wife for treatment for tuberculosis. By way of consolation he wrote, "Twenty five years ago when my best friend my mother departed from me and last words she lefted for us children that God will taking care of us." John now said those same words to Minnie and the children.[5]

Minnie had to bear up under the ordeal of searching for the body. Early on May 28 a group of Alex's friends, headed by an expert diver named Fred Wiswell, left Muskogee to begin the search, but they returned the next day because the river was too high. Minnie

Alex Posey, 1908. Courtesy of Daniel F. Littlefield, Jr.

Minnie and Wynema Posey, 1910. From Minnie H. Posey, comp., The Poems of Alexander Lawrence Posey *(Topeka: Crane, 1910).*

offered a reward of seventy-five dollars for the body. Identifying features were precisely described: straight black hair, gray suit, black vest, patent leather shoes, a diamond ring on the left hand, and a horseshoe stickpin of emeralds and pearls in the tie. Watchers maintained a vigil along the river. The searchers continued for several days under the direction of John Posey, and on June 4 they found the body of Joel Scott, Alex's boatman, who had also died at the break in the railroad. Wiswell and Elliott Howe, a brother of Robert Howe, nearly drowned when their boat capsized in the swift waters, and the search was finally given up because of the high water. The river did not go back into its banks until late June. In the second week of July, Minnie and Nancy organized a search party that began from the site of the drowning. Nancy, in her sixtieth year, walked the banks of the river, looking for the remains of her son.[6]

They were not found until July 20. Young Jud Newton, who was hunting squirrels near the Rock Ford not far from Eufaula, found them in a pile of driftwood about a hundred yards from the river. Minnie went to Eufaula that night, and on July 22 she accompanied the body to Muskogee, where it was buried in Green Hill Cemetery. Nancy and Conny were the only members of the family from Eufaula to attend the services.[7]

As soon as news of his death appeared, tributes came from all directions. George Riley Hall, Minnie's brother-in-law, who called Alex his "best and closest friend," wrote: "Posey was absolutely and always loyal. He never wavered. His was the soul so great and noble that bitterness never found place therein. Nobility became him— rested as naturally upon him as a halo fits a star."[8] Charles Gibson, fellow Creek and longtime friend, in a brief tribute titled "Gone Over to See," viewed Alex's death fatalistically: "But as the red men say, it was in the beginning ordained that he should retire from this life as he did."[9] Ora Eddleman Reed, Cherokee and former editor of the *Twin Territories*, where Alex had published many of his works, called him "one of the most brilliant men the Indians of any tribe have produced," whose "death is a thing to be lamented over, not alone by his own people, but by all who knew him and admired him for his deep, true, sturdy nature."[10]

The tributes continued at the burial. A local minister conducted the services, and Minnie invited statements from S. M. Rutherford, the former mayor of Muskogee, and J. S. Holden, editor of the *Fort Gibson Post*, both of whom gave glowing eulogies. The stone finally placed at Alex's grave was inscribed with his poem "To a Daffodil":

> When Death has shut the blue skies out from me,
> Sweet Daffodil,
> And years roll on without my memory,
> Thou'lt reach thy tender fingers down to mine of clay,
> A true friend still,
> Although I'll never know thee till the judgment day.[11]

Alex had "gone over to see," but his friends and family, reluctant to let him go, clung tenaciously to his memory and jealously guarded his reputation. Among the tributes to Alex was one that contained a statement Minnie and others believed was damaging to Alex's memory. A correspondent for the Kansas City *Star* had written from Eufaula that Alex did not believe in God or in the existence of the soul.[12] In addition to the unnerving matter of searching for Alex's body, Minnie found it necessary to ask friends to answer what she perceived as an attack on his character.

The first to do so was George Riley Hall. Hall had to admit that there was "a more or less well founded belief" that Alex had been skeptical concerning "orthodox religion," but, Hall insisted, Alex "did believe in God and in the existence of a soul." He wrote, "That soul that reveled in the beauties and spotless purity of the humble flowers of the wildwood, that soul that heard the voice of God in the wind, or listened to the pulsing throb of the world's great heart in the stillness of a summer evening, is a part of eternity and can never die. Posey loved the best and purest of God's creation." Hall added, "He was a child of nature, and had a soul attuned to all the sweet and varied harmonies of the universe."[13]

At the graveside, Minnie asked Rutherford to address the issue in the final tribute to Alex. Like Hall, Rutherford could not defend his orthodoxy: "Alex did not observe the conventionalities of religion, refusing to subscribe to what he considered idle ceremonies; his house of worship was all nature and was as broad and comprehensive as nature itself. He loved nature and in the silence of his own heart and in his own way worshiped nature's God." Alex had been an original thinker who looked inward "for the truths that are wrapped in the mysteries of nature, stripped of the ceremonial and glamor with which so many surround their devotion." With early French anticlerical writers as a major source of his ideals, he arrived at a belief in "a universal religion" and "assumed the responsibility of working out his own salvation, sensibly realizing the responsibilities of life and courageously accepting them. He saw and acknowledged in all the hand of divinity." [14]

That Alex took a dim view of Christianity and organized religion is certain. In 1912 George J. Remsburg, who had corresponded with the youthful Alex in the early 1890s, claimed that only a year before his death, Alex had told him that his religious views were basically what they had been while he was at Bacone. In his tribute to D. N. McIntosh, delivered at McIntosh's funeral in 1895, Alex reflected his reading of Thomas Paine, calling the Bible a "man-written book to which the world hangs in its ignorance" and the Christian God "the imaginary monster who rewards the few in heaven—who tortures the many in perdition." [15] In later years the institutionalized church took many jabs from the pen of Fus Fixico.

Whatever his religious views at the end of his life, the matter was not laid to rest with Alex. In the July issue of *Sturm's Oklahoma Magazine*, editor O. P. Sturm plagiarized the article from the *Star*: "One of the remarkable things about him was, lover of nature that he was, gentle, humorous and kind, he did not believe in the existence of a supreme being or the existence of a soul." Minnie annotated her copy of Sturm's article, writing "false" in the margin next to the statement. Elsewhere in the margin, echoing Hall's defense of Alex, she wrote that though he was skeptical concerning orthodox religion, "those that knew him best know that he felt God in all nature & his religious duties were in acts of charity, love & mercy." [16] Two weeks after his first statement, and in response to Sturm, Hall reaffirmed his earlier comments and added that Alex's religious belief was basically that of Thoreau. He concluded, "This story was undoubtedly circulated by some ignorant or bigoted person, and may be with a view to injure Mr. Posey in the estimation of church people." [17] But why would anyone wish to do that?

In the many tributes to Alex there had been no hint that he had enemies. All were testimonies to his altruism and his literary achievements. Rutherford had said of him, "To his own people he was ever looked up to as a comforting guide and to none will his death be a greater blow. He was born and lived through all his life amongst his own Creek people whom he loved and protected. He lived to see but the beginning of the end of that once proud and courageous nation, however, and in the dim distance clearly saw the result, the absolute absorption and changing of his people and his people's institutions by the resistless onward sweep of that higher and nobler civilization of this Christian age."[18] Those are the words of a white man. Like others who praised Alex, Rutherford failed to see the inconsistency of this view and that of Alex the land and oil man dealing in Indian allotments.

All who praised Alex remembered him not as a land dealer but only as a poet and the creator of Fus Fixico. They ignored the apparent materialism and remembered earlier, more idealistic sentiments. "I would rather have a $10 sofky bowl in my parlor to gaze upon than a $200 rug," he had said. "Had I the millions of Rockefeller I would not have expensive things that are not necessary to life." Another time he had written, "The rattlesnake, when he has swallowed a rabbit, crawls in the shade and is satisfied. The hawk, when he has caught a young chicken, stops circling above the barnyard and gives the old hen a rest. But man, when he has hoarded away enough of this world's goods to keep his stomach full and body clothed here and hereafter, wants more and continues to prey upon his brethern unto the day he turns his toes up to the daisies." Those who praised him perhaps ignored the irony of another of Alex's earlier statements: "When a man becomes so good that he is in nobody's way; when everybody is prompt to say but well of him, I tell you, sir, you can put it down, and safely too, that the world can move on without him."[19]

There were those who believed the world could indeed move on without Alex. Some Creeks, among them a few of his relatives in the Tuskegee and Artussee communities, resented his land dealings and felt he had somehow betrayed them. His continued association with the Palo Alto Land Company and his public statements concerning the conservative Creeks could only have heightened the sense of betrayal. Some thought they saw a sign in his death, and one distant relative said that perhaps it was a good thing. That it was the Oktahutche, which Alex loved, that killed him was not lost on Charles Gibson: "On the bosom of the stream that at last swallowed him he had often paddled his bark. He loved the old river that in a moment of rage extinguished his young life. . . . The roar of the old stream put him to sleep and sent him to his long home." And in his fatalistic Creek way, Gibson said it was meant to be.[20] There were no doubt others who thought the same and some who were unwilling to deny that some medicine was at work in the event.

A public perception that Alex was becoming wealthy through extensive landholdings was fed by exaggerated accounts in the press. On the day he died Congress had passed legislation that opened the way to a clear title to thousands of acres of Creek lands. Shortly after his death, one published report said that Alex owned 10,000 acres. A few days later a court decision upheld the validity of titles to land sold by those inheriting from full-bloods. The *Indian Journal* reported that the decision greatly increased the value of Alex's estate because he had "acquired extensive interests in such titles," and the report estimated the value of his estate at $25,000 to $30,000.[21] It was true, and it should be said in Alex's defense, that those allotments Alex had purchased for himself, other than those of his immediate family, were bought from the heirs of deceased allottees. But rumor had greatly exaggerated the extent of his holdings. If the stories about his personal wealth had been true, Alex would have died a wealthy man.

The truth is that Alex's estate was "land poor." He had borrowed money for which there were notes to be paid. He had assumed his brother John's debts to a Muskogee finance company, apparently in return for part of his allotment, and those debts were still outstanding. There were funeral and legal expenses and taxes. The oil venture at Bald Hill had come to nothing, and the land was not being improved. When Minnie finally settled the estate in 1910, the sale of his real estate did not raise enough money to pay all his debts. She was forced to sell a city lot that Alex owned in Muskogee as well as the Emma Posey allotment at Wagoner, the Lucy Washington allotment near Weleetka, and what Alex had owned of John's and Conny's allotments at Bald Hill. Ironically, nearly all of this property was sold to the officials of the Palo Alto Land Company, who also paid Minnie a pittance for Alex's interest in the company as well as his interest in certain other Creek allotments.[22]

Alex had also left unfinished plans in the literary field. One of his objectives in becoming editor of the *Indian Journal* had been to do "literary work," but he had written very little during the preceding year and a half. Some of his work in the *Journal* in 1908 suggests he was having difficulty regaining his productivity. The style of the *Journal* lacked the originality it had formerly displayed when he was editor. Though his humor was sharp, it came through only occasionally in the local news items: "Lewis Deer bounded into Eufaula this week to do some trading," or "Woxie Harjo was in our city Monday from the west riding a two hundred pound filly which was sway-backed and wobbling with Woxie's three hundred pounds of brawn and sinew and renderings." Perhaps Alex did not exert himself full force as an editor because he intended his tenure at the *Journal* to be short. According to one family member, he had been offered an editorial position with the Kansas City *Star*.[23]

The Fus Fixico letters also lacked the spark of earlier years. Two of them, as well as a piece titled "A New Home—A New Country," derived from the content of Fus Fixico letters of an earlier period. Alex had apparently decided some months earlier to put Fus Fixico away for good. Hotgun had died in January, and Alex had published a piece titled "The Passing of 'Hot Gun'" in the Kansas City *Star*. In the article, which was reprinted in the *Journal*, he reviewed Hotgun's career as "a philosopher, carpenter, blacksmith, fiddler, clockmaker, worker in metals, and a maker of medicines." He prefaced the article with the poem "Hotgun on the Death of Yadeka Harjo," in form, content, and tone perhaps the best of his poems. The most significant statement in the article, however, was Alex's past tense comment on the characters of the Fus Fixico letters: "Hot Gun, Wolf Warrior, Kono Harjo, and Fus Fixico were a quartet of Creek philosophers who used to spend much time together, and their criticisms became as proverbs among their fellow Indians." Many of the issues they had discussed had become moot points with statehood. Alex's language suggests he intended to retire these characters. He revived them, however, apparently for their usefulness in the McIntosh County seat fight, and continued using them to attack such issues as the wrangling of petty politicians in the Oklahoma legislature, the Oklahoma dispensary law as a means of getting around prohibition, and inane legislative debates on such topics as whether women should ride astride or sidesaddle or the length of bed sheets in hotels.[24]

There are intimations of other directions in his literary career. Evidence in the *Journal* suggests that he intended to mine the vast store of experiences he had accumulated during his years of work with the Dawes Commission. A piece called "Lost from His Tribe

for Many Years," for instance, was a revision of the transcript of testimony he had taken from Itshas Harjo in the Cherokee Nation in
1907. Also, he was said to have been collecting Creek traditions and
folklore just before his death. Such literature had interested him for
many years. In 1901 and 1902 he had published some "fables," and
he had used other Creek legends and tales in his Fus Fixico letters. Alex had long believed that many of the Uncle Remus stories
originated among the Creeks and were told among his people before the Africans arrived in the New World. As late as September
1907 he had discussed assembling a collection of Creek stories for
publication, saying he already had enough material for a thousand
pages. Alex was familiar with William E. Connelley's collection of
Wyandot legends and may have thought to pattern his collection
after that. He had written some stories in which the characters bore
Creek names, such as Chuffee the rabbit and Yaha the wolf. Ever
mindful of the similarities between the Creek stories and the Uncle
Remus tales, he wrote across one manuscript that it was too much
like Joel Chandler Harris's story and needed to be rewritten.[25]

Alex's interest was also directed toward recording Creek history.
The recent death of Pleasant Porter made Alex fear that he had
already missed good opportunities to gather information. As a young
man Porter had been secretary and interpreter for one of the Creek
leaders who had died during a trip to Washington. The dying man
dictated a message for Porter to take back to the Creek Nation.
Though Porter had never put it in writing, he had repeated it to
Alex many times. Nor had Porter written down his speech to his
warriors at the beginning of the Green Peach War. Alex believed
both the speeches were bits of Creek history that should have been
preserved.[26]

Besides these, he may have had other literary intentions. Only
days before he died, he received a letter from the Cherokee writer
and syndicated cartoonist Royal Roger Eubanks, who proposed to
oversee the publication of a volume of Alex's work, which Eubanks
would illustrate with pen-and-ink drawings. Also, in recent years
Alex had considered some of his earlier productions immature and
had intended to revise them. Some who knew his work agreed with
his self-evaluation, at least in regard to his poetry, laying blame
for his literary immaturity on his isolation in the Indian Territory
and his refusal to seek a wider audience: "Unhappily, Posey died in

the early springtime of his career. He had scarcely felt the thrill of literary ambition. He lived apart from men whose knowledge of his art would have been helpful to his craftsmanship. His little songs were sung as a boy sings in the fields. That the years would have brought him strength and vigor in lyrical expression is the belief of those who knew him." [27]

His literary plans may have been grander than simply continued writing or revision of his earlier works. The acquisition of land and the search for oil were apparently meant to produce the wealth that would give him the life style he had dreamed of a decade earlier. After his death, George Riley Hall said that Alex had intended to build a home at Bald Hill where he could entertain "authors, poets, and kindred souls, where close to nature they could commune." In reality, he had planned to build the home, to be called Tulledega Lodge, in the Tulledega Hills near the Oktahutche.[28]

To some there was no need to ask what Alex might have done— he had already earned a place in the literary annals of the West. George Riley Hall's assessment was typical: "As a classic English scholar he had no superior in the West. His memory was marvelous. His relish for the best literature was remarkable, even while he was yet a boy." Hall concluded: "The state may grow great and proud in art and literature, but the impress he left on the literature of his day cannot be effaced. It will live. 'To live in hearts we leave behind is not to die' and Posey will live as long as Oklahomans live and read." Alex's fellow workers at the *Indian Journal* wrote: "Alex Posey has sung the beauty and glory of his Indian country in verse that will live as long as the name of Oklahoma shall endure on her monuments. He has woven the names of the rivers, mountains, valleys and plains into song and story which will inspire the young patriots of other generations and brighten the pages of the nation's literature." [29]

For the Indian writers of Oklahoma, however, Alex's death dashed hopes of literary greatness for the American Indian. B. N. O. Walker, the Wyandot poet and storyteller who wrote under the name Hentoh, believed that Alex's "maturer years would have produced something yet more worthy of his talents" than his poetry or the Fus Fixico letters. Ora Eddleman Reed, a Cherokee, called him "one of the most brilliant men the Indians of any tribe have produced," one whose friends "were very ambitious for him, recognizing in him a rare power." Had he not died, "his name would unquestionably have become one of national prominence." In his poems "he was the dreamer, the lover of nature in all her moods—in short, the Indian poet, who saw all things with clear eyes—heard the music of the birds and the rippling of the streams, and, understanding, interpreted in words that were all music." Charles Gibson said simply, "He was one of the few Indian writers of North America."[30]

A writer's success can be measured in part by what he leaves and by his imitators. As a poet, prose writer, journalist, and humorist, Alex left a corpus greater in variety than that of any Indian writer and greater than most in volume. Those who believed Alex's literary renown rested on his poetry simply shared his romantic tastes. Because of their admiration, they could not see that he had done little that was distinctive in his poetry and nothing that deserved imitation. They failed to realize that he had already secured his place in American Indian literary history through his prose depictions of the landscapes, life, and character of the Creek Nation.

Of these depictions, the Fus Fixico letters would have the most lasting value. Writers of Alex's day recognized their value and imitated them. Some copied his style and letter format. Editors adapted his letters to their own local political issues. Shortly before his death, Alex compared the products of his imitators in the Checotah and Hoffman papers to "the wooden aborigine," a "product of the white man's factory" that bore "no resemblance to the real article." The Fus Fixico letters influenced other Creek writers, including Jesse McDermott, who worked for the Dawes Commission when Alex did and claimed to be his disciple; Acee Blue Eagle, a Creek-Pawnee artist, who also wrote dialect poetry; and most important, Thomas E. Moore, whose William Harjo letters appeared as a regular column called "Sour Sofkee" in an Oklahoma City newspaper in the late 1930s. Alex's influence was apparent as well in the dialect works of other tribal writers who were familiar with the Fus Fixico letters: the "Nights with Uncle Ti-ault-ly" stories by Royal Roger Eubanks, Cherokee; the lectures and writings of E. M. Landrum, Cherokee, who wrote under the persona Bill Kantfraid; and the poems and tales of Bertrand N. O. Walker, Wyandot.[31]

The land and people that Alex knew, loved, and captured in his writing are much changed. Yet something of the world he moved in survives—perhaps more than he could have imagined. Like many intellectuals of his time, Alex believed one had to possess certain skills and attitudes to survive in the age of "multiplicity," whose advent Henry Adams had announced in 1907. Such thinking led him to some erroneous conclusions about the passing of Creek culture. Not simply the cultural conservatives, but Creeks in general have maintained a strong sense of identity. Though the significance of such matters as clan and kinship declined, Creek towns, as social and cultural entities, survived the allotment debacle as well as statehood, with its political structures based on the new geographic units of county, district, and state.[32] Town identity often depended in part—perhaps ironically—on the Christian church, which bound town members in close-knit units. As one writer put it near mid-century, "The Creek church has either superseded the old ceremonial square ground or exists side by side with it, the two being separated by only a mile or two. The important thing is that the town organization has tended to hang on; its ceremonial center is simply changing from the square ground to the church."[33] Some towns remain largely intact. Ceremonial grounds are maintained at Alabama Quasarte, Greenleaf, and Fishpond, for example, and Thloplocco was federally recognized as a tribe after its members adopted a constitution in 1938. Its independence from the Creek Nation of Oklahoma was recognized by the Bureau of Indian Affairs in 1989.

Today Tuskegee Canadian, which gave Alex his identity as a Creek, is an entity whose significance reaches far beyond a point on a map. The hub of the community is the Baptist church, which sits at the edge of the old square ground, encircled by small camp houses. The families that maintain them gather each summer for their annual encampment, which serves their sense of spiritual renewal and community well-being in much the same way the busk served their ancestors. Services in Creek throughout the decades have done much to preserve the language and, presumably, the cultural ideas that go with it. Thus in the English speech of Creeks in the Tuskegee community there can still be heard an occasional expression reminiscent of Fus Fixico.

Though the Oktahutche Alex knew is gone, its ancient banks far below the surface of Lake Eufaula, the bolder surrounding landscape survives. Highway U.S. 69 crosses the lake not far from the flooded site of Posey Hole. Clearly visible from there, to the west, across the lake and above the far tree line, Bald Hill rises blue against the sky, and farther to the north and west, darker and low on the horizon, lie the Tulledega Hills.

Postscript

· ·

When a man dies as suddenly and dramatically as Alex did, he leaves the odds and ends of his life for someone else to sort out and deal with, and those who must do the sorting are sometimes unequal to the task and victimized by others who sense their vulnerability. Though it is impossible to know exactly what hopes and dreams Alex had cherished for Minnie, Yohola, and Wynema, it can safely be said that they did not include the events that unfolded during the five decades after his death.

Alex had not been dead a week when Minnie received inquiries concerning his literary estate. Z. T. Walrond, her attorney at Muskogee, first asked her to compile Alex's works for publication, but shortly thereafter it was announced that Walrond was arranging for the publication, to be supervised by John Beauregard Torrans, the poet friend after whom Alex had named Wynema. Through J. N. Thornton, an inquiry also came from Frederick S. Barde, a correspondent for the Kansas City *Star*, with whom Alex had been on

familiar terms as early as 1903. Barde was probably responsible for
the many notices of Alex as a writer and newspaper man that had appeared in the *Star*. He was concerned that Alex's work in manuscript be preserved: "Some day, with proper editing, it could be published in a little book as a memorial to Posey and for the benefit of his family." Minnie assured Barde that every bit of Alex's work would be saved and that she expected to compile and publish it "at an early date." That fall the *Muskogee Phoenix* announced the imminent publication of "a little volume" of Alex's poems in Creek and English. Whether this was the product of Walrond's and Torrans's efforts is uncertain. Whether it appeared is also uncertain, but almost twenty years later, two copies of a Creek-English edition were alleged to exist.[1]

During the next two years, Minnie worked to get a large edition of the poems into print. She collected 105 poems in a volume titled "Song of the Oktahutchee and Other Poems," which Houghton Mifflin, McClurg, and Scribner rejected. She had no assistance in preparing the collection and had included pieces that she thought "pretty" but that she believed Alex would probably have rejected because he was "very modest & placed little value on any thing that he wrote." By early 1910, however, William E. Connelley of Topeka, former director of the Kansas State Historical Society, had offered his assistance in getting the volume published. It appeared late that year as *The Poems of Alexander Lawrence Posey*, published by Crane and Company of Topeka. To celebrate publication, Mrs. A. C. Lawrence set some of the poems to music and gave a recital in Muskogee on December 13.[2] To introduce the volume, Connelley supplied a long "Memoir of Alexander Lawrence Posey," for which Minnie supplied a good deal of information. Until now it has stood as the authoritative statement on his life, and much of what has been written about him since its publication has been derived from it. Of course, it presents Alex as Minnie saw him. The *Poems* volume has also stood as the authoritative version of his poetry, but Minnie made serious errors in transcription in some poems and significant revisions in others.

At the time the volume appeared, Minnie had just settled Alex's personal estate and was facing financial difficulties. Those who first encouraged her in the publication project hoped the book sales would be profitable, but they were not. Notices of the publication appeared locally and in places as far-flung as Galveston and Baltimore, but sales were limited and slow. They were so bad, in fact, that the publisher ultimately destroyed the stock of books and plates and returned the copyright to Minnie. Thus Minnie had to look for work to rear the children, so she entered government service, first at the Sequoyah Orphan Training School near Tahlequah.[3] During the years that followed, Minnie moved from place to place, working some years at federal Indian schools, including those at Carlisle and Phoenix, managing to survive and to educate the children.

It had been so difficult to find a publisher for the poems that Minnie gave up her original plan to publish other works, including a volume of the Fus Fixico letters and perhaps a volume of the legends, stories, field notes, and journals. Among the latter was part of what she called the "River Journal," which Alex had kept when he, Thornton, and Doc Williams floated down the Oktahutche in summer 1901. He had later published the first chapter in the *Indian Journal* but had not continued because Thornton objected. When Barde approached Thornton shortly after Alex's death, he was particularly interested in the "River Journal," part of which Alex had once showed him, and which he considered "good stuff." Barde had wanted to publish it and had asked Alex about it; Alex "was timid, however, and declined to let it be published," according to Barde.[4]

Barde persisted in his quest to obtain the journal. He repeatedly asked Minnie for that and other materials. Pleased at the interest in Alex's work, she sent him photographs and offered to let him come to her home and look at Alex's manuscripts and her scrapbooks. In early 1910, when Barde planned an article, she sent him a biographical sketch she had prepared as well as snapshots and manuscript copies of poems. At that time the collection of poems she had prepared was circulating to publishers, and she believed an article might promote it. Barde then offered to write an introduction to the collection, but Minnie was apparently not interested. By then Barde had become quite persistent. In 1915 he finally prevailed, and Minnie sent him the "River Journal" to read, asking that he return it. Barde died shortly thereafter, and several years later, when Barde's papers were donated to the Oklahoma Historical Society, the journal was alleged to be among them. Barde's widow arranged to have it copied for Minnie, who objected to both the copying and its in-

clusion in Barde's collection. The Historical Society sent her a copy,
which she claimed was incomplete, and on learning that Barde had
published part of the journal in the Kansas City *Star*, she accused
him of violating her copyright. The manuscript was never returned
to her. If it still exists, it is hidden from public view.[5]

For the rest of her life Minnie was sought out by opportunists, and
she was little more successful in resisting them than she had been
in resisting Barde and the officials of the Palo Alto Land Company
in settling Alex's literary and personal estates. After her experience
with Barde, however, she was more cautious. From her home in Arizona, where she retired, she gave vague and noncommital responses
to inquiries concerning Alex's manuscripts. In 1949 she placed what
remained of his papers in the Thomas Gilcrease Institute of American History and Art at Tulsa.[6]

Besides his manuscripts, there was great interest in his well-known
collection of Indian artifacts. In 1913 Minnie had placed the collection on loan at the University of Oklahoma, with the stipulation
that she or her children could reclaim it at any time. It consisted
of eighty-two items, including bows and arrows, pottery, wooden
spoons and paddles, the loom Alex had bought from Artus Hotiye
in 1906, ball sticks, tortoise-shell rattles, and other items. In 1917
Minnie reclaimed the collection, minus a few pieces that could not
be accounted for, and put it on display at a city-run museum in the
Union Indian Agency building at Muskogee. The city had invited
Minnie to become manager of the museum but could not pay her a
salary. She accepted, and the collection was on display for a short
time in 1918. Minnie ran a little tearoom in connection with the
museum to support herself and the children.[7]

Perhaps because of her retrieval of the artifacts, Minnie caught
the attention of Edward Everett Dale, an instructor in history at the
University of Oklahoma. He approached her ostensibly for two reasons: to obtain her assistance in gathering Indian arts and crafts for
what he called the "Dale Collection" at the university and to seek
her advice on Indian matters for a series of "Indian" stories he was
writing. Like others before him, he also expressed an interest in
Alex's manuscripts. Minnie had been frustrated in her own ambitions. After the failure of the 1910 edition of Alex's poems, she had
given up on getting more of his works into print. Her experience
as a teacher in the federal Indian schools had convinced her that

Indian children were losing touch with their heritage. She had argued that they should be taught Indian history and had proposed to
write a series of life stories of famous Indian men and women, have
the stories published by the Indian school press, and distribute them
to the students. But her ideas had been rejected by school officials.
She had also hoped to complete the Creek stories that Alex had left
unfinished and to have Yohola illustrate them, but she finally concluded that she would never do it.[8] Perhaps she thought Dale could
help her, so she encouraged him when he inquired.

Throughout spring 1918 they corresponded frequently, and a
strong friendship developed. She read the stories that ultimately became his *Tales of the Teepee* (1920) and gave him advice. She sent
him copies of stories by Charles Gibson as well as some of Alex's
tales in manuscript. Dale made a brief visit to her home and looked
at the remaining manuscripts. When he asked her to let him copy
Alex's journals, she reluctantly sent them to him, trusting that he
would not "publish a line" of them without her consent. She also
invited him to her home in June for a two-week visit so that he could
read, write, and look through the manuscripts at his leisure.[9] Shortly
thereafter Dale went to Harvard to pursue his doctoral studies, and
a few months after that Minnie left Muskogee to seek salaried em-
ployment once more. Her friendship with Dale ceased abruptly in
early 1919.

The friendship with Dale had caused Minnie to examine her life.
When Dale discovered her birthdate in one of Alex's journals, she
remembered "how sunny those birthdays were." Now at midlife, she
looked toward old age with misgiving, and perhaps she was thinking
of Alex when she affirmed her belief in the line, "Those the Gods
love die young." Yet she was not bitter. Alex had been dead for ten
years, and she could now talk about him and fondly remember their
life together. When she moved to Muskogee, for the first time in six
years she was able to unpack her books and set up her library, where
she liked to sit and read. Those books held associations of the past for
her. Now and then a mark or a note in a margin would speak warmly
from the page. In one book she found a letter Alex had written her
when he was in the field for the Dawes Commission. "These things
do not make me sad," she said. "They give me a glimpse of a happy
past—and then I look again to the future and wonder what the next
day will bring. My days have brought some wonderful things." She

could say of Alex's poems, "They are the tender thoughts of a tender heart now dead—how sweet to remember a life so filled with
beautiful thoughts." [10]

Minnie wondered if she had betrayed Alex through judgment
blurred by love and memory. Each thought in his poems was pure
and sweet to her. Where others read a single thought, she read volumes in his lines. Because he had been so sensitive and modest about
his works, she regretted, as she grew older, having published some
of them. When Dale broached the subject of publishing the journals,
she hesitated. "It's a foolish nature that I have, I know," she wrote,
"of not wanting them copied—as they are they seem so much an
intimate part of his young life that was only known and understood
by me. . . . Every note tells a story to me no matter how short." She
believed she might never consent to their publication, for she no
longer trusted her judgment regarding which of Alex's works should
be published.[11]

Time undermined her resolve. In 1955 she sought to get the poems
into print once more. She had renewed her copyright in 1938 and
wanted to publish a new edition before the copyright ran out. She
had been sent a manuscript of the poems with an introduction prepared in the 1930s by Orlando Swain of Okmulgee and Edith Connelley Clift of Oklahoma City. Swain had known Alex in 1906 and
1907, had greatly admired his poetry, and had attempted for many
years to get a collection of the poems into print. Mrs. Clift was the
daughter of William E. Connelley, who had written the introduction
for the 1910 edition. Realizing that radio and television had replaced
reading as a pastime, Minnie knew it would be difficult to find a
publisher and was willing to help finance the publication. Because
of her age and extremely poor health, she turned to her one-time
friend E. E. Dale, then retired and a professor emeritus at the University of Oklahoma, for help in getting the Swain-Clift manuscript
into print.[12]

Dale immediately brought up again the subject of publishing
Alex's journals. He and Muriel Wright, editor of the *Chronicles of
Oklahoma*, the journal of the Oklahoma Historical Society, decided
it would be advantageous to publish the journals in the *Chronicles*,
save the type, and reissue them in pamphlet form for publicity and
profit. Afraid that publication in the *Chronicles* would limit reader-
ship to subscribers, Minnie warmed to the idea of the pamphlets,

which could be circulated widely. Money was not her concern; she simply wanted Alex's name before the public once more. Still, she hesitated in giving her consent.[13]

Minnie complicated the matter for Dale and Wright by asking for the return of some photographs, a child's chair, a platter decorated with scenes from *Ivanhoe*, two baskets, and a bracelet that were with Alex's collection of artifacts, which she had lent to the Oklahoma Historical Society in 1925. Wright handled the affair for the society. She asked Dale to intercede, arguing that Minnie was requesting the return of some of the "best" items in the collection. To stall Minnie, Wright sent her copies of the photographs and informed her that since 1942 the society had considered the collection a gift, not a loan. Dale was concerned about losing the collection, but more concerned about the bad publicity the society might receive if Minnie's wishes were denied. He believed that the society had no legal right to retain the collection and that if Minnie chose to sue for it, she would win. Dale and Wright did not want to jeopardize the chances of obtaining Minnie's permission to publish the journals. Thus Dale proposed a solution to the directors of the society: offer Minnie two or three items, not including the bracelet or the baskets, to placate her. They agreed, and Wright wrote to her offering the chair and the platter. In reality, Minnie wanted the society to have the collection and wanted to retrieve only a few pieces for Wynema and Wynema's daughter. Minnie accepted Wright's terms and released the rest of the collection to the society. Dale realized the moral implications of what they had done and told Wright, "That is exactly the procedure the white man followed in dealing with the Indian for centuries." Longtime historian of the Indian that he was, Dale saw the situation clearly, but the society was in what he repeatedly called an "embarrassing situation." [14]

Besides donating the collection, Minnie also reluctantly gave Dale permission to edit and publish the journals. A sense of having betrayed Alex still nagged at her. She recalled how shy he was, "almost to a fault," about his works. "I still feel a little guilty and that I have in a way betrayed the trust that Alex had in me in allowing the Journals to be published," she wrote to Dale, who was urging publication. "He would not have approved of my publishing many of the poems of the Crane edition either but I agree with you." Thus during the next year she assisted him in clarifying Alex's difficult handwriting, identifying people, places, and events for annotations,

and correcting the typescript of the journals. Perhaps in his old age
it had slipped Dale's mind that he had published one of Alex's journals in 1930 without Minnie's consent or, apparently, knowledge. He
also failed to alert Wright, who claimed editorially, when the journal
was published in the *Chronicles*, that it was being published for the
first time.[15]

However disagreeable the affair may seem to the outsider, reread-
ing the journals in detail had revived Minnie's fond memories of
Alex and their life together. Her admiration for him shines through
her letters to Dale. At times the pain is also there. Of Pachina, their
son who died in 1900, she wrote, "I think of him as my baby still who
never grew up." By early 1957 she had given up the idea of publishing the poems; it was simply too risky an undertaking for publishers.
She recognized the singularity of her life and wanted to write her
autobiography so that, as she said, her "children & friends will know
the person that they have lived with yet never really known." [16]

Time had divested Minnie of practically everything related to
Alex's dreams and ambitions except the memory of them and the
children. She had lived for more than twenty years with Wynema
and her husband at Phoenix. Yohola, who became an engineer, had
entered government service, moving around with his assignments
and retiring finally at Las Cruces, New Mexico. Distance and old
age had made Minnie vulnerable to the maneuverings of the likes
of Dale and Wright, and she died in November 1961, not knowing
she could have had not only the items she asked for but the entire
collection of artifacts had she wanted it. Neither did she live to see
the publication of the journals, which did not appear until 1967 and
1968.[17] In his wildest flights of imagination, Alex could not have
anticipated what Minnie went through in the aftermath of his death.

Neither could he have imagined what happened to the Posey lands
at Bald Hill. Large tracts had gone when Minnie settled the estate.
By that time sales agreements had been made for most of the other
Posey surplus allotments, including Nancy's. Because the Posey children were half Creek, their forty-acre homestead allotments were
restricted from sale. Most of the children applied to the secretary of
interior for removal of restrictions and sold their homesteads as well.
By the mid-1920s, the remaining homesteads had sold. In addition to
Alex's lands, much of the other Posey land fell into the hands of offi-

cials of the Palo Alto Land Company. By 1910 all of the family had left Bald Hill; at that time Nancy lived at Dustin. Ella, Alex's youngest sister, returned and was the only one of his siblings to remain on Posey land, though not on her own allotment, which had been sold.[18] So much for Alex's belief that Creeks like him and his siblings would easily make the transition from Creek to United States citizenship. Even his family was not immune to the lure of the quick cash that land would bring and the different life-style it would buy. What a turn of events! The very land company he had helped to obtain the allotments of other Indians now owned much of his own cherished family ranch and the seat of the land empire on which he had hoped to build his family's future.

By 1918 Nancy was at Mounds with her aunt, Lydia Tiger, who was well over one hundred years old. Lydia died late that year, and having had only one child, whom she survived, she left Nancy her allotment of 160 acres, containing several oil wells, and an estimated $40,000 in oil and gas royalties, then in the custody of Gabe E. Parker, commissioner to the Five Civilized Tribes. After a legal challenge by her distant relatives and by her sister Winey's children, Nancy was awarded the estate in 1919. She immediately sold half of the allotment for $24,000. The Tiger allotment was on the edge of the Glenpool field, one of the richest oil discoveries the world has ever known. It was worth a fortune. Yet the Tiger estate was apparently never settled. In 1981 a Tulsa County court dismissed the case, and it was placed in the dead file. What happened to the estate between 1919 and 1981 is unclear. Family members say that Nancy, who could not read, write, or speak English, lost the land and the money through mismanagement and possible illegalities by her son Darwin. There was talk of prosecution, but Nancy forbade it, believing Darwin would go to jail. He might have, indeed, for he had been convicted earlier of taking money under false pretenses.[19]

With Lydia Tiger passed Nancy's last close connection to the old Creek world. Her brother Cumsey had died in 1903, Lewis in 1908, and Johnson in 1914. By 1918 Winey also was dead.[20]

Nancy now moved from place to place, legally dependent on Melissa Emery, whose husband, John, had formerly held Nancy's power of attorney. In 1929, a few months before the stock market crash, she was persuaded to buy two lots and build a home at Wewoka, where she would take in boarders to make a living. But the oil boom declined with the onset of the depression. In 1930 she deeded the property to her grandson J. Gladstone Emery, who promptly mortgaged it. Emery deeded the property back to her in early 1932, but unable to meet the financial obligations attached to it, she lost it through a sheriff's auction in early 1936. She then moved with the Emerys to Heavener in what had been the old Choctaw Nation, and there she lived out her days. The public fascination with Alex led reporters to her, and she reminisced about his childhood, youth, and manhood. She pictured him always the same: sensitive, devoted, kind, and protective. After nearly thirty years, those who spoke with her still sensed the terrible void his death had left in her life. Nancy died in March 1938 at the home of Melissa Emery. The funeral was held at Bald Hill, and she was buried in the old family plot on its slope.[21]

As she approached the end of her life, how bewildering were the changes time had brought Nancy through![22] How differently she lived than when the green corn ceremony dominated the ceremonial life at Tuskegee during her early years. How far in the past must have seemed those war years in dreary exile with Thlee-sa-ho-he and Lydia in Kansas, the coming of Christianity to Tuskegee, and those years with Hence on Limbo Creek, where her first and favorite child was born. What had happened to the ranch Hence had worked so hard to build at Bald Hill? What had become of his plans to prepare his children to meet the challenges of the changing social order? Ironically, strangers owned the Bald Hill ranch, while in the remoter rural areas of the neighboring hills the conservative Creeks still farmed their little patches, ran their livestock in the woods, made their sofky, and built grave houses over the resting places of the departed as they had done for centuries.

And what had happened to the promise embodied in her children? Bill, John, Mattie, and Conny had died. Frank was serving life imprisonment for murder.[23] The remaining children were scattered. The greatest loss, however, had apparently been Alex, in whom Nancy and Hence had placed such great store. He had believed in and helped bring about the new social order that had transformed the land and brought strangers to Bald Hill. Though widely acclaimed for many accomplishments, he had died before his personal ambitions, whatever they might have been, could come to fruition. Nancy had witnessed his praise by contemporaries, as well as the recognition by subsequent generations that, as a Creek, his life was singular. Privy, no doubt, to her son's expectations for the future, Nancy understood as perhaps no one else could—even Minnie—the significance of the loss of so talented a Creek at such a critical point in Creek history.

Notes

· ·

ABBREVIATIONS

AMD-OHS—Archives and Manuscripts Division,
  Oklahoma Historical Society, Oklahoma City
Gilcrease—Alexander L. Posey Collection,
  Thomas Gilcrease Institute of American History
  and Art, Tulsa, Oklahoma
NAMP—National Archives Microfilm
  Publications, National Archives, Washington,
  D.C.
NARG—National Archives Record Group,
  National Archives, Washington, D.C.
RG75NA-OHS—Record Group 75, National
  Archives, Oklahoma Historical Society,
  Oklahoma City
WHC—Western History Collections, University of
  Oklahoma

1. "Specter of Death Still Haunts Water Hole," *Tulsa Daily World*, February 7, 1932, sec. 5, p. 3; William Elsey Connelley, "Memoir of Alexander Lawrence Posey," in Minnie H. Posey, comp., *The Poems of Alexander Lawrence Posey* (Topeka: Crane, 1910), 43; *Muskogee Times-Democrat*, May 28, 1908.

2. Connelley, "Memoir," 43–44.

3. Connelley, "Memoir," 44, 56.

4. Connelley, "Memoir," 44–46; "Specter of Death," *Indian Journal*, May 29, 1908.

5. Connelley, "Memoir," 46–48; "Specter of Death."

6. Connelley, "Memoir," 48–50; *Henryetta Free-Lance*, June 5, 1908.

7. Connelley, "Memoir," 50–53; "Specter of Death."

8. Connelley, "Memoir," 53–56; *Muskogee Times-Democrat*, May 28, 1908; "Specter of Death."

9. "Fancy," in Poems by Posey (p. 20), item 4026.8259, Gilcrease. This poem was not published during his lifetime. The popularly published poem, usually titled "My Fancy," was an earlier version. The one reprinted here was Posey's last.

10. "Specter of Death"; La-Vere Shoenfelt Anderson, "Getting Acquainted with Oklahoma Bards," *Tulsa Daily World*, February 11, 1934, sec. 4, p. 7; Nyna Stone, "Soul of the West in Heart of Indian Poet," *Wewoka Times-Democrat*, April 29, 1934.

CHAPTER ONE

1. J. N. B. Hewitt, *Notes on the Creek Indians*, ed. John R. Swanton, Bureau of American Ethnology Bulletin 123 (Washington, D.C.: Government Printing Office, 1939), 127–28; Harry Austin, Interview, *Indian-Pioneer History* (AMD-OHS), 28:183; Claims of Phillips Families, Samuel Brown Collection, Loyal Creek Claimants, AMD-OHS; Affidavit of Nancy Posey, December 24, 1937, typescript copy in author's files from original lent by Alexander Posey's granddaughter, Ginger Blaine Moore.

2. Affidavit of Nancy Posey.

3. Creek Census Card 497 (Lydia Tiger), Enrollment Cards for the Five Civilized Tribes, 1898–1914, NAMP M1186; Claims of Phillips Families, Samuel Brown Collection, AMD-OHS.

4. Affidavit of Nancy Posey; Creek Census Card 497 (Lydia Tiger). For clarifying insights into the ethnic diversity that made up the people known as Creeks, see J. Leitch Wright, Jr., *Creeks and Seminoles: The Destruction and Regeneration of the Muscogulge People* (Lincoln: University of Nebraska Press, 1986), especially chap. 1.

5. Hewitt, *Notes on the Creek Indians*, 128; Frank G. Speck, *The Creek Indians of Taskigi Town* (Millwood, N.Y.: Kraus Reprint, 1974), 117.

6. 50th Congress, 1st session, *Senate Executive Document 198*, 9; "Census of the Creek Nation, East," 23d Congress, 1st session, *Senate Executive Document 512*, 4:239, 260, 261; Affidavit of Nancy Posey; William McCombs, "History of Tuskegee Church," undated typescript in the possession of Leona Colbert, Eufaula, Oklahoma.

7. 50th Congress, 1st session, *Senate Executive Document 198*, 18; Angie Debo, *The Road to Disappearance* (Norman: University of Oklahoma Press, 1941), 98–99; *Land Location Registers, ca. 1834–86* and *Location Registers and Certifications of Contracts, ca. 1834–36*, in Creek Removal Records and *Schedules of Unpatented Creek Lands, 1878* in Records concerning Patents and Deeds, Records of the Bureau of Indian Affairs, NARG 75; entries for section 1, township 17 north, range 22 east, and sections 1 and 6, township 17 North, range 23 east, Tract Book, Probate Judge's Office, Macon County, Alabama. For history of the Creeks in the removal era, see Michael D. Green, *The Politics of Indian Removal: The Creek Government and Society in Crisis* (Lincoln: University of Nebraska Press, 1982). The story of the land fraud in Alabama is told in Mary Elizabeth Young, *Redskins, Ruffleshirts, and Rednecks: Indian Allotments in Alabama and Mississippi, 1830–1860* (Norman: University of Oklahoma Press, 1961).

8. Debo, *Road to Disappearance*, 100, 106; Jackson Lewis, informant, "Creek Ethnologic and Vocabulary Notes, Oct. 1910," Creek 1806, and "Creek Notes," Creek 4200, National Anthropological Archives, Smithsonian Institution.

9. Speck, *Creek Indians*, 134–44; Hewitt, *Notes on the Creek Indians*, 149–54.

10. See Cases 697 and 1488, *Records relating to the Loyal Creek Claims, 1869–70*, in Records relating to Civil War Claims of Loyal Indians, Records of the Bureau of Indian Affairs, NARG 75; Debo, *Road to Disappearance*, 112. For changes among the Creeks as a result of European contact, see Wright, *Creeks and Seminoles*, chap. 2.

11. Elliott Howe, Interview, Tulsa, Oklahoma, July 31, 1990. The theory of ethnic divisions among the Creeks is presented in Wright, *Creeks and Seminoles*, 14–19, 306–7. For the details of Opothleyohola's trek to Kansas, see John Bartlett Meserve, "Chief Opothleyahola," *Chronicles of Oklahoma* 9 (December 1931): 440–53; Edwin C. Bearss, "The Civil War Comes to Indian Territory, 1861: The Flight of Opothleyoholo," *Journal of the West* 11 (January 1972): 9–42; Charles Bahos, "On Opothleyahola's Trail: Locating the Battle of Round Mountains," *Chronicles of Oklahoma* 63 (Spring 1985): 58–89.

12. Case 992, *Records relating to the Loyal Creek Claims, 1869–70*. For conditions in the camps, see Dean Banks, "Civil-War Refugees from Indian Territory in the North, 1861–1864," *Chronicles of Oklahoma* 41 (Autumn 1963): 286–98.

13. See LeRoy H. Fischer and William L. McMurry, "Confederate Refugees from Indian Territory," *Chronicles of Oklahoma* 57 (Winter 1979–80):

457. For a firsthand account of the conditions prevailing on the Creeks' return to the Canadian River district, see W. David Baird, ed., *A Creek Warrior for the Confederacy: The Autobiography of Chief G. W. Grayson* (Norman: University of Oklahoma Press, 1988), 120–23.

14. Austin, Interview, 183; McCombs, "History of Tuskegee Church"; Leona Colbert, Interview, Eufaula, Oklahoma, June 15, 1988; Fischer and McMurry, "Confederate Refugees from Indian Territory," 457; Case 991, *Records relating to the Loyal Creek Claims, 1869–70*, NARG 75.

15. R. M. Loughridge, comp., *Muskokee Hymns*, 5th ed. (Philadelphia: Presbyterian Board of Christian Education, 1937; reprint, Okmulgee, Okla.: B. Frank Belvin, 1970), 1–2. English translation is by George Bunny, Oklahoma City.

16. The story of Takosar Harjo's conversion is told in Austin, Interview, 183; McCombs, "History of Tuskegee Church."

17. "History of Tuskegee Indian Church," *Indian Journal*, bicentennial special edition, June 1976; "Tuskegee Indian Baptist Church," typescript, 1976, in History File, *Indian Journal* Office, Eufaula, Oklahoma, copy in author's file; McCombs, "History of Tuskegee Church."

18. "Tuskegee Indian Baptist Church"; Austin, Interview, 183; "Reverend William McCombs," *Chronicles of Oklahoma* 8 (March 1930): 138.

19. Jones Gladstone Emery, *Court of the Damned; Being a Factual Story of the Court of Judge Isaac C. Parker and the Life and Times of the Indian Territory and Old Fort Smith* (New York: Comet Press Books, 1959), 183–84; Leona Colbert, Interview, Eufaula, Oklahoma, February 9, 1989.

20. William Elsey Connelley, "Memoir of Alexander Lawrence Posey," in *The Poems of Alexander Lawrence Posey*, comp. Minnie H. Posey (Topeka: Crane, 1910), 6; "Specter of Death Still Haunts Water Hole," *Tulsa Daily World*, February 7, 1932, sec. 5, p. 3.

21. Connelley, "Memoir," 10; Ora Eddleman Reed, "Alexander Posey, the Creek Poet," *Indian School Journal* 11 (June 1911): 13; "Death of L. H. Posey," *Eufaula Gazette*, undated (January 1902), clipping, Scrapbook, item 4626.31, Gilcrease (this source should be viewed with question, for a part of the newsprint has been cut out and the information regarding Posey's birth penciled in. The newspaper is not extant, so verification is impossible; Elliott Howe, Interview, Tulsa, Oklahoma, July 31, 1990; Eugene Current-Garcia and Dorothy B. Hatfield, eds., *Shem, Ham and Japheth: The Papers of W. O. Tuggle* (Athens: University of Georgia Press, 1973), 43.

22. Creek Census Card 892 (Lewis H. Posey), NAMP M1186; "Specter of Death Still Haunts Water Hole"; Reed, "Alexander Posey," 13; Connelley, "Memoir," 6; Emery, *Court of the Damned*, 181; George Riley Hall, "East Side Landmark of Creek Indians Torn Down," undated clipping, Scrapbook, item 4626.31, Gilcrease.

23. Connelley, "Memoir," 6–7.

24. Ibid., 7, 10; "Death of L. H. Posey," *Eufaula Gazette*, undated (January 1902), clipping, Scrapbook, item 4626.31, Gilcrease.

25. Free Inhabitants in Indian Lands West of Arkansas, Creek Nation,

Schedule 14, 1860 Census Schedules, NAMP M653; Lewis H. Posey Record, First Creek Mounted Volunteers, Compiled Service Records of Confederate Soldiers Who Served in Organizations Raised Directly by the Confederate Government, NAMP M258; Bearss, "Civil War Comes to Indian Territory, 1861," 24–26; Hall, "East Side Landmark."

26. Affidavit of Nancy Posey; Wynema Posey Blaine to George H. Shirk, January 30, 1953, and Shirk to Blaine, February 10, 1953, Alexander Posey Vertical File, Library, Oklahoma Historical Society; Creek Census Card 1762 (Mitchell Yargee, brother of Posey's first wife), NAMP M1186; "Notes and Documents," *Chronicles of Oklahoma* 33 (Autumn 1955): 392. Connelley (pp. 7–8) establishes the date of marriage and says that Nancy was fifteen years old at the time. Subsequent accounts of Posey's life and career have repeated those statements. However, Nancy said she was born in 1848. Creek enrollment records and Oklahoma census records indicate that she was born sometime about 1850. See Affidavit of Nancy Posey.

27. Laurel Pitman, Interview, *Indian-Pioneer History* (AMD-OHS), 40: 108; Alexander L. Posey's Journal (p. 9), item 3626.183a, Gilcrease.

CHAPTER TWO

1. George Riley Hall, "Alexander Posey, Indian Poet of the Transition, Was Sensitive Lover of Nature," *Daily Oklahoman*, April 23, 1939; Posey's Journal (p. 19), item 3626.183a, Gilcrease. Over thirty years ago, the Oklahoma Historical Society marked the Hence Posey site at Mellette as the birthplace of Alex, but the identification is incorrect. Posey's journal indicates the site near present Lenna, close to the trail that led from the Choctaw Nation to Okmulgee, as does an undated (1905) letter from Alex to his wife in the possession of Posey's granddaughter, Ginger Moore, photocopy in the author's file. The latter site was reaffirmed by Alex's brother-in-law after Alex's death in "In Memoriam," *Henryetta Free-Lance*, June 5, 1908.

2. Chinnubbie Harjo, "Tulledega," undated newspaper clipping, Scrapbook, item 4626.31, Gilcrease.

3. William Elsey Connelley, "Memoir of Alexander Lawrence Posey," in *The Poems of Alexander Lawrence Posey*, comp. Minnie H. Posey (Topeka: Crane, 1910), 9, 10; "Nancy Posey, Mother of Famed Indian Poet, Faces Loss of Her Wewoka Home," *Daily Oklahoman*, June 28, 1936, C5.

4. "This Indian Is Gaining Fame as a Poet," *Press* (Philadelphia), November 4, 1900, quoting Posey (clipping, Scrapbook, item 4627.32, Gilcrease).

5. Connelley, "Memoir," 10–11.

6. "Nancy Posey, Mother of Famed Indian Poet," C5; Connelley, "Memoir," 16–17.

7. "Nancy Posey, Mother of Famed Indian Poet," C5.

8. Frank G. Speck, *The Creek Indians of Taskigi Town* (Millwood, N.Y.: Kraus Reprint, 1974), 145–59.

9. Charles Gibson, "Creek Summer Resorts," *Indian Journal*, June 27, 1902; Chinnubbie Harjo, "Two Famous Prophets," *Twin Territories* 2 (September 1900): 181; Harry Austin, Interview, October 15, 1937, *Indian-Pioneer History* (AMD-OHS), 28:178–79.

10. Speck, *Creek Indians of Taskigi Town*, 114.

11. Chinnubbie Harjo, "Two Famous Prophets," 180.

12. "Famous Rain-Maker," *Muskogee Times*, undated (December 28, 1904?) clipping, Scrapbook, item 4627.32, Gilcrease.

13. Chinnubbie Harjo, "Two Famous Prophets," 181–82.

14. Connelley, "Memoir," 13; *Indian Journal*, April 18, 1902; Mary Hays Marable and Elaine Boylan, *Handbook of Oklahoma Writers* (Norman: University of Oklahoma Press, 1939), 77; Nyna Stone, "Soul of the West in Heart of Indian Poet," *Wewoka Times-Democrat*, April 29, 1934.

15. *Indian Journal*, April 18, 1902.

16. *Indian Journal*, April 18, 1902; Chinnubbie Harjo, "Two Famous Prophets," 180; Connelley, "Memoir," 12.

17. "Biographical," *Twin Territories* 2 (May 1900): 108. Posey gave the same story to the newspapers in fall 1900. See, e.g., *Kansas City Star*, September 27, 1900, p. 5.

18. 46th Congress, 3d session, *House Executive Document 1*, pt. 5: 216; 47th Congress, 1st session, *House Executive Document 1*, pt. 5: 161; 47th Congress, 2d session, *House Executive Document 1*, pt. 5: 149–50; 48th Congress, 1st session, *House Executive Document 1*, pt. 5, p. 148; 48th Congress, 2d session, *House Executive Document 1*, pt. 5, p. 144; *Indian Journal*, April 22, 1886.

19. Alex Posey told a version of this story in "Two Famous Prophets," 180–81. Another version was attributed to William Collins, Chalogee's grandson, in "Famous Rain-Maker," *Muskogee Times*, undated (December 28, 1904?) clipping, Scrapbook, item 4627.32, Gilcrease.

20. The date is uncertain. Some sources say Alex was born there: "Specter of Death Still Haunts Water Hole"; Marable and Boylan, *Handbook of Oklahoma Writers*, 77. Others say that Hence moved to Bald Hill when Alex was a small child: Minnie Posey to George H. Shirk, December 12, 1952, Alexander Posey Vertical File, Oklahoma Historical Society. But Alex himself establishes beyond doubt that he spent his childhood at the home on Limbo Creek: Posey's Journal (p. 19), item 3626.183a, Gilcrease. As late as 1884, Hence's ranch was still fifteen miles west of Eufaula on the North Canadian, considerably farther than Bald Hill is from Eufaula. By early 1886 the ranch was described as ten miles from Eufaula, more like the distance to Bald Hill. See Hence's brand advertisements, *Indian Journal*, June 12, 1884, and March 11, 1886.

21. A useful source in deriving the foregoing abstract of Creek history in the postwar period is Angie Debo, *The Road to Disappearance*, (Norman: University of Oklahoma Press, 1941), 177–284. The theory of the Muskogee/non-Muskogee division in the Green Peach War and thereafter is presented

in J. Leitch Wright, Jr., *Creeks and Seminoles: The Destruction and Regeneration of the Muscogulge People* (Lincoln: University of Nebraska Press, 1986), 308–9.

22. Election Returns, September 20, 1881, and L. H. Posey to Samuel Checote, February 22, 1882, documents 31827 and 31843; document 26043, Eufaula District Court Documents, Creek National Records, RG75NA-OHS.

23. *Indian Journal*, August 27 and September 3, 1885, and September 9, 1886; *Indian Chieftain*, November 22, 1888; *Muskogee Phoenix*, September 6 and November 15 and 29, 1888; Appearance Docket and cases 104, 105, and 106, United States District Court, Kansas, Second Division Criminal, 1883–88, National Archives, Federal Records Center, Kansas City, Missouri.

24. "Robert Sewell in Muskogee," undated (1906?) newspaper clipping, Scrapbook, item 4627.32, Gilcrease; *Indian Journal*, February 22, 1906.

25. *Indian Journal*, March 12 and 19, August 27, and December 3, 1885, and January 10, 1886. Hence's membership in the livestock association was of long duration. He was a delegate to the Cattlemen's Association meeting at St. Louis in 1885 and to the one at Fort Worth in 1890. See *Indian Journal*, April 8, 1886, and December 9, 1889; *Muskogee Phoenix*, March 13, 1890. Like Hence, McIntosh and Berryhill were avid horse racers and may have taken a special interest in these thieves. Berryhill had charged Mitchell Collins with horse stealing on at least one earlier occasion. See document 26032, Eufaula District Court Documents, Creek National Records, RG75NA-OHS.

26. Posey's Journal (pp. 19, 22), item 3626.183a, Gilcrease; Chinnubbie Harjo, "Jes 'Bout a Mid'lin', Sah," *Twin Territories* 2 (April 1900): 77.

27. Loyal Creek Claims 1224–26, Special Series A, General Records, 1907–39, Records of the Bureau of Indian Affairs, NARG 75.

28. Creek Census Cards 2183 and 2184, Enrollment Cards for the Five Civilized Tribes, 1898–1914, NAMP M1186.

29. Creek Census Cards 270, 275, 1853, 2028, 2347, and 2775, NAMP M1186; "Sarah Scott Phillips," June 16, 1937, *Indian-Pioneer History* (AMD-OHS), 40:6; Loyal Creek Claim 2342, Special Series A, General Records, 1907–39, Records of the Bureau of Indian Affairs, NARG 75; Creek Nation Enumeration District 69, 1900 Census Schedules, NAMP T623.

30. Creek Census Cards 109, 425, and 3149, NAMP M1186.

31. In later years, families erected camp houses. Nancy's camp was just west of the church. For early church history, see "History of Tuskegee Indian Church," *Indian Journal*, Bicentennial Edition, June 1976. Information on the location of Nancy's camp was given by Leona Colbert, Tuskegee Church secretary, June 15, 1988.

32. Documents 32473, 32897, 32921, and 32976, Creek National Records, RG75NA-OHS; Austin, Interview, 183–84; William McCombs, Jr., Interview, June 10, 1937, *Indian-Pioneer History* (AMD-OHS), 34:424–25.

33. Vol. 10, Eufaula District Court, 1882–91, and vol. 12, Eufaula District Court, 1890–98, Creek National Records (RG75NA-OHS), throughout, but especially pp. 1 and 5 in the latter. See also vol. 40, North Fork District Court, 1868–69, pp. 31 ff.

34. George Riley Hall, "Memoirs" (unpublished typescript, copy in author's file), 55; Debo, *Road to Disappearance*, 325; *Indian Journal*, July 28 and October 21, 1887; Harjo, "Jes 'Bout a Mid'lin', Sah," 77; Leona G. Barnett, "Este Cate Emunkv," *Chronicles of Oklahoma* 46 (Spring 1968): 22; "Death of L. H. Posey," *Eufaula Gazette*, undated (January 1902) clipping, Scrapbook, item 4627.32, Gilcrease.

35. Hall, "Memoirs," 54.

36. "Biographical," 108; Connelley, "Memoir," 10; Posey's Journal (p. 1), item 3626.183a, Gilcrease.

37. "Biographical," 108; *Press*, November 4, 1900.

38. Connelley, "Memoir," 14.

39. "Biographical," 108; *Press*, November 4, 1900.

40. *Muskogee Phoenix*, November 1 and 22, 1888; Hall, "Alexander Posey, Indian Poet of the Transition."

41. *Indian Journal*, April 22, September 30, and December 8, 1886.

42. *Indian Journal*, April 22 and May 20, 1886; May 12, 1887; and January 3, 1889.

43. *Muskogee Phoenix*, November 22, 1888. Hence was well established in Eufaula by early 1889. *Indian Journal*, January 3 and April 4, 1889, and August 21, 1890.

44. Few copies of the newspaper are extant for this period. This episode is based on statements by Charles J. Shields, one of Alex's schoolmates. Shields, "Pioneer Days in Okmulgee," undated (1923?) clipping, Scrapbook, item 4627.32, Gilcrease. Shields may refer to early 1889 when it was reported that Wortham was recovering from "a long siege of congestion of the brain." See *Muskogee Phoenix*, February 21, 1889. At that time, however, Wortham had an able associate editor, George W. Grayson. *Indian Journal*, January 3, 1889.

CHAPTER THREE

1. George Riley Hall, "Alex Posey—Creek Poet," January 28, 1938, typescript, Oklahoma Biography—Alexander Posey, Vertical File, Muskogee Public Library, Muskogee, Oklahoma (copy also in Alexander L. Posey File, Grant Foreman Collection, AMD-OHS); Hall, "Alexander Posey, Indian Poet of the Transition, Was Sensitive Lover of Nature," *Daily Oklahoman*, April 23, 1939; "Showcase," *Oklahoma City Times*, July 4, 1971.

2. Hall, "Alexander Posey, Indian Poet of the Transition."

3. "The Board of Education," undated clipping, Scrapbook, item 4626.31,

Gilcrease; Ella M. Hayes, "History of Bacone," *Baconian* 11 (May 1908): 8;
Coeryne Bode, "The Origin and Development of Bacone College" (M.A.
thesis, University of Tulsa, 1957), 18.

4. Autograph Book, item 5326.440, Gilcrease; Posey to Anna Lewis,
June 19, 1890, reprinted in *Chronicles of Oklahoma* 45 (Autumn 1967):
334; *Muskogee Phoenix*, June 12 and 26, 1890.

5. *Muskogee Phoenix*, June 12, 1890; Posey to Lewis, June 19, 1890.

6. Posey to Lewis, June 28, 1890, reprinted in *Chronicles of Oklahoma* 45
(Autumn 1967): 335. Anna Lewis died in 1896 while attending the Baptist
Missionary Training School in Chicago. See "Miss Anna Lewis, Teacher of
Alexander Posey at Bacone University, 1889–1890," *Chronicles of Oklahoma*
45 (Autumn 1967): 335.

7. Posey to Lewis, June 19, 1890.

8. Posey to George J. Remsburg, October 21, 1890, "Letters Written by
A. L. Posey and Charles Gibson, Creek Indians and Newspaper Clippings
pertaining to the Former," AMD-OHS.

9. Posey to Remsburg, October 21, 1890. In later life Remsburg lived at
Porterville, California. See *Historia* 8 (July 1919): 5.

10. *Muskogee Evening Times*, March 2, 1901.

11. Posey to Remsburg, September 12, 1892, "Letters Written by A. L.
Posey and Charles Gibson," AMD-OHS.

12. Posey to Remsburg, October 31, 1892, "Letters Written by A. L. Posey
and Charles Gibson," AMD-OHS.

13. Diploma of Alexander L. Posey, June 17, 1891, display case, Bacone
College Library.

14. *Indian Journal*, February 26, 1891.

15. Bode, "Origin and Development of Bacone College," 20.

16. "Biographical," *Twin Territories* 2 (May 1900): 108; William Elsey
Connelley, "Memoir of Alexander Lawrence Posey," in *The Poems of Alexander Lawrence Posey*, comp. Minnie H. Posey (Topeka: Crane, 1910), 19.

17. Posey to Remsburg, September 12 and October 31, 1892, "Letters
Written by A. L. Posey and Charles Gibson," AMD-OHS.

18. An undated clipping of this story in Scrapbook, item 4627.33, Gilcrease, is set in the distinctive type of the *B.I.U. Instructor*.

19. "The Indian: What of Him?" *Indian Journal*, undated clipping (June
1892), Scrapbook, item 4626.31, Gilcrease.

20. Ibid.; a copy of the pamphlet is in Scrapbook, item 4626.31, Gilcrease.

21. "Col. McIntosh's Speech," *Indian Journal*, undated clipping (July?
1892), Scrapbook, item 4626.31, Gilcrease.

22. Frances Berry to Posey, February 11, 1898, Scrapbook, item 4627.32,
Gilcrease.

23. John H. Phillips to Anna Lewis, August 7, 1892, Alexander L. Posey
File, Bacone College Library.

24. See various clippings, Scrapbook, item 4626.31, Gilcrease, and Posey's personal library, Bacone College Library.

25. Posey's Journal, "Notes on English Authors," item 3626.185, Gilcrease.

26. See various clippings, Scrapbook, item 4626.31, Gilcrease.

27. Posey to Remsburg, October 31, 1892, "Letters Written by A. L. Posey and Charles Gibson," AMD-OHS.

28. Posey to Remsburg, November 25, 1892, "Letters Written by A. L. Posey and Charles Gibson," AMD-OHS.

29. Posey to Remsburg, October 31, 1892, "Letters Written by A. L. Posey and Charles Gibson," AMD-OHS.

30. "Posey a Believer," *Indian Journal*, July 17, 1908.

31. Bode, "Origin and Development of Bacone College," 20.

32. Connelley, "Memoir," 19–20, dates these works. A copy of the pamphlet is in Scrapbook, item 4626.31, Gilcrease.

33. "Chinnubbie Scalps the Squaws," *B.I.U. Instructor*, 2 (May 20, 1893), unpaged.

34. According to Connelley, "Memoir" (p. 56), all these tales were printed in pamphlet form. No copies of the first and last have been found. A pamphlet version of "Chinnubbie and the Owl" is in Scrapbook, item 4627.33, Gilcrease, and a single poor copy survives of "Chinnubbie Scalps the Squaws" as it appeared in the *B.I.U. Instructor*, author's file.

35. *Cherokee Advocate*, July 22, 1893.

36. *Muskogee Phoenix*, June 22, 1893; *Cherokee Advocate*, July 22, 1893; *Red Man* 12 (July–August, 1893): 8; *Daily Oklahoma State Capital*, July 11, 1893.

37. Bode, "Origin and Development of Bacone College," 20.

38. Alexander Posey, *The Alabama Prophet* (Bacone: Indian University Press, 1893?).

39. Connelley, "Memoir," 20.

40. A copy of "Death of a Window Plant" (from the *B.I.U. Instructor*) is in Scrapbook, item 4626.31, Gilcrease. Connelley (p. 20) says the poem was Alex's first to attract wider than local attention. "This was published far and wide," Connelley says, "with comments most flattering to the young poet," but no evidence for these assertions has been found. In fact, Alex later named "O, Oblivion" as his first poem to receive public notice.

41. Connelley, "Memoir," 20.

42. *Twilight* (Bacone: Indian University Press, n.d.). Clippings of the shorter poems are in Scrapbook, item 4626.31, Gilcrease. Although certain dating is impossible, the distinctive type of the *Instructor* indicates the source of the first two. The last is also from his Bacone years, probably the last, as indicated by the use of dialect. It is also signed "Alexander Posey," a name he did not use except once on poems that he offered for publication after he left Bacone.

43. *Indian Journal*, February 20, March 1 and 15, and June 1, 1894.

44. *Indian Journal*, March 1, 8, and 29 and May 11 and 25, 1894.

45. *Indian Journal*, February 22 and May 4, 11, and 18, 1894.

46. *Indian Journal*, April 12, May 11, and June 1, 1894.

47. *Muskogee Phoenix*, June 14 and 21, 1894.

48. "Room at the Top," *Indian Journal*, July 6, 1894.

49. Ibid.

50. *Muskogee Phoenix*, June 21, 1894; *Indian Journal*, June 29 and July 6, 1894.

51. *Indian Journal*, July 13, 1894.

52. Ibid.

53. *Indian Journal*, July 20 and 27, 1894.

54. Bode, "Origin and Development of Bacone College," 20.

55. "Note," *Twin Territories* 2 (August 1900): 158. Some of Henry B. Sarcoxie's doggerel appeared as "Rhymes Written at Las Vagas [*sic*]," *Twin Territories* 2 (September 1900): 193. He had traveled to the West for his health in 1900. His journal of this trip appeared as "Westward Ho!" in the August and September issues (158–59, 191–92). Sarcoxie, who suffered from tuberculosis, died at Bartlesville, Cherokee Nation, in early 1901. See Mrs. H. B. Sarcoxie to Posey, January 27, 1901, Scrapbook, item 4627.32, Gilcrease.

56. Untitled essay, signed "A. L. Posey," Scrapbook, item 4626.31, Gilcrease.

57. Hall, "Alexander Posey, Indian Poet of the Transition."

CHAPTER FOUR

1. *Indian Journal*, October 5, 1894.

2. *Indian Journal*, December 14, 1894.

3. *Muskogee Phoenix*, October 6, 1894; *Indian Journal*, December 7, 1894, and January 4, February 15 and 22, and April 5, 1895.

4. George Riley Hall, "Memoirs" (unpublished typescript, copy in author's file), 48, 49, 51, 54.

5. Mrs. Florence Berry to Posey, February 11, 1898, Scrapbook, item 4627.32, Gilcrease.

6. Alexander L. Posey, "Col. McIntosh," manuscript, April 1895, owned by Elliott Howe, copy in author's file.

7. Hall, "Memoirs," 54–55.

8. Angie Debo, *Road to Disappearance*, (Norman: University of Oklahoma Press, 1941), 345–46.

9. *Indian Journal*, February 22, 1894.

10. *Indian Journal*, March 1, 1894; *Muskogee Phoenix*, July 11, 1895.

11. *Indian Journal*, February 22, 1894.

12. *Indian Journal*, March 1, 1894.

13. *Muskogee Phoenix*, June 29, 1895.

14. Posey's Appointments, June 22 and 24, 1895, items 5126.600 and 4026.8211, Gilcrease; Debo, *Road to Disappearance*, 361; *Muskogee Phoenix*, May 19, June 19, and July 11, 1895.

15. Debo, *Road to Disappearance*, 354–56; document 33196, Creek National Records, RG75NA-OHS; Posey's Appointment, July 25, 1895, item 5126.601, Gilcrease.

16. Debo, *Road to Disappearance*, 356–57.

17. David Harry to National Council, September 3, 1895, item 3826.2174, Gilcrease.

18. Debo, *Road to Disappearance*, 358; Appointments of Posey, September 8 and 24 and November 27, 1895, items 5126.602–4, Gilcrease; Bond of A. L. Posey, December 4, 1895, Alexander Posey File, Section X, AMD-OHS; documents 39356–58 and 39362, Creek National Records, RG75NA-OHS.

19. Posey's Appointment to Copy Census, undated, item 5126.620, Gilcrease; *Muskogee Phoenix*, September 26, 1895; Hall, "Memoirs," 55; Hall, "Alexander Posey, Indian Poet of Transition, Was Sensitive Lover of Nature," *Daily Oklahoman*, April 23, 1939.

20. Debo, *Road to Disappearance*, 362; documents 33240 and 33242, Creek National Records, RG75NA-OHS; *Muskogee Phoenix*, October 10, 1895.

21. Debo, *Road to Disappearance*, 361–70.

22. Hall, "Memoirs," 56; Hall, "Alexander Posey, Indian Poet of the Transition;" Payment Schedule, 1895–96, document 37324, and documents 24399, 24400, 24401, 24403, and 36132, Creek National Records, RG75NA-OHS.

23. Hall, "Memoirs," 56; *Muskogee Phoenix*, November 9, 1893.

24. Hall, "Memoirs," 56–57; Hall, "Alexander Posey, Indian Poet of the Transition."

25. Posey's Journal (pp. 3–4), item 3626.183a, Gilcrease; Minnie H. Posey to E. E. Dale, October 31, 1955, folder 15, box 53, Edward Everett Dale Collection, WHC. Minnie Harris was the daughter of Milton D. and Sarah M. Harris, who lived between Fayetteville and Farmington, Arkansas. Besides Minnie, the Harrises had daughters Mary, Josephine, and Catherine and sons Harve, Robert, El Cavey, Herbert, and Meril. See Enumeration District 216, Washington County, Arkansas, 1880 Census Schedules, NAMP T9, and Enumeration District 111, Washington County, Arkansas, 1900 Census Schedules, NAMP T623.

26. Posey's Journal (p. 3), item 3626.183a, Gilcrease; Hall, "Memoirs," 57; document 37896, Creek National Records, RG75NA-OHS; Minnie H. Posey to E. E. Dale, October 31, 1955, folder 15, box 53, Edward Everett Dale Collection, WHC.

27. Untitled poem, item 4026.8219a, Gilcrease.

28. Posey's Journal (p. 3), item 3626.183a, Gilcrease; Hall, "Memoirs," 57; William Elsey Connelley, "Memoir of Alexander Lawrence Posey," in

The Poems of Alexander Lawrence Posey, comp. Minnie H. Posey (Topeka: Crane, 1910), 22; Minnie Posey's statement, from Connelley, "Memoir," 23; Leona G. Barnett, "Este Cate Emunkv," *Chronicles of Oklahoma* 46 (Spring 1968): 23.

29. Hall, "Memoirs," 57; Hall, "Alexander Posey, Indian Poet of the Transition."

30. Posey's Journal (pp. 8, 17, 24, 36), item 3626.183a, Gilcrease.

31. Posey's Journal (pp. 1, 2, 3, 6–7, 8, 10), item 3626.183a, Gilcrease.

32. Posey's Journal (pp. 5, 8–9, 10, 21, 28), item 3626.183a, Gilcrease; Hall, "Alex Posey—Creek Poet" (unpublished typescript of speech, January 28, 1938), Oklahoma Biography—Alexander Posey, Vertical File, Muskogee Public Library (copy also in Alexander L. Posey File, Grant Foreman Collection, AMD-OHS).

33. Posey's Journal (pp. 3, 11, 20, 21, 22, 28, 29, 32, 33), item 3626.183a, Gilcrease.

34. Posey's Journal (pp. 2, 3, 4–5, 7, 13, 14, 16), item 3626.183a, Gilcrease.

35. Posey's Journal (pp. 10, 11, 21, 24–25, 27, 28–29), item 3626.183a, Gilcrease.

36. Posey's Journal (pp. 1, 5–6, 8, 12, 16, 17, 18, 19–20, 21, 25, 26, 27, 33, 35, 40, 43), item 3626.183a, Gilcrease.

37. Posey's Journal (pp. 24–25, 30, 33, 34, 36, 37), item 3626.183a, Gilcrease.

38. Posey's Journal (pp. 1, 5, 17, 25, 26–27), item 3626.183a, Gilcrease.

39. Posey's Journal (pp. 20, 25, 27), item 3626.183a, Gilcrease.

40. Posey's Journal (pp. 22, 23, 34), item 3626.183a, Gilcrease.

41. Posey's Journal (pp. 3, 5, 8, 34), item 3626.183a, Gilcrease.

42. Posey's poem "Cuba Libre" appeared in *Muskogee Phoenix*, December 24, 1896, and "The Indian's Past Olympic" appeared on December 17. Further evidence that the last poem was an earlier work is the use of his name rather than Chinnubbie or Chinnubbie Harjo, as he had signed all his works in the last two years.

43. Posey's Journal (pp. 3, 7, 13, 25, 30, 31, 35, 36), item 3626.183a, Gilcrease; Poems, items 4026.8220, 4026.8281, and 4016.8292, Gilcrease.

44. Posey's Journal (pp. 12–13), item 3626.183a, Gilcrease.

45. Posey's Journal (pp. 7, 8, 11, 16, 27, 28, 35, 36), item 3626.183a, Gilcrease; Hall, "Alexander Posey, Indian Poet of the Transition."

46. Posey's Journal (pp. 16, 27, 28, 29, 30, 37, 39, 40), item 3626.183a, Gilcrease; Frank G. Speck, *The Creek Indians of Taskigi Town* (Millwood, N.Y.: Kraus Reprint, 1974), 117.

47. Posey's Journal (p. 18), item 3626.183a, Gilcrease; documents 24414 and 24481, Creek National Records, RG75NA-OHS.

48. Posey's Journal (pp. 7, 24, 33, 35, 38), item 3626.183a, Gilcrease.

49. Posey's Journal (pp. 14, 17, 23, 27, 29, 37), item 3626.183a, Gilcrease; Hall, "Memoirs," 57; Hall, "Alexander Posey, Indian Poet of the Transition."

50. Posey's Journal (pp. 13, 23, 24, 25, 35), item 3626.183a, Gilcrease.

51. Posey's Journal (pp. 18, 22, 23, 26, 27, 28, 31, 35, 43), item 3626.183a, Gilcrease.

52. Posey's Journal (pp. 4, 18, 20, 25, 29, 30), item 3626.183a, Gilcrease; Hall, "Memoirs," 57.

53. From "Lines to Hall," item 4026.8292, Gilcrease.

54. Posey's Journal (pp. 6, 12, 15, 22, 26, 28), item 3626.183a, Gilcrease.

55. Posey's Journal (pp. 19, 22, 26, 32, 40–41), item 3626.183a, Gilcrease.

56. Posey's Journal (pp. 17, 19, 22, 26, 32, 33, 41, 43), item 3626.183a, Gilcrease.

57. Posey's Journal (pp. 19, 22, 33), item 3626.183a, Gilcrease.

58. Posey's Journal (p. 19), item 3626.183a, Gilcrease.

59. Posey's Journal (pp. 17, 18, 19, 34), item 3626.183a, Gilcrease.

60. Posey's Journal (pp. 31, 37), item 3626.183a, Gilcrease.

CHAPTER FIVE

1. Posey's Journal (pp. 37, 44, 46), item 3626.183a, Gilcrease; document 36167, Creek National Records, RG75NA-OHS; *Muskogee Phoenix*, June 22, 1893.

2. Posey's Journal (pp. 38–42), item 3626.183a, Gilcrease; *Muskogee Phoenix*, May 13, 1897.

3. Posey's Journal (pp. 33, 41), item 3626.183a, Gilcrease.

4. Posey's Journal (pp. 40, 42–43, 44–45, 46), item 3626.183a, Gilcrease.

5. Posey's Journal (pp. 37, 39, 43), item 3626.183a, Gilcrease.

6. Posey's Journal (p. 44), item 3626.183a, Gilcrease; "Sea Shells" appeared in *Muskogee Phoenix*, December 23, 1897.

7. Posey's Journal (pp. 45, 46), item 3626.183a, Gilcrease; George Riley Hall, "Memoirs" (unpublished typescript, copy in author's file), 57–58; Minnie H. Posey to E. E. Dale, October 31, 1955, folder 15, and November 7, 1956, folder 16, box 53, Edward Everett Dale Collection, WHC.

8. Bond for Posey, December 17, 1897, Alexander L. Posey Papers (MS 85-72), AMD-OHS; document 36273, Creek National Records, RG75NA-OHS; Posey's Appointment, December 21, 1897, item 5126.606, Gilcrease; *Indian Journal*, April 29, 1886.

9. Hall, "Memoirs," 58.

10. Statement of W. A. Rentie, February 5, 1898, and Statement of A. G. W. Sango, February 8, 1898, documents 36171 and 37335, Creek National Records, RG75NA-OHS; *Muskogee Phoenix*, October 10 and 24, 1895, and January 13, 1898.

11. Posey's Statement, undated, document 37335, Creek National Records, RG75NA-OHS; *Muskogee Evening Times*, April 15 and June 13, 1898.

12. Hall, "Memoirs," 58; F. B. Posey to Isparhecher, May 26, 1898, Posey's Statement, undated, and Upler Bird et al. to Principal Chief, October 12,

1897, documents 36172, 37335, and 36164, respectively, Creek National
Records, RG75NA-OHS.

287

Notes

to Pages

103–109

13. Hall, "Memoirs," 60; *Muskogee Phoenix*, August 24, 1899; *South McAlester Capital*, August 31, 1899.

14. "The Poet's Song," item 4026.8236, Gilcrease.

15. Posey's Journal (p. 40), item 3626.183a, Gilcrease.

16. Posey's Journal (pp. 39, 40, 42, 43), item 3626.183a, Gilcrease; Poems, items 4026.8221–24, Gilcrease; "The Boston Mountains," undated clipping, *Indian Journal*, Scrapbook, item 4626.31, Gilcrease. "To a Humming Bird" appeared in *Muskogee Phoenix*, December 23, 1897.

17. Poems, items 4026.8222 and 4026.8259 (p. 20), Gilcrease.

18. "Verses Written at the Grave of McIntosh," item 4026.8260, Gilcrease.

19. Poems, items 4026.8225–29, Gilcrease.

20. "To a Cloud" appeared in Minnie H. Posey, comp., *The Poems of Alexander Lawrence Posey* (Topeka: Crane, 1910), p. 148, as "To a Summer Cloud," with a serious error in transcription.

21. Poems, items 4026.8226, 4026.8230, 4026.8232, 4026.8239, and 4026.8241, Gilcrease.

22. The publication record for 1898 is sketchy because of a lack of extant copies of the *Indian Journal* and the *Checotah Enquirer*, the two publications to which he sent poems during this period. However, some published works that cannot be dated with certainty may have appeared in 1898: "The Homestead of Empire," "On the Piney," "Tulledega," and "When Molly Blows the Dinner Horn."

23. William Elsey Connelley, "Memoir of Alexander Lawrence Posey," in Posey, *Poems of Alexander Lawrence Posey*, 24.

24. Connelley, "Memoir," 23–24.

25. Connelley, "Memoir," 25.

26. From "What I Ask of Life," item 4026.8257, Gilcrease.

27. "What My Soul Would Be," item 4026.8286, Gilcrease.

28. From "My Hermitage," item 4026.8256, Gilcrease.

29. J. N. Thornton to Mrs. Alex Posey, February 4, 1911, Scrapbook, item 4627.32, Gilcrease.

30. Hall, "Alexander Posey, Indian Poet of the Transition, Was Sensitive Lover of Nature," *Daily Oklahoman*, April 23, 1939; Hall, "Posey a Believer," *Indian Journal*, July 17, 1908.

31. Minnie H. Posey to F. S. Barde, February 3, 1910, Poets and Poetry—Oklahoma #1, Frederick S. Barde Collection, AMD-OHS; Hall, "Posey a Believer"; Hall, "Alex Posey—Creek Poet" (unpublished typescript of speech), January 28, 1938, Oklahoma Biography—Alexander Posey, Vertical File, Muskogee Public Library, Muskogee, Oklahoma (copy also in Alexander L. Posey File, Grant Foreman Collection, AMD-OHS).

32. Connelley, "Memoir," 23.

33. Minnie H. Posey to E. E. Dale, April 1, 1918, and October 31, 1955,

folder 15, and November 7, 1956, folder 16, box 53, Edward Everett Dale Collection, WHC.

34. United States Department of the Interior, *Laws, Decisions, and Regulations Affecting the Work of the Commission to the Five Civilized Tribes, 1893–1906* (Washington, D.C.: Government Printing Office, 1906), 14–29; Angie Debo, *And Still the Waters Run* (Princeton: Princeton University Press, 1972), 32–33.

35. From "The Decree," *Red Man* 16 (April, 1900): 3.

36. *Claremore Courier*, September 1, 1899, typescript, M23, Mrs. Alfred Mitchell Collection, WHC; John D. Benedict to Isparhecher, August 23, 1899, document 36394, Creek National Records, RG75NA-OHS; *Muskogee Phoenix*, October 12, 1899.

37. *Muskogee Phoenix*, August 24 and October 12, 1899; Posey's Appointment, December 5, 1899, item 5126.609, Gilcrease; *South McAlester Capital*, August 31, 1899.

38. Hall, "Alexander Posey, Indian Poet of the Transition."

39. Documents 24444 and 36396, Creek National Records, RG75NA-OHS; Hall, "Memoirs," 63–64.

40. Hall, "Alexander Posey, Indian Poet of the Transition."

41. From "Memories (Inscribed to George R. Hall)," item 4026.8223, Gilcrease.

42. Posey's Journal (pp. 46, 47), item 3626.183a, Gilcrease.

43. George Washington Grayson, "Creek Vocabulary and Verb Paradigms with Occasional Ethnographic Notes, June–August 1885," 568-a Creek, National Anthropological Archives, Smithsonian Institution. For an account of Grayson's career through the 1890s, see W. David Baird, ed., *A Creek Warrior for the Confederacy: The Autobiography of Chief G. W. Grayson* (Norman: University of Oklahoma Press, 1988).

44. Posey's Journal (p. 47), item 3626.183a, Gilcrease.

45. Posey's Journal (p. 47), item 3626.183a, Gilcrease; Poems, items 4026.8261, 4026.8265, 4026.8270, 4026.8273, 4026.8279, Gilcrease.

46. *Muskogee Phoenix*, November 2 and 11, 1899; John W. Stailey to Chinnubbie Harjo, December 7, 1899, Scrapbook, item 4627.32, Gilcrease; St. Louis *Republic*, November 26, 1899, Magazine:7; "Pohalton Lake," *Twin Territories* 1 (November 1899): 246. "Pohalton Lake" had previously appeared in the *Indian Journal*, date uncertain.

47. Elaine Goodale Eastman to Posey, January 16 and 19 and May 15, 1900, and undated clipping about Nashville *Daily American* (1900), Scrapbook, item 4627.32, Gilcrease; "Biographical," *Twin Territories* 2 (May 1900): 108; "My Hermitage," *Red Man* 15 (February 1900): 2; "The Decree," *Red Man* 16 (April 1900): 3.

48. Isparhecher to Alex McIntosh, July 23, 1900, document 37345, Creek National Records, RG75NA-OHS; Posey's Appointment, June 11, 1900, item 5127.610, Gilcrease; *Muskogee Phoenix*, July 12, 1900; Connelley, "Memoir," 26.

49. Undated clipping, Scrapbook, item 4627.32, and undated clipping from *Checotah Enquirer*, Scrapbook, item 4627.33, Gilcrease.

50. *Indian Journal*, November 30, 1900; Notes Afield (pp. 1–8), item 3627.187, Gilcrease.

51. Elaine Goodale Eastman to Posey, September 7, 1900, William R. Draper to Posey, September 28, 1900, and E. Leslie Gilliams to Posey, October 3, 1900, Scrapbook, item 4627.32, Gilcrease; *Kansas City Star*, September 27, 1900.

52. "Biographical," *Twin Territories* 2 (May 1900): 108.

53. *Press* (Philadelphia), November 4, 1900, clipping, Scrapbook, item 4627.32, Gilcrease.

54. *Press* (Philadelphia), November 4, 1900, clipping, Scrapbook, item 4627.32, Gilcrease; "O, Oblivion!" undated clipping, Scrapbook, item 4626.31, Gilcrease.

55. E. MacDonald to Posey, December 10, 1900, and Harold Goddard Rugg to Posey, November 18, 1900, Scrapbook, item 4627.32, Gilcrease.

56. Draper to Posey, January 26, 1901, and "Chinnubbie Harjo, the Creek Indian Poet," undated clipping, St. Louis *Republic*, Scrapbook, item 4627.32, Gilcrease.

57. *Press* (Philadelphia), November 4, 1900, clipping, Scrapbook, item 4627.32, Gilcrease; Ora Eddleman Reed, untitled article, *Sturm's Oklahoma Magazine* 6 (July 1908): 15; Minnie H. Posey to F. S. Barde, February 3, 1910, and Barde, "Biographical Sketch of Alex Posey," Poets and Poetry—Oklahoma #2, Frederick S. Barde Collection, AMD-OHS; Minnie H. Posey to Cora Case Porter, April 20, 1937, Oklahoma Biography—Alexander Posey, Vertical File, Muskogee Public Library.

58. O. P. Sturm, "The Passing of the Creek Poet," *Sturm's Oklahoma Magazine* 6 (July 1908): 14.

59. Eastman to Posey, September 7, 1900, Scrapbook, item 4627.32, Gilcrease.

60. From "The Call of the Wild," item 4026.8282, Gilcrease.

61. Poems by Posey, item 4026.8359, Gilcrease.

62. Posey to Barde, May 15, 1903, reprinted in Mary Hays Marable and Elaine Boylan, *A Handbook of Oklahoma Writers* (Norman: University of Oklahoma Press, 1939), 79.

63. Posey to Barde, May 15, 1903, reprinted in Marable and Boylan, *Handbook*, 79.

64. Posey, "The Cruise of the Good Vrouw from a Diary of One of the Crew," *Indian Journal*, July 25, 1902; "An Indian Poet's Tale of a River Trip," *Kansas City Star*, October 3, 1915.

65. Certificates of Selection, November 24, 1899, and Allotment Deeds, September 2 and 3, 1902, items 5127.611–14 and 5126.607–8, Gilcrease; *Indian Journal*, October 26 and November 16, 1900.

66. Notes Afield (pp. 9–12), item 3627.187, Gilcrease.

1. *Indian Journal*, January 24, 1902; Probate Case 3617, Court Clerk's Office, McIntosh County, Oklahoma.

2. *Indian Journal*, February 14, 1902.

3. George Riley Hall, "Memoirs" (unpublished manuscript, copy in author's files), 71; *Indian Journal*, January 17 and 31, 1902; Creek Newborn Census Card 4 (Wynema Torrans Posey), Enrollment Cards for the Five Civilized Tribes, 1898–1914, NAMP M1186. For over twenty-five years, John Beauregard Torrans managed the art department of the Turner Hardware Company at Muskogee. He left Muskogee in 1917 and died at Los Angeles on December 21, 1934. *Muskogee Phoenix*, January 10, 1935.

4. *Indian Journal*, February 14, April 11, May 9 and 12, July 4, and August 1, 1902.

5. *Indian Journal*, June 13, 1902.

6. *Indian Journal*, April 25, June 26, and August 1 and 22, 1902.

7. *Indian Journal*, February 14 and April 4 and 11, 1902.

8. *Indian Journal*, May 2, July 18, August 22, October 3, and December 26, 1902; January 2, March 13 and 20, May 22, June 12 and 26, July 3, 10, and 24, and August 14, 1903.

9. *Indian Journal*, January 13, 1903.

10. *Indian Journal*, August 1, 1902; February 13, March 6, and June 12, 1903.

11. *Indian Journal*, June 27 and July 4, 1902.

12. *Indian Journal*, January 2, 1903.

13. *Indian Journal*, January 9, 1903.

14. *Indian Journal*, March 7 and 14 and April 4, 1902.

15. *Indian Journal*, February 14 and 22, April 4, May 2 and 9, June 13, 20, and 27, June 20 and 27, July 18, August 8 and 22, September 4, 12, and 29, October 3, 10, 17, 24, and 31, November 14, 21, 28, 1902; January 9 and February 13, 1903.

16. *Indian Journal*, February 27, March 2 and 28, April 4 and 18, May 30, July 4 and 18, August 1, September 4, October 24 and 31, 1902; February 27 and March 13, 20, and 27, 1903.

17. *Indian Journal*, April 4, June 20, July 4 and 18, August 22, September 9, and October 10, 1902; June 12 and August 14 and 28, 1903.

18. *Indian Journal*, July 18, 1902.

19. *Indian Journal*, January 2, 1903.

20. "On the Capture and Imprisonment of Crazy Snake," in Minnie H. Posey, comp., *The Poems of Alexander Lawrence Posey* (Topeka: Crane, 1910), 88.

21. *Indian Journal*, January 31, February 7 and 21 and April 18, 1902.

22. *Indian Journal*, February 7, 21, and 28, March 7, and April 11, 1902.

23. *Indian Journal*, February 28, 1902.

24. *Indian Journal*, March 7, 1902.

25. *Indian Journal*, April 11, 1902.

26. *Indian Journal*, April 11, 1902.

27. *Indian Journal*, August 1, October 3, and December 5, 1902; March 13, May 1 and 8, and August 14, 1903.

28. *Indian Journal*, March 7, August 1 and 15, October 24, and November 7, 1902; May 8, June 12, and September 25, 1903.

29. *Indian Journal*, March 6, 1903.

30. *Indian Journal*, May 2, 1902.

31. *Indian Journal*, May 16, 1902.

32. *Indian Journal*, May 23, 1902.

33. W. David Baird, ed., *A Creek Warrior for the Confederacy: The Autobiography of Chief G. W. Grayson* (Norman: University of Oklahoma Press, 1988), 163–64. Grayson's autobiography ends with the establishment of the Dawes Commission and, unfortunately, does not cover the years of his friendship with Posey.

34. *Indian Journal*, June 27 and July 11, 1902.

35. *Indian Journal*, July 4 and November 7, 1902; January 9, 1903.

36. Paul Nesbitt, ed., "Governor Haskell Tells of Two Conventions," *Chronicles of Oklahoma* 14 (June 1936): 193–94.

37. Pleasant Porter to Green McCurtain, October 13, 1902, series I-B, box 2, Green McCurtain Collection, WHC; *Indian Journal*, September 19 and 26 and October 3 and 24, 1902.

38. *Indian Journal*, October 3 and November 14, 1902; January 9, 1903.

39. *Indian Journal*, October 17, 1902.

40. *Indian Journal*, October 24, November 7, 14, and 21, and December 5, 1902; *Five Civilized Tribes Protest Congressional Legislation Contemplating Annexation of Indian Territory to Oklahoma or Territorial Form of Government prior to March 4th, 1906* (Kinta, Indian Territory, 1902).

41. *Indian Journal*, December 19, 1902.

42. *Indian Journal*, December 5, 12, and 19, 1902; January 2 and 9 and March 20, 1903.

43. G. W. Grayson, "With Secretary Hitchcock," *Indian Journal*, May 15, 1903; *Muskogee Daily Phoenix*, May 8 and 9 and June 24, 1903.

44. McCurtain to Governor, March 14, 1903, and Porter to McCurtain, March 16, 1903, series I-B, box 2, Green McCurtain Collection, WHC; *Indian Journal*, May 22, 1903.

45. *Indian Journal*, May 22 and 29, 1903; *Muskogee Daily Phoenix*, May 21 and 22, 1903; Posey's Appointment, May 18, 1903, item 5127.615, and Green McCurtain to Posey, May 28, 1903, Scrapbook, item 4627.32, Gilcrease; *Chief Executives of Five Civilized Tribes Adopt Plans for a Prohibition State: Protest against Territorial Form of Government or Annexation to Oklahoma* (n.p., 1903).

46. Posey to McCurtain, May 25, 1903, series I-B, box 2, Green McCurtain Collection, WHC; *Indian Journal*, June 5 and 26, July 3, and September 4, 1903; *Muskogee Daily Phoenix*, July 11, 1903.

47. *Indian Journal*, December 12, 1902; March 27, April 3 and 17, May 1, 8, and 29, and July 10, 1903.

48. *Muskogee Daily Phoenix*, June 18 and July 10, 1903.

49. *Indian Journal*, May 1 and August 28, 1903.

50. *Indian Journal*, March 13 and 27, April 3, and May 1, 8, and 22, 1903.

51. *Indian Journal*, June 26, 1903.

52. *Indian Journal*, July 24, 1903.

53. *Indian Journal*, August 14, 1903.

54. *Indian Journal*, August 14 and 28, and September 4, 1903; Pleasant Porter to Posey, September 4, 1903, item 3827.2243, Gilcrease; Frederick Webb Hodge, ed., *Handbook of American Indians North of Mexico* (Washington, D.C.: Government Printing Office, 1912), 2:287; Eugene Current-Garcia and Dorothy B. Hatfield, eds., *Shem, Ham and Japheth: The Papers of W. O. Tuggle* (Athens: University of Georgia Press, 1973), 47.

55. *Muskogee Daily Phoenix*, May 30 and August 6 and 8, 1903; *South McAlester Capital*, July 16, 1903.

56. *Indian Journal*, July 24 and August 14, 1903.

57. *Indian Journal*, April 25, 1902; 59th Congress, 2d session, *Senate Report 5013*, part 2, 1908–9.

58. *Indian Journal*, April 4, 1902.

CHAPTER SEVEN

1. See, e.g., *Indian Journal*, July 11 and 18, and September 19, 1902; January 16, 1903.

2. *Indian Journal*, August 22 and September 19, 1902.

3. *Indian Journal*, March 20, 1903.

4. *Indian Journal*, March 20, 1903.

5. *Indian Journal*, February 13, March 13, May 29, and August 14, 1903.

6. *Indian Journal*, February 13 and March 6 and 13, 1903.

7. *Indian Journal*, March 14, 1902; March 6 and May 29, 1903.

8. *Indian Journal*, March 20, April 3, May 1 and 15, June 26, and July 24, 1903.

9. *Indian Journal*, March 14, 1902; February 27, March 13, April 3, and May 8, 1903.

10. *Indian Journal*, May 1 and June 12 and 26, 1903; *Fort Smith Times*, October 15, 1903; *Muskogee Daily Phoenix*, July 17, 1902.

11. *Indian Journal*, July 4 and 18, 1902.

12. *Indian Journal*, September 4, 1902.

13. *Indian Journal*, September 4 and October 10 and 24, 1902.

14. *Indian Journal*, November 7, 1902.

15. "Fus Fixico's Letter," *Indian Journal*, March 20, 1903.

16. Alex Posey, "The Passing of 'Hot Gun,'" *Indian Journal*, January 24, 1908.

17. "Fus Fixico's Letter," *Indian Journal*, November 21, 1902.

18. "Fus Fixico's Letter," *Indian Journal*, December 19, 1902, and February 20, 1903.

19. "Fus Fixico's Letter," *Indian Journal*, December 12, 1902, and February 27, 1903.

20. "Fus Fixico's Letter," *Indian Journal*, November 21, 1902.

21. "Fus Fixico's Letter," *Indian Journal*, December 19, 1902, and January 2, 1903.

22. "Fus Fixico's Letter," *Indian Journal*, January 16 and March 6, 1903.

23. "Fus Fixico's Letter," *Indian Journal*, January 16, 1903.

24. "Fus Fixico's Letter," *Indian Journal*, March 27 and May 8, 1903.

25. "Fus Fixico's Letter," *Indian Journal*, May 22, 1903, and *Tahlequah Arrow*, May 30, 1903.

26. "Fus Fixico's Letter," *Tahlequah Arrow*, June 6, 1903.

27. "Fus Fixico's Letter," *Indian Journal*, June 12 and July 3, 1903.

28. "Fus Fixico's Letter," *Indian Journal*, January 2, February 20, and March 20, 1903.

29. *Indian Journal*, March 27, 1903; "Fus Fixico's Letter," *Indian Journal*, April 3 and 17 and May 1, 1903.

30. "Fus Fixico's Letter," *Indian Journal*, May 8 and June 26, 1903.

31. "Fus Fixico's Letter," *Indian Journal*, June 26, July 10, and August 6, 1903; "Fus Fixico's Letter," *Fort Smith Times*, September 10, 1903.

32. *Indian Journal*, April 11 and July 11, 1902; April 10 and August 14, 1903.

33. *Indian Journal*, April 25, May 2, July 11 and 25, and October 3, 1902; March 20 and April 24, 1903.

34. "From Fus Fixico," *Indian Journal*, October 24, 1902; "Fus Fixico's Letter," *Indian Journal*, December 26, 1902.

35. *Indian Journal*, February 20, March 3 and 20, and April 10 and 17, 1903.

36. "Fus Fixico's Letter," *Indian Journal*, February 27 and April 24, 1903.

37. *Indian Journal*, July 11, 1902; July 10, 1903.

38. "The Creek Sage Writes," *Muskogee Daily Phoenix*, July 17, 1903.

39. *Indian Journal*, July 24, 1903; *Vinita Daily Chieftain*, August 15, 1903, clipping, NARG 200, Ethan Allen Hitchcock Papers, box 43, Scrapbook, 1:66.

40. *Indian Journal*, August 14, 1903.

41. *Indian Journal*, August 28, 1903; *Leavenworth Times*, August 18, 1903, clipping, NARG 200, Ethan Allen Hitchcock Papers, box 43, Scrapbook, 1:3; 50th Congress, 2d session, *Senate Document 189*, 5, 7, 8.

42. *Leavenworth Times*, August 18, 1903; *Indian Journal*, August 28, 1903; 50th Congress, 2d session, *Senate Document 189*, 12–15.

43. "Fus Fixico's Letter," *Fort Smith Times*, August 26, 1903.

44. *Vinita Daily Chieftain*, August 18, 1903; *Kansas City Journal*, August 21, 1903, South McAlester *Daily Capital*, August 24, 1903, and *Indian*

Republican, September 4, 1903, clippings, NARG 200, Ethan Allen Hitchcock Papers, box 43, Scrapbook, 1:82, 90b, 97, 158; *Indian Journal*, August 28 and September 4, 1903; "Fus Fixico's Letter," *Fort Smith Times*, September 10, 1903.

45. *Kansas City Journal*, August 21, 1903, New York *Weekly Progress*, August 29, 1903, *Kansas City Star*, August 31, 1903, and *Kansas City Times*, September 4, 1903, clippings, NARG 200, Ethan Allen Hitchcock Papers, box 43, Scrapbook, 1:90a, 131, 140, 156.

46. *Indian Journal*, September 4 and 11, 1903; *Muskogee Daily Phoenix*, September 3, 1903; *Washington Times*, August 27, 1903, clippings, NARG 200, Ethan Allen Hitchcock Papers, box 43, Scrapbook, 1:117; *Cherokee Advocate*, October 10, 1903.

47. *Indian Journal*, September 11 and 25, 1903; *Washington Post*, September 28, 1903, clippings, NARG 200, Ethan Allen Hitchcock Papers, box 43, Scrapbook, 2:62.

48. *Indian Journal*, September 4, 11, and 25, 1903; "Fus Fixico's Letter," *Fort Smith Times*, September 10, 1903; 50th Congress, 2d session, *Senate Document 189*, 5.

49. *Washington Post*, August 18, 1903, clipping, NARG 200, Ethan Allen Hitchcock Papers, box 43, Scrapbook, 1:81; *Indian Journal*, September 4 and 25, 1903; "Fus Fixico's Letter," *Fort Smith Times*, October 25, 1903; *Muskogee Daily Phoenix*, November 22 and December 11 and 19, 1903; "Fus Fixico's Letter," *Muskogee Evening Times*, December 16, 1903; "Fus Fixico's Letter," *Vinita Weekly Chieftain*, December 31, 1903; *Muskogee Daily Phoenix*, March 6 and 29, 1903; 50th Congress, 2d session, *Senate Document 189*, 5–7.

50. *St. Louis Daily Globe-Democrat*, July 1, 1903, Okmulgee *Capital News*, July 9, 1903, and *St. Louis Post-Dispatch*, September 15, 1903, clippings, NARG 200, Ethan Allen Hitchcock Papers, box 43, Scrapbook, 1:24, 32, and 2:39; P. B. Porter to Arthur P. Murphy, December 26, 1902, and Murphy to E. A. Hitchcock, December 28, 1902, "Attorney for Creek Nation—1902" file, NARG 200, Ethan Allen Hitchcock Papers, box 35; Murphy to Mr. Secretary, April 28, 1905, "Indian Territory—Shoenfelt, Wright, Murphy, Jenkins—1905" file, NARG 200, Ethan Allen Hitchcock Papers, box 37; 50th Congress, 2d session, *Senate Document 189*, 15–20; *Muskogee Times-Democrat*, May 1 and June 8, 1907.

51. *Muskogee Daily Phoenix*, March 9, 1904; *Muskogee Evening Times*, March 22, 1904, clipping, NARG 200, Ethan Allen Hitchcock Papers, box 43, Scrapbook, 2:108; 50th Congress, 2d session, *Senate Document 189*, 22, 39–40; H. Craig Miner, *The Corporation and the Indian: Tribal Sovereignty and Industrial Civilization in Indian Territory, 1865–1907* (Norman: University of Oklahoma Press, 1989), 108–209. Miner's work explores the involvement of Five Tribes members in the corporate development of the Indian Territory. Chapter 10 analyzes the relationship between the bureau-

crats and the corporations and places the scandal of 1903 in the context of other developments in the territory.

52. Frank Post to Posey, June 12, 1903; Robertus Love to Posey, July 6, 1903; J. I. C. Clark to Posey, July 8, 1903; A. D. Howard to Posey, July 6, 1903; E. Leslie Gilliams to Posey, July 8, 1903; M. Glen Fling to Posey, July 13, 1903; H. D. Jones to Posey, August 11, 1903; G. R. Rucker to Posey, July 20, 1903; Clara H. Winterstien to Posey, July 6, 1903; J. O. Brant-Sera to Posey, August 3, 1903; J. S. Jones to Posey, July 15, 1903; Winslow Whitman to Posey, undated (July 1903); Esther Ripley to Posey, August 31, 1903; J. Oscar Long to Posey, June 19, 1903; Henry U. Swinnerton to Posey, September 1, 1903; James Walter Smith to Posey, August 17, 1903; Mrs. W. H. French to Posey, August 15, 1903; Anne S. Davis to Posey, July 8, 1903; Horace W. Shephard to Fus Fixico, June 27, 1903; John H. Smithwick to Posey, July 18, 1903; H. A. Juen to Posey, July 23, 1903; Lillimay Perkins to Posey, August 15, 1903; Fred Camplin to Posey, August 7, 1903; and R. Ingalls to Posey, July 31, 1903, all in Scrapbook, item 4627.32, Gilcrease; *Kansas City Journal*, June 19, 1903; *New York Times*, September 1, 1903, 2:6.

53. *Indian Journal*, October 31, 1902, and April 3 and 24, May 5, and June 26, 1903; *Muskogee Daily Phoenix*, April 21, 1903; *Kansas City Journal*, July 19, 1903.

54. *Kansas City Journal*, July 19, 1903; *South McAlester Capital*, July 16, 1903; G. R. Rucker to Posey, June 20, 1903; J. F. Henry to Posey, October 14, 1903; R. Ingalls to Posey, July 31, 1903; J. O. Brant-Sera to Posey, August 3, 1903, Scrapbook, item 4627.32, Gilcrease.

55. *South McAlester Capital*, July 16, 1903; *Indian Journal*, August 14, 1903; Henry to Posey, October 14, 1903, Scrapbook, item 4627.32, Gilcrease.

56. See, e.g., *Indian Journal*, February 2, April 4, and July 25, 1902.

57. *Indian Journal*, February 7, July 4, 11, and 25, September 4, and October 3, 1902; April 10 and 24, May 15, June 5, and August 14, 1903; Mrs. L. F. Woodward to Posey, March 1, 1902, and J. K. Cole to Posey, October 19, 1902, Scrapbook, item 4627.32, Gilcrease; Florence Bledsoe Crofford, "A Real Indian Poet, 'Chinnubbie Harjo,'" *Criterion* 3 (September 1902): 37–38.

CHAPTER EIGHT

1. *Muskogee Democrat*, June 24 and 25; July 2, 11, 19, and 30; August 19 and 17; September 6, 1904.

2. "Fus Fixico's Letter," *Muskogee Evening Times*, January 1904 (exact date undetermined for lack of original source), clipping 34 in Scrapbook, item 4627.32, Gilcrease.

3. *Indian Journal*, August 28 and September 4, 11, and 25, 1903; Angie Debo, *And Still the Waters Run* (Princeton: Princeton University Press, 1972), 111–20; Clinton Rogers Woodruff, "The Present Status in Indian Territory," *Christian Work and Evangelist*, March 26, 1904, clipping, NARG 200, Ethan Allen Hitchcock Papers, box 43, Scrapbook, 2:111.

4. "Fus Fixico's Letter," undated (April? 1904), clipping 42, Scrapbook, item 4627.32, Gilcrease.

5. "Fus Fixico's Letter," *Muskogee Daily Phoenix*, April 17, 1904.

6. "Fus Fixico's Letter," *Muskogee Daily Phoenix*, April 17, 1904.

7. "Fus Fixico's Letter," *Muskogee Daily Phoenix*, May 1, 1904.

8. "Fus Fixico's Letter," *Cherokee Advocate*, May 28, 1904.

9. "Fus Fixico's Letter," *Cherokee Advocate*, May 28, 1904.

10. "Fus Fixico's Letter," *Muskogee Evening Times*, undated (January 1904), clipping 34, Scrapbook, item 4627.32, Gilcrease.

11. "Fus Fixico's Letter," *Muskogee Daily Phoenix*, May 29, 1904.

12. *Muskogee Democrat*, October 11, 15, 22, 27, and 31 and November 1 and 4, 1904; *South McAlester Capital*, November 17, 1904; "Crazy Snake," *Kansas City Journal*, undated (1904) clipping, Scrapbook, item 4627.32, Gilcrease.

13. Posey's Journal (p. 1), item 3826.183a, Gilcrease; *Muskogee Democrat*, November 4, 15, 19, and 22, and December 22, 1904; Tulsa *Indian Republican*, December 2, 1904.

14. Posey's Journal (pp. 2, 3, and 11), item 3826.183a, Gilcrease; quotation is from *Muskogee Democrat*, December 22, 1905.

15. Posey's Journal (pp. 2, 6, 8, 9, 12, 13, and 15), item 3826.183a, Gilcrease; "Back from the Woods," undated (November 1905) clipping, Scrapbook, item 4627.32, Gilcrease.

16. J. N. B. Hewitt, *Notes on the Creek Indians*, ed. John R. Swanton, Bureau of American Ethnology Bulletin 123 (Washington, D.C.: Government Printing Office, 1939), 144–45; *Dustin Dispatch*, June 3, 1905; *Red Fork Derrick*, June 24, 1905.

17. Posey's Journal (pp. 3 and 8), item 3826.183a, Gilcrease; Posey to Henry Hains, March 22, 1905, item 3827.2247a and b, Gilcrease; "Back from the Woods" and "Where They Were," undated clippings, Scrapbook, item 4627.32, Gilcrease; *Muskogee Democrat*, December 21, 1905.

18. Posey's Journal (pp. 6, 8, 9, and 13), item 3826.183a, Gilcrease; *Indian Journal*, May 15, 1908; *Henryetta Free-Lance*, June 23, 1905.

19. Posey's Journal (pp. 5, 6, 7, 9, and 12), item 3826.183a, Gilcrease; *Muskogee Democrat*, August 3, 1905.

20. Papa to My Dear Mamma, undated (1905) letter, in the possession of Ginger Moore, Posey's granddaughter, photocopy in author's file; Letter: To Mamma from Papa, undated (July? 1906), item 3826.2270, Gilcrease.

21. *Muskogee Democrat*, April 29, 1905; Posey's Journal (pp. 4 and 5), item 3826.183a, Gilcrease.

22. Posey's Journal (p. 10), item 3826.183a, Gilcrease; *Henryetta Free-Lance*, October 20, 1905.

23. *Muskogee Phoenix*, April 13 and June 1, 1905; May 3, 1906.

24. *Dustin Dispatch*, June 3, 1905; *Red Fork Derrick*, June 24, 1905; *Muskogee Democrat*, June 15, 1905; "New Born" Creeks, item 5127.616, Gilcrease.

25. *Muskogee Democrat*, June 15, 1905; *Red Fork Derrick*, June 24, 1905; *Indian Republican*, April 14, 1905; *Muskogee Phoenix*, April 20, 1905; Posey's Journal (p. 2), item 3826.183a, Gilcrease.

26. *Henryetta Free-Lance*, July 21, 1905; *South McAlester Capital*, July 27, 1905; *Broken Arrow Ledger*, July 27, 1905.

27. *Muskogee Times-Democrat*, May 15, 1906; *Holdenville Times*, May 18, 1906.

28. *Muskogee Democrat*, January 5 and 11 and April 29, 1905; *Holdenville Tribune*, October 4, 1906; "A Gathering of Snakes," clipping, January 12, 1905, and "Testifies While in Saddle," "Alex Posey Here," "Back from the Woods," "Hunting Lost Indians" (November 1905), and "Search for Lost Creeks" (October 1906), undated clippings, Scrapbook, item 4627.32, Gilcrease.

29. *Indian Journal*, January 31, February 21, April 4 and 25, and May 9, 1902; March 6 and May 1 and 29, 1903.

30. *Muskogee Democrat*, March 15, November 24, and December 22, 1905; *South McAlester Capital*, November 30, 1905; Tams Bixby to Posey, June 27, 1905, Scrapbook, item 4627.32, Gilcrease.

31. Jackson Lewis, informant, "Creek Ethnographic and Vocabulary Notes, October, 1910," Creek 1806, National Anthropological Archives, Smithsonian Institution; Posey's Journal (pp. 5, 12, 14–15, and 16), item 3826.183a, Gilcrease; "Arbekas Meet the Eufaulas," *Muskogee Phoenix*, October 19, 1905; "Yahdeka Harjo of Hickory Ground," undated (October 1905) clipping, Scrapbook, item 4627.32, Gilcrease; *Tulsa Democrat*, October 27, 1905; *Muskogee Times-Democrat*, February 21, 1906.

32. *Muskogee Democrat*, December 22, 1905; *Cherokee Advocate*, January 27, 1906.

33. Posey's Journal (pp. 13 and 16), item 3826.183a, Gilcrease; "Back from the Woods" and "Modern Zenobia," undated clippings, Scrapbook, item 4627.32, Gilcrease; *South McAlester Capital*, December 8, 1904; *Indian Republican*, December 9, 1904.

34. *Henryetta Free-Lance*, July 27, 1906; Hall, "Alexander Posey, Indian Poet of the Transition, Was Sensitive Lover of Nature," *Daily Oklahoman*, April 23, 1939.

35. See, e.g., Posey's Journal (p. 2), item 3826.183a, Gilcrease; *Muskogee Democrat*, December 22, 1905.

36. Reported in *Muskogee Democrat*, January 22, 1906, and *Cherokee Advocate*, January 27, 1906.

37. Posey's Journal (p. 16), item 3826.183a, Gilcrease; *Indian Journal*, November 11, 1904.

38. Bixby to Posey, July 3, 1906, item 3827.2249, Gilcrease; *Henryetta Free-Lance*, July 27, 1906; *Holdenville Tribune*, August 2, 1906.

39. *Henryetta Free-Lance*, July 27, 1906; "Yahdeka Harjo of Hickory Ground," undated (October 1905) clipping, Scrapbook, item 4627.32, Gilcrease; Hewitt, *Notes on the Creek Indians*, 125, 128; Frank G. Speck, *The Creek Indians of Taskigi Town* (Millwood, N.Y.: Kraus Reprint, 1974), 115.

40. Posey's Journal (pp. 8, 9, 11, and 13), item 3826.183a, Gilcrease; *Muskogee Democrat*, March 15, 24, and 27, 1905, and January 22, 1906; Letters, items 3827.2245b, 3827.2246a, 3827.2247b, and 3827.2248b, Gilcrease; *Tahlequah Arrow*, January 27, 1906; *Muskogee Times-Democrat*, March 8, 1906; "Creek Nation Has a Graceful Poet," *Globe-Democrat*, undated (February 1905) clipping, Scrapbook, item 4627.32, Gilcrease; "Three Indian Writers of Prominence," *Sturm's Oklahoma Magazine* 1 (October 1905): 84–91.

CHAPTER NINE

1. *Muskogee Phoenix*, October 5, 1905.

2. C. N. Haskell to Posey, March 8, 1906, Scrapbook, item 4627.32, and Letter: To Momma from Papa, undated (July? 1906), item 3826.2270, Gilcrease.

3. *Muskogee Daily Phoenix*, July 22, 1903; *Indian Journal*, September 4, 1903; W. H. Ansley to Posey, September 3 and November 16, 1903, items 3827.2242 and 3827.2244, Gilcrease; *Talala Topic*, November 18, 1904. Ansley, the chairman of the committee, did not live to see the statehood convention. In April 1905 he apparently cut his throat and jumped into the Arkansas River near Fort Smith, Arkansas. *Holdenville Tribune*, April 20, 1905.

4. Henry Ansley to McCurtain, May 27, August 27, October 7 and 17, and November 21, 1903, and January 19, 1904, and Committee to the Editor, September 21, 1903, series I-B, box 2, Green McCurtain Collection, WHC; Angie Debo, *And Still the Waters Run* (Princeton: Princeton University Press, 1972), 161–62.

5. "Fus Fixico's Letter," *Muskogee Daily Phoenix*, January 1, 1905.

6. *Muskogee Democrat*, July 18, 1905; "Posey Talks," *Muskogee Phoenix*, August 3, 1905.

7. "Fus Fixico's Letter," *Muskogee Phoenix*, August 10, 1905.

8. "Fus Fixico's Letter," *Dustin Dispatch*, August 26, 1905.

9. "Fus Fixico's Letter," *Muskogee Phoenix*, August 31, 1905.

10. Debo, *And Still the Waters Run*, 162–63; H. Wayne Morgan and Anne

Hodges Morgan, *Oklahoma: A Bicentennial History* (New York: W. W. Norton, 1977), 77–78.

11. "Fus Fixico's Letter," *Muskogee Phoenix*, September 7, 1905.

12. *Constitution of the State of Sequoyah* (Muskogee: Phoenix, 1905); Amos Maxwell, "The Sequoyah Convention," *Chronicles of Oklahoma* 28 (Autumn 1950): 327.

13. Morgan and Morgan, *Oklahoma*, 79–80; *Muskogee Phoenix*, August 24 and 31, 1905. Green McCurtain of the Choctaws did not attend this planning session. Stung by the failure in 1903 and 1904 of the other tribes to do their part in planning a convention, he threatened to withdraw his name from the first call to convention, which he claimed had been issued without his consent. He refused, he said, to be a political scapegoat. After appeals by Haskell, Robert L. Owen, and others, he reluctantly gave his approval to the meeting and a few days later apparently joined the movement when he saw that the other chiefs would act. See McCurtain to Pleasant Porter, July 11, 1905; A. W. Robb et al. to McCurtain, July 12, 1905; McCurtain to Owen, July 13, 1905, and McCurtain to Porter, July 13, 1905, series I-B, box 2, Green McCurtain Collection, WHC.

14. Morgan and Morgan, *Oklahoma*, 80; *Muskogee Phoenix*, August 24 and 31 and September 7, 1905; Paul Nesbitt, ed., "Governor Haskell Tells of Two Conventions," *Chronicles of Oklahoma* 14 (June 1936): 196–98.

15. "Constitutional/Statehood Convention," undated manuscript, box H-26, Charles N. Haskell Collection, WHC; *Muskogee Phoenix*, August 10, 1905. Posey's alleged influence on the style of the constitution is argued by William Elsey Connelley, "Memoir of Alexander Lawrence Posey," in Minnie H. Posey, comp., *The Poems of Alexander Lawrence Posey* (Topeka: Crane, 1910), 40.

16. "Fus Fixico's Letter," *Dustin Dispatch*, August 5, 1905.

17. Morgan and Morgan, *Oklahoma*, 79; William H. Murray, "The Constitutional Convention," *Chronicles of Oklahoma* 9 (June 1931): 129–30. For a brief history of the Sequoyah constitution, see Maxwell, "The Sequoyah Convention" (parts 1 and 2), *Chronicles of Oklahoma* 28 (Summer 1950): 161–92, and 28 (Autumn 1950): 299–340. See also 59th Congress, 1st session, *Senate Document 143*, 1–27.

18. "Fus Fixico's Letter," *Muskogee Phoenix*, November 2, 1905.

19. *Muskogee Phoenix*, October 26, 1905; "Fus Fixico's Letter," *Dustin Dispatch*, August 26, 1905.

20. "Fus Fixico's Letter," *Muskogee Phoenix*, September 7, 1905.

21. *Muskogee Phoenix*, November 2, 1905.

22. *Muskogee Phoenix*, September 14 and December 7, 1905.

23. "Fus Fixico's Letter," *New-State Tribune*, March 8, 1906.

24. "Fus Fixico's Letter," *New-State Tribune*, March 8, 1906, and *Indian Journal*, March 16, 1906.

25. "Fus Fixico's Letter," *New-State Tribune*, March 15, 1906.

26. "Fus Fixico's Letter," *New-State Tribune*, March 15, 1906, and *Indian Journal*, March 23, 1906.

27. "Fus Fixico's Letter," *New-State Tribune*, March 22, 1906, and *Indian Journal*, March 30, 1906.

28. "Fus Fixico's Letter," *New-State Tribune*, March 29, 1906.

29. "The Indian Part by Alex Posey," *Holdenville Times*, June 29, 1906.

30. *Muskogee Times-Democrat*, October 1, 1906.

31. *Muskogee Times-Democrat*, October 1, 1906; *Holdenville Tribune*, October 4, 1906; *Indian Journal*, October 5, 1906; "Search for Lost Creeks," undated (October 1906) clipping, Scrapbook, item 4627.32, Gilcrease.

32. "Fus Fixico's Letter," *New-State Tribune*, March 8, 1906.

33. "Hotgun on the New State," *Kansas City Star*, June 24, 1906; "The Indian Part by Alex Posey," *Holdenville Times*, June 29, 1906.

34. "Fus Fixico's Letter," *Holdenville Tribune*, November 29, 1906.

35. *Muskogee Phoenix*, March 8, 1906; *Muskogee Times-Democrat*, January 3, 1907.

36. "Letter of Fus Fixico," *Indian Journal*, January 11, 1907.

37. Mrs. Posey's Journal (pp. 1–6 and 9), item 3627.184, Gilcrease; *Muskogee Times-Democrat*, January 3 and 5, 1907.

38. Mrs. Posey's Journal (pp. 9–21), item 3627.184, Gilcrease.

39. Mrs. Posey's Journal (pp. 21–22, 23–30), item 3627.184, and "Cat a Double Header," undated clipping, Scrapbook, item 4627.32, Gilcrease.

40. Mrs. Posey's Journal (pp. 30–33, 34), item 3627.184, and Statement of Itshas Harjo, January 10, 1907, item 5127.686, Gilcrease; Posey, "Lost from His Tribe for Many Years," *Indian Journal*, May 15, 1908.

41. Mrs. Posey's Journal (pp. 23, 33–49), item 3627.184, Gilcrease.

42. *Indian Journal*, February 22, 1907.

CHAPTER TEN

1. Angie Debo, *And Still the Waters Run* (Princeton: Princeton University Press, 1972), 138, 139–41.

2. Debo, *And Still the Waters Run*, 141–57; 59th Congress, 2d session, *Senate Report 5013*, 1:v–vi.

3. Debo, *And Still the Waters Run*, 168.

4. *Indian Journal*, July 5 and 12, 1907.

5. The best treatment of fraud in the sale of land of the Five Civilized Tribes is Debo, *And Still the Waters Run*.

6. *Indian Journal*, July 5, 1907; Mrs. Posey's Journal (p. 57), item 3627.184, Gilcrease.

7. *Muskogee Times-Democrat*, February 11, 1907; "To Turn Grafter" and "Poet Will Sell Land," undated (1907) clippings, Scrapbook, item 4627.32, Gilcrease.

8. *Muskogee Daily Phoenix*, April 23, May 7 and 17, and July 9 and 29

and October 7, 1903, and May 25, 1905; *Muskogee Democrat*, January 29,
Tribune, November 29, 1906; *Muskogee Times-Democrat*, November 17 and
December 18, 1906.

10. Articles of Agreement and Incorporation of the Posey-Thornton Oil
and Gas Company, United States Court Records (AMD-OHS, microcopy
USC 17), book 3, p. 268.

11. *Muskogee Daily Phoenix*, July 21 and October 7, 1903; *Indian Journal*,
nal, July 12, 1907, and May 15, 1908; *Muskogee Democrat*, September 21,
1904; "A New Land Company," undated (1907) clipping, Scrapbook, item
4627.32, Gilcrease; Articles of Agreement and Incorporation of Palo Alto
Land Company, United States Court Records (AMD-OHS, microcopy USC
17), book 3, p. 354; Decree of Sale of Personal Property, October 9, 1909,
Probate Case 197, Court Clerk's Office, Muskogee County, Oklahoma.

12. *Indian Journal*, July 12 and 26 and August 9 and 16, 1907; *Muskogee
Times-Democrat*, August 3, 1907; Debo, *And Still the Waters Run*, 170–71.

13. Mrs. Posey's Journal (pp. 56–67), item 3627.184, Gilcrease; *Indian
Journal*, August 14, 1903, and December 13, 1907; John H. Phillips to
Mrs. A. L. Posey, June 9, 1908, Scrapbook, item 4627.32, Gilcrease; *Mus-
kogee Democrat*, June 25, 1904.

14. County Clerk's Office, McIntosh County, Oklahoma, Deed Books
3D:347, 545, 610; 4D:131, 377; 5D:597, 614–15; 6D:433; 8D:319; 10D:628;
12D:117; 14D:67–68, 70–71, 73; Miscellaneous Books 1:36–37, 45–46, 77;
3:255, 290, 296, 332, 417, 422, 434, 436; 6:59–60; 10:353; and 14:533. See
also County Clerk's Office, Hughes County, Oklahoma, Deed Book A:264;
County Clerk's Office, Okfuskee County, Oklahoma, Deed Books 3:161–62
and 6:302–3 and Transcript Books 14:449, 458; 18:506; and 19:217–23; and
Appraisal before Sale of Lands at Private Sale, October 27, 1909, and Decree of Sale, October 9, 1909, Probate 197, Court Clerk's Office, Muskogee
County, Oklahoma.

15. Debo, *And Still the Waters Run*, 168–70.

16. Mrs. Posey's Journal (pp. 55–65), item 3627.184, Gilcrease.

17. From "To My Wife," item 4026.8280, Gilcrease.

18. Mrs. Posey's Journal (pp. 55–65), item 3627.184, Gilcrease.

19. County Clerk's Office, McIntosh County, Oklahoma, Miscellaneous
Records Book 3:66, 69; *Indian Journal*, April 10, 1908.

20. *Muskogee Times-Democrat*, March 30, 1908; *Indian Journal*, April 10,
1908; Order Vesting Ownership of Certain Shares in a Corporation in Minnie Posey, August 4, 1910, Probate 197, Court Clerk's Office, Muskogee
County, Oklahoma; *Henryetta Free-Lance*, April 3, 1908.

21. *Indian Journal*, April 10, May 8 and 22, and June 5, 1908; *Tulsa Daily
World*, February 7, 1932; Leona Colbert, Interview, Eufaula, Oklahoma,
February 6, 1989.

22. Posey's Journal (p. 3), item 3826.183a, Gilcrease.

23. *Indian Journal*, April 17 and 24; May 1, 8, 15, and 22, 1908.

24. "Checotah," *Indian Journal*, May 1, 1908.

25. "O'Blenness," *Indian Journal*, May 8, 1908.

26. "Fus Fixico's Letter," *Indian Journal*, April 10 and 24, 1908.

27. "An Address by the Principal Chiefs," in *Addresses and Arguments by Prominent Men in Favor of Separate Statehood for Indian Territory* (Kinta, Indian Territory: Kinta Separate Statehood Club, 1905), 1–2; *Muskogee Phoenix*, October 5, 1905.

28. Debo, *And Still the Waters Run*, 166–67.

29. Debo, *And Still the Waters Run*, 173–79; *Indian Journal*, April 10, 1908.

30. *Indian Journal*, April 10, 1908.

31. *Indian Journal*, April 24, 1908.

32. "Is Russell Sage of the Creeks," *Indian Journal*, April 24, 1908; "Tumsee Culba," and "A Self-Made Man," *Indian Journal*, May 15, 1908.

33. "Lobbyists at Nation's Capital," *Indian Journal*, April 10, 1908.

34. "Indian Brave of the Old School," *Indian Journal*, April 10, 1908; "Snakes Meet at Busk Ground," *Indian Journal*, April 24, 1908; "Gathering of the Snakes," *Indian Journal*, May 22, 1908.

35. "A New Home—A New Country," *Indian Journal*, April 17, 1908.

36. "Future of the 'Snakes,'" *Indian Journal*, April 24, 1908; "A New Home—A New Country," *Indian Journal*, April 17, 1908; *Muskogee Times-Democrat*, June 25, 1906.

37. "Re-opening the Tribal Rolls," *Indian Journal*, April 24, 1908.

38. Posey's Journal (pp. 38–40), item 3626.183a, and R. B. Harris to Posey, June 5, 1897, item 3826.2241, Gilcrease; *Muskogee Phoenix*, January 2, 1890; For Harris's early efforts to establish an Indian colony in Mexico, see *Wagoner Record*, May 20, 1895. In 1906 the conservative Creeks established a commission to select lands in Mexico, allegedly at the invitation of President Diaz. *Wagoner Record*, March 1, 1906.

39. "A New Home—A New Country," *Indian Journal*, April 17, 1908; "Future of the 'Snakes,'" *Indian Journal*, April 24, 1908; "Good Country for Indians," *Indian Journal*, May 22, 1908.

40. "The Homestead of Empire," clipping, Scrapbook, item 4627.33, Gilcrease.

41. See Brian W. Dippie, *The Vanishing American: White Attitudes and U.S. Indian Policy* (Middletown, Conn.: Wesleyan University Press, 1982), especially 244–50.

42. Diversity of the peoples comprising the Creek Nation is analyzed in J. Leitch Wright, Jr., *Creeks and Seminoles: The Destruction and Regeneration of the Muscogulge People* (Lincoln: University of Nebraska Press, 1986); see chap. 10 for treatment of the Creek Nation in the West, especially 309–10, 320–21. For treatment of the Creeks and the other Civilized Tribes, see W. David Baird, "Are There 'Real' Indians in Oklahoma? Historical Perceptions of the Five Civilized Tribes," *Chronicles of Oklahoma* 68 (Spring 1990): 4–25, especially 7–10.

43. *Purcell Register*, June 26, 1891; *Muskogee Phoenix*, April 19, 1894.

44. 58th Congress, 2d session, *Senate Document 189*, 26–27, 35–36.

45. Debo, *And Still the Waters Run*, 179.

46. James A. Clifton, for example, presents the problems that arise from confusing race and ethnicity in defining "Indianness." He argues that racial terms, though used by Indians themselves, were creations of the Europeans, specifically the English and French, which "reflected exclusively European preoccupations with racial classification." See his "Alternate Identities and Cultural Frontiers" in *Being and Becoming Indian: Biographical Studies of North American Frontiers* ed. James A. Clifton (Chicago: Dorsey Press, 1898), 26–27.

47. Wright, *Creeks and Seminoles*, 320; Baird, "Are There 'Real' Indians in Oklahoma?" 18.

48. See their magazine, *The Supercivilized Indian* 1 (June 1926), published at Oklahoma City, and its longer-lasting apparent successor at Tulsa, *The American Indian*, which began publication in October 1926.

49. What constitutes Indian identity has been a problem for tribes, bureaucrats, authors, and scholars throughout this century. For a general historical survey of the issue, see William T. Hagan, "Full Blood, Mixed Blood, Generic, and Ersatz: The Problem of Indian Identity," *Arizona and the West* 27 (Winter 1985): 309–26. The subject is pervasive in the life and works of many contemporary Indian writers; see, e.g., Brian Swann and Arnold Krupat, ed., *I Tell You Now: Autobiographical Essays by Native American Writers* (Lincoln: University of Nebraska Press, 1987), and Joseph Bruchac, ed., *Survival This Way: Interviews with American Indian Poets* (Tucson: University of Arizona Press, 1987). It is also a point of some concern in scholarly works about Indian writers. See, for instance, Terry P. Wilson's comments in reference to John Joseph Mathews in "Osage Oxonian: The Heritage of John Joseph Mathews," *Chronicles of Oklahoma* 59 (Fall 1981): 267–68; Matthias Schubnell's analysis of the issue regarding N. Scott Momaday in *N. Scott Momaday: The Critical and Literary Background* (Norman: University of Oklahoma Press, 1985), 3–11; and Baird's analysis regarding George W. Grayson specifically, and the Five Civilized Tribes generally, in "Are There 'Real' Indians in Oklahoma?" See Clifton's "Alternate Identities and Cultural Frontiers," pp. 1–33, for a recent attempt to unravel the knotty problem of defining what it means to be "Indian." Indian leaders and others, he argues, use "Indian" status as a bargaining chip in the "game" of "interest-group politics" (25). Clifton and others have taken this issue a step further by arguing that anthropologists, historians, writers, artists, and bureaucrats have involved themselves in "interest-group politics" by presenting stock interpretations of Indian experience, creating what he calls "cultural fictions." See James A. Clifton, ed., *The Invented Indian: Cultural Fictions and Government Policies* (New Brunswick, N.J.: Transaction, 1990), especially Clifton's chapters 1 and 2. Chapter 2 also appeared as "Cultural Fictions," *Society* 27 (May–June 1990): 19–28.

1. *Indian Journal*, April 24, May 1, 5, and 22, and June 19, 1908; *Henryetta Free-Lance*, June 5, 1908.

2. *Tulsa Daily World*, February 7, 1932; William Elsey Connelley, "Memoir of Alexander Lawrence Posey," in Minnie H. Posey, comp, *The Poems of Alexander Lawrence Posey* (Topeka: Crane, 1910), 43; *Muskogee Times-Democrat*, May 28, 1908.

3. *Muskogee Times-Democrat*, May 28 and 30, 1908; *Indian Journal*, May 29, 1908.

4. "To Our Baby, Laughing," item 4026.8263, Gilcrease.

5. *Muskogee Times-Democrat*, May 28, 1908; John H. Phillips to Mrs. A. L. Posey, June 9, 1908, Scrapbook, item 4627.32, Gilcrease.

6. *Muskogee Times-Democrat*, May 29 and 30 and June 3, 5, and 6, 1908; *Indian Journal*, June 5 and 26 and July 3, 1908; *Muskogee Daily Phoenix*, July 5, 1908; Nyna Stone, "Soul of the West in Heart of Indian Poet," *Wewoka Times-Democrat*, April 29, 1934.

7. *Muskogee Daily Phoenix*, July 21 and 23, 1908; *Indian Journal*, July 24, 1908; *Henryetta Free-Lance*, July 24, 1908. According to Elliott Howe, the family believed that when the location of Alex's body was reported, local scavengers raced ahead and plundered his remains. His ring finger was missing and the diamond ring gone. Interview, Tulsa, Oklahoma, July 31, 1990.

8. *Henryetta Free-Lance*, May 29, 1908.

9. *Indian Journal*, June 5, 1908.

10. Ora Eddleman Reed, untitled article, *Sturm's Oklahoma Magazine* 6 (July 1908): 14–15.

11. *Muskogee Phoenix*, November 2, 1899, Century Edition, p. 56.

12. *Kansas City Star*, June 7, 1908.

13. Hall, "Posey a Believer," *Indian Journal*, July 17, 1908.

14. S. M. Rutherford, "A Tribute to Alex Posey," *Indian Journal*, July 24, 1908.

15. George J. Remsburg to W. P. Campbell, April 1912, "Letters Written by A. L. Posey and Charles Gibson, Creek Indians and Newspaper Clippings pertaining to the Former," AMD-OHS; Alexander L. Posey, "Col. McIntosh," manuscript, April 1895, owned by Elliott Howe, copy in author's file.

16. O. P. Sturm, "The Passing of the Creek Poet," *Sturm's Oklahoma Magazine* 6 (July 1908): 14; Mrs. Posey's annotated copy of the same article, Scrapbook, item 4627.32, Gilcrease.

17. Hall, "Alex Posey's Belief," *Henryetta Free-Lance*, undated clipping, Scrapbook, item 4627.32, Gilcrease.

18. "A Tribute to Alex Posey," *Indian Journal*, July 24, 1908.

19. "Simple Life for Posey," undated clipping, and Chinnubbie Harjo, "Epigrams," two undated clippings, Scrapbook, item 4627.32, Gilcrease.

20. Leona Colbert, Interview, Eufaula, Oklahoma, February 6, 1989; Gibson, "Gone Over to See," *Indian Journal*, June 5, 1908.

21. *Muskogee Daily Phoenix*, June 30, 1908; *Indian Journal*, July 3, 1908.

22. Various records, Probate 197, Court Clerk's Office, Muskogee County, Oklahoma; *Muskogee Times-Democrat*, October 1, 1908; see County Clerk's Office, McIntosh County, Oklahoma, Deed Books 16D:15 and 18D:67–68, 70–71, and 73, and Miscellaneous Records Books 5:572, 9:191, and 15:547, 552.

23. *Indian Journal*, April 10 and 24, 1908; Elliott Howe, Interviews, Tulsa, Oklahoma, July 19 and 31, 1990.

24. *Indian Journal*, January 24, 1908; "Fus Fixico's Letter," *Indian Journal*, April 17 and May 8 and 22, 1908.

25. *Indian Journal*, May 15, 1908; "Fable of the Foolish Young Bear," *Indian Journal*, March 22, 1901; "A Fable," *Indian Journal*, January 31, 1902; "A Fable," *Indian Journal*, February 7, 1902; "Posey Biography and Tribute by Orlando Swain and Others," item 4926.429, Gilcrease; "The Creek Uncle Remus," undated clipping, and Charles J. Shields, "Pioneer Days in Okmulgee," undated clipping (1923), Scrapbook, item 4627.32, Gilcrease; Minnie H. Posey to E. E. Dale, January 18, 1918, folder 15, box 53, Edward Everett Dale Collection, WHC.

26. "Posey Biography and Tribute by Orlando Swain and Others," item 4926.429, Gilcrease.

27. R. Roger Eubanks to Posey, May 1, 1908, Scrapbook, item 4627.32, Gilcrease; "Late Creek Indian Poet and Two of Oklahoma Literary Associates," *St. Louis Republic*, November 20, 1910. The quotation is from Frederick S. Barde, "A Creek Indian Poet," typescript, Alexander Posey no. 1, Frederick S. Barde Collection, AMD-OHS.

28. "Alex Posey Drowned," *Henryetta Free-Lance*, June 5, 1908; Minnie H. Posey to F. S. Barde, February 3, 1910, Poets and Poetry—Oklahoma #2, Frederick S. Barde Collection, AMD-OHS.

29. *Henryetta Free-Lance*, May 29, 1908; *Indian Journal*, June 5, 1908.

30. Hen-toh, "Noted Indian Passes Away," *Indian School Journal* 9 (June 1908): 19; Reed, untitled article, 14–15; *Indian Journal*, June 5, 1908.

31. "Mus Nixico's Letter (with Apologies to Alex Posey)," *South McAlester Capital*, January 7, 1904; " 'Fus Fixico' Again," *Bartlesville Weekly Examiner*, April 28, 1906; "With Apologies to Fus Fixico," *Johnston County Democrat*, April 17, 1908; *Indian Journal*, May 1, 1908; "Creek Politics by a Fullblood," *Muskogee Times-Democrat*, August 10, 1906; "Fullblood," clipping (source undetermined), March 22, 1910, Jessie McDermott File, Frederick S. Barde Collection, AMD-OHS; Acee Blue Eagle, "Indian Poetry," in *The Creek Nation Journal Centennial Edition* (Okmulgee, 1967), unpaged; William Harjo, *Sour Sofkee* (Muskogee, Okla.: Hoffman, 1983); R. Roger Eubanks, "How the Terrapin Beat the Rabbit," *Osage Magazine* 1 (May 1910): 72–74, and "The Ball Game of the Birds and Animals," *Osage Magazine* 2 (September 1910): 45–47; "Late Creek Indian Poet and Two

of Oklahoma Literary Associates," *St. Louis Republic*, November 20, 1910; "Cherokee Full Blood Airs Political Views," *Muskogee Times-Democrat*, September 14, 1906; "Extracts from Senator Landrum's Lecture," *Renfrew's Record*, August 1, 1919; Bertrand N. O. Walker, *Tales of the Bark Lodges, by Hen-Toh, Wyandot* (Oklahoma City: Harlow, 1919) and *Yon-doo-shah-we-ah (Nubbins) by Hen-Toh (Wyandot)* (Oklahoma City: Harlow, 1924).

32. Morris Edward Opler, "The Creek 'Town' and the Problem of Creek Indian Political Reorganization," in *Human Problems in Technological Change*, ed. Edward H. Spicer (New York: Russell Sage Foundation, 1952), 172–79; Alexander Spoehr, "Changing Kinship Systems: A Study in the Acculturation of the Creeks, Cherokee, and Choctaw," *Publications of the Field Museum of Natural History*, Anthropological Series, 33 (1947): 153–235 (also Millwood, N.Y.: Kraus Reprint, 1976), 210–11.

33. Opler, "Creek 'Town' and the Problem of Creek Indian Political Reorganization," 211.

POSTSCRIPT

1. Z. T. Walrond to Mrs. Alex Posey, June 1, 1908, and F. S. Barde to J. N. Thornton, June 4, 1908, Scrapbook, item 4627.32, Gilcrease; *Muskogee Times-Democrat*, June 27, 1908; Alex Posey to Barde, January 24, 1904, and Minnie Posey to Barde, June 24, 1908, Poets and Poetry—Oklahoma #2, Frederick S. Barde Collection, AMD-OHS; *Indian Journal*, October 28, 1908; W. F. Jones, Interview, July 21, 1937, *Indian-Pioneer History* (AMD-OHS), 31:464; Posey to Barde, May 15, 1903, in *Handbook of Oklahoma Writers*, by Mary Hayes Marable and Elaine Boylan (Norman: University of Oklahoma Press, 1939), 79–80.

2. Minnie H. Posey to Barde, January 29 and February 3 and 6, 1910, Poets and Poetry—Oklahoma #2, Frederick S. Barde Collection, AMD-OHS; Program, Song Recital, December 13, 1910, Scrapbook, item 4627.32, Gilcrease.

3. Publication notices, *Galveston News*, October 23, 1910, and *Baltimore American*, October 17, 1910; Minnie H. Posey to Joseph B. Thoburn, July 27, 1914, Alexander Posey File, Joseph B. Thoburn Collection, AMD-OHS; Minnie H. Posey to E. E. Dale, September 1, 1955, folder 16, box 53, Edward Everett Dale Collection, WHC; Cherokee County, Oklahoma, 1910 Census Schedules, NAMP T264.

4. Minnie Posey to Barde, June 24, 1908, Poets and Poetry—Oklahoma #2, Frederick S. Barde Collection, AMD-OHS; Barde to Thornton, June 4, 1908, Scrapbook, item 4627.32, Gilcrease; Posey to Barde, May 15, 1903, in Marable and Boylan, *Handbook of Oklahoma Writers*, 79–80.

5. Minnie H. Posey to Barde, February 3 and 6, 1910, and May 7, 1915, Poets and Poetry—Oklahoma #2, Frederick S. Barde Collection, AMD-OHS; Barde to Minnie Posey, February 4, 1910, Scrapbook, item 4627.32,

Gilcrease; Minnie Posey to Thoburn, March 11 and July 16, 1921, Alexander Posey File, Joseph B. Thoburn Collection, AMD-OHS; "An Indian Poet's Tale of a River Trip," *Kansas City Star*, October 31, 1915.

6. Wynema Posey Blaine to E. E. Dale, October 14, 1966, Alexander Posey File, Section X—Creek, AMD-OHS; Minnie H. Posey to Carolyn Thomas Foreman, April 1934, Alexander L. Posey File, Grant Foreman Collection, AMD-OHS; Minnie Posey to Cora Case Porter, April 20 and November 30, 1937, Oklahoma Biography—Alexander Posey, Vertical File, Muskogee Public Library, Muskogee, Oklahoma; *Tulsa Daily World*, June 26, 1949.

7. *Muskogee Daily Phoenix*, November 15 and 30, and December 13, 1917, and January 5 and 23, 1918; Minnie Posey to Joseph B. Thoburn, December 19, 1913, July 27, 1914, and March 12, 1918, Alexander Posey File, Joseph B. Thoburn Collection, AMD-OHS.

8. Minnie H. Posey to E. E. Dale, January 18, 1918, folder 15, box 53, Edward Everett Dale Collection, WHC.

9. Minnie H. Posey to Dale, February 18, 1918, folder 3, box 211; and January 1, April 1, April 18, and April 19, 1918, folder 15, box 53, Edward Everett Dale Collection, WHC.

10. Minnie H. Posey to Dale, February 9, 1919, folder 15, box 53; February 18, 1918, folder 3, box 211; and August 10, 1918, folder 16, box 53, Edward Everett Dale Collection, WHC.

11. Minnie H. Posey to Dale, April 18, 1918, folder 15, box 53, Edward Everett Dale Collection, WHC.

12. Minnie H. Posey to Dale, September 1, 1955, folder 16, box 53, Edward Everett Dale Collection, WHC.

13. Minnie H. Posey to Dale, October 31, 1955, folder 15, box 53, Edward Everett Dale Collection, WHC.

14. Muriel H. Wright to Minnie H. Posey, October 6, 1955; Wright to E. E. Dale, October 25, 1955; Dale to Wright, October 25, 1955; Dale to Wright, October 25, November 7, and November 28, 1955; and Minnie Posey to Dale, November 2, 1955, Alexander Posey File, Section X—Creek, AMD-OHS. Loan of the artifacts was reported in *Muskogee Times-Democrat*, July 18, 1925; *Daily Oklahoman*, July 12, 1925; and "Annual Report of Czarina C. Conlan, February 2, 1926," *Chronicles of Oklahoma* 4 (March 1926): 70.

15. Minnie H. Posey to E. E. Dale, November 20, 1955, and November 7, 1956, folder 16, box 53, Edward Everett Dale Collection, WHC; Edward Everett Dale and Jesse Lee Rader, *Readings in Oklahoma History* (Evanston, Ill.: Row, Peterson, 1930), 669–77; "Journal of Creek Enrollment Field Party 1905 by Alexander Posey," *Chronicles of Oklahoma* 46 (Spring 1968): 2–15.

16. Minnie H. Posey to E. E. Dale, February 11, 1957, folder 16, box 53, Edward Everett Dale Collection, WHC.

17. *Sooner State Press*, November 18, 1961; "The Journal of Alexander

Lawrence Posey, January 1 to September 4, 1897," *Chronicles of Oklahoma* 45 (Winter 1967–68): 393–432; "Journal of Enrollment Field Party 1905 by Alexander Posey," 2–15. The reader should use these editions of Posey's journals with caution. They contain numerous errors in transcription, and the first omits an entire paragraph.

18. See various transactions, County Clerk's Office, McIntosh County, Oklahoma, Deed Books 4:377, 5:242, 7:266, 9:53, 73, 172, 177, 564, 19:377, 415, 12:543, 14:52, 258, 275, 484, 495, 16:477, 617, 17:189, 570, 18:67, 68, 70, 71, 73, 344, 572, 22:108, 273, 462, 27:132, 35:540, 36:93, 592, 38:571, 41:183; Miscellaneous Books 3:253, 5:349, 474, 476, 517, 6:97, 171, 7:36, 246, 357, 351, 9:87, 90, 191, 12:541, 13:506, 15:36, 547, 552; Hughes County, Oklahoma, 1910 Census Schedules, NAMP T264.

19. Court Clerk's Office, Tulsa County, Oklahoma, Probate 2705; Elliott Howe, Interviews, Tulsa, Oklahoma, July 19 and 30, 1990; *Eufaula Republican*, September 22, 1911.

20. *Eufaula Republican*, July 17, 1908; *Eufaula Democrat*, September 15, 1914.

21. County Clerk's Office, Seminole County, Oklahoma, Deed Records 424:266, 268, 445:403, 470:293, and 563:150; "Nancy Posey, Mother of Famed Indian Poet, Faces Loss of Her Wewoka Home," *Daily Oklahoman*, June 28, 1936, C5; untitled clipping, March 4, 1938, Oklahoma Biography— Alexander Posey, Vertical File, Muskogee Public Library.

22. "Nancy Posey, Mother of Famed Indian Poet," C5.

23. Elliott Howe, Interviews, Tulsa, Oklahoma, July 19 and 30, 1990.

Bibliography

. . . .

Published Works by Posey (Works Cited Only)

The Alabama Prophet. Bacone: Indian University Press, n.d. ;
"Chinnubbie Scalps the Squaws." *B.I.U. Instructor* 2 (May 20, 1893), un-
    paged.
"The Creek Sage Writes." *Muskogee Daily Phoenix*, July 17, 1903.
"The Cruise of the Good Vrouw from the Diary of One of the Crew."
    Indian Journal, July 15, 1902.
"Cuba Libra." *Muskogee Phoenix*, December 24, 1896.
"The Decree." *Red Man* 16 (April 1900): 3.
"A Fable." *Indian Journal*, January 31, 1902.
"A Fable." *Indian Journal*, February 7, 1902.
"Fable of the Foolish Young Bear." *Indian Journal*, March 22, 1901.
"From Fus Fixico." *Indian Journal*, October 24, 1902.
"Fus Fixico's Letter." *Cherokee Advocate*, May 18, 1904.
"Fus Fixico's Letter." *Dustin Dispatch*, August 26, 1905.
"Fus Fixico's Letter." *Fort Smith Times*, August 26, 1903; September 10,
    1903; October 25, 1903.
"Fus Fixico's Letter." *Holdenville Tribune*, November 29, 1906.
"Fus Fixico's Letter." *Indian Journal*, November 21, 1902; December 12,

1902; December 19, 1902; December 26, 1902; January 2, 1903; January 16, 1903; February 20, 1903; February 27, 1903; March 6, 1903; March 20, 1903; March 27, 1903; April 3, 1903; April 17, 1903; April 24, 1903; May 1, 1903; May 8, 1903; May 22, 1903; June 12, 1903; June 26, 1903; July 3, 1903; July 10, 1903; August 6, 1903; March 16, 1906; March 23, 1906; March 30, 1906; April 10, 1908; April 17, 1908; April 24, 1908; May 8, 1908; May 22, 1908.

"Fus Fixico's Letter." *Muskogee Daily Phoenix*, April 17, 1904; May 1, 1904; May 29, 1904.

"Fus Fixico's Letter." *Muskogee Evening Times*, December 16, 1903.

"Fus Fixico's Letter." *Muskogee Phoenix*, August 10, 1905; August 31, 1905; September 7, 1905; November 2, 1905.

"Fus Fixico's Letter." *New-State Tribune*, March 8, 1906; March 15, 1906; March 22, 1906; March 29, 1906.

"Fus Fixico's Letter." *Tahlequah Arrow*, May 30, 1903; June 6, 1903.

"Fus Fixico's Letter." *Vinita Weekly Chieftain*, December 31, 1903.

"Hotgun on the New State." *Kansas City Star*, June 24, 1906.

"The Indian Part by Alex Posey." *Holdenville Times*, June 29, 1906.

"An Indian Poet's Tale of a River Trip." *Kansas City Star*, October 3, 1915.

"The Indian's Past Olympic." *Muskogee Phoenix*, December 17, 1896.

"Jes 'Bout a Mid'lin', Sah." *Twin Territories* 2 (April 1900): 76–77.

"Lost from His Tribe for Many Years." *Indian Journal*, May 15, 1908.

"My Hermitage." *Red Man* 15 (February 1900): 2.

"Note." *Twin Territories* 2 (August 1900): 158.

"The Passing of 'Hot Gun.'" *Indian Journal*, January 24, 1908.

"Pohalton Lake." *Twin Territories* 1 (November 1899): 246.

"Room at the Top." *Indian Journal*, July 6, 1894.

"Sea Shells." *Muskogee Phoenix*, December 23, 1897.

"Sequoyah." *Muskogee Phoenix*, June 22, 1893; *Cherokee Advocate*, July 22, 1893; *Daily Oklahoma State Capital*, July 11, 1893; *Red Man* 12 (July–August 1893): 8.

"To a Humming Bird." *Muskogee Phoenix*, December 23, 1897.

Twilight. Bacone: Indian University Press, n.d.

"Two Famous Prophets." *Twin Territories* 2 (September 1900): 180–82.

Manuscripts and Archival Materials

Bacone College, Muskogee, Oklahoma
    Alexander L. Posey File, Indian Collection
    Alexander L. Posey's Personal Library
Federal Records Center, Kansas City, Missouri
    United States District Court, Kansas, Second Division, Criminal, 1883–88

Muskogee Public Library, Muskogee, Oklahoma
  Oklahoma Biography—Alexander Posey, Vertical Files
National Anthropological Archives, Smithsonian Institution, Washington, D.C.
  Creek File Numbers 568-a, 1806, 4200
National Archives, Washington, D.C.
  Ethan Allen Hitchcock Papers (Record Group 200)
  Records of the Bureau of Indian Affairs (Record Group 75)
    Creek National Records (maintained by Archives and Manuscripts Division, Oklahoma Historical Society)
    Creek Removal Records
    Records concerning Patents and Deeds
    Records relating to Civil War Claims of Loyal Creek Indians
    Special Series A, General Records, 1907–39
National Archives Microfilm Publications
  Compiled Service Records of Confederate Soldiers Who Served in Organizations Raised Directly by the Confederate Government (Microcopy 258)
  Enrollment Cards for the Five Civilized Tribes, 1898–1914 (Microcopy M1186)
  1860 Census Schedules (Microcopy M653)
  1880 Census Schedules (Microcopy T9)
  1900 Census Schedules (Microcopy T623)
  1910 Census Schedules (Microcopy T624)
Oklahoma Historical Society, Archives and Manuscripts Division, Oklahoma City
  Alexander L. Posey Papers (MS 85-72)
  Creek National Records (National Archives Record Group 75)
  Frederick S. Barde Collection
  Grant Foreman Collection
  Indian-Pioneer History Papers
  Joseph B. Thoburn Collection
  "Letters Written by A. L. Posey and Charles Gibson, Creek Indians and Newspaper Clippings pertaining to the Former"
  Samuel Brown Collection, Loyal Creek Claimants
  Section X (Alexander Posey)
  United States Court Records
Oklahoma Historical Society, Library
  Alexander Posey Vertical Files
Thomas Gilcrease Institute of American History and Art, Tulsa, Oklahoma
  Alexander L. Posey Collection
Western History Collections, University of Oklahoma, Norman, Oklahoma
  Edward Everett Dale Collection
  Charles N. Haskell Collection

Green McCurtain Collection
Mrs. Alfred Mitchell Collection

Miscellaneous Unpublished Sources

Bode, Coeryne
"The Origin and Development of Bacone College." M.A. thesis, University of Tulsa, 1957.
Colbert, Leona
Interviews: Eufaula, Oklahoma, June 15, 1988, and February 6, 1989.
McCombs, William. "History of Tuskegee Church" (undated typescript).
Hall, Hugh C.
Hall, George Riley. "Memoirs" (typescript, 1942).
Howe, Elliott
Interviews: Telephone, July 19, 1990; Tulsa, Oklahoma, July 31, 1990.
Posey, Alexander L. "Col. McIntosh" (manuscript dated April 1895).
Indian Journal Newspaper Office (Eufaula, Oklahoma)
"Tuskegee Indian Baptist Church" (typescript, 1976), History File.
Moore, Ginger Blaine
Affidavit of Nancy Posey, December 24, 1937 (typescript).
Posey to Wife (letter), undated (1905?).

County Records

Alabama
Macon County, Probate Judge's Office, Probate Records
Oklahoma
Hughes County, County Clerk's Office, Deed Books
McIntosh County, County Clerk's Office, Deed Books and Miscellaneous Books; Court Clerk's Office, Probate Records
Muskogee County, Court Clerk's Office, Probate Records
Okfuskee County, County Clerk's Office, Deed Books and Transcript Books
Seminole County, County Clerk's Office, Deed Books
Tulsa County, Court Clerk's Office, Probate Records

Government Publications

Hewitt, J. N. B. *Notes on the Creek Indians*, Ed. John R. Swanton. Bureau of American Ethnology Bulletin 1233. Washington, D.C.: Government Printing Office, 1939.
Hodge, Frederick Webb. *Handbook of American Indians North of Mexico*. Washington, D.C.: Government Printing Office, 1912.

    23d Congress, 1st session. *Senate Executive Document 512.*   *Bibliography*
    46th Congress, 3d session. *House Executive Document 1.*
    47th Congress, 1st session. *House Executive Document 1.*
    47th Congress, 2d session. *House Executive Document 1.*
    48th Congress, 1st session. *House Executive Document 1.*
    48th Congress, 2d session. *House Executive Document 1.*
    50th Congress, 1st session. *Senate Executive Document 198.*
    59th Congress, 2d session. *Senate Report 5013.*
United States Department of the Interior. *Laws, Decisions, and Regulations Affecting the Work of the Commission to the Five Civilized Tribes, 1893–1906.* Washington, D.C.: Government Printing Office, 1906.

Newspapers and Magazines

The American Indian (Tulsa, Oklahoma), 1926
Baltimore American, 1910
Bartlesville Weekly Examiner, 1906
Broken Arrow Ledger, 1905
Cherokee Advocate (Talequah, Cherokee Nation), 1893, 1903, 1904
Daily Oklahoman (Oklahoma City, Oklahoma), 1925, 1936, 1939
Daily Oklahoma State Capital (Guthrie, Oklahoma Territory), 1893
Dustin Dispatch, 1905
Eufaula Democrat, 1914
Eufaula Republican, 1908
Fort Smith Times, 1903
Galveston News, 1910
Henryetta Free-Lance, 1905, 1906, 1908
Holdenville Times, 1905, 1906
Holdenville Tribune, 1906
Indian Chieftain (Vinita, Cherokee Nation), 1888
Indian Journal (Eufaula, Creek Nation and Oklahoma), 1884, 1885, 1886, 1887, 1889, 1890, 1891, 1894, 1895, 1896, 1900, 1901, 1902, 1903, 1906, 1907, 1908, 1976
Indian Republican (Tulsa, Creek Nation), 1904
Johnston County Democrat (Tishomingo, Oklahoma), 1908
Kansas City Journal, 1903
Kansas City Star, 1906, 1908, 1915
Muskogee Daily Phoenix, 1902, 1903, 1904, 1905, 1908, 1917, 1918
Muskogee Democrat, 1904, 1905, 1906
Muskogee Evening Times, 1898, 1901, 1903
Muskogee Phoenix, 1888, 1889, 1890, 1893, 1894, 1895, 1897, 1898, 1899, 1900, 1903, 1905, 1906, 1935
Muskogee Times-Democrat, 1906, 1907, 1908, 1925

New-State Tribune (Muskogee, Creek Nation), 1906
New York Times, 1903
Oklahoma City Times, 1971
Purcell Register, 1891
Red Fork Derrick, 1905
Renfrew's Record (Alva, Oklahoma), 1919
St. Louis Republic, 1899, 1910
Sooner State Press (Norman, Oklahoma), 1961
South McAlester Capital, 1899, 1903, 1904, 1905
The Supercivilized Indian (Oklahoma City, Oklahoma), 1926
Tahlequah Arrow, 1903, 1906
Talala Topic, 1904
Tulsa Daily World, 1908, 1932, 1934, 1949
Tulsa Democrat, 1905
Vinita Weekly Chieftain, 1903
Wagoner Record, 1895
Wewoka Times-Democrat, 1934

Books and Pamphlets

Addresses and Arguments by Prominent Men in Favor of Separate Statehood for Indian Territory. Kinta, Indian Territory: Kinta Separate Statehood Club, 1905.

Baird, W. David, ed. *A Creek Warrior for the Confederacy: The Autobiography of Chief G. W. Grayson*. Norman: University of Oklahoma Press, 1988.

Bruchac, Joseph, ed. *Survival This Way: Interviews with American Indian Poets*. Tucson: University of Arizona Press, 1987.

Chief Executives of Five Civilized Tribes Adopt Plans for a Prohibition State: Protest against Territorial Form of Government or Annexation to Oklahoma. N.p., 1903.

Clifton, James A., ed. *Being and Becoming Indian: Biographical Studies of North American Frontiers*. Chicago: Dorsey Press, 1898.

——. *The Invented Indian: Cultural Fictions and Government Policies*. New Brunswick, N.J.: Transactions, 1990.

Constitution of the State of Sequoyah. Muskogee: Phoenix, 1905.

Current-Garcia, Eugene, and Dorothy B. Hatfield, eds. *Shem Ham and Japheth: The Papers of W. O. Tuggle*. Athens: University of Georgia Press, 1973.

Dale, Edward Everett, and Jesse Lee Rader. *Readings in Oklahoma History*. Evanston, Ill.: Row, Peterson, 1930.

Debo, Angie. *And Still the Waters Run*. Princeton: Princeton University Press, 1972.

————. *The Road to Disappearance*. Norman: University of Oklahoma Press, 1941.

Dippie, Brian W. *The Vanishing American: White Attitudes and U.S. Indian Policy*. Middletown, Conn.: Wesleyan University Press, 1982.

Emery, Jones Gladstone. *Court of the Damned; Being a Factual Story of the Court of Judge Isaac C. Parker and the Life and Times of the Indian Territory and Old Fort Smith*. New York: Comet Press Books, 1959.

Five Civilized Tribes Protest against Congressional Legislation Contemplating Annexation of Indian Territory to Oklahoma or Territorial Form of Government prior to March 4th, 1906. [Kinta?], Indian Territory, 1902.

Green, Michael D. *The Politics of Indian Removal: Creek Government and Society in Crisis*. Lincoln: University of Nebraska Press, 1982.

Harjo, William. *Sour Sofkee*. Muskogee: Hoffman, 1983.

Loughridge, R. M., comp. *Muskokee Hymns*. 5th ed. Philadelphia: Presbyterian Board of Christian Education. Reprint. Okmulgee, Okla.: B. Frank Belvin, 1970.

Marable, Mary Hays, and Elaine Boylan. *Handbook of Oklahoma Writers*. Norman: University of Oklahoma Press, 1939.

Miner, H. Craig. *The Corporation and the Indian: Tribal Sovereignty and Industrial Civilization in Indian Territory, 1865–1907*. Norman: University of Oklahoma Press, 1989.

Morgan, H. Wayne, and Anne Hodges Morgan. *Oklahoma: A Bicentennial History*. New York: W. W. Norton, 1977.

Posey, Minnie H., comp. *The Poems of Alexander Lawrence Posey*. Topeka: Crane, 1910.

Schubnall, Matthias. *N. Scott Momaday: The Cultural and Literary Background*. Norman: University of Oklahoma Press, 1985.

Speck, Frank G. *The Creek Indians of Taskigi Town*. Millwood, N.Y.: Kraus Reprint, 1974.

Swann, Brian, and Arnold Krupat, eds. *I Tell You Now: Autobiographical Essays by Native American Writers*. Lincoln: University of Nebraska Press, 1987.

Walker, Bertrand N. O. *Tales of the Bark Lodges, by Hen-Toh, Wyandot*. Oklahoma City: Harlow, 1919.

————. *Yon-doo-sha-we-ah (Nubbins), by Hen-Toh (Wyandot)*. Oklahoma City: Harlow, 1924.

Young, Mary Elizabeth. *Redskins, Ruffleshirts, and Rednecks: Indian Allotments in Alabama and Mississippi, 1830–1860*. Norman: University of Oklahoma Press, 1961.

Articles

"Alexander Posey, the Creek Poet." *Indian School Journal* 11 (June 1911): 11–14.

"Annual Report of Czarina C. Conlan, February 2, 1926." *Chronicles of Oklahoma* 4 (March 1926): 70–73.

Bahos, Charles. "On Opothleyahola's Trail: Locating the Battle of Round Mountains." *Chronicles of Oklahoma* 63 (Spring 1985): 58–89.

Baird, W. David. "Are There 'Real' Indians in Oklahoma? Historical Perceptions of the Five Civilized Tribes." *Chronicles of Oklahoma* 68 (Spring 1990): 4–23.

Banks, Dean. "Civil-War Refugees from Indian Territory, in the North, 1861–1864." *Chronicles of Oklahoma* 41 (Autumn 1963): 286–98.

Barnett, Leona G. "Este Cate Emunkv." *Chronicles of Oklahoma* 46 (Spring 1968): 20–35.

Bearss, Edwin C. "The Civil War Comes to Indian Territory, 1861: The Flight of Opothleyoholo." *Journal of the West* 11 (January 1972): 9–42.

"Biographical." *Twin Territories* 2 (May 1900): 108.

Blue Eagle, Acee. "Indian Poetry." In *The Creek Nation Journal Centennial Edition*. Okmulgee, Okla., 1967.

Clifton, James A. "Cultural Fictions." *Society* 27 (May–June 1990): 19–28.

Crofford, Florence Bledsoe. "A Real Indian Poet, 'Chinnubbie Harjo.'" *Criterion* 3 (September 1902): 37–38.

Eubanks, R. Roger. "The Ball Game of the Birds and Animals." *Osage Magazine* 2 (September 1910): 45–47.

———. "How the Terrapin Beat the Rabbit." *Osage Magazine* 1 (May 1910): 72–74.

Fischer, LeRoy H., and William L. McMurry. "Confederate Refugees from Indian Territory." *Chronicles of Oklahoma* 57 (Winter 1979–80): 451–62.

Hagan, William T. "Full Blood, Mixed Blood, Generic, and Ersatz: The Problem of Indian Identity." *Arizona and the West* 27 (Winter 1985): 309–26.

Hayes, Ella M. "History of Bacone." *Baconian* 11 (May 1908): 1–11.

Hen-toh. "Noted Indian Passes Away." *Indian School Journal* 9 (June 1908): 19.

Historia 8 (July 1, 1919): 5.

"The Journal of Alexander Lawrence Posey, January 1 to September 4, 1897." *Chronicles of Oklahoma* 45 (Winter 1967–68): 393–432.

"Journal of Creek Enrollment Field Party 1905 by Alexander Posey." *Chronicles of Oklahoma* 46 (Spring 1968): 2–15.

Maxwell, Amos. "The Sequoyah Convention." *Chronicles of Oklahoma* 28 (Summer 1950): 161–92; 28 (Autumn 1950): 299–340.

Meserve, John Bartlett. "Chief Opothleyahola." *Chronicles of Oklahoma* 9 (December 1931): 440–53.

"Miss Anna Lewis, Teacher of Alexander Posey at Bacone University, 1889–1890." *Chronicles of Oklahoma* 45 (Autumn 1967): 332–35.

Murray, William H. "The Constitutional Convention." *Chronicles of Oklahoma* 9 (June 1931): 126–38.

Nesbitt, Paul, ed. "Governor Haskell Tells of Two Conventions." *Chronicles of Oklahoma* 14 (June 1936): 189–217.

"Notes and Documents." *Chronicles of Oklahoma* 33 (Autumn 1955): 384–409.

Opler, Morris Edward. "The Creek 'Town' and the Problems of Creek Indian Political Reorganization." In *Human Problems in Technological Change*, ed. Edward H. Spicer, 165–80. New York: Russell Sage Foundation, 1952.

Reed, Ora Eddleman. [Untitled]. *Sturm's Oklahoma Magazine* 6 (July 1908): 14–17.

"Reverend William McCombs." *Chronicles of Oklahoma* 8 (March 1930): 137–40.

Sarcoxie, Henry B. "Rhymes Written at Las Vagas [*sic*]." *Twin Territories* 2 (September 1900): 193.

———. "Westward Ho!" *Twin Territories* 2 (August 1900): 158–59; 2 (September 1900): 191–92.

Spoehr, Alexander. "Changing Kinship Systems: A Study in the Acculturation of the Creeks, Cherokee, and Choctaw." *Publications of the Field Museum of Natural History*, Anthropological Series, 33 (1947): 153–235. Millwood, N.Y.: Kraus Reprint, 1976.

Sturm, O. P. "The Passing of the Creek Poet." *Sturm's Oklahoma Magazine* 6 (July 1908): 13–14.

"Three Indian Writers of Prominence." *Sturm's Statehood Magazine* 1 (October 1905): 84–85.

Wilson, Terry P. "Osage Oxonian: The Heritage of John Joseph Mathews." *Chronicles of Oklahoma* 59 (Fall 1981): 264–93.

Index

. . . .

Aesop's Fables, 100
Afro-American League, 103
Ahlincha faction, 146
Alabama Town, 222
Alabama Prophet, 26
Aldrich, Thomas Bailey, 93
Alex, Freeland G., 55
Allotment, 6, 109; Chinnubbie on,
    75–76; conservative Creeks and,
    240–41; Creek agreement for,
    147; Creek resistance to, 73–74;
    Five Civilized Tribes' resistance
    to, 74–75
Allotments: Creek deeds for, 147–
    50, 164, 168; enrollment of
    newborns for, 198–99; fraud in
    Creek, 173–83; Posey family,
    123; restrictions on, 149–50,
    226–30; sale of Creek, 226–27;
    speculation in, 174–75, 227–30
Ansley, W. Henry, 210, 298n.3

Arabian Nights' Entertainments, 86
Arbekas, 201
Arkansas Gazette, 87
Artus Hotiye, 199, 202, 222, 265
Artussee, Creek Nation, 14, 33,
    141, 142, 232
Artussee Indian Baptist Church,
    142, 196

Bacone Indian University, 5; Posey
    at, 41–56; rules of conduct at, 58.
    See also *B.I.U. Instructor*
Baker, John, 200
Bald Hill, 71, 111, 114, 123, 140,
    141–42, 196, 232; location of,
    29, 32; oil exploration at, 234,
    255; Posey allotments at, 269–70,
    271; Posey ranch at, 29, 278n.20;
    Posey's visits to, 94–96
Bald Knob Oil and Gas Com-
    pany, 234

Ball game between Arbekas and Eufaulas, 201

Barde, Frederick S., 262–63, 264–65

Barnes, George W., 231

Barnes Investment Company, 235

Barnett, Billy, 165

Basketry, 201

Beavers, J. J., 187

Bell, H. H., 231

Bell, L. B., 74

Benedict, John D., 110, 115, 180

Berryhill, Dick, 31, 32

Bird, Jim, 199

Bird Creek, Mandy, 233

B.I.U. Instructor, 15–16, 50–53

Bixby, Tams, 165, 176, 178, 223; and land fraud, 177, 179–80

Blacks, 9, 29. *See also* Creek freed-men

Blue Eagle, Acee, 259

Bonaparte, Charles J., 232, 244; investigation by, 180–83; report of, 182–83

Boone, Thomas, 99

Boudinot, E. C., 74

Bradley, C. M., 180, 229

Bradley Real Estate Company, 180, 231

Brannon, Tom, 2, 3

Brant-Sera, J. Ojijatekha, 184

Breckenridge, Clifton R., 178, 179; and land fraud, 177

Brosius, S. M., 178, 179; investigation by, 177–78

Brown, A. J., 210

Brown, John F., 70, 212

Buel, James William, 86

Buffington, T. M., 153

Burns, Robert, 86, 87

Burroughs, John, 121

Bush, Jonas, 32

Busk, 143. *See also* Green corn ceremony

Byrd, L. L., 220

Caine, Hall, 88

Callahan, Samuel Benton, 86, 137

Callahan, Sophia Alice, 137

Canadian, Choctaw Nation, 140

Canadian Valley Trust Company, 177, 178, 179–80

Capeche Emarthla, 200

Carlisle Indian Industrial School, 115

Carter, Charles D., 220

Cass, Frank H., 31

Cathay, Oklahoma, 1

Chalogee, 26, 27, 29

Checotah, Creek Nation, 140; and county seat contest, 235–37; intertribal council at, 73

Checotah Enquirer, 89, 118

Cheparney, 13

Cherokee Advocate, 51

Cherokee Indians, 57

Cherokee Oil and Gas Company, 178

Chicago Columbian Exposition, 49

Childers, Ellis B., 76, 80

Chinnubbie: on allotment, 75; as persona, 54–55

Chinnubbie Harjo, 50–51, 118, 165

Chitto Harjo, 4, 143–47, 166, 167, 168, 169, 201, 202–3, 204; arrest of, 144–45; as candidate for chief, 155, 172; Fus Fixico letter on, 190–91; poem about, 144; Posey's interview with, 193, 197–98; speech of, 227

Choela, 167, 168, 193

Chofolop Harjo, 202

Cimeter, 102

Cinda, 202

Clift, Edith Connelley, 267

Cobb, Guy P., 177

Colbert, Benjamin, 178, 179

Colbert, Louis, 166

Colbert, Thompson, 239

Collins, Mitchell, 32, 279n.25

Concharte Micco, 74

Connelley, William E., 257, 263, 267
Coon Creek, 32, 56
Coosie Harjo, 33
Coppick, W. C., 4
Cosmopolitan, 87
Council Hill, 201
County seats: contests for, 235–37; and Sequoyah convention, 216
Creek culture, survival of, 260
Creek freedmen, 30, 31, 32, 35, 95, 102, 155, 239; stories about, 56–57, 122
Creek Indians: economy of, 14; changing culture of, 243–44; in Cherokee Nation, 223–24; in Civil War, 15–16; cultural diversity among, 12, 15, 244; after statehood, 237–44. *See also* Ahlincha faction; Loyal Creeks; Snake faction
Creek Nation: constitutionalism in, 30; land use in, 108; political patronage in, 80, 101–2, 109; political turmoil in, 29–30, 77–80; politics in, 35; ranch life in, 28–29
Creek Orphan Asylum, 5, 79, 81
Creek towns. *See names of towns*
Criterion, 185
Current Literature, 87, 123
Curtis, Charles, 118
Curtis Act, 109
Cussetah Yohola, 200

Daily Indian Journal, 164, 183
Daily Muskogee Phoenix, 164
Daily Oklahoma State Capital, 51
Dale, Edward Everett, 265–66, 267–69
Davidson, Charles A., 177
Davidson, J. P., 103
Dawes, Henry L., 74
Dawes Commission, 6, 53, 264; creation of, 73; Creek resistance to, 77, 80; Creeks visited by, 73–74; Five Civilized Tribes' resistance to, 109; and land fraud, 172–73, 183; and land sales, 227; Posey works for, 159; scandal involving, 175–83
Deer, James H., 220
Deere, Ben, 200
Deere, Lawyer, 153
Dialect: of Fus Fuxico, 165–66, 184; Posey on, 87; Posey's early works in, 165–66; Posey's use of, 53, 57
Diaz, Porfirio, 146
Dickinson, Emily, 86
Douglas, Clarence B., 155, 182; firing of, 176
Doyle, Arthur Conan, 88, 123
Draper, William R., 116
Duncan, DeWitt Clinton (Too-qua-stee), 185
Dustin, Creek Nation, 198, 205, 232
Dustin Townsite Company, 232

Eastman, Charles A., 115, 119, 246
Eastman, Elaine Goodale, 115, 119
Eddleman, Ora V. *See* Reed, Ora V. Eddleman
Education, in Creek Nation, 110
Election, Creek national, 154–57
Eliza. *See* Thlee-sa-ho-he
Emery, J. Gladstone, 271
Emery, John E., 81, 82, 112, 141–42, 232
Emery, Melissa Posey, 35, 37, 42, 81, 82, 141–42, 270–71
Essex, A. J., 55
Eubanks, Royal Roger, 257, 259
Eubanks, William, 185
Eufaula, Creek Nation, 29, 37, 194; boarding school at, 5; and county seat contest, 235–37; intertribal council at, 76; Posey's boosting of, 139–41; statehood convention at, 151, 153, 210

Eufaula District courthouse, 76
Eufaula High School, 112
Eufaula Trust Company, 177, 179
Eufaulas, 201
Eu-pock-lotte-kae, 13, 34
Evans, Robert M. (Bob), 33, 142
Evans, Winey Phillips, 12, 16, 33, 142, 270

Fahnee, 202
Fame, Creek Nation, 141, 142
Fife, James, 35
First Regiment of Creek Volunteers, 20
Fish kill, 71–72
Fisher, William, 136
Flynn, Dennis, 108
Forest Hotel, 37
Fort Gibson, Cherokee Nation, 57
Fort Gibson Post, 252
Fox, Finis, 179
Francis, Minkey, 33
Fus Fixico, 260; dialect of, 165; and Joe Harjo, 165; literary antecedents of, 165
Fus Fixico letters, 6, 8, 55, 137, 164–86, 205, 233, 240, 253, 256; on allotment deeds, 168–69; characters in, 167; and Christianity, 191; on conservative Creeks, 188–95; on county seats, 215–16, 236–37; on Creek allotment, 174–75; on Creek election, 171–73; in *Fort Smith Times*, 182; on Indians in politics, 222; on land leasing, 174; on land scandals, 176–83; literary achievement in, 185–86; literary influence of, 259; and Mexican emigration, 242; in *Muskogee Evening Times*, 182, 183; in *New-State Tribune*, 217–19, 221; on Oklahoma statehood, 221; on party politics, 219–22; play on names in, 169, 178; popularity of, 183–86; race issue in, 173;

on statehood, 169–71, 209–10, 218–19; and State of Sequoyah, 211–14, 215–17; and urbanism, 192–93

General Allotment Act, 73
Gentry, Bob, 31
Gibson, Charles, 185, 200, 201, 236, 254–55, 259, 266; on allotment, 174–75; as candidate for chief, 155, 172; tribute to Posey by, 251
"Gibson's Rifle Shots," 185
Gilliams, E. Leslie, 117
Gilliams Press Syndicate, 84
Goat, John R., 77, 86, 171
Goodykoontz, A. P., 31
Grayson, Aunt Cook, 32
Grayson, Dick, 32, 95, 162, 165
Grayson, George W., 48, 74, 172, 229, 235; on allotment, 148–49, 174–75; and Bureau of American Ethnology, 113; essays by, 185; with Hitchcock, 152–53; as Informal Club member, 113; and land trust companies, 175–76
Grayson, Jennie, 33
Grayson, Moses, 32
Grayson, Richard, 32
Grayson, Sam, 78, 102
Grayson, Will, 32, 95, 165
Greek Anthology, 123
Green corn ceremony, 14. *See also* Busk

Greenleaf Mountain, 223
Green Peach War, 30–31, 35, 200, 228

Hains, Henry, 205
Hall, Catharine (Kittie) Harris, 91, 98, 112, 196; marriage of, 137
Hall, George Riley, 48, 59, 79, 98, 99, 101, 107–8, 112, 258; at Arbeka, 71–72; at Coweta,

101–5; and dialect, 87; as editor
of *Henryetta Free-Lance*, 196;
friendship with Posey, 71–72, 92–
93; as Informal Club member,
113–14; marriage of, 137; musical
ability of, 91; at Orphan Asylum,
81–97; poems by, 93; and Posey,
40–41; on Posey's religion, 252;
tribute to Posey by, 251
Hall, Jefferson, 86, 93, 96, 101, 112
Halputta Micco, 153
Hanna, Creek Nation, 198, 208
Harjo, H. Marcey, 103
Harjo, Joe, 165
Harris, Milton, 99; family of,
284n.25
Harris, Red Bird, 242
Harte, Bret, 93, 100
Haskell, Charles N., 209–10, 214–
16, 220, 225; as publisher, 217; at
Sequoyah convention, 213
Hickory Ground, 143, 144, 201,
222, 239
Hitchcock, Ethan A., 162, 163,
178; Indian Territory visited by,
152–53; and land fraud, 180–81
Hoffman, Creek Nation, 194
Hoffman Herald, 236
Holathoye, 222
Holden, J. S., 252
Hope, Witty, 162
Hopkins, G. W., 177
Hotgun, humiliation of, 146
Hotgun (character), 164, 167–68,
169–73, 176, 181, 182, 188–95,
202, 211–14, 216–17, 218–19,
221–22, 236
Hotulke Emarthla, 48, 74, 76,
78, 79
Howe, Elliott, 251
Howe, Mattie Posey, 36, 96, 114,
123, 141, 271
Howe, Robert D., 1–4, 234, 248,
251
Huckleberry, James H., 177, 179

Huckleberry, James H., Jr., 177
Humor: in Fus Fixico letters, 164;
Indian, 72, racial, 155
Hutche Chuppa, 112, 222
Hymn, 17

Iconoclast, 87
The Iliad, 86
Illinois Station, Cherokee Nation,
223
Indian identity: debate on,
303nn.46, 49; definition of,
244–46
Indian International Fair, 37
Indian Journal, 6, 46, 47, 87, 89,
115, 116, 120, 255; Posey as editor
of, 137–59, 160–64, 168–82, 234–
36; Posey's reports to, 54–55, 56;
Posey's sale of, 157, 182, 185
Indian Journal Printing Com-
pany, 234
Indian Territory Press Associa-
tion, 164
Indians: songs and poems of, 117; as
writers, 115
Indian's Friend, 115
Informal Club, 113–14
Ingersoll, Robert, 49
International Banking Trust Com-
pany, 177
International Land Company, 229
Irving, Washington, 86, 90
Isparhecher, 30, 48, 74, 76, 77,
80, 242, 243; as candidate for
chief, 73
Itshas Harjo, 224, 257

Jameson, Bud, 233
Jamestown Exposition, 234
Jefferson Trust Company, 179
Jessie, Billie, 33
Joe Harjo letters, 165–66
Johnston, Douglas H., 212
Judge, 87

Kansas, refugee Indians in, 15–16
Kansas City Journal, 116, 117,
 183, 184
Kansas City *Star*, 87, 118, 123, 256,
 263, 265
Keetoowahs, 146
Kelly, John, 197, 202
Kernels, Temiye, 201
Kipling, Rudyard, 88
Kite, Abe, 157
Kono Harjo (character), 164,
 188, 189

Lah-tah Micco, 146
Land: speculation in, 173–83, 230;
 trusts, 177–78
Land, J. H., 101
Land fraud: in Indian Territory,
 173–83; investigation of, 180–
 83; in leasing, 179; means used
 in, 180
Landrum, E. M., 259
Larney, Joe, 202
Lawrence, Mrs. A. C., 263
Lee, Lillie, 81, 91, 98
Lee, Rosa, 91, 112–13, 118
Lenna, Creek Nation, 23, 140, 141
Lerblance, E. H., 78, 79
Lewis, Anna, 41–43, 58, 281 n.6
Lewis, Jackson, 201, 235
Little, Thomas, 153
Little Fish, 202
Limbo Carr Ferry, 94
Limbo Creek, 20, 24, 26, 29,
 107, 271
Lochar Harjo, 30
Loyal Creek claims, 29, 141, 193
Loyal Creeks, 16

McCombs, David, 34, 142
McCombs, Milla, 34
McCombs, Sallie, 34
McCombs, William, 17, 18, 20, 34,
 76, 110, 142
McCoy, Joseph, 178

McCurtain, D. C., 220
McCurtain, Green, 74, 210, 215,
 220, 299n.13; at Sequoyah Con-
 vention, 213; and statehood,
 151–54, 170–71
McDermott, Jesse, 259
McIntosh, Alex, 103, 110–11
McIntosh, Cheesie, 153
McIntosh, Chilly, 18
McIntosh, Cub, 32
McIntosh, D. N., 47, 48, 74, 136,
 253; death of, 72
McIntosh, Freeland, 31
McIntosh, Louis, 33
McIntosh, Luke G., 110, 165
McIntosh, Roley, 77, 78, 79
McWilliams, Thomas, 18
Mayes, Samuel, 74
Mele Thlocco, 201
Mellette, Creek Nation, 141,
 142, 232
Mellette, William, 176–77
Mewike (John Killer), 224
Mexico: proposed Creek emigra-
 tion to, 241–42; proposed Indian
 emigration to, 168, 302n.38
Midland, 87
Midland Oil and Gas Company,
 179
Miller, Joaquin, 93, 100
Miner, H. Craig, 183
Mingo, Emma, 103
Mingo, Joseph, 103
Mingo, Robert, 103
Mitchell, Donald Grant, 86, 100
Monroe, Harriet, 49
Moore, John, 35
Moore, N. B., 78
Moore, Thomas E., 259
Morgan, Gideon, 169
Morrow, J. S., 55
Murphy, A. P., 182
Murray, William H., 210, 212,
 214–16, 225; at Sequoyah con-
 vention, 213

Muskogee, Creek Nation, 29, 157–58; federal bureaucracy at, 175
Muskogee Democrat, 205
Muskogee Phoenix, 87, 114, 155, 156, 176, 263
Muskogee Times, 158
Muskogee Title Company, 177
Myers, James B., 204, 220, 223–24

Nakdimen, I. H., 235
Nancy, 12
Narkomey, 13, 18
National Hotel, 37, 45
Needles, Thomas B., 178, 179; and land fraud, 177
New-State Tribune, 217
Newton, Jud, 251
New York *Evening Sun*, 118

Okemah, Creek Nation, 223, 224
Oklahoma: constitutional convention of, 219–22, 225, 235; first elections in, 233; statehood act for, 219
Oklahoma City, statehood conventions at, 152, 169
Oklahoma Historical Society, 264
Okmulgee, Creek Nation, 232
Oktahutche (North Canadian River), 24
Opothleyohola, 15–16, 20
Otawa Harjo, 12
Owen, Robert L., 238

Paden, Creek Nation, 198, 205
Pahosa Harjo. *See* Phillips, Pahosa Harjo
Pahose Micco, 13
Paine, Thomas, 49, 72, 253
Palo Alto Land Company, 231, 232, 233, 235, 254, 255, 270
Pecan Creek school, 102–3
Perryman, Legus C., 78–79; African ancestry of, 156; as candidate for chief, 154–57, 172–73; im-

peachment of, 78
Philadelphia *Press*, 117
Phillips, Abbie, 33
Phillips, Benjamin, 16, 33, 34
Phillips, Betsy, 142, 232
Phillips, John H., 48, 55, 142, 196, 232, 248
Phillips, Johnson J., 12, 18, 33, 142, 166, 196, 239, 270
Phillips, Lewis, 12, 33, 232, 270
Phillips, Pahosa Harjo, 12–14, 17–18, 33, 34, 78, 80, 142, 243; family of, 13–14
Phillips, Sarah, 142, 166
Phillips, Taylor, 33
Phillips, Tecumseh, 12, 16, 33, 35, 48, 270
Phillips, Winey. *See* Evans, Winey Phillips
Pike, Albert, 88
Plutarch, 86, 87
The Poems of Alexander Lawrence Posey, 263
Pokagon, Simon, 115, 119
Posey, Alexander L.: on allotment, 75–76; allotments of, 123, 234; artifact collection of, 43–45, 265, 268; artistic limitations on, 93; at Bacone Indian University, 41–56; bigotry of, 155–57; birth of, 11, 20–21; birthplace of, 23, 277n.1; boyhood stories by, 89; bribery charges against, 102; burial of, 251–52; on Burroughs, 121; career of, surveyed, 5–9; character of, 38–39; in Cherokee Nation, 223–24; childhood described by, 117; as Chinnubbie Harjo, 50–51; and Chitto Harjo, 144–47; collected works of, 120; and conservative Creeks, 6, 8–9, 143–47, 238–44; on Creek culture, 44–45, 200–203; Creek dislike for, 235; Creek fables by, 205; at Creek Orphan Asy-

Posey, Alexander L. (*cont.*)
lum, 81–97, 98–101; and Creek
progress, 44; curriculum studied
by, 41, 45, 50, 51; as Dawes Commission agent, 187–204, 220,
222–25; death of, 2–4, 248; as
delegate to statehood convention, 152; democratic politics
of, 156, 161; early childhood of,
23–27; early education of, 36–
38; edited journals of, 308n.17;
as editor, 137–59, 160–64, 168–
82; editorial policy of, 138–39;
and election of 1903, 154–57;
as escort for treasurer, 79–80;
estate of, 255, 263–64; at Eufaula
boarding school, 110–15; eulogy
for McIntosh by, 72–73; fables
collected by, 257; first poem of
note by, 118; friendship of, with
Hall, 92–93; friendships sought
by, 112–14; and games, 91; and
Hitchcock, 152–53; home of,
106, 196; humor of, 54–55; as
humorist, 164; humorous poem
by, 105; as intertribal council
delegate, 77; journalistic style of,
160–64; journalists' admiration
for, 157; journals of, 267; as land
dealer, 254; on land fraud, 175–
76, 178, 181; land holdings of,
255; as landlord, 108; limericks
by, 236; linguistic skills of, 36–
37, 77; literary estate of, 262–69;
literary influences on, 95; literary plans of, 255–57; literary
production by, 111–12, 205–6;
literary reputation of, 8, 51, 258–
59; literary self-consciousness
of, 118, 185; literary sensibili-
ties of, 59; literary signature of,
282n.42, 285n.42; literary style
of, 43, 54; literary tastes of, 41;
manuscripts of, 265; marriage
of, 83; metrical experiments by,

105–6; musical tastes of, 91; and
nature, 107–8, 122–23; newspaper work by, 38; opposition of,
to Porter, 148–51; as orator, 51;
oratory by, 46–47, 55–56, 76–
77; as poet, 112; poetic sensibility
of, 107, 121; poetic skills of, 105;
as political candidate, 73, 76–
77; and politics, 94; and popular
literature, 87–88; on preaching,
85; and progress, 6, 8–9, 139,
142–43, 158–59, 203–4, 242–
43; and progressive Creeks, 72;
publication of poems by, 262–63;
publication record of, 287n.22;
publicity for, 114–15, 116–20,
183–85, 205; racial attitudes of,
9; reading habits of, 40–41, 48–
49, 86–88, 100; reading voice of,
90; as real estate agent, 226–35;
religious skepticism of, 49–50,
252–53; remains of, 304n.7; and
Republicans, 156; reputation of,
4; resentment against, 254; river
journal of, 264–65; river trip by,
122–23; romantic influences on,
117–18, 120–21; search for body
of, 248, 251; in Seminole Nation,
70–71; sense of humor in, 85; and
Sequoyah convention, 212; siblings of, 36, 37, 95–96; on Snake
faction, 239–44; and statehood,
150–54, 210; at Stidham, 103–9;
subjects of poems by, 105–6; as
superintendent of public instruction, 101–6; temperament of, 155;
in Texas, 100; on Thoreau, 121;
tombstone of, 252; tributes to,
251–52; at Wetumka National
School, 116, 122; on Whitman,
121; and world affairs, 88; writing
habits of, 106–7, 108
Posey's works: "A Creek Fable,"
114, 122; "All the While," 118;
"An Outcast," 114; "Autumn,"

105; "A Vision of June," 118; "Bob White," 114, 116; "Callie," 89; "Chinnubbie and the Owl," 50; "Chinnubbie Harjo, the Evil Genius of the Creeks," 50; "Chinnubbie Scalps the Squaws," 50–51; "Cuba Libra," 88; "Daisy," 89; "Death of a Window Plant," 52–53, 54; "Death of the Poets," 53; "Fancy," 5; "Happy Times for Me an' Sal," 53; "Hotgun on the Death of Yadeka Harjo," 43, 256; "Jes 'Bout a Mid'lin', Sah," 89, 121; "June," 104; "Kate and Lou," 105; "Limbo," 114; "Lines to Hall," 89, 93–94; "Loweyna," 83; "Mellette," 176–77; "Memories," 113, 118; "Moonlight," 118; "Mose and Richard," 89, 122; "My Fancy," 105; "My Hermitage," 107, 115; "Nightfall," 114; "Ode to Sequoyah," 114; "O, Oblivion!" 118; "Pohalton Lake," 114; "The Red Man's Pledge of Peace," 53; "Room at the Top," 55–56; "Sea Shells," 100, 104; "Shelter," 114; "Song of the Oktahutche," 114, 116; "Spring in Tulwa Thlocco," 114; "The Alabama Prophet," 52; "The Athlete and the Philosopher," 105; "The Blue Jay," 114, 116; "The Boston Mountains," 104; "The Burial of the Alabama Prophet," 52; "The Conquerers," 89; "The Decree," 109, 115; "The Homestead of Empire," 242; "The Idle Breeze," 104; "The Indian's Past Olympic," 88–89; "The Indian: What of Him?" 46; "The Mockingbird," 114; "The Origin of Music According to the Creek Medicine-Men," 46; "The Passing of 'Hot Gun,'" 256; "The Two Clouds," 89; "To a Cloud," 105; "To a Daffodil," 114, 252;

"To a Humming Bird," 104; "To a Morning Warbler," 114, 118; "To a Robin," 116; "To an Over-stylish Miss," 105; "To My Wife," 234; "To Our Baby, Laughing," 248; "To the Century Plant," 104; "To the Crow," 105; "Twilight," 53, 118; "Two Famous Prophets," 89, 122; "Uncle Dick and Uncle Will," 56–57; "Uncle Dick's Sow," 89, 121; "Verses Written at the Grave of McIntosh," 105; "Wildcat Bill," 71

Posey, Cornelius (Conny), 36, 95, 114, 123, 141, 255, 271

Posey, Darwin, 95, 127, 270

Posey, Ella, 94, 123, 270

Posey, Emma, 233, 255

Posey, Frank, 36, 95, 101, 141, 271; at Coweta, 101–5; marriage of, 103

Posey, Harriett, 19

Posey, James Blaine, 37, 101, 112, 118, 136; death of, 111

Posey, John, 36, 85, 114, 123, 141, 251, 255, 271

Posey, Horace, 37, 114, 123

Posey, Lewis Henderson (Hence), 11, 23, 35, 38–39, 41, 82, 83, 101, 102, 114, 117, 123, 271, 272; as bounty hunter, 31; character of, 36; death of, 136; early life of, 19–20; education of, 36; education stressed by, 36–37; as farmer-rancher, 28–29; as horse racer, 37–38, 279n.25; as hotelkeeper, 37, 45; as light-horseman, 31; in livestock association, 279n.25; marriages of, 20; obituary of, 276n.21; political activities of, 35; politics of, 73; ranching activities of, 32; stories told by, 95; violent acts by, 31–32

Posey, Mattie. See Howe, Mattie Posey

Posey, Melissa. *See* Emery, Melissa
Posey
Posey, Mendum, 95, 123
Posey, Minnie Harris, 82, 101,
105, 106, 107, 111, 116, 137, 188,
196–97, 223–25, 233–34, 247,
248, 251–52; at Creek Orphan
Asylum, 83–97; family of, 99;
farm managed by, 108; friendship of, with Dale, 265–66; at
Indian schools, 264; as matron
at Eufaula, 112; Posey's artifacts loaned by, 265; after Posey's
death, 262–69; Posey's estate
settled by, 255; and Posey's journals, 268–69
Posey, Nancy, 11, 23, 27, 36, 38, 41,
82, 83, 96, 101, 123, 141, 142,
251, 272; age of, 277n.26; allotment of, 269; character of, 24;
Christian beliefs of, 18–19; Civil
War experiences of, 15–16; death
of, 271; early life of, 14; family of,
12–14, 32–34; later years of, 270–
72; marriage of, 20; stories told
by, 24–25
Posey, Pachina Kipling, 123, 269;
allotment of, 233, 248; birth of,
111; death of, 116, 120
Posey, William, 19
Posey, William (Bill), 36, 95,
101, 271
Posey, Wynema Torrans, 223–25,
233, 262, 269; birth of, 137
Posey, Yahola Irving, 105, 106, 111,
116, 123, 223, 233, 269; allotment
of, 233, 234, 248; birth of, 90
Posey Hole, 5
Posey-Thornton Oil Company,
231, 233
Possum Flat, 123; Posey's farm at,
96, 99
Prohibition, 170
Puck, 87

Raker, George, 234
Red Man, 51, 115, 119
The Red Man and Helper, 116
Reed, Henry C., 102
Reed, Ora V. Eddleman, 185, 258;
tribute to Posey by, 251
Reeves, Ira, 158
Remsburg, George J., 43–44, 45; on
Posey's religion, 253
Rentie, W. A., 102–3
Reuter, P. G., 177
Review of Reviews, 87, 123
Riley, Betsy, 33
Riley, Hettie, 33
Riley, James Whitcomb, 93
Rogers, William Connell, 210, 211;
at Sequoyah convention, 213
Roosevelt, Theodore, 169, 178, 217;
Posey's dislike for, 156
Rutherford, S. M., 253–54; on
Posey's religion, 252–53; tribute
to Posey by, 251–52

St. Louis *Globe-Democrat*, 205
St. Louis *Republic*, 114, 116, 118
Sallisaw, Cherokee Nation, 223,
224
Sands, 30
Sango, A. G. W., 102
Sarcoxie, Henry B., 58–59, 283n.55
Sasakwa, Seminole Nation, 70
Scott, Joel, 2, 3, 251
Scott, Sarah, 33
Senora, 93, 94, 96, 112, 144
Sequoyah, 51
Sequoyah Constitution, 214; Has-
kell's role in, 214–16; Murray's
role in, 214–16
Sequoyah Statehood convention,
213–17; 235; Posey's role in,
214–15
Severs, F. B., 20
Sewell, William, 31–32
Shakespeare, William, 86

Shelley, Percy, 100; Posey's poem about, 105
Shoenfelt, J. Blair, 176, 178, 212
Simpson, John F., 136
Skaggs, Drennen, 187, 193, 194, 195, 196, 197, 198, 199, 201, 203
Smith, Reverend John, 17
Snake faction, 118, 143–47, 167–68, 193; allotments assigned to, 194; communal farms of, 199; legal arguments of, 203; Posey's efforts to enroll, 193–200; Posey's rapport with, 204–5; resistance to enrollment by, 197–200; after statehood, 239–44
Soletawa, 146
Soper, Pliny, 178; and land fraud, 177–78, 180
South McAlester Capital, 156, 185
Spokogees, 200
Stanley, W. E., 179
Statehood: in Fus Fixico letters, 169–71; movement for separate, 150–54; Republican opposition to, 150
Stidham, 140, 141
Sturm, O. P., 253
Sturm's Oklahoma Magazine, 205, 253
Sulphur, Tom, 26–28, 37, 117, 144, 196
Swain, Orlando, 267

Tallassees, 13
Takosar, 13
Takosar Harjo, 13, 14, 17, 18, 33, 34, 142
Tchadahkey (Tchadahky McIntosh), 33
Teller, Henry, 118
Te-wah-tah-li-che, 12
Thlee-sa-ho-he (Eliza), 12, 14; death of, 33

Thomas Gilcrease Institute of American History and Art, 265
Thompson, March, 239
Thoreau, Henry David, 56, 253; Posey's reading of, 205
Thornton, D. P., 230
Thornton, John N., 95, 107, 137, 161, 262; as Informal Club member, 113; river trip by, 122–23
Tie-e-tah-kee, 33
Tiger, J. C., 81
Tiger, Jackson, 144
Tiger, Johnson, 98, 101
Tiger, Lydia, 12, 14, 16, 101; estate of, 270
Tiger, Moty, 232
Tina, 13
Tishomingo Trust Company, 179
Tobler, Jake, 31
Tobler, Joe, 31
Toche, 202
Tompkins, Joe, 84, 85
Tookpafka Micco (character), 164, 170, 171, 176, 181, 182, 188–95, 211–14, 216–17, 218–19, 221–22, 236
Torrans, John Beauregard, 137, 262, 263, 290n.3
Tossinnichee, 13
Town and Country Club, 181
Town lot fraud, 182
Towns, Creek, 260. *See also* names of towns
Tribal Development Company, 177, 178, 180
Tribal rolls, 204
Triggs, Mrs. P. A., 102
Truth, 87
Tuckabatchee, 12, 14
Tulledega Hills, 23, 24, 94, 104, 107, 258; lore about, 25; medicine men in, 25–26
Tulmachussee, 14
Tulope Tustenuggee, 157

Tulsa Canadian, 14
Tuskegee (Tuskegee Canadian),
    5, 32–33, 73, 141, 142, 232,
    260, 270; Baptist Church at, 34,
    279n.31; Christianity at, 11–12,
    14, 16–19; green corn ceremony
    at, 17; political division in, 16
Tuskegee Baptist Church, 17–18
Tussekiah Hutke, 13, 14, 17, 33, 34
Tustenuggee Chupco, 13, 34
Tustenuggee Thlocco, 201
Twine, W. H., 102
Twin Territories, 114, 116, 117, 120,
    121, 185, 251

Uncle Remus stories, 257
Union Bureau of News, 184
Up to Date, 87
Upper Creeks, 14

Verdigris Oil and Gas Com-
    pany, 179
Vest, George, 88

Wacache, 147, 168
Wadsworth, Ben, 76
Wadsworth, Benjamin W., 85
Wadsworth, Mitchell, 103
Waetcah Micco, 75
Wagoner, Creek Nation, 29
Walker, Bertrand N. O., 258, 259
Walrond, Z. T., 262, 263
Warner, Charles Dudley, 86
Washington, Booker T., 156
Washington, Lucy, 233, 255

Washington, Watson, 166
Wauhillau Outing Club, 181
Welch Gas and Oil Company, 179
Weleetka, Creek Nation, 194, 232
Whitman, Walt, 100, 105
Williams, Charley, 162
Williams, Doc, 122, 123
Wilson, Bean, 37
Wisdom, Dew M., 78
Wiswell, Fred, 248, 251
Wolf Warrior (character), 164,
    172, 188
Women's Christian Temperance
    Union, 210
Woodruff, Clinton Rogers, 181, 244
World's Work, 123
Wortham, Albert, 38
Wright, Belle, 98, 99, 101
Wright, J. George, 178
Wright, Muriel, 267–69
Writers, Indian, 185, 245–46
Wynema, 137
Wysee, 33

Yadeka Harjo, 43, 48, 201–2, 205
Yaha Hocochie, 146
Yargee, Captain, 20
Yargee, Polly, 20
Yohola, Thomas, 76
Yokes, Samuel, 146
Young, M. G., 231

Zeveley, J. W., 182
Zitkala-Sa, 115, 119, 246

Other volumes in the
American Indian Lives
series include: